Managing Data Protection

Second edition

Dr Chris Pounder
Freddy Kosten

Butterworth–Heinemann Ltd
Linacre House, Jordan Hill, Oxford OX2 8DP

 PART OF REED INTERNATIONAL BOOKS

OXFORD LONDON BOSTON
MUNICH NEW DELHI SINGAPORE SIDNEY
TOKYO TORONTO WELLINGTON

First published 1987
Second edition 1992

British Library Cataloguing in Publication Data
A CIP catalogue record for this book is available from the British Library
ISBN 0 7506 0355 0

Published in association with Hoskyns

Printed and bound in Great Britain by
Thomson Litho Ltd, East Kilbride, Scotland

Contents

Foreword

In writing the second edition of MANAGING DATA PROTECTION, our principal aim has again been to share our knowledge and experience of the Data Protection Act with all those who are struggling to implement the legislation, and who may well feel isolated as they contemplate the work that needs to be done. In many cases the Act's implications, let alone its potential benefits, have yet to be appreciated by management, and those responsible for this work may be left without resources, facilities and moral support. We dedicate this book to all who find themselves in this predicament.

A further aim is to assist those who need to anticipate the changes that will result from a harmonisation of European Data Protection laws. Accordingly, we have added much that illuminates the impact of Data Protection in an international market place; our hope is that this will enable readers to steer a clear path through all the possibilities for change, and to identify the new procedures that Data Users and Computer Bureaux might need to adopt. We trust that the book will thus provide some cover under which all can safely weather any Data Protection turbulence!

We hope that our book will also prove to be of use to a far wider audience, and that we have provided relevant practical advice, guidance and ideas in a form that is intelligible, ready to use and effective. The following are examples of such topics:

- what is likely to happen post-1992 to the Data Protection Act;
- data protection procedures in practice;
- how to check compliance with each Data Protection Principle;
- how to ensure that staff know their legal obligations;
- how to use the more complex implications of the Act to best advantage;
- what course of action to take if the Police request a disclosure of personal data;
- the requirements for holding personnel data which can be agreed with staff and with trades unions.

Looking back at the First Edition, we realise that much has changed since its publication in 1987. Data Protection has become an established factor in the life of hundreds of thousands of organisations and individuals, and, as anticipated in that book, the debate has not subsided. At a 'personal data' level, the Greater London Council, which had the foresight to form a Data Protection Unit and bring the authors together, has faded into memory, and two co-authors of the First Edition (S. Papadopoulos and A. Rickard) have moved on. We wish to 'register' our debt to our 'current and past' colleagues and employers.

We would also like to thank the many others who helped us in our endeavours with this book: our typing support (who suffered grievously at our hands); the Data Protection Registrar's Office who, with unfailing politeness, answered our probing questions; and all those who widened our horizons by telephoning us with their enquiries, thereby ensuring that the murkier aspects of Data Protection saw the light of day. Finally, we must mention the patience of Peter Dixon at Heinemann, and the skill of Gary Borrett in producing the finished version of the text; as with all our published work, your comments are invited on any aspect of its contents.

Dr. Chris Pounder
Freddy Kosten
August 1991

Summary of contents

In the eleven chapters that follow we have made only one assumption: that the reader has access to a copy of the Act, and to Registration forms, Guidelines and other information available free from the Data Protection Registrar. This has allowed us to restrict quotes from these sources to a minimum, and to allocate space to a detailed contents list and comprehensive index. After Chapter Two, we assume that the reader is familiar with the basic terms. For consistency with the Act, with the material from the Registrar, and with the proposed European Commission Directive we have used data as a plural noun, and we emphasise, through the use of capital letters (direct quotations excepted) that concepts such as Data User, Data Subject, the Principles, Register Entry etc have specific and formally defined meanings.

Chapter One, entitled 'Understanding the Act', provides a historical perspective: from the Younger Committee, where the Data Protection Principles first surfaced, to their incorporation into the Council of Europe Convention and ultimately into our own Data Protection Act. The five Parts of the Act are then described from a practical viewpoint, with particular emphasis on the definitions and on the Registrar's powers to enforce compliance with the Principles; the exemptions from the Act are also summarized.

Chapter Two focuses on the role of management, on the work of a Data Protection Officer (ie the person generally 'volunteered' to be responsible for implementing the Act), and on a Data User's responsibilities towards the Data Protection Principles. There is a detailed description of the Registration process, and the options that face a Data User when applying for Registration are also discussed.

Chapter Three comprises a comprehensive review of the pitfalls associated with Registration; from the preliminaries of the procedure to the checks, reappraisals and amendments once an application for Registration has been accepted by the Registrar. We provide examples of the complex issues that surround the structure and content of a Register Entry, and of the message which such an Entry can send to Data Subjects, to pressure groups and to those members of the public interested enough to consult the Register.

Chapter Four explains how to evaluate and implement each Data Protection Principle. The three part structure of this Chapter gives due prominence to Subject Access without divorcing this topic from the other Principles: we are aware that for many Data Users Data Protection is limited to Registration (the Second and Third Principles) and Subject Access (half of the Seventh Principle). As a result the five and a half other Principles are frequently overlooked - a situation that needs remedy.

The Chapter deals with each Principle in turn and, after an explanation of what the Principle means in practice, lists the 'Procedural Review' questions that management has to resolve to ensure compliance. At the end of the Chapter, we summarize audit issues in relation to the Principles, and also the Registrar's role in ensuring compliance; additionally we show how the changes proposed by the European Community could affect the 'Review' questions. Chapter Four(A) deals solely with Subject Access; from the first hint of an Access request to what should be done if the Data Subject complains or threatens legal action. Chapter Four(B) comprises case studies of events, relevant to one or more Principles, which could have brought the Data User before the Courts, or made answerable to the Registrar for what had occurred.

Chapter Five provides commentaries on several important Codes of Practice and compares these, where appropriate, to related Council of Europe Recommendations (eg concerning Direct Marketing, Personnel, Police). It explains what the Registrar expects from these Codes, and directs attention to the likely European standards for certain key sectors.

Chapter Six is intended primarily for Training Officers. We include the complete text of a basic training course for all staff, which we have used successfully in many consultancies. In addition, we indicate the contents of more detailed training courses suitable for a wide variety of specialist staff, including a Data Protection Liaison Team, managers, programmers, housing staff, health workers, social workers, police officers, probation services staff, magistrates courts staff, education staff, and councillors and board members.

Chapter Seven details what each exemption in the Act means in practice. We have tried to ensure that all implications are clearly understood; we indicate the live issues that need to be resolved, and we provide advice on the necessary structures and procedures. Where appropriate, we have mentioned related legislation (eg the Access to Health Records Act 1990).

Chapter Eight relates to security. Since many comprehensive security books are available, we concluded that it would be wrong to re-invent the wheel. Consequently we have limited our discussion to Computer Bureaux, to the effect of the Eighth Principle and other Sections of the Act related to security, and to related legislation (eg the requirements of the Computer Misuse Act 1990, or Sections 68 and 69 of the Police and Criminal Evidence Act 1984).

Chapter Nine provides a critique of the Act and includes summaries of the changes proposed by the Registrar, the Home Office, and the European Community. In this way, readers can see where Data Protection may be going and, by noting areas of agreement (and disagreement), prepare themselves for the changes which can be expected towards the middle of the decade.

The Appendices contain extracts from our quarterly Data Protection News (dealing with Court and Tribunal cases), also guidance notes and forms that have survived the test of time. These notes have been extensively used, criticised and refined; we believe the basic problems have been sorted out. The final Appendix provides a guide to some of the problems associated with transfer of information across national boundaries.

Chapter One: Understanding the Act

1. The concept of Data Protection

1.1 Before exploring any legislation it is important to understand how it relates to the way society functions; in the case of Data Protection or Privacy legislation to understand why it has been found necessary to defend these rights. As each country is likely to deal with such subjects in a way rooted in its history and culture, differences in approach can emerge, and these can impose barriers to the international trade in goods and services upon which today's complex society increasingly relies. For instance, Section 1 of the relevant French legislation links these issues in language which echoes the revolutionary fervour of 1789: 'Data processing shall be at the service of every citizen. It shall develop in the context of international cooperation. It shall infringe neither human identity, nor the rights of man, nor privacy, nor individual or public liberties'.

1.2 Most adults living in continental Europe today will have personal experience (or through a member of their family) of living under, or escaping from, military occupation; Spaniards, Portuguese and Greeks will respectively recall the dictatorships of Franco and Salazar, or the junta of Greek Generals. Thus the collective European cultural experience is that individual rights need protecting because they have been abused by totalitarian authorities or police states; for example, the average German who lived under the East German Communist regime has a different appreciation of a national security apparatus than, say, the average UK citizen, and is therefore more attuned to the need for safeguards.

1.3 In general, serious abuse of individual rights has been largely absent from UK political and social life, with the result that our approach to legislating for such rights has been evolutionary rather than revolutionary. This goes some way towards explaining the traditional British reluctance for legal intervention in this area, and could account for the impression that many have: that Data Protection is a topic characterised by form-filling and bureaucratic nit-picking. Those who see the subject in this light, as something unnecessary or 'to get round', miss the real point: that Data Protection is primarily about preserving the fundamental human right to privacy.

1.4 Privacy itself is an intangible commodity; vital to the quality of life, almost impossible to define, and often categorised in a negative sense (for example privacy is 'invaded', a confidence is 'breached', or a trust is 'broken'). Judge Cooley attempted a definition in 1888, and established the classic 'the right to be let alone'. Sixty years later, the European Convention on Human Rights, adopted after the Second World War when the realities of life under the Axis Dictatorships became clear, reinforced Cooley's requirement to preserve individual privacy; Article 8, for example, states that 'everyone has the right to respect for his private and family life, his home and his correspondence'. Data Protection can be seen as being firmly rooted in that Convention.

1.5 However, these traditional concepts of individual privacy are increasingly being eroded by advances in technology. For example, with a modern camera and telephoto lens, it has been known for a person (ie a member of the paparazzi) to take a photograph, from a mile away, of an individual on a beach and claim that 'I took the photograph in full view of that individual'. A video surveillance camera can improve office security after hours, but the same technology can also be used to monitor staff at work. A directional microphone may be useful to record bird-song; it is also vital equipment that allows others to eavesdrop a conversation. These examples typify the conflict between the use and abuse of technology. Note that technology is not an essential prerequisite for this kind of conflict: pressures on the popular press to titillate its readership often means that an article that is meant 'to interest the public' may not be 'in the public interest'. In summary, whilst the use and abuse of computers and personal data is a relatively new phenomenon, it merely reflects age-old concerns; it should not be seen in isolation and is just one problem amongst many which modern-day society has to resolve.

1.6 There is, however, one major difference; democratic societies have attempted, through legislation, to differentiate between use and abuse of computers. Technological developments have hastened these attempts, as through the use of computers it is possible to monitor purchases made, record who has telephoned whom, deduce the nature of the telephone conversations, log the movements of individuals, and thereby to compile comprehensive information about patterns of consumption, personal lifestyles and preferences. The same technology allows the collection of lifestyle data on every adult based on information collected for another purpose (eg Community Charge); facilitates direct marketing by storing the details of millions of telephone subscribers or voters on a single CD Disk; collates over 42 million records relating to the creditworthiness of individuals; provides facilities for the official vetting of one percent of the adult population every year; could link Government databases via a network, and assists the Police to compile ever larger databases. Such activities, whether harmless or positively beneficial in themselves, cannot be equated with Judge Cooley's notion of 'being let alone'. The fact that modern society depends for its very survival on the use of personal information (and that this use is increasingly assuming a multi-national dimension), adds fuel to these problems.

1.7 Sometimes other fundamental rights are affected. For example, direct marketing activities create two profound conflicts, of which those involved can be blissfully unaware.

Conflict (A) arises from the fact that the more an organisation knows about a potential customer's preferences, choices, behaviour and spending patterns, the better it can target its marketing efforts at the people most likely to buy, thus ensuring greater chances of sales and lower promotional costs (and less chance that individuals will be troubled with information that they don't want). However, this provides an incentive to obtain ever increasing quantities of information about individuals, to the extent that it can constitute an invasion of privacy.

Conflict (B) involves the spectre of censorship and interception of correspondence, if the right of an organisation to communicate with an individual is restricted in any way. Article 10 of the Human Rights Convention states that 'Everyone has the right to freedom of expression' and that this right 'shall include freedom to ... impart information', whilst Article 8 deals with 'the right to respect for ... correspondence' and states that 'there shall be no interference by a public authority' with correspondence unless interception is for a specific purpose in the national interest (eg national security, policing matters etc).

1.8 The resolution of such conflicts can be fundamental to the way a business can operate (or whether it operates at all). For example one member of staff at Hoskyns had been refused credit in a furniture shop. By means of an application under Section 158 of the Consumer Credit Act, it was discovered that the refusal was based on personal data which related to the address in question, but concerned an ex-partner (who had had a bad debt recorded against the name in 1985). This person had left the address before accruing the bad debt, but was still shown at the address according to the 1987 Electoral Register.

1.9 Several queries arise from these facts. Is it fair to allow personal data that relate to one partner to be interpreted in relation to the other partner? Note that this question involves not **how** the data should be processed but **whether** the data should be processed at all. Similarly, in this situation, can personal data that relate to one individual be accepted as relevant when applied to another? Is it excessive to the purpose to hold such data? And is the absence of similar personal data, relating to the partner who was actually seeking credit, an indication that the personal data in question are inadequate for the purpose of refusing credit? Can the Electoral Register be relied on to be up to date? If not, how can a credit reference agency that relies on this Register keep personal data up to date? How long will the agency retain personal data relating to the other partner (for comparison, after 5 years some convictions are spent under the terms of the Rehabilitation of Offenders Act: does this mean that society takes bad debt more seriously than some crimes)? Finally, the disclosure of personal data to one person at an address, about another person who no longer lives there, raises further privacy problems.

1.10 Data Protection legislation attempts to resolve such conflicts by changing the nature of the privacy debate; this transformation recognises that organisations must use personal data but preserves the balance by providing individuals with several important levers to control that use. Being aware that these levers exist, why they exist and knowing how they can be activated is usually the first step in ensuring that Data Protection aspects receive proper consideration. Thus the debate has to resolve certain crucial questions; for example:

(a) Should certain information be collected in the first place and, if so, how?

(b) Should the data be disclosed and, if so, can this be done safely?

(c) Are the personal data accurate and of high quality, and how does the organisation assess these factors?

(d) Are the data relevant, and how is this established?

(e) Are the data securely held? How long should they be retained?

(f) Does the individual concerned need to know of, or consent to, certain data processing activities?

(g) How can individuals obtain a copy of their personal data, and how can inaccurate data be corrected or erased?

(h) Can the organisation justify why certain data should not be corrected or erased?

(i) How are staff trained to use equipment reliably and to follow established procedures?

1.11 Those involved in Data Protection must be prepared to answer such questions by instigating changes to procedures and, where necessary, by raising major issues of corporate ethics and policy.

1.12 The second important step is to accept that the UK has a Data Protection Act, and to recognise that in a democracy one cannot pick and choose which laws are obeyed. The Act **is** enforceable and its form and content **are** here to stay unless Parliament decides otherwise and legislates further. Until that happens there is no choice but to 'honour and obey' (and to add 'love' if at all possible).

2. A brief history of Data Protection in the UK

2.1 For the Government, arriving at a suitable structure for legislation has not been an easy task. The issues surrounding Data Protection in the UK have a long and controversial history (see Table 1), with every prospect of an equally eventful future. It can safely be expected that the major Government Inquiries to date - the Younger Committee on 'Privacy' (1970-1972), the Lindop Committee on 'Data Protection' (1976-1978), the consultations over the workings of the Act in the UK (1988-89), and the public discussions over the proposals for a European Directive (1990-91) will not be the last!

2.2 In the UK, it was the Younger Report (July 1972) that started the 'official' ball rolling. Although the Report was limited to the private sector and contained only one chapter on computers, it concluded that the problem of privacy with regard to computers was one of 'apprehensions and fears and not so far one of facts and figures'. However, Younger recognised the potential for the misuse of information stored and processed by computer, and consequently concluded:

> 'We found that the computer facility to store, link, manipulate and provide access to information gave rise to suspicions that complete personal profiles on a great number of people could be compiled; that information could be used for a purpose for which it was not initially collected; that some information could be inaccurate; that it facilitated access to confidential information by many people scattered over a wide area; that its powers of correlation were so superior to traditional methods that it made practicable what had hitherto been impracticable' (paragraph 581).

2.3 As a result, the Younger Committee took the unusual step of exceeding its terms of reference by making recommendations with respect to the public sector. It suggested that:

> 'the more credible of these apprehensions, however, relate to the use or possible use of computers by central or local government, in particular to those in the hands of the police, the Inland Revenue and the health and social services, all of which are outside our terms of reference' (paragraph 582).

2.4 Consequently, Younger suggested an investigation that would include the public sector.

> 'We suggest that in the light of what we say and of the outcome of its own review of computerised personal information stores held by Departments, the Government should consider the desirability of including both the public and private sectors within the purview of the standing commission which we recommend' (paragraph 628).

In paragraphs 592 to 599, Younger suggested means of controlling the use of personal data via ten 'Principles for handling personal information'.

Table 1: Important data protection dates

1961	Right of Privacy Bill (Lord Mancroft)
1967	Right of Privacy Bill (Alex Lyon MP)
1969	Data Surveillance Bill (Kenneth Baker MP) Personal Record (Computer) Bill (Lord Windlesham) Right of Privacy Bill (Brian Walden MP)
1970	Younger Committee appointed
1971	Control of Personal Information Bill (Les Huckfield MP)
1972	Younger Report (Cmnd 5012)
1975	White Paper: Computers and Privacy (Cmnd 6353) Supplement: Computers; Safeguards for Privacy (Cmnd 6354)
1976	Rights of Individuals; European Parliament Resolution Lindop Committee appointed
1978	Lindop Report (Cmnd 7341)
1979	Protection of the Rights of Individuals - European Parliament
1980	OECD Guidelines on Privacy and Transborder Flows of Personal Data
1981	Council of Europe Convention open for signature
1982	Data Protection - White Paper issued (Cmnd 8539) Presentation of Data Protection Bill
1983	Data Protection Bill reintroduced following 1983 General Election
1984	Data Protection Act 1984 - Royal Assent 12.7.84
1987	Data Protection Act 1984 (Amendment) Bill (Harry Cohen MP) Data Protection Act 1984 - fully in force 11.11.87
1988	Data Protection Act 1984 (Amendment) Bill (Harry Cohen MP) Data Protection Structure Review (by Government)
1989	Data Protection (Amendment) Bill (Eddy Loyden MP) 'What Are Your Views?' (review by the Data Protection Registrar)
1990	Data Protection Draft Directive from the European Commission

2.5 Following the work and suggestions of the Younger Committee and of the White Papers three years later, the Government set up a special committee under Sir Norman Lindop to study and advise on the question of data protection in the public and private sectors. The Lindop Committee collected and considered evidence from a wide range of sources and reported in 1978 (Cmnd 7341).

2.6 The Lindop Report proposed that:

(a) legislation should cover all automatic handling of personal data by any data user or data handling bureau in the private and public sectors;

(b) a Data Protection Authority, independent from government or Ministerial control but accountable to the Courts or Parliament should be established to administer the legislation;

(c) the Data Protection Authority would attempt to ensure that any personal data processing would conform to fourteen statutory principles;

(d) the Data Protection Authority should maintain a public register of all data users, enforce rules for data users, investigate complaints from data subjects and prosecute where necessary;

(e) statutory Codes of Practice, tailored by the Data Protection Authority, should be produced to balance the interests of data users, data subjects and the community, and to explain to data users what their legal obligations were.

2.7 Lindop's Codes of Practice were unpopular with Government. According to Timothy Raison, then Minister of State at the Home Office:

> 'The fact is (Lindop's) Codes of Practice were in reality major extensions of the criminal law, creating a whole host of new offences. We do not believe it is desirable to enlarge the criminal law in this way. We do not think it is constitutionally right to confer responsibility for drafting a whole sector of the criminal law on an independent authority, or that the proposed procedures would be acceptable. Nor do we believe that an independent authority would have the competence to undertake a task which is essentially one for government and Parliament.' (Computing, 22.10.81).

2.8 A less charitable interpretation, which was current at the time, was that the Government was not prepared to let Lindop's proposed Data Protection Authority have so much independence that it could produce Codes of Practice unacceptable to Government. In addition, the advent of a new Conservative Government committed to removing bureaucracy was not the appropriate time to establish a large, let alone powerful, quango.

2.9 Meanwhile there were significant movements on the international stage. By October 1980 the Organisation for Economic Co-operation and Development (OECD) had produced a 'Recommendation ... concerning guidelines governing the protection of privacy and transborder flows of personal data'. Eighteen of the twenty-four participating OECD countries adopted this Recommendation which would ease the passage of personal information between member countries, and yet ensure the privacy of individuals with respect to information held in both manual and automated forms. These Guidelines defined eight 'Basic Principles of National Application'; paragraph 19 stated that 'Member countries should in particular endeavour to .... adopt appropriate domestic legislation'. At that time, the United Kingdom was one of the six countries which abstained from signing the Recommendation.

2.10 In 1981, the next most important step occurred when the Government signed the Council of Europe Convention 'for the protection of individuals with regard to automatic processing of personal data'. The purpose of the Convention is to secure in the territory of each signatory for all individuals, whatever their nationality or residence, respect for their rights and fundamental freedoms, and in particular their right to privacy with regard to automatic processing of personal data relating to them. As each party to the Convention had to take the necessary legislative measures, signature meant that the UK Government was committed to some kind of Data Protection legislation.

2.11 Thus by the early eighties, international pressure was beginning to oblige Government to legislate; the Departments responsible for Trade and Industry were becoming increasingly concerned about the possibility that restrictions and embargoes would be placed on the transfer of data to the UK by countries who already had data protection legislation, whilst the Younger and Lindop Reports had raised expectations that the various privacy problems that arose from the use of computers would be resolved.

2.12 In determining the form the legislation would take the Government had to take account of the twenty Articles of the Convention. The most significant of these form the basis of the Data Protection Principles found in the Act, and can be summarised as follows:

Article 3 - Scope

The Convention applies to all public and privately owned automated personal data files and may be extended by any State to manual files.

Article 5 - Quality of data

Personal data shall be:

obtained and processed fairly and lawfully;

stored for specified and legitimate purposes and not used in a way incompatible with those purposes;

adequate, relevant and not excessive in relation to the purposes for which they are stored;

accurate and, where necessary, kept up to date;

preserved in a form which permits identification of the Data Subjects for no longer than is required for the purposes for which these data are stored.

Article 6 - Special categories of data

Personal data revealing racial origin, political opinions, religious or other beliefs, health or sexual life, as well as personal data relating to criminal convictions, may not be processed automatically unless domestic law provides appropriate safeguards.

Article 7 - Data security

Appropriate security measures for personal data shall be taken against accidental or unauthorised destruction or accidental loss as well as against unauthorised access, alteration or dissemination.

Article 8 - Additional safeguards for the Data Subject

Any person has a right to:

establish the existence of an automated personal data file, its main purposes, and the name and address of the controller of the file;

know whether a data file has information relating to that person and obtain the contents of that information at reasonable intervals and without excessive delay or expense;

obtain the rectification or erasure of such data if these have been processed contrary to a basic set of data protection principles.

Article 9 - Exceptions and restrictions

Exceptions from the provisions listed above are allowed in order to:

protect public safety, State security or monetary interests of the State, or the suppression of criminal offences;

protect the Data Subject or the rights and freedoms of others.

2.13 The Government's signing of the Convention was followed by a further White Paper (Cmnd 8539), published in April 1982, which outlined the general principles of the proposed legislation. (The Council of Europe Convention, originally published in 1981 as Cmnd 8341, was republished as Cm 1329 in December 1990).

2.14 The 1982 White Paper stated that statutory Codes of Practice (over four years after Lindop proposed them) were now unacceptable to the Government because time was pressing, although voluntary codes could provide useful guidance. Paragraph 8 of the White Paper stated that the Government saw:

> 'some value in codes of practice in this field and expects that some professional bodies, trade associations and other organisations may wish to prepare such codes as a guide to their members. But the Government does not consider that these codes should have the force of law or that it would be practicable, without imposing an unacceptable burden on resources, to cover the whole field of personal data systems with statutory codes of practice within any reasonable timescale'.

2.15 Following this White Paper, a Data Protection Bill was published in December 1982; this fell with the dissolution of Parliament in May 1983. After the General Election, the Bill was re-introduced in June 1983 in a modified form, and a further amended version finally received Royal Assent on 12 July 1984. Although, after 23 years of debate, proposals for data protection became law, Table 1 indicates that arguments over the form of the law still continue.

2.16 The Data Protection Act 1984 has five Parts and four Schedules, each with a unique function. In outline:

(a) Part I defines crucial concepts and refers to the Principles underlying the legislation;

(b) Part II sets out the Registration process, the main criminal offences found in the Act, the enforcement powers of the Registrar, and the appeals against those powers;

(c) Part III deals with the rights of Data Subjects to access personal data and to obtain compensation;

(d) Part IV deals with exemptions to parts of the Act;

(e) Part V contains general rules concerning the duties and powers of the Registrar, the role of Government Departments and Chief Constables of Police, other important definitions used in the text of the Act, and various administrative procedures timetabling the introduction of the legislation in the UK;

(f) the four Schedules provide further details on the Principles and their interpretation, the status of the Data Protection Registrar, the rules associated with appeals against the Registrar's use of powers, and on the conditions that must apply to enable the Registrar to obtain a search warrant.

2.17 From the viewpoint of the individual, the Act provides for certain rights in relation to personal data held about that individual in the files and databases of any computer. These rights allow individuals to obtain a copy of their own personal data, to have inaccurate personal data corrected or erased and, in appropriate cases, to seek redress for any damage caused. The Act provides a mechanism by which individuals can make formal complaints about any aspect of the use, disclosure, collection, security etc (ie **all** operational procedures) of any personal data held by others and, if substantiated, to have those complaints investigated by an independent body.

2.18 From the viewpoint of an organisation or individual controlling the contents and use of personal data, the Act obliges them to provide a structured description of those data, and of the purposes for which they are held, to a public body (the Office of the Data Protection Registrar). These details, once accepted, are then placed in the public domain and can be obtained, at no cost, by any member of the public. In addition, eight 'Data Protection Principles' (which together define a code of conduct for the processing of personal data) must be followed; the Registrar has powers to ensure that the statutory responsibilities with respect to these Principles are not neglected.

2.19 To assist compliance, the Registrar has produced several publications about the Data Protection Act, some of which are quoted in this book. A complete list of these publications is provided below; all, except the annual reports, are available at no cost from the Registrar's Office.

(a) **Guidelines**: there are eight Guidelines (blue covers) published in February 1989. There have been no revisions so far; readers who have copies of the earlier red-cover Guidelines, Questions and Answers (1-20) and Questions and Answers

(21-34) are reminded that all these were superseded.

(b) **Guidance Notes**: there are over 20 specialist Notes that treat specific issues more fully than the Guidelines. We recommend readers to obtain a complete set; for example even though the subject matter of Guidance Note 24 (on Financial Services) at first sight would not interest public sector authorities, much of its content reinforces other guidance about direct marketing techniques, and is therefore of wider application.

(c) **Annual reports**: these are published every July and are only available from HMSO; the 'First Report of the Data Protection Registrar' appeared in 1985. The reports are highly recommended as providing insight to the Registrar's concerns and possible actions. In Part B of the Fifth Report (1989) the Registrar published the results of the 'What are your views?' exercise; this was also published separately.

(d) **Forms**: there are five kinds of application forms associated with Registration. These are: DPR.1 (the familiar Parts A and B); DPR.2 (Alteration or Removal of Register Entry); DPR.3 (Renewal); DPR.3A (Renewal reminder); and DPR.4 (Simplified Application for Registration (Small Businesses)). There is also a Magistrates Court Guidance Pack. The DPR.1 forms can be obtained in a 'Registration Pack' which also contains a booklet (brown covers) 'NOTES to help you apply for Registration'.

(e) **Ad-hoc publications**: these comprise the 'Update' series (Issue No. 4 was dated March 1991); information for Data Subjects (eg the blue leaflet 'If there's a mistake on a computer about you'); a card for new Data Users (eg for use at exhibitions to encourage Data Users to get further details about the Act), and a news briefing for journalists. The Registrar also issues Press Releases to publicise his views on significant Data Protection events.

3. Part I of the Data Protection Act

3.1 The first Section of the Act deals with fundamental definitions: 'Data Users' (persons who control the contents and use of the information to be processed), 'Data Subjects' (living individuals whose details are recorded), 'Computer Bureaux' (who provide computer services), and what constitutes 'data', 'personal data' and the activities of 'processing' and 'disclosing'. The definition of data hinges on the form in which the information is recorded, and limits the legislation to information that can be processed automatically; manual systems (ie non-automated files) are outside the scope of the Act.

3.2 The definitions need careful study; they are frequently referred to in the Act and are the key to understanding its provisions. Thus, for example, to understand this extract from Section 4(1) of the Act: 'The Registrar shall maintain a register of data users who hold ... personal data' the reader must fully appreciate what the terms 'data users' and 'personal data' really mean. Whilst Section 1 of the Act, with its nine subsections, can be read in about three minutes it takes a great deal longer to apply these definitions to practical situations!

3.3 In practice, each definition can be taken to pose one or more test questions. For example as regards the first definition ('Data'): in what form is the information recorded? If the answer shows that the constraints of the definition are met (ie the information is processable by automatically operated equipment), then the next definition should be tested (ie are the data personal data?). If all such tests posed by the definitions are confirmed, then the information is subject to the other Sections of the Act, unless an exemption applies. Individuals who administer the Act must ensure that they fully comprehend the definitions; failure to understand the implications of each definition will inevitably lead to non-compliance with other provisions of the Act. As will be seen, the answers to these test questions are not straightforward.

3.4 **Data**

3.4.1 **Text of definition**: ' "Data" means information recorded in a form in which it can be processed by equipment operating automatically in response to instructions given for that purpose.' (Section 1(2) of the Act).

3.4.2 Crucial to this definition is linkage of the word 'information' with the 'form' in which it is 'recorded' to allow automatic processing to proceed. Thus, to be 'data', there must be equipment to perform such automated processing and instructions which cause the processing to occur. If information cannot be processed automatically, then the information is not 'data', and if it is not 'data', then that information cannot be subject to the Act. Note that the word 'recorded' is generally accepted as meaning that the information is not of a transient nature (eg data recorded on magnetic media but not data fleetingly held in computer memory), and that the concept of 'data' extends beyond text-files in ASCII or EBCDIC. Thus other examples of data as defined here could include: the information on a tape recorder, the pictures recorded on a video cassette, the grey scales that result from the scanning of a picture, or the digital representation of analog data collected by a voice analyser.

3.4.3 The most obvious example of the type of equipment mentioned in the definition is a 'computer'. However, the Act does not define (or use) the word 'computer', an omission which means that data can be processed by many other types of electronic (or even mechanically operated) equipment. Thus data processing equipment that could pass the test posed by this first definition includes: automatic microfiche readers, equipment that checks security passes, electronic laboratory equipment that assists in the analysis of samples, tachometers that monitor the use of vehicles, automatic telephone logging equipment, bar-code scanners and, in particular, the ubiquitous optical character recognition devices. It is, therefore, important to check **all** electronic equipment in any survey of 'data' processing, and not to limit enquiries to computers - some weighing machines can process data, and some photocopiers have microchips that collect and analyse information about usage!

3.4.4 Note that this definition includes the word 'processed', a term which is defined in Section 1(7) of the Act. It is the application of this latter definition which excludes most electronic devices (eg 'simple' photocopiers or 'basic' fax machines) from the legislation. More electronically sophisticated photocopiers, as well as fax machines if allied to appropriate software, could process data (such fax machines would provide automatic input of information while the software would provide the potential for word-searching the text: see also the Registrar's Guideline 2, paragraph 12.4).

3.4.5 Section 39(5) of the Act states that the Act does not apply to any data processed wholly outside the UK and not used or intended for use in the UK.

3.5 Personal Data

3.5.1 **Text of definition**: ' "Personal Data" means data consisting of information which relates to a living individual who can be identified from that information (or from that and other information in the possession of the data user), including any expression of opinion about the individual but not any indication of the intentions of the data user in respect of that individual.' (Section 1(3) of the Act).

3.5.2 Note the linkage of 'personal' with 'data'; thus **the information must also be 'data'** as defined in Section 1(2). Consequently this definition elucidates when 'data' are 'personal data' and, as before, if the information is not personal data then the obligations towards personal data found in the Act cannot apply.

3.5.3 The first test to apply is 'whether the information relates to a living individual'. Information about people who have died can never be personal data, and 'individual' cannot mean a company or a corporate body; so, for example, information about the Government, Hoskyns and other corporate bodies can never be personal data.

3.5.4 The second test is whether the information relates to a living individual 'who can be identified from that information'. Note that an individual need not be identified by name, but that this criterion is also met if it is possible to identify an individual from the context of the information; for example, the individual is clearly identified if the information is 'The first woman Prime Minister of the United Kingdom'. Additionally, the means by which the individual is identified need not rely solely on the information constituting the data, but can include any 'other information in the possession of the data user'. Note that the latter use of the word 'information' is not qualified in any way and therefore can include information contained in manual records. Thus to make 'data' into 'personal data' the identity of the individual does not have to be clear from the data themselves, but can be derived from a combination of the data and 'other information' held by the data user, anywhere and in any form. (The term 'data user' refers to the person in control of the data and is itself defined in Section 1(5) of the Act).

3.5.5 To illustrate the second test consider an organisation's payroll system that uses a works number set by the Finance Department, whilst the Personnel Department has a manual file that links the works number to a name; does the payroll system contain personal data? The answer is 'yes', because the Personnel Department can identify the employees concerned from their works number; the Department has the key (ie the 'other information') through which the individuals in the payroll system can be identified by the organisation (ie by the Data User with respect to these personal data).

3.5.6 An example of a less clear situation, which may well have to be settled by legal argument, arises in the case of data, relating to property, which can be used in conjunction with the Electoral Register to find the names of residents in a particular area. As this additional information is in the public domain (eg in Public Libraries) and thus **available** to any Data User, it could be claimed that 'other information' came into the **possession** of the Data User when the Register was consulted. Thus a visit to the Library could translate the data into personal data!

3.5.7 The purchase of equipment, equipment upgrading or the provision of new or improved software could also have data protection implications; these acquisitions may include facilities that allow the manipulation of data in new ways that relate to individuals, so that the data become personal data. For example, the purchase of an Optical Character Recognition (OCR) device (or automated micro-fiche reader, desktop electronic filing system etc) could bring manual files under the ambit of the Act as the device transforms printed material (eg typing) into 'data'. The input to the OCR, the information on the paper, is clearly 'in a form that can be processed automatically in response to instructions' (Section 1(2) of the Act) and passes the test of data. However, the question remains whether the data are personal data; the answer will depend on how the data (ie the typed manuscript, manual files, perhaps in future handwriting etc) are subsequently processed. If the data are structured and searched in such a way that they can provide information on specific individuals, so that the definition of 'processing' is satisfied (Section 1(7) of the Act), then the data are personal data.

3.5.8 Some data may not look like personal data. For example, the data may, at first sight, refer only to businesses or to anonymous holders of certain posts. However, lists of customers or suppliers usually include some sole traders or self-employed persons, whilst the description of certain posts may identify specific individuals (eg 'the Manager of Division X'). If identification is possible, the data are personal data. Often, in these cases, it can be less time-consuming to register the required details, and bring in the controls of the Act (organisations at any rate tend to keep such information confidential), than to search for confirmation that none of the data are personal data, and then have to worry that somebody will discover that an error was made.

3.5.9 There will always be some electronic equipment that records data which **could** be related to individuals. What may at first seem to be purposes associated with, say, the management of inanimate objects or the output of statistics may, through additional use, involve the processing of personal data to identify living individuals. For example, software that measures the number of key depressions, or corrections, made on a word processor, or computes the output of a machine in a factory, may also be capable of determining who is the 'fastest' typist (worrying information if the typing pool is to be rationalised), or the 'best' machine operator. Electronic security equipment, whose function is to allow access to a location, can be used to monitor who has entered that location and when (thus effectively establishing the movement of staff).

3.5.10 The safest course of action, in this and the many other 'grey areas' of interpretation, will be to err on the side of caution and to assume that the test has been passed. Particularly where large Data Users are concerned, it would be very difficult to discover every compendium, book or directory which could have the effect, under this definition, of transforming anonymous data into personal data that are covered by the Act.

3.5.11 The final test is to identify a Data User's 'intentions', which by definition are excluded from the Act, as distinct from 'opinions' - which are included. The definition specifies that what a Data User may wish to do, with respect to an individual (eg 'I will not employ, promote, rehouse, etc Joe Bloggs', or 'We will place Jim Smith at the top of the list') is not classed as personal data. By contrast, the Data User's opinions (eg 'Joe Bloggs is unemployable, not promotion material, adequately housed' etc) are personal data and therefore subject to the Act, even though the opinion may imply the intention (as in the cases mentioned above). Note that the intentions of anyone other than the Data User are not 'intentions' as defined by the Act.

3.5.12 At first sight this distinction creates a large loophole; what is to stop a Data User from casting opinions in the form of intentions? In practice, however, this may be difficult to do. For example, 'I shall not promote Joe Bloggs because he is a communist' consists of both an 'intention' and an alleged 'fact'. The words 'because he is a communist' form no part of an 'intention' and are subject to the Act. In addition, it could be argued at some stage that the statement 'I shall not promote Joe Bloggs' has become a 'fact' and is no longer an 'intention', on the grounds that

Joe Bloggs has not been promoted. Consequently both the nature of the data and the way they are being used could determine whether an 'intention' may really be an 'opinion'.

3.5.13 Suppose an organisation holds certain personal data in the form of intentions: for example 'Joe Bloggs will not be promoted by us' or 'Our company will not give credit facilities to Fred Smith'. If these data do constitute the organisation's intentions towards an individual, then the data are not personal data as defined by the Act. This means that the data are not subject to Registration by the organisation (the 'Data User'), nor to the Data Protection Principles, to Subject Access or to any enforcement powers of the Data Protection Registrar.

3.5.14 As will be seen, this position is legally different to an exemption under the Act. Such an exemption can only be exercised on the basis of strict conditions laid down by the legislation; and in relation to Subject Access, Section 25(2) of the Act provides a Court with the power to inspect any data held in order to determine whether an exemption has been properly applied. By contrast, only one test can be applied by a Court to determine whether data constitute an 'intention': whether the data truly describe an 'intention' of the Data User in respect of an individual.

3.5.15 Consequently, a Data User who holds data which comprise intentions towards individuals should be prepared to justify such holding to the Courts, and should be aware that the Registrar has indicated publicly (and in Guideline 2, paragraph 3.4) that he will be watching the situation carefully to ensure that the Act is not undermined by a potential loophole. It does seem that the 'intention' qualification to the definition of personal data has opened the way to legal controversy which could, on occasion, be resolved to the detriment of the Data User.

3.6 Data Subject

3.6.1 **Text of definition**: ' "Data subject" means an individual who is the subject of personal data.' (Section 1(4) of the Act).

3.6.2 Since personal data must, by virtue of Section 1(3) relate to living individuals, it follows that a Data Subject is alive! Note that the Data Subject definition carries no inference concerning nationality or territory. Consequently, a Data User who processes personal data about individual members of remote Indian tribes would still be subject to the Act (eg would need to register). Also the concept of Data Subject rights is established as 'individual rights', exercisable only by the subject of personal data. Thus corporate bodies, partnerships etc cannot exercise the rights of Subject Access, or of claiming damages under the Act.

3.7 Data User

3.7.1 **Text of definition**: ' "Data user" means a person who holds data, and a person "holds" data if -

(a) the data form part of a collection of data processed or intended to be processed by or on behalf of that person as mentioned in subsection (2) above; and

(b) that person (either alone or jointly or in common with other persons) controls the contents and use of the data comprised in the collection; and

(c) the data are in the form in which they have been or are intended to be processed as mentioned in paragraph (a) above or (though not for the time being in that form) in a form into which they have been converted after being so processed and with a view to being further so processed on a subsequent occasion.' (Section 1(5) of the Act).

3.7.2 This three part definition of Data User, which is expressed in terms of data (not personal data), is complex; it can be condensed into two conditions both of which need to be satisfied. Firstly the data must have been processed or be in a form in which they are intended to be processed; the actual form in which they are stored (eg on tape or disk) is immaterial. Secondly a Data User must be a 'person' (this is legal terminology for the legal entity, either an organisation or an individual, who 'holds' the data and thereby controls their contents and use). Note that one component relates to the processing of the collection of data, and the other to the status of the person who determines what happens to the data.

3.7.3 Parts (a) and (c) of the definition ensure that no matter where, or how, the data are stored, they are still data if they can be processed, are intended to be processed or are in a form in which they have been processed and can be processed again in future. For example, suppose a Police Force uses optical disks to archive a criminal investigation: are the data held? The answer is 'yes', because the data have been processed (during the investigation) and have been retained (to allow the investigation to be re-opened); thus there always will be the possibility (and legal requirement as the Court of Appeal could order a review) to process on a subsequent occasion. Consequently the data are held and the Police Force is a Data User with respect to that collection of data.

3.7.4 It is this definition that catches 'archived data' as being held by a Data User. Data archives may be kept by a Data User for a variety of reasons (internal record keeping, statutory requirements, future research etc), and although the Data User will not normally use such data for day to day operations, the data are clearly in the form in which they have been processed and could again be processed in future. Thus a collection of data includes both the current and the archived data (this has serious implications for Subject Access).

3.7.5 Note that the words 'by or on behalf of' in part (a) of the definition mean that to 'hold' data the Data User need not have a computer! For example, a District Council may control the contents and use of certain data on the County Council's computer, or a small business may instruct a Computer Bureau - 'please run my payroll every month, here is a list of my staff, their bank accounts, salary details etc'. In each case the Data User tells the Bureau what to do and when to do it, and controls how the personal data are processed. For example, if the Manager of the small business phones the Bureau and says 'please alter the payments made to Joe Bloggs', the Bureau would comply with the request. Thus the small business controls the contents and use of the personal data and clearly satisfies the definition of Data User - without owning a computer.

3.7.6 The definition also allows for the same collection of data to be held by more than one Data User, and where facilities and personal data are shared between Data Users the question of whether one or more Data Users control the contents and use of the data **must** be resolved. Do **not** assume that only one Data User can be legally responsible.

3.7.7 In some cases establishing who is a Data User is very difficult, even though a Data User must be a legal entity. For example a District Council comprises several legal entities (eg an Electoral Registration Officer, a Rent Officer). Sometimes public policy creates legal entities; for example, the formation of self-managing Hospitals changes their relationship to the computing services provided by the District Health Authority. No longer are the Hospitals part of the same Data User (ie the District Health Authority); they have become, through statute, individual legal entities (ie the Hospital, if it holds personal data, has become a Data User).

3.7.8 In the private sector, the situation can be far more complex. For example, suppose Company A has two divisions or subsidiaries; are these separate Data Users or are they just names used in a marketing strategy? The answer will depend on whether they are constituted as separate companies, with their own company Registration - an important legal distinction. If Head Office of Company A receives a copy of personal data from a subsidiary, could this constitute a disclosure of personal data to a different Data User? Is Head Office a Data User that controls the contents and use of the personal data? As will be seen later, getting the answers to such questions wrong could result in criminal offences.

3.7.9 The message is very clear: if a Data User is involved with a parent organisation, or organisation of similar type (eg Regional Authorities with District Authorities, companies with divisions of companies etc), it is very important to take advice (eg from a legal officer or Company Secretary) should there be any doubt as to the legal standing of the respective organisations.

3.7.10 Two final points: a Data User has to control **both** contents and use of the data. With networked access to data, some organisations may only read data (ie they use data but cannot control the contents). Secondly, although a Data User is defined in terms of data, all the Data User's obligations under the Act relate to personal data (except where the Data User responds to a Subject Access request to tell the Data Subject that no personal data are held).

3.7.11 Section 39 of the Act deals with those circumstances when data are held wholly or partly outside the United Kingdom. In summary, if the data are controlled from outside the UK (eg a German company holding data in the UK) **and all** of the data are used **wholly outside the UK**, then the provisions of the Act do not apply. If the data are controlled from outside the UK, and some of the data are used within the UK, then the provisions of the Act do apply to the latter data. If the data are controlled from the UK, used in the UK, but are processed abroad (eg a UK company holding data on a German computer) then the data are subject to the Act. In all cases, the key query is 'what happens **in the UK**?'. Complex situations of this kind require careful thought; for example, if a person who is not a UK resident processes personal data in the UK through an agent, then that agent can assume the obligations of Data User (it all depends on where the personal data are used, what the agent does and the relationship between the agent and the controller of the data).

3.8 Computer Bureau

3.8.1 **Text of definition**: 'A person carries on a "computer bureau" if he provides other persons with services in respect of data, and a person provides such services if -

(a) as agent for other persons he causes data held by them to be processed as mentioned in subsection (2) above; or

(b) he allows other persons the use of equipment in his possession for the processing as mentioned in that subsection of data held by them.' (Section 1(6) of the Act).

3.8.2 A Computer Bureau provides computer services to individuals or organisations ('persons', in legal jargon) by causing data to be processed (this is normally taken to mean on the Bureau's equipment; see Guideline 2, paragraph 6.2), or by allowing other persons to use equipment, in the Bureau's possession, for processing of data. By inference, and in contrast to the definition of Data User, a Computer Bureau only follows the instructions of its clients and does not control the collection, dissemination or use of data. As a Computer Bureau cannot 'hold' data, to confirm the status solely of Computer Bureau it is advisable to ensure both that the definition of Data User **cannot** apply to the data, as well as positively confirming that the definition of Bureau **does** apply.

3.8.3 Data Users who own computers, or any organisation with computing facilities, can sometimes additionally acquire Bureau status without a deliberate decision to this effect. For example, Local Authorities and Health Authorities may agree to provide micros for voluntary groups to process their data, a school or hospital may 'opt-out' of Authority control and yet still use the Authority's computing services, and organisations may enter into arrangements for reciprocal back-up (ie if the computer at one site goes down, the other site will assist with the data processing). These and similar arrangements fall within the definition of Computer Bureau, and any Data User who implements such a service is, therefore, performing the functions of a Bureau. If this is done 'knowingly or recklessly', a criminal offence is being committed unless and until Bureau status is registered under the Data Protection Act. In many organisations, notably in the private sector, Computer Departments are separate legal entities, and will thus be in a Bureau relationship with their parent bodies.

3.8.4 Care has to be taken as to the meaning of 'the use of equipment in his possession' as it extends beyond the narrow concepts associated with 'ownership'. Consequently the test of 'Computer Bureau' may be satisfied by certain leasing arrangements (especially if the leasing arrangement extends beyond a simple rental contract). It is therefore important for any leasing organisation to consider the range of services provided to clients, in order to confirm whether or not that organisation is a Bureau.

3.8.5 Section 39 of the Act also has a bearing on the responsibilities of a Bureau towards the data it processes. If a person in the UK (ie the Data User) uses the computing services of a German company, then the German company is not subject to UK law (although the Data User is). A UK company providing computing services in relation to personal data controlled by a German company would remain a Computer Bureau, because the processing takes place in the UK. As with the cases described in paragraph 3.7.11, careful thought is required to define the responsibilities of the parties involved; for example, depending on the relationship between the person exercising control and the agent, the agent could assume the obligations of Data User (ie as well as Computer Bureau).

3.9 Processing

3.9.1 **Text of definition**: ' "Processing", in relation to data, means amending, augmenting, deleting or re-arranging the data or extracting the information constituting the data and, in the case of personal data, means performing any of those operations by reference to the data subject.' (Section 1(7) of the Act).

3.9.2 Although the definition of processing includes a series of operations (eg deleting or extracting), these words are not used in the Act in their technical context. For example, it is well known that to 'delete' a file is a logical 'delete', leaving the contents of the file on disk but removing the entry from the disk's catalog of files (eg the File Allocation Table). In reality, the file is not 'deleted' but made 'non-accessible', and is only truly destroyed if another file overwrites the freed disk space. Often 'deleted' files are readily recoverable via an UNDELETE program!

3.9.3 These technicalities will generally not be relevant to Court proceedings: to understand what 'delete' means in law, one would have to turn to a good English dictionary and not to the computer manual. 'Delete' will mean what the 'man on the Clapham Common omnibus' would understand by 'delete' and is not restricted to the understanding of a computer specialist; in theory all the technical operations are covered by the combination of words found in Section 1(7). For example, 'to copy' could be described in the language of the definition by 'data are extracted from one part of a disk, and another part of a disk will be augmented by these data'.

3.9.4 However, the principal impact of this definition is through the use of the words 'by reference to the Data Subject'. To process personal data, a Data User must want to find out something that relates to a Data Subject (ie a living individual). If a Data User does not have that objective with respect to a particular collection of personal data, then these personal data are not processed, and because they are not processed as defined in Section 1(7), they cannot be 'held' as defined in Section 1(5). Since Section 4(1) obliges the Registrar to maintain a Register of Data Users who hold personal data, there is then no need to register this collection of personal data. Only personal data that are processed by reference to the Data Subject need to be registered.

3.9.5 The effects of this important conclusion can, on occasion, be difficult to anticipate. Consider a local education scheme whose collection of data consists of a list of schools, the amount of asbestos found in each school, the estimated cost of clearing the asbestos, when the work can commence, and the name of the schools inspector who found the asbestos. In this example personal data are processed, but are they processed 'by reference to the Data Subject'? The answer to this question is 'it depends on how the data are used!'.

3.9.6 If the data are processed to answer questions like 'which school has the most asbestos?', or 'we have £3,000; which school can we clear?', or 'when did the work at St Mary's Junior School begin?' then that is not processing by reference to the Data Subject - even though the name of the inspector may appear on a VDU or printout as the consequence of such processing. Thus using the argument in paragraph 3.9.4: if personal data are not 'processed by reference to the data subject', they can't 'form part of a collection of data processed or intended to be processed'; as these data are not 'held', it follows there is no Data User, nor any obligation under the Act with respect to these data. If, however, the data are processed to answer questions such as 'who is the best asbestos spotter?', or 'who found the asbestos at St Mary's?' then personal data are being processed by reference to a Data Subject and are fully subject to the Act.

3.9.7 Situations like this create problems of management and control. It is possible, for example, for a new manager to decide that the personal data concerning asbestos removal from schools, can be used (without any programming change) to provide information to assess staff performance. Without prior Registration, it could be illegal to use the personal data for such a purpose.

3.9.8 It is for this reason that the uses of personal data which are **not** processed by reference to the Data Subject, but **could be**, need to be monitored. Data Protection Officers should alert line managers who have the **capability but not the intention** to process personal data in this way to be very careful as to what they actually do with the information, and make it clear that any intended change of use, or purpose, should be reported immediately. In many cases, the best course will be to bring the personal data under the 'data protection' umbrella from the outset.

3.9.9 Free text retrieval (the ability to 'word search' a database) is another headache. With many such systems available it is now possible to browse through much data, almost at the whim of the operator, dependent only on the nature of the enquiry. With these systems, the Data Protection Officer has to concentrate attention not on the data themselves, but on the uses of the data. Consequently, data management controls will have to be built around use rather than data content. In summary, whenever the objective is to use personal data to find out something about an individual, then the personal data are processed 'by reference to the Data Subject'. If **not, and there is no prospect of such use**, then the personal data are not processed by reference to the Data Subject (and are therefore not held and are not subject to the Act etc); however, guaranteeing this abstinence could be difficult.

3.9.10 In many cases, software capability to process with respect to an individual will co-exist with a manager's view that there is no likelihood of this being done. Data Protection Officers should note that this is dangerous ground. 'Why', a Court may ask, 'should somebody spend money to acquire the capability to process data in a flexible way, without at least some intention of using this capability?'. In general, it will be safer to assume that data that **can** be processed by reference to the Data Subject **will** be so processed some time in the future, rather than to run the risk of processing personal data illegally.

3.10 Not processing

3.10.1 **Text of definition**: 'Subsection (7) above shall not be construed as applying to any operation performed only for the purpose of preparing the text of documents.' (Section 1(8) of the Act).

3.10.2 This definition constitutes the misnamed 'word processor exemption'. Word processors are not exempt from the Act; however, processing 'only for the purpose of preparing the text of documents' is.

3.10.3 The word 'only' is vital. If personal data are kept for other purposes then the word 'only' does not match the actual processing of the data. 'Only' means just this; consequently the extension of the definition of 'processing' to what is 'not processing' is very limited. As in paragraph 3.9.4 above, the argument applies that if personal data are not 'processed' - they cannot be 'held' - and therefore are not subject to the Act.

3.10.4 Processing **only** for the preparation of the text of documents means that the sole use of any personal data is as text. However, the more complicated the manipulations of the text (eg using the mail merge, word search, or sort facilities), the more difficult it is to claim that the personal data are used **only** for the purpose of preparing the text of documents (the Registrar's Guideline 2, Section 8 provides more details on such borderline cases).

3.10.5 It is reasonable to assume that software developments will make this Section of the Act redundant. There is a trend towards integrated packages, for example combining spreadsheets and databases. It is easy to imagine an integrated word processor/database package or word processor/enquiry package which would answer questions such as 'what did I say in my last letter to Joe Bloggs?' or 'how many times have I written to Joe Bloggs?'. Even though one result will be a further letter sent to Joe Bloggs, the personal data are already being used for purposes other than text preparation.

3.10.6 Difficulties will arise when a line manager invests in a new software package, unknown to the Data Protection Officer, or receives such a package from the manufacturer, via a routine upgrade. Unless management appreciates the particular limitations of this Section, the new software features could result in illegal processing of personal data. Consequently, a Data Protection Officer should always monitor carefully the application of word processors within the organisation, the procedures for updating their software, and the use of personal data on such systems.

3.11 Disclosing and transferring

3.11.1 **Text of definition**: ' "Disclosing", in relation to data, includes disclosing information extracted from the data; and where the identification of the individual who is the subject of personal data depends partly on the information constituting the data and partly on other information in the possession of the Data User, the data shall not be regarded as disclosed or transferred unless the other information is also disclosed or transferred.' (Section 1(9) of the Act).

3.11.2 The important point here is that disclosure is defined in terms of data and 'information extracted from the data'. Thus disclosures can occur in non-computerised form, and need not consist of the whole of the personal data. Examples of disclosures are: in response to a member of the public who telephones to ask for information about a bill or method of payment; as special comments printed on an invoice, to assist delivery; as bills or salary slips in the form of computer print-out; as verbal information on staff salaries provided to a manager; as lists of trades union subscriptions, or of new staff, provided to a union representative. All of these are disclosures under the Act, and all have to be under proper management control through appropriate authorisation procedures.

3.11.3 Unless an exemption applies, disclosures to third parties are amongst the particulars that have be registered by a Data User. Hence a distinction arises between an internal disclosure (ie within the Data User; this could, however, result in a new **use** of personal data which will need to be registered), and an external disclosure (ie made to a person who is not the Data User; this may need to be registered as a disclosure). In large Data User organisations, tracing disclosures to see whether they are internal or external can be a problem; for example, suppose personal data held by the Data User (eg by a Housing Department) were extracted and sent in the form of a memo to the Legal Department where the information was incorporated into a letter sent to a Doctor. In this case, the Legal Department would be making a disclosure, as defined by the Act, on behalf of the Data User (without necessarily being aware of this fact). If the Legal Department used the memo for a non-housing purpose this could be a new use of personal data by the Data User.

3.11.4 Disclosures made inadvertently are often capable of causing damage to Data Subjects, as well as indicating lax security (in contravention of the Eighth Principle). In one example, a large Local Authority had a procedure in which builders were advised, by means of a job sheet, of the work to be done each day. These job sheets often included special notes of the kind: 'Mrs Smith keeps the key under the mat', or 'Mrs Jones is deaf - please knock loudly', this information having been extracted from a free text field of a database associated with Work Planning and Management. Thus, if a workman lost a job sheet, or in the pub at lunch was overheard saying 'Mrs Smith at No. 10 Acacia Avenue is taking a risk keeping the key under the mat, she could easily be robbed', this would be a disclosure. In addition, as the disclosure would be unauthorised, damages could be awarded if Mrs Smith was actually robbed by a person who overheard the remark.

3.11.5 For personal data to be disclosed, information that identifies the individual must be also disclosed. Note also the use of the word 'information' at the end of the definition; this means that the identification of the individual need not be contained in the disclosed data, but could be contained in a manual file that is also disclosed (not necessarily at the same time). Where the data do not identify an individual, no disclosure (as defined by the Act) has taken place unless and until other information that identifies the individual has also been disclosed. For example, suppose a Data User processes a list of names and addresses of individuals, and rents to be paid. If details concerning addresses or rents are disclosed to another organisation, this is not a disclosure regulated by the Act. However, if a name on its own is subsequently linked to an address or rent, perhaps during a telephone enquiry (eg "who owes the £96.00 at 55 Acacia Avenue?"), then a disclosure of personal data has taken place.

3.11.6 Nevertheless, even if only details of addresses and rents are disclosed, should the Data User have to take into account that the recipient of the information can reconstitute the personal data by visiting the local library to examine the Electoral Register? As in the case of the definition of personal data (paragraph 3.5.6 above), there could be legal argument regarding the meaning of the words 'other information in the possession of the data user'. Could this phrase be taken as describing the fact that the Data User knew, or could guess, that the recipient would use the Electoral Register to reconstitute the personal data? If so, it could also be argued that the Data User had 'other information' that what was disclosed were personal data, even though the names were not actually disclosed.

3.11.7 The paragraph above does not mean that the Data User should 'second-guess' what every disclosee would do with the data they receive; Data Users should, however, consider all disclosures carefully.

3.11.8 Understanding the definition of 'disclosure' is crucial to the proper Registration of disclosures, and in determining what an authorised or unauthorised disclosure is. Unauthorised disclosures, as will be seen later, could make a Data User liable to claims for damages.

3.11.9 In the Act, several sections refer to overseas transfer of data; unfortunately the word 'transfer' is not defined and certain relevant criteria have to be deduced. For example, the word 'transfer' is always linked to the word 'data'; thus what is transferred must be data, namely information in an automatically processable form (eg information contained on disk or tape). The word 'overseas' means the territory or country outside England, Scotland, Wales or Northern Ireland; note that UK Embassies abroad are UK territory whilst foreign Embassies in the UK are 'overseas'. In the majority of references involving overseas transfer, there is a link (either explicit or implicit) to the words 'personal data': thus what is transferred must also satisfy the requirements of Section 1(3). Accordingly, the transfer abroad of anonymised data on disk, coupled with sending a manual file that holds the key to unlock the anonymity of the data, would be an overseas transfer. Finally, in the era of portable computers, international travel and multi-national networks, note that the sending abroad of an electronic mail message about colleagues, or taking a computerised list of customers on an overseas trip, involve overseas transfers of personal data. In most cases, an overseas transfer implies a disclosure to another person; however, if the list of customers is kept in **total confidence** there would be no disclosure.

3.12 Part I of the Act contains the first mention of the Eight Data Protection Principles and their Interpretations, found in Schedule 1 to the Act; these precepts form the heart of the Act. The Principles are general guidelines, derived from the Council of

Europe Convention (see paragraph 2.12 above), which together define a Data User's responsibilities when processing personal data. The Secretary of State may modify the Principles to provide additional safeguards in relation to certain kinds of potentially controversial personal data (Section 2(3) of the Act); since 1984 these powers have not been exercised.

Table 2: Key questions arising from the definitions

(a) Is the information recorded in a form in which it can be processed by equipment operating automatically?

(b) Do the data relate to living individuals?

(c) Are the individuals identifiable, even though the means of identification is held elsewhere within the Data User's organisation?

(d) Do the data contain facts, opinions, conjectures, thoughts etc (anything except intentions) that relate to living individuals?

(e) Is the organisation responsible for the collection of personal data? Does it control the contents and use of personal data (eg their processing and disclosure)? Are other organisations involved in controlling the contents and use of personal data?

(f) Are the personal data in the form in which they have been processed, or could they be processed in the future?

(g) Are the personal data processed, or can they be processed, to find out something about a Data Subject?

(h) Are the personal data processed as part of a service provided to other persons?

3.13 In outline, the Principles state that personal data must be obtained fairly and lawfully, be accurate, relevant to the purpose for which the data are collected, not excessive for that purpose, held no longer than is necessary, not disclosed without proper authority and securely held. They also state that there must be a right of correction of personal data that are found to be incorrect and that there must be a right of access by the Data Subjects to their own personal data. In particular, the Principles state that the purposes for which personal data are used must be specified, and that the disclosures that are made must be compatible with those purposes.

4. Part II of the Data Protection Act

4.1 Article 5 of the Convention states that 'Personal data shall be ... stored for specified and legitimate purposes', and Article 8 states that 'Any person has a right to ... establish the existence of an automated personal data file, its main purposes, and the name and address of the controller of the file'; in the Data Protection Act, both these objectives are designed to be met, in part, through Registration. Part II of the Act defines what information about Data Users and Computer Bureaux needs to be specified, and establishes how this is to be achieved: by means of a Register maintained by a Data Protection Registrar. The criminal offences associated with Registration, the Registrar's powers of supervision, and his general duties are also detailed here (the duties to promote the observance of the Data Protection Principles are described in Part V of the Act).

4.2 According to Section 4 of the Act, all uses of personal data (bar those few that are exempt) will have to be registered and Data Users will be committing an offence if they hold personal data and are not registered. An application for Registration must state whether the person wishes to be registered as a Data User, as a Computer Bureau, or as both, and must provide an address to which Data Subjects may write for access to their personal data (Subject Access). If a Data User holds personal data for two or more purposes, separate applications for Registration may be made for any of those purposes; once accepted, these details will form an Entry (or Entries) in the Register. Each Entry contains basic information about the Data User and information which describes, for each purpose, the personal data held (ie the types of individuals whose personal data are held, and the kinds of information held about them), from whom the personal data may need to be obtained and to whom the personal data may need to be disclosed; any territories outside the UK to which personal data may be transferred also have to be listed. Note that all these other descriptions (ie sources, disclosures etc) are related to specific purposes, and can be seen as fleshing out each purpose. A Data User may make changes to these particulars at any time.

4.3 Within 6 months of receipt of the application for Registration, the Registrar must notify the applicant whether the application has been accepted, refused or whether more time is necessary to consider the application. The Registrar may not refuse an application unless he considers the information provided to be insufficient or he believes the applicant is likely to contravene any of the Data Protection Principles. If an application is refused, the Registrar must state his reasons and inform the applicant of the rights of appeal to the Data Protection Tribunal (see paragraph 4.6).

4.4 To enable the Registrar to supervise compliance with the Principles the Registrar may -

(a) issue an Enforcement Notice if he believes a Data User has contravened any of the Principles, thus in effect forcing the Data User to comply with the Principles in question. The Enforcement Notice will contain a statement of the Principle(s) which the Registrar is satisfied have been or are being contravened, his reasons for reaching this conclusion, and particulars of the rights of the Data User to appeal to the Data Protection Tribunal.

(b) issue a De-registration Notice. This deletes the whole or part of a Data User's Register Entry, and thus has the effect of making illegal the processing of the relevant personal data. A De-registration Notice will contain a statement of the Principle(s) which the Registrar is satisfied have been or are being contravened, his reasons for deciding that compliance cannot be adequately achieved by the issue of an Enforcement Notice, the date on which he intends to remove particulars from the Register, and details of the appeals procedure to the Tribunal. Once a De-registration Notice has come into effect, the Data User concerned faces further difficulties, outlined in Section 7 of the Act, on any subsequent (within two years) application for Registration. Essentially, the normal arrangements whereby a Data User can assume 'acceptance by the Registrar unless told otherwise', do not apply. Instead, the Data User will have to wait, for a period not exceeding two months, for the Registrar's acceptance of the application (ie for approval to renew the processing of the personal data concerned).

(c) issue a Transfer Prohibition Notice, which has the effect of prohibiting a particular transfer of personal data to a territory outside the UK, if the Registrar is satisfied that a contravention of any of the Principles may result from the transfer. Transfer Prohibition Notices will contain statements of the Principle(s) which the Registrar believes are likely to be contravened, his reasons for believing so, the date on which the Notice is to take effect and details of the appeals procedure to the Data Protection Tribunal.

(d) apply to a circuit judge for a warrant to empower the Registrar to enter and search premises, to examine and test any data equipment found there, and to inspect and seize any documents that may provide relevant evidence. A warrant may not be issued unless the Registrar has reasonable grounds to suspect that an offence under the Act is being committed, or that the Data Protection Principles have been, or are being, contravened. In addition, the Registrar must have been refused entry to the premises, have given seven days notice of his demand for access, and have notified the occupier of the Registrar's application for a warrant (unless the judge is satisfied that these provisions would defeat the object of the entry)! As can be seen, there are many hurdles to jump before the Registrar can exercise these particular powers.

4.5 Failure to comply with an Enforcement or Transfer Prohibition Notice can lead to a criminal prosecution, in which a Data User can offer the defence that 'all due

Table 3: Membership of the Data Protection Tribunal (1990)

Part-time Chairman	J.A.C. Spokes QC Crown Court Recorder
Part-time Deputy Chairmen	Professor A.L. Diamond Law Department Queen Mary College, London
	Rear Admiral J.W.T. Walters, CB Barrister

Part-time Members

M.C.J. Barnes	Director, United Kingdom Immigrants Service
R.H. Barton QPM	Retired member of HM Inspectorate of Constabulary
Professor T.F. Carbery OBE	Head of Department of Office Organisation, University of Strathclyde
B. Chandler	Life Offices Association
A.B. Cowling	Association of Market Survey Organisations
Mrs K. Foss	Ex-member of National Consumer Council
J. Hanson	Retired Director of Social Services, Dorset County Council
Professor W.W. Holland MD, FRCGP, FRCP, FFCM	Department of Community Medicine, St Thomas' Hospital Medical School
K. Holroyd	APEX Official
B. Kelly	Former National Secretary, National Federation of Self Employed and Small Businesses Limited
G. Lanchin	Member of the Consumers Association

A. Lawrence	Principal Lecturer, Buckinghamshire College of Higher Education
P. Lumb	General Manager, Leeds Permanent Building Society
P.R. Oglesby	Retired Deputy Secretary, DHSS
H.A. Osborne	Retired Head of Law Section, Barclays Bank PLC
L. Peach	Director of Personnel, NHS Management Board (formerly Director of Personnel, IBM)
D.L. Perrot LLB, BCL	Reader in Business Law, University of Exeter; and Director, Exeter Enterprise Limited
L. Plowman CBE	Retired Secretary of the Association of Metropolitan Authorities
A. Pragnell CBE, DFC	Former Deputy Director General of the IBA
J.C. Richards MBE, IPFA, FPMI	Director of Pensions Administration, Water Authorities Superannuation Fund
J.A.M. Ross	Partner, KPMG Peat Marwick McLintock
V. Ross	Retired Chairman, Reader's Digest Association Limited
M.H. Smith	National Consumer Council
A.C. Sullivan	TGWU Official
E. Thomas	General Manager - Marketing, Compower Limited
A.W. Walker	Retired Chairman, Air Products Limited
N. Watson	National Association of Citizens Advice Bureaux
Professor G.J. Zellick MA, PhD	Professor of Public Law, University of London

Secretary

Miss S.M. Swinborne	Home Office, 50 Queen Anne's Gate London SW1H 9AT

diligence' was exercised to comply with the Notice. When a De-registration Notice has been served, no deletion may be made from the Register until there has been time to appeal and, if there is an appeal, until the Tribunal has reached its decision.

4.6 The Data Protection Tribunal is established for the hearing of appeals on the grounds that the Registrar has exceeded his powers in serving an Enforcement Notice, De-registration Notice or Transfer Prohibition Notice, or in refusing to accept or alter a Register Entry. Section 3 of the Act states that the Tribunal will consist of a Chairman and Deputy Chairman (of legal standing); Schedule 3 states that in Appeal Proceedings there shall be, additionally to the Chair, an equal number of Tribunal members to represent Data Users and Data Subjects. The list of Tribunal members, as presently appointed, is found in Table 3.

4.7 The Tribunal provides a balance to the Registrar's powers, and tests whether the Registrar was justified in his action. Whatever the Tribunal decides during an appeal can be taken to the Courts, by either party, on a point of law, and it is, therefore, possible for the Registrar and Tribunal to hold one view, and for the Courts to hold another.

4.8 This prospect is a consequence of the separation of powers in the UK. In terms of the Data Protection Act it is Parliament who passed the Act, it is the Registrar who polices the Act and offers guidance, but it is the Courts who decide what the Act means in reality. On the whole it is likely that the Registrar's guidance and the Tribunal's interpretation of the Registrar's decisions will be supported by the Courts. However, the ultimate arbiter of the Data Protection Act will be the Courts, and as a result a Data Protection Officer should keep abreast of any judicial interpretation of the Act.

4.9 Besides issuing Enforcement Notices, the Registrar (or Director of Public Prosecutions) may prosecute Data Users who:

(a) hold personal data and are unregistered or have not applied for Registration when they should have;

(b) knowingly or recklessly obtain, hold, use, disclose or transfer personal data other than as described in a Register Entry;

(c) fail to comply with any Notice issued by the Registrar;

(d) deliberately supply the Registrar with false or misleading information; or

(e) fail to keep the registered address up to date.

4.10 Proceedings may be taken against Computer Bureaux who:

(a) knowingly or recklessly operate as a Computer Bureau and process personal data without being registered as such;

(b) knowingly or recklessly disclose personal data without the Data User's authority;

(c) fail to keep the registered address up to date; or

(d) fail to comply with any Notice issued by the Registrar.

4.11 Proceedings may be taken against any person who:

(a) intentionally obstructs a person executing a warrant, or fails to help reasonably a person executing a warrant given under the terms of the Act (Schedule 4, Section 12 of the Act).

(b) knowingly or recklessly holds personal data for purposes not included in a Register Entry (Section 5 of the Act).

(c) knowingly or recklessly contravenes the Register Entry and obtains, uses, discloses or transfers personal data in a way at variance with the Register Entry (Section 5 of the Act).

4.12 As well as the individual liability outlined immediately above, Section 20 of the Act deals specifically with the liability of senior officers of an organisation (eg directors, managers etc) and states:

> 'Where an offence under this Act has been committed by a body corporate and is proved to have been committed with the consent or connivance of or to be attributable to any neglect on the part of any director, manager, secretary or similar officer of the body corporate or any person who was purporting to act in any such capacity, he as well as the body corporate shall be guilty of that offence and be liable to be proceeded against and punished accordingly'.

4.13 In most cases the maximum penalty is a fine (which is unlimited and therefore depends on the circumstances), with minor offences being subject to a maximum fine of £2,000. Jail sentences are only possible where contempt of Court is involved.

4.14 Section 38 of the Act notes that Government Departments are subject to the same obligations under this Act as a private person, although Departments are not liable to prosecution. However, it is possible for proceedings to be taken against individuals within a Department, and in some cases transgressors are likely to find themselves also in breach of the Official Secrets Act 1989. Some disclosures of information covered under the old Section 2 of the Official Secrets Act 1911, have been reintroduced in other legislation (eg disclosures from the Department of Social Security and Inland Revenue can be offences under the Social Security Act 1989 and the Finance Act 1989; in relation to the Census, the Census (Confidentiality) Act 1991). Each Department is to be treated as separate from any other Department and persons in the public service of the Crown will be treated as employees of their Department.

4.15 Data Subjects also have some 'clout' in persuading Data Users to comply with the Act. Besides complaining to the Registrar that a Data User is contravening a Data Protection Principle, they can apply to the Courts to:

(a) oblige a Data User to comply with a request to provide an individual with Subject Access;

(b) award compensation against a Data User, for damage and resulting distress caused by reason of the use of inaccurate personal data;

(c) award compensation against a Data User for damage and resulting distress caused by unauthorised access to, or loss, destruction or disclosure of personal data;

(d) order a Data User to rectify or erase inaccurate data;

(e) require any information sought by the Data Subject, via Subject Access, to be made available to the Court for inspection, before deciding whether Subject Access can proceed according to the provisions of the Act.

5. Part III of the Data Protection Act

5.1 Part III outlines a Data Subject's rights in detail. These rights include 'Subject Access' - allowing Data Subjects to ascertain whether personal data are held by a Data User, and to have a complete copy of their own personal data provided by that Data User. Subject Access is obtained through a formal procedure which may include payment of a fee, and the provision by the Data Subject of sufficient information to allow the Data User to ensure the identity of the Data Subject and to help locate the Data Subject's personal data. No aspect of this procedure can be so onerous or demanding as to frustrate the exercising of this right.

5.2 In addition, a Data Subject can seek damages from a Data User because the personal data are inaccurate or have been improperly disclosed, accessed or lost. Under the terms of the Act, a Data Subject must show actual damage; distress alone is not sufficient although if damage has occurred, compensation for distress can be taken into account. These actions can be brought before the Civil Courts, and the Registrar has no formal part to play in these proceedings, except that any investigation by the Registrar may be used in evidence.

5.3 Section 22 of the Act establishes a Data Subject's entitlement to compensation if personal data are 'incorrect or misleading as to any matter of fact', and if it can be proved to a Court's satisfaction that the inaccurate data caused damage to the Data Subject. A major defence available to the Data User is to prove to a Court's satisfaction that the User's operational procedures were of sufficient quality to establish that 'reasonable care' was taken to ensure the accuracy of the personal data.

5.4 Section 22 also outlines other means available to the Data User, to guard against the award of damages. As long as the data received or obtained by the Data User have been **recorded** accurately, damages cannot be awarded if the personal data have been marked as received from a Data Subject or third party, and if the personal data are always used with these markers. If the Data Subject has complained about the accuracy of personal data, this too must be indicated by a marker. As long as the meaning of the marker is clear, or explained to the recipient of the data, a marker need not be complex; it may be a simple character, or the name of the actual source of the data, or perhaps a set of initials.

5.5 Section 23 of the Act provides for compensation to be paid to the Data Subject if that Data Subject can prove to a Court's satisfaction that damage resulted from unauthorised loss, disclosure, access or destruction of personal data. The defence most likely to be advanced by a Data User will be that all reasonable steps that could be taken to prevent the damage were in fact taken.

5.6 Thus in most cases before the Courts (or investigations by the Registrar), the burden of proof will be on the Data User to demonstrate 'reasonable care' (ie that the Data User had the proper procedures in place at the material time, and actively monitored the effectiveness of these procedures). In this way the Act encourages Data Users to develop adequate quality control, security and privacy procedures in relation to the use of all personal data. Note that without documentary evidence, it will be difficult for a Data User to prove that procedures were changed, checked or reliably managed.

5.7 Section 24 outlines the conditions under which a Court can order the Data User to rectify or erase the personal data, and Section 25 states the conditions under which a Court can examine any personal data, including those for which a Subject Access exemption has been claimed by a Data User, to determine whether the Data Subject is entitled to receive the data. (A similar effect can be achieved by the Registrar serving an Enforcement Notice with respect to the Seventh Principle; if the Data User appeals to the Tribunal against the Notice, the Tribunal has powers to see the personal data).

6. Part IV of the Data Protection Act

6.1 Part IV outlines three categories of exemption from the Act: from Part II (Registration and Supervision of Data Users) and Sections 21 to 24 (Rights of Data Subjects); from the provisions of Subject Access (Section 21); and from the various non-disclosure provisions. The first exemption effectively means that, where it applies, the Data User should abide by the Data Protection Principles, but need not register, provide Subject Access or be subject to the enforcement powers of the Registrar in relation to the Principles or Registration. The Subject Access exemption means that the Data User need not provide a Data Subject with access to personal data covered by the exemption, nor inform the Data Subject that such personal data are held. Non-disclosure exemptions apply to disclosures which do not have to be described in a Data User's Register Entry.

6.2 All exemptions are limited by law and are only valid if specific stringent conditions are met; they are by no means easy to understand, whether in theory or in practice, and only a brief list and explanation is provided here (see Chapter 7 for comprehensive exposition of each exemption). The three categories of exemption will be considered in turn.

6.3 **Exemptions from Part II and Sections 21-24 of the Act**

6.3.1 These exemptions relate to personal data which are used for the purpose of National Security (Section 27 of the Act); or for domestic, family or personal affairs (Section 33); or to personal data that have to be made public by law (Section 34(1)). Personal data used for maintaining accounts, calculating payroll, pensions, keeping records for purchases, sales, and other management forecasts are exempt under Section 32, and some mailing lists, and unincorporated clubs, are also exempt under Section 33.

6.3.2 Under these exemptions, there is no need to register and no need to provide Subject Access to personal data. In addition, the Registrar cannot serve an Enforcement Notice and a Data Subject cannot claim damages. Consequently, to ensure that these privileges are not abused, all the exemptions have stringent statutory conditions which are usually defined in terms of 'if' and 'only'. These 'ifs' and 'onlys' **must be rigorously applied**.

6.3.3 For example, personal data used for the calculation of pay, pensions and other remuneration, or personal data used for business accounting purposes, are exempt if the personal data are used only for these purposes, otherwise they must be registered. In addition, to qualify for the exemption the personal data can only be disclosed in specific circumstances, and if any other disclosure is made that is not in accord with these circumstances (eg disclosure to an engineer for the purpose of computer maintenance) then this exemption **does not** apply (and the particulars under which the personal data are used are fully subject to the Act, eg must be registered etc). The disclosures described as permitted under the terms of this exemption are:

(a) to any person, other than the Data User, by whom the remuneration or pensions in question are payable;

(b) for the purpose of obtaining actuarial advice;

(c) for research into occupational diseases or injuries;

(d) for audit purposes;

(e) for the purpose of providing information about the Data User's finances; or

(f) if the Data Subject has consented to the disclosure.

6.3.4 In the first instance it will be the Data User who says 'this exemption applies to me'; it can be either a Court or the Registrar who may ask the Data User to substantiate that claim. Thus, for example, it could be insufficient for a Data User to claim 'I have an accounts system, therefore by virtue of Section 32 the personal data are exempt'. The Courts and the Registrar could expect Data Users to be able to demonstrate that they had acted reasonably in claiming the exemption (eg performed some kind of analysis, preferably in a well-documented form, of the personal data that were processed and the disclosures that were made). Failure to do this could invite prosecution for holding unregistered personal data.

6.3.5 Note that if the conditions of an exemption are infringed at a future date (eg the Data User decides to sign a computer maintenance contract), Registration must precede this, since otherwise the Data User is processing personal data illegally. If there is no relevant Register Entry, and anything untoward happened (eg an unauthorised disclosure which caused damage), to be shown to be processing personal data outwith the terms of the Act would certainly compound the Data User's problem in presenting a defence to a Court. In general, large Data Users, who have to register anyway, will find these exemptions to be so tightly specified that they will derive little or no benefit from claiming them.

6.4 Exemptions from Subject Access

6.4.1 Under these exemptions, a Data User need not inform a Data Subject, following a Subject Access request, that personal data are held, nor provide a copy of the requested personal data. In addition, the Registrar cannot serve an Enforcement Notice to allow Subject Access. Note, however, that by virtue of Section 25 a Court may require to inspect the personal data. Similarly, the Data Protection Registrar or

Tribunal may become involved in confirming that the conditions surrounding a Subject Access exemption do actually apply. This means that a Data User should be prepared to justify why a Subject Access exemption applies.

6.4.2 There are many Subject Access exemptions. The complete list is as follows:

(a) if a Minister of the Crown certifies that the exemption is required for the purposes of safeguarding national security (Section 27);

(b) if the personal data are held by an individual and used only for personal tasks or for recreational, domestic or household purposes (Section 33(1));

(c) if the personal data are held by an unincorporated members' club, only relate to the members of the club, only consist of names and addresses, and are used only for the purpose of distributing articles to the Data Subjects, **and** if each Data Subject whose personal data are to be used in this way has agreed to this (Section 33(2)-(5));

(d) if the personal data are required by law to be made publicly available (Section 34(1));

(e) if the personal data are held for the purpose of making judicial appointments (Section (31));

(f) if the personal data consist of information which is claimed to be protected by legal privilege (Section 31);

(g) if the personal data are held only for preparing statistics or for carrying out research, providing that the information is not disclosed for any other purpose and that the results of the research are presented in a form which does not identify any of the Data Subjects (Section 33(6));

(h) if the personal data are available to the Data Subject through the provisions of the Consumer Credit Act 1974 (Section 34(3));

(i) if compliance with a request for access would expose the Data User to proceedings for an offence under any other Act (Section 34(9));

(j) if the personal data are kept only for the purpose of replacing other data which may be lost or destroyed (ie back-up data: Section 34(4));

(k) if the personal data are held by certain regulatory bodies or by bodies exercising statutory functions designated by Order of the Home Secretary (eg the Bank of England), or if such functions are designed to protect members of the public against financial loss (Section 30 of the Data Protection Act and Section 190 of the Financial Services Act 1986: relevant Orders to date are the 'Data Protection (Regulation of Financial Services etc) (Subject Access Exemption) Order' (S.I. 1987 No. 1905), and the 'Data Protection (Regulation of Financial Services etc) (Subject Access Exemption) (Amendment) Order' (S.I. 1990 No. 310);

(l) if Subject Access would prejudice the prevention or detection of crime, the apprehension or prosecution of offenders, the assessment or collection of any tax or duty (Section 28: this exemption is inevitably controversial because of the very nature of policing);

(m) if the Home Secretary lays an Order before Parliament in relation to personal data consisting of information as to the physical or mental health of the Data Subject (Section 29: the relevant Subject Access Modification Order is S.I. 1987 No. 1903);

(n) if the Home Secretary lays an Order before Parliament in relation to personal data that are held by government departments or local authorities or voluntary organisations, and if Subject Access would prejudice the carrying out of Social Work (Section 29: the relevant Subject Access Modification Order is S.I. 1987 No. 1904);

(o) if the Home Secretary lays an Order before Parliament that states that the restriction of Subject Access rights ought to prevail over the interests of the Data Subject or any other individual (Section 34(2): the relevant Subject Access Modification Order is S.I. 1987 No. 1906);

(p) if the personal data are held for a purpose relating to sperm and egg donors (Section 32 of the Human Fertilisation and Embryology Act 1990).

6.4.3 Note that via Section 2(3) the Secretary of State may by Order modify the Subject Access provisions, for the purpose of providing additional safeguards, where the data consist of the racial origin of Data Subjects, their political opinions or religious or other beliefs, their criminal convictions, their physical or mental health, or their sexual life. Orders made by the Home Secretary that have the effect of changing Subject Access have to be approved by both Houses of Parliament.

6.5 Non-disclosure exemptions

6.5.1 Under these exemptions, a disclosure can legally take place but an indication of that disclosure need not appear in the Register Entry; in addition, the Registrar cannot issue an Enforcement Notice in relation to that disclosure. However, if an individual suffers damage by reason of the non-disclosure provisions, compensation can only be awarded against a Data User if a Court deemed that the incorrect application of the non-disclosure provisions led to an unauthorised disclosure of personal data.

6.5.2 The conditions surrounding a non-disclosure exemption need to be followed rigorously, as there is a very thin line between an unauthorised disclosure or unregistered disclosure (which can result in damages being paid or in prosecution), and a perfectly valid 'non-disclosure exempted' disclosure. What separates the two will be defined by the procedures adopted by a Data User towards the disclosure of the personal data.

6.5.3 The non-disclosure provisions can cover the following disclosures:

(a) to individual Data Subjects or any individual acting on their behalf or at their request or with their consent (Section 34(6));

(b) to servants or agents of the Data User or Bureau to allow those servants or agents to perform their function, providing that the use of the personal data is lawful (Section 34(6));

(c) to prosecuting or revenue agencies if there are reasonable grounds for believing that non-disclosure would prejudice the prevention or detection of crime or the apprehension or prosecution of offenders or the assessment or collection of any tax or duty (Section 28: this disclosure is inevitably controversial because of the very nature of policing);

(d) to any person acting in an emergency to prevent injury or damage to the health of any person (Section 34(8));

(e) required by or under any enactment, by any rule of law or by the order of a Court (Section 34(5));

(f) to safeguard national security (Section 27);

(g) to obtain legal advice, or to participate in legal proceedings (Section 34(5));

(h) any disclosures specified in Sections 32 ('Payrolls and accounts') and Section 33 ('Domestic or other limited purposes'), if the exemption from Part II and Sections 21 to 24 is claimed.

6.5.4 In general, as far as disclosures of personal data are concerned, it is also the duty of the Data User to ensure that any disclosures are:

(a) only to the person(s) or organisations listed in the relevant Register Entry;

(b) only to territories outside the UK specified in the relevant Register Entry;

(c) made by a Computer Bureau (if a Bureau is used) only with the prior authority of the person for whom the bureau services are being provided.

7. Part V of the Data Protection Act

7.1 Part V of the Act outlines the duties of the Registrar (Section 36). These include promoting the observance of the Principles, considering complaints from Data Subjects, disseminating guidance about the operation of the Act, promoting voluntary Codes of Practice, and reporting annually (at least) to Parliament. Note that the Registrar can use his Annual Report to point out deficiencies in the Act, whilst the duty to consider Data Subjects' complaints will be the main trigger for exercising his enforcement powers.

7.2 Other Sections in Part V tie up the 'loose ends' of the legislation. They deal with the status of the Registrar with respect to the Council of Europe Convention (Section 37); application of the Act to Government Departments and to the Police (Section 38); the territorial scope of the legislation (Section 39) and how Ministerial Orders will be laid before Parliament (Section 40). The latter Section, for example, allows the Secretary of State for the Home Department to set the fees for Subject Access, for an application for Registration and for a certified copy of a Register Entry. Section 41 contains other definitions to assist with the general interpretation of the Act, and Section 42 describes a (now redundant) timetable for the Act to come into effect.

7.3 In essence, therefore, the Act has a straightforward structure. Part 1 outlines the conditions for compliance, Part II the mechanism of compliance and the penalties for non-compliance, Part III the rights of Data Subjects, Part IV the exemptions from parts of the Act, and Part V the duties of the Registrar. Unfortunately, in the experience of most Data Users, the work necessary to ensure compliance with the Act is not so straightforward.

Chapter Two: Getting the Act together

1. Managing Data Protection

1.1 The easiest way for a Data User to demonstrate that the Data Protection Act is being taken seriously, is to adopt a Data Protection Policy. This policy need not be a complicated statement; a commitment to the Data Protection Principles and to procedures for compliance should suffice. In organisational terms, the policy should delegate a board level manager to be responsible for implementing the Act; that manager should call for regular progress reports on the implications for the Data User that arise from the Act, and report, as appropriate, to the board. All staff should be made aware that Data Protection Policy ranks as an integral part of their conditions of service (eg it is as important to the organisation as commercial confidentiality).

1.2 Ultimately this senior manager will probably delegate day to day work to a member of staff who has received the necessary specialised training - the 'Data Protection Officer'. Depending on the size of the Data User, this might involve a full time post; however, if the Officer also has other work to do, a high priority must be given to the Act (as compliance with its provisions is a statutory duty of all Data Users). The Officer must have sufficient support from management to ensure that things get done; consequently management's first task is to determine how much time the Officer can spend on Data Protection work.

1.3 Regrettably, in many cases even this basic assessment is not made and Data Protection Officers find themselves working in limbo; not having been given the tools for the job. In such circumstances it is important for an Officer to regain control by reporting this fact to the line manager. Having agreed the situation, a period should be set aside (eg 5 days) to produce a report which identifies and describes the work that needs to be done. One resultant recommendation would define the length of time (in a rolling programme of work) which the Officer should devote to Data Protection over a period of three months (eg an average of 1 day per week); a further recommendation would set out the appropriate reporting structure. If these basic procedures cannot be agreed and implemented, or if management repeatedly offers little real support, Officers should for their own protection (rather than data protection) record in clear terms that they cannot take responsibility should the worst happen.

1.4 In a sizeable organisation with a well-established and perhaps complex structure, it is likely that a Liaison Team, made up of representatives from each relevant department, will be needed. Such a Team should meet on a regular basis, perhaps with the senior manager in the chair and the Data Protection Officer as Secretary, to review the work in progress. The Team should never be disbanded, although obviously membership of the Team will change, and the frequency of its meetings will reflect the scale of the work to be done. In other organisations there might be no formal Liaison Team, and meetings between the Data Protection Officer and managers would only take place as and when specifically needed. In the latter case, the Policy must expressly state that it is the duty of all managers to cooperate with the Data Protection Officer.

1.5 Both arrangements must incorporate a formal reporting system; this is essential to the formulation of an adequate defence against any action under the Act brought by a Data Subject or by the Registrar. Periodical reports should, therefore, be made to the senior manager (or to the full board if appropriate) concerning any changes in relevant procedures, or in the use and Registration of personal data, and on the status of any Subject Access requests. Progress reports should also be prepared on the work necessary to conform with other aspects of the Data Protection Principles. The Data Protection Officer is advised to keep a diary of meetings arranged, their aims, decisions taken, conclusions drawn, actions agreed and any other significant details that surround compliance with any aspect of Data Protection. This diary represents valuable evidence that the Officer did indeed carry out Data Protection tasks within the given resources.

1.6 Progress reports to the senior manager will be based either on the results of meetings of the Liaison Team, or of meetings between the Data Protection Officer and managers. In both cases details about the work in progress within each department should be collated and reported formally. Any serious difficulty (eg managers who do not adequately respond to Data Protection initiatives) should be reported as it is encountered. Objectives should be also be formally minuted for action and reported to the senior manager (or to the board if appropriate).

1.7 Management must be prepared to act on these reports and to recognise and resolve the problems that face the Data Protection Officer. The Officer should not underestimate the amount and range of work that has to be done, and should be prepared to argue for the resources that are necessary; it is essential that the Officer has the time, authority, resources and expertise to complete the tasks. If, at the end of the day, management decides that a proposal is too expensive in terms of resources etc, then that decision lifts managerial responsibility from the Officer's shoulders.

1.8 The Data Protection Officer need not be a computer expert. The major attributes required, apart from courtesy and common sense, are a sufficient knowledge of the workings of the Act and its underlying Principles, to allow its interpretation in the context of the organisation's data processing activities. As the Officer is an agent of change, good interpersonal and communication skills are required, as is the ability to produce clear documentation, to use the management structure and to design new operational procedures. The Officer's principal duties can be summarised as follows:

(a) **Understand the Act**

This is not easy. It means understanding abstruse phrases such as 'exempt from the non-disclosure provisions' and deciphering the definitions or strict exemptions. The Officer will have to comprehend the Act's specific provisions in relation to data processing, and to evaluate how best to organise the work in relation to the organisation's structure.

(b) **Identify key personnel**

Key managers and personnel, expert within their area of work, should be identified; such contacts could form the nucleus of any Data Protection Liaison Team. The co-operation, assistance, and goodwill of these contacts is vital to present and future developments, and to the evaluation of necessary changes in work practices, new security routines and other procedures.

(c) **Inform management**

Managers must know what their responsibilities are in relation to the Act. They should know that a change in their operations may require some Data Protection advice. They should be able to recognise problem areas and know that they need to discuss the options necessary to deal with problems. A manager should be provided with sufficient information to be able to advise staff on appropriate procedures (eg in relation to disclosures). Above all, there should be a clear line of communication between managers and the Data Protection Officer (or the relevant member of the Liaison Team) so that, as far as possible, the statement 'I did not know ...' will be avoided.

(d) **Draw up a timetable for the work**

Periodic reviews of Registration particulars (incorporating sample checks on the accuracy of the Registration) are necessary. The frequency of such checks will be determined by the complexity of the Data User's activities and by how often these activities are modified with respect to the use of personal data. Additionally time must **always** be found for ad hoc amendments in response to impending changes in the use of personal data. Reviews to check compliance with other aspects of the Data Protection Principles should be implemented; an action timetable agreed at meetings will ensure that work in relation to the Principles is carried out in good time.

(e) **Perform a census**

All holdings of personal data should be identified and a census of the data conducted. If this was not done comprehensively before initial Registration, it needs to be done as soon as possible thereafter, and checked at appropriate intervals (see above). The value of a proper census of the data is immeasurable and should provide a clear and concise picture of data processing within the organisation; it can also be combined with a hardware or software inventory. The census should be completed by all staff who are in charge of sections which have particular functions that relate to the processing of personal data, and can assist in the evaluation of procedures to meet the requirements of Copyright legislation, of the Computer Misuse Act 1990, and of other aspects which involve computer security.

(f) **Maintain the Register Entries**

Most Data Users will have registered as both Data User and Computer Bureau; Registration has to be renewed on payment of the appropriate fee after a three year period. A Data User's Registration must provide a description of the purposes for which personal data are used, the types of data to be held, from whom the data may need to be obtained, to whom they may need to be disclosed, any territories to which the data may be transferred, and an address to which Data Subjects may write for access to their data. As outlined in paragraphs (e) and (f) above, the Data Protection Officer is responsible for keeping all Entries in the Register up to date, for repeating parts (or all) of the census, as necessary, and for checking the accuracy of current Entries. All managers should have a copy of the Entry or Entries that relate to the personal data for which they are responsible. Checking an Entry is especially important if the original Registration was carried out in haste or after cursory enquiry (say, to meet a deadline); such Registrations tend to contain errors, and may also show signs that the Data User was unsure about (or perhaps took insufficient care to satisfy) the legal obligations.

(g) **Ensure compliance with Data Protection Principles**

The Data Protection Officer is responsible for advising on the organisation's compliance with all Data Protection Principles, and on its adherence to the Data Protection Policy. The Officer should be able to detect any weak links, and inadequate or incorrect procedures, and should be involved in establishing new procedures and monitoring their effectiveness. The Officer must be able to report regularly to senior management, and to ensure that identified difficulties are properly resolved. Compliance with the Principles (and monitoring such compliance) will form the bulk of the work that needs to be done by all concerned with the Act.

(h) **Evaluate staff awareness and training requirements**

Appropriate seminars, lectures, workshops and discussions should be undertaken to introduce staff to the Principles of Data Protection. These sessions should highlight staff responsibilities, and their obligations under this legislation. Staff should know which Register Entry or Entries apply to their work and be properly trained in the disclosure of personal data. Leaflets, posters and stickers may help remind staff of their obligations. The Data Protection Officer should be involved in training courses (including induction courses for new staff), and liaise with Trades Unions and with Personnel sections regarding any impact of the Act on changing work patterns or on changes in conditions of employment. A high level of staff awareness is essential if the Data User is to avoid falling foul of the Act; all staff should be aware of the criminal offences created by this legislation.

(i) **Keep up to date with guidance and with case law**

The Data Protection Officer will need to 'read, mark, learn and inwardly digest' all the Registrar's Guidelines and Guidance Notes. In addition, the Officer should keep up with the decisions of the Courts, Registrar and Data Protection Tribunal; discussion with a Legal Officer should assist in achieving this. A cuttings service may be available to some Data Users; the computing trade press often carries relevant incidents and anecdotes missed by the nationals. (Data Protection News, a quarterly magazine produced by the authors of this book, is devoted to this aspect of the work).

(j) **A focus within the Data User**

The Data Protection Officer should be well known and clearly identifiable within the Data User; it is a high profile job. If staff and managers do not know who the Officer is, or where the Officer works, then how are they to seek advice, and what chance has the hapless Data Subject who wants Subject Access? What opinion would the Registrar form of this arrangement following a complaint by a Data Subject?

1.9 Implementation of the Data Protection Act will involve some or all of the following staff:

(a) **Data Protection Officer** - to establish how the Data User measures up to the requirements of the legislation, and to provide administrative support.

(b) **Line Managers/Liaison Officers** - to represent the various departmental activities of the Data User, to define current procedures, to be involved in designing new procedures, to help monitor compliance within their departments, and to draw attention to new procedures and systems so that Register Entries can be amended in good time.

(c) **Technical Staff** - to ensure new procedures are technically feasible, especially where security, computer operations and accuracy of personal data are concerned.

(d) **Personnel Department** - to contribute whenever personnel considerations are at issue (Trades Union representatives may also need to be consulted).

(e) **Senior Management** - to determine priorities, monitor progress, thump the table if nothing happens, and ensure the correct composition of any Data Protection Team by co-opting the necessary skills.

(f) **Internal Auditor** - to ensure that procedures and policies are compatible with the established audit guidelines.

(g) **Legal Officer** - to be present if it looks likely that the Data User will become embroiled with the Courts, Data Protection Tribunal or with the Registrar, or following legal action by a Data Subject.

2. Outline of the work that needs to be done

2.1 A major task will be to ensure that the Data User conforms to the Eight Data Protection Principles. Some aspects of these Principles are by no means clear, and seem to comprise noble but vague exhortations towards unobtainable ideals. For example, what is 'appropriate security' (Eighth Principle) and how can anybody assess what is meant by 'adequate, relevant and not excessive' (Fourth Principle)? To meet this problem of interpretation, and to supplement the Registrar's publications, in-house guidance on appropriate standards and practices, relevant to the departments concerned, needs to be produced. In many cases, Codes of Practice written by trade associations or representative bodies will provide useful advice.

2.2 To satisfy the requirements of the First Principle that the 'personal data shall be obtained, and personal data shall be processed, fairly and lawfully', the Data User should not knowingly deceive or mislead any person as to the purposes for which personal data are processed. Wherever feasible, the Data User should give an indication of such purposes on any forms used to collect data, and train staff to understand, and to explain where necessary, why personal data are being collected. In addition, the Data User should seek to ensure that no unfair pressure is used in order to obtain the information.

2.3 The Second and Third Principles are satisfied by Registration, and by making certain that the registered details are, in themselves, **all** lawful. Consequently, the Data User should review the holding of personal data, ensure that the Register Entries are properly monitored and kept up to date and, as necessary, ensure that they contain:

(a) particulars that adequately describe all processing of the personal data held by the Data User; that explain as fully as possible the purpose(s) for which the personal data are held by the Data User; that indicate the types of personal data, the sources and disclosures involved, and any overseas transfers;

(b) information that, to the extent permitted by the Registration format, is neither ambiguous nor confusing to the Data Subject.

2.4 The Data User should designate a person or persons (usually the Data Protection Officer) to be responsible for Registration, and to answer questions from Data Subjects pertaining to any Register Entry. In addition, the Data User should ensure that:

(a) by establishing sound operational procedures, all uses and disclosures of personal data are lawful and compatible with the Register Entry;

(b) personal data can lawfully and safely be disclosed, in accordance with procedures that identify the disclosees;

(c) all uses and disclosures of personal data are regularly monitored and reviewed to see if they are appropriate;

(d) staff are at all times aware of the particular responsibilities pertaining to the uses and disclosures of personal data, are properly trained, and will not use or disclose personal data without following established procedures.

2.5 The Data User should acknowledge that certain personal data may require special safeguards (see Section 2(3) of the Act). Consequently the Data User should recognise that an enhanced level of care pertains to any personal data which relate to an individual's racial origin, political opinions, religious or other beliefs, physical or mental health or sexual life, and criminal convictions. (Note: some other countries add consumer credit and trade union membership to this list).

2.6 The Fourth Principle involves the Data User in examining the personal data held to ensure that they are 'adequate, relevant, and not excessive' in relation to every purpose for which the data are processed. Data Users should be prepared to explain why personal data are held, and to justify that each and every item of data is necessary to the relevant registered purpose.

2.7 The Fifth Principle implies that a Data User should establish procedures to verify that personal data are accurate and, where necessary, kept up to date in relation to the purpose for which the personal data are used. In addition, the Data User should take account of properly notified corrections to personal data, and rectify, as may be necessary, such incorrect data. (Section 22 of the Act allows for compensation to be paid to a Data Subject who suffers damage by reason of inaccurate personal data).

2.8 The Data User should also undertake to establish procedures which allow rectification or erasure of personal data, in compliance with formal requests from Data Subjects. Where personal data have been received from a third party, the Data User should consult, where practicable, with that third party before instigating any change.

2.9 The Data User should provide procedures to allow a Data Subject to question a decision not to correct or erase a Data Subject's personal data. These procedures will be in addition to the Data Subject's statutory right to complain to the Registrar. In addition, the Data User should attempt to correct any action that was based on incorrect personal data, advise disclosees of such corrections whenever practicable and train staff in proper recording practices.

2.10 To comply with the Sixth Principle, a Data User should review the length of time that personal data are kept, monitor whether personal data are still required, adhere to such legal requirements as may be in force for keeping certain personal data for specific lengths of time, and dispose of those personal data that are no longer required. Where personal data are kept for historical or statistical purposes the Data User should undertake, where appropriate, to render the data anonymous, and to keep under review the justification of these purposes.

2.11 The Seventh Principle requires a Data User to satisfy Data Subject Access, and to be prepared to correct or erase personal data. The Data Subject has a right (unless Access is restricted through the application of a Subject Access exemption):

(a) to be informed whether or not a Data User holds personal data about a Data Subject;

(b) to receive, within 40 days following a valid request for Access, a copy of the personal data expressed in terms that are intelligible to the Data Subject, including an explanation of any coded information contained in the data.

2.12 In satisfying a Subject Access request, the Data User's obligation to supply a copy of the information does not commence until the request has been received in writing, the identity of the individual making the request has been adequately established, and the Data User has received from the Data Subject appropriate assistance (should this be necessary) to locate the personal data. Payment of the fee (if applicable) has to be made before the information is released to the Data Subject.

2.13 If a Data User has separate Entries in the Register 'in respect of data held for different purposes' (see Section 21(3) of the Act), then the Data Subject must make a separate request, and pay a separate fee (if applicable), in respect of each Entry to which Subject Access is requested.

2.14 Following Subject Access, or the failure to obtain Subject Access (and perhaps as a challenge to the application of a Subject Access exemption), a Data Subject may:

(a) seek a Court order to force the Data User to comply fully with a Subject Access request (if the Data Subject has grounds for believing that some personal data have been unlawfully withheld);

(b) seek a Court order to have personal data rectified, erased or supplemented by a statement of the true facts, if the Data User has refused a request to this effect; or

(c) complain to the Data Protection Registrar that the Data User is in breach of the Seventh Principle.

2.15 The Eighth Principle requires a Data User to take appropriate security measures to guard against unauthorised access to the personal data held, or alteration, disclosure or destruction, or accidental loss or destruction of these personal data. Such measures will take account of the nature of the personal data, the potential harm to a Data Subject that would result from a security breach, the reliability of staff having access to the data and the existing security measures already taken by the Data User.

2.16 Consequently, the Data User should ensure that security of computer equipment, networks, programs, data and documentation is maintained at a high standard, and that access to data and equipment is at all times restricted to appropriate staff. The Data User should train staff in proper practices and procedures, and ensure that such procedures are monitored and reviewed. In addition, the Data User should undertake to establish procedures to guard against accidental disclosures, to recover from disasters and, where necessary, to provide emergency stand-by arrangements (Section 23 of the Act allows for compensation to be paid to Data Subjects who suffer damage by reason of personal data being held in an insecure fashion).

2.17 When compliance with the Eighth and Fifth Principles is being monitored, it is especially important that progress is formally recorded. Such a record could play a crucial part in any defence against charges that the personal data were inaccurate or kept in an insecure manner, or that improper procedures resulted in a Data Subject suffering damage (Part III of the Act outlines the liabilities involved).

2.18 In cases where compensation is claimed, the Act allows a primary defence, should the matter come before the Courts. This is that the Data User took 'such care as in all the circumstances was reasonably required' to prevent what occurred from occurring. Thus, if the worst happens, documentary evidence of meetings and decisions could be used to prove to a Court that the issue was taken seriously by the Data User, and that what happened was, say, a genuine accident, and not attributable to the negligence of the Data User.

2.19 An important concern will be a good working relationship with staff; not only because the work could affect current practices, but also because of the need to explain to staff their own and the Data User's liabilities under the Act. Staff should be alerted to the fact that, in certain circumstances, it is possible for employees to be prosecuted for criminal offences under the Act. In addition, senior managers who the Courts decide have neglected their duty under the Act (eg to sufficiently inform or train staff, or to monitor staff reliability) could also face criminal proceedings. Staff who make unauthorised disclosures of information and who work in Central Government may face prosecution under the Official Secrets Act 1989, the Finance Act 1989, the Social Security Act 1989 or the Census (Confidentiality) Act 1991.

2.20 Staff must be given clear instructions, and trained to keep personal data confidential and solely for the purpose of their work. Defining responsibilities of staff within the workplace is important; everyone must be aware why new procedures are being introduced, and of the possible consequences should, for example, staff fail to follow instructions and there is an unauthorised disclosure of personal data. Staff should be instructed not take personal data from the workplace unless formally authorised to do so by management (eg so that the arrangements for an equivalent level of 'appropriate security' can be made).

2.21 In summary, all procedures that relate to personal data should be formally assessed. Any new procedure should be:

(a) **R**easonable	(not excessive or restrictive)
(b) **E**ffective	(in solving the problem)
(c) **S**imple	(as easy to operate as the current procedure)
(d) **C**ompared	(not out of step with common practice)
(e) **U**nderstood	(to appreciate why the change is necessary)
(f) **E**ncouraged	(through training in the new procedure)
(g) **S**crutinised	(to ensure that the procedure works).

2.22 This approach, established with the help of the Data Protection Officer, **RESCUES** the Data User from the maze of the legislation. Formal reports protect the Data User from allegations of acting unreasonably or making little attempt to comply with the Principles. Checking the status of the Register Entries, taking action on those which require amendments, and ensuring that all staff are aware of the implications that arise from Registration will help to protect the Data User (and staff) from accusations that they offended 'knowingly or recklessly'.

3. Understanding and controlling the Registration process

3.1 Obtaining the information

3.1.1 The first stage in performing a census is to identify where all personal data are held. In some organisations an inventory of data processing equipment will first need to be taken; this would involve every manager responsible for such equipment in answering some simple questions: Who is the manager responsible? What is the equipment? Where is it located? Is the equipment used in conjunction with information that could relate to, or identify, any living individual? Some Data Users may take this opportunity to ask other useful questions: eg what software is being used? (in order to check whether copyright has been infringed and whether unauthorised copies of software have been made); what are the serial numbers of the equipment and peripherals? (useful to have on the record in case of theft or an insurance claim).

3.1.2 Having identified where and by whom personal data might be held, the next stage is to move to a census of personal data proper. The problem is that what ultimately will be registered is an not inventory of computer applications or even of the computers themselves, but the purposes for which the Data User holds personal data. The differences between an equipment inventory and a personal data census can be profound; for example an inventory may show ten terminals and fifteen microcomputers in a large office; however, with respect to personal data they all could be used for the same purpose and for the same set of Data Subjects. Conversely there might be one small office with a single micro that uses personal data for ten purposes each involving a different set of Data Subjects. In addition, output containing personal data and originating in one office may be sent to another office which has no computer, to be used in the second office for another purpose (whereas the location would not be shown in any equipment inventory). Care will also be required since computing equipment is only one example of equipment that can process personal data (see the discussion of the definition of 'data' and 'personal data' in Chapter 1). Even in smaller organisations, where some personal data could currently be exempt from Registration, a census should be taken; it is the only way of ensuring that an exemption has been properly applied and checked by the Data User. Thus, to keep control over what personal data processing takes place, all applications that use personal data must be included in the census.

3.1.3 A copy of the census form should be sent to all managers who are in charge of a section, function or activity which is involved in the processing of personal data. These managers must decide whether other members of their staff also need to complete such a form (for example, in a large office where all the equipment is used to process personal data for one purpose, only one census form might be needed; however if personal data are used for different purposes then census forms may have to be widely distributed). The census should provide the Data Protection Officer with all the necessary information to check existing Register Entries, compile a new Register Entry, or amend an existing Entry. It should, therefore, ask for:

(a) the name, signature, date of completion of the census and location of the person (ie the respondent) who is responsible for the section's use of personal data. This not only demonstrates (if necessary to a Court) that a census took place, it ensures that any future enquiry about the application or about the census form can be answered by the person most directly involved;

(b) the name or description of the computer application and equipment used, so that any census forms filled in by different respondents, but relating to the same or similar use of personal data, can be grouped together;

(c) a description, in the respondent's own words, of the specific purposes (ie not the 'Standard Purposes' established by the Registrar) for which the personal data are held for each computer application supervised by the respondent (for example, purpose A - payment of weekly wages; purpose B - keeping sickness returns, purpose C - production of staff mailing list). If no personal data are processed by the section, then this fact should be clearly stated;

(d) the classification of the data fields held in relation to each of the purposes outlined in (c) above (for example, purpose A fields: name, national insurance number, salary; purpose B fields: name, date illness began, date returned to work; purpose C fields: name, location, telephone number). An alternative would be to ask for sample inputs, or printouts that describe the personal data. The census should note any personal data which the Act indicates are of a special nature (criminal convictions, mental or physical health, racial origin, sexual life, political opinions or religious or other beliefs) in case an Order is made under Section 2(3) of the Act. Personal data held for the purpose of carrying out Social Work also need to be identified, as Social Work records often contain personal data in these categories, and because such personal data may be exempt from Subject Access (Section 29). In some cases it is possible to infer, from the context in which the personal data are used, that they may require particular safeguards; thus it is important to leave a free text space for the respondent to comment (eg to explain any doubts);

(e) the sources of personal data for each of the purposes outlined in (c) above. It will be useful to include internal sources, as the first step towards checking compliance with the First Principle, and for tracing from where within the organisation the personal data are obtained;

(f) the disclosees of personal data for each of the purposes outlined in (c) above. It is useful to include internal disclosures in the census (ie disclosures to different departments or sections of the Data User), so that the Data Protection Officer can check that personal data are not disclosed by the Data User via a secondary route. Additionally, if personal data are sent from Department A to Department B, Department B's use may require an additional purpose to be registered);

(g) a description of the types of Data Subjects for each of the purposes outlined in (c) above (in the examples given, the Data Subject in every case is an employee);

(h) the name of any territory outside the United Kingdom to which the personal data are transferred in machine readable form (note that the Channel Islands and the Isle of Man are defined as being outside the UK).

3.1.4 In conducting the census, decisions will often have to be taken with respect to 'grey areas' which may or may not fall within the scope of the Act. In such cases, the following scenario can usually obtain the correct result. Ask the relevant member of staff involved with the 'grey area' to imagine that the Police, urgently investigating a matter of life and death, need to identify a particular living individual from the data in question. They approach the manager for help and ask one basic question: "Can you identify this individual from these data, or from these data used in combination with manual files known to you?". If the answer to this question is "yes" (note that "I could, if pushed" means "yes"), then the next question is whether the personal data are actually processed by reference to any living individual. Only if the answer is an emphatic "**NEVER**" should the census not be taken any further; Table 2 of Chapter 1 (located after paragraph 3.11.9) lists the complete set of questions to be asked.

3.1.5 The completed census returns should be grouped to reflect the Data User's structure and data processing activities. The returns in each group will then be used to complete an application for Registration, and will eventually constitute a Register Entry. The advice of respondents will also be useful to determine training requirements, and when arranging for Procedural Reviews. All Data Users will find it useful to repeat the census, in whole or in part, on a regular basis.

3.2 The Register Entry format

3.2.1 Having performed the census, the complications of the Registration process have yet to be mastered. One consideration in determining how many Register Entries a Data

User should have is how Subject Access will be administered by the Data User. For example, if all the Data User's activities are entered in one Register Entry, then, as a consequence of Section 21(3) of the Act, a single Subject Access application will entitle Data Subjects to a copy of all their personal data used in any or all of these activities. If the organisation has a complex data processing structure, this might make it not only very inconvenient, but also very expensive in resources to retrieve the data.

3.2.2 At first glance, the answer to this problem would seem to be to have as many Register Entries as possible. However, quite apart from the expense involved (currently £75 per Entry, for a period of up to three years), the Registrar has pointed out that the number of Register Entries should not be such as to frustrate Data Subject Access ('NOTES to help you apply for Registration', page 2). In practice, therefore, a reasonable balance between these opposing considerations is required.

3.2.3 Clarity in the Register Entries is an important factor. This is because Sections 5(3) and 20(1) of the Act state that offences under the Act can be committed by individual members of staff as well as by the organisation (ie by the Data User). It is therefore important to have Register Entries that are, as far as possible, easy for staff to understand in relation to their duties. In addition, as Register Entries are publicly available, an Entry which is clear may be sufficiently informative to deter Data Subjects from exercising their right of Subject Access.

3.2.4 The first step in the Registration process is to obtain one or more Registration packs, as necessary, from the Office of the Data Protection Registrar. Each pack consists of one Part A form, three Part B forms, a 45-page booklet of 'NOTES' to assist completion of these forms, two address labels and a return envelope. Additional Parts A and B are also available on request from the Registrar, as are Registration forms in Welsh. Simplified Registration packs are available for use by 'small businesses' with limited data processing activities.

3.2.5 Three ingredients of the Registration pack are quite easy to explain. One address label is used to advise the Data User of the receipt of the application for Registration, and the other is used to advise the Data User if the Registration has been accepted onto the Register, or rejected; if accepted the Data User also receives one free copy of the Register Entry. The 'NOTES' booklet contains detailed guidance on how to complete Parts A and B and provides explanations and descriptions of the 'Standard Purposes' and 'Data Classes' (which relate solely to a Part B). The envelope saves making errors in the Registrar's address.

3.2.6 The simple explanations stop now! Part A of the form is used to describe the Data User (eg the Data User's address and Company Registration Number). Part B is used to describe what that Data User does with the personal data (eg purposes, sources and disclosures). Details entered into a Part A and associated Parts B by a Data User constitute an 'Application for Registration' and, if the Application is successful, are available free from the Registrar, for anyone to inspect. Most Data Users (about two-thirds) have only one simple Register Entry, ie one Part A plus one or at most a few Parts B, whereas large organisations may have many complex Entries, ie many Parts A each with a number of Parts B.

3.2.7 The Part A and Part B forms can be structured in various ways to fit a Data User's organisation and data processing activities. Consider a Data User who uses personal data for three distinct purposes (purpose X, purpose Y and purpose Z). The Data User could decide to have three separate Register Entries by completing a Part A describing the Data User and a Part B for the details associated with purpose X, a Part A (describing the same Data User) and a Part B for purpose Y, and yet another Part A and Part B combination for purpose Z, making three simple Part A - Part B combinations in all.

3.2.8 Alternatively, the Data User could choose to have one Part A describing the Data User and combine that with three Parts B (one Part B for each of purposes X, Y and Z). Thus, the Data User will have to choose whether it is best to have three distinct Register Entries each with one purpose, or one Entry with three purposes. Clearly, a further option, in this instance, is to submit one Part A combined with two Parts B, and a simple Part A plus Part B combination.

3.2.9 In the case of a large Data User, the final choice of combination of Part A and Part B can be exercised in a more sophisticated way, to reflect the structure or functions of the organisation. Not only can one Part A be associated with one or more Parts B, but each Part A or Part B can be associated with a particular data processing function or geographical location. The following example should make this clear. Consider a Data User who has branches in Inverness, Birmingham and Penzance, and suppose that each of these three branches performs **different**, single, data processing functions. Then the Data User could decide to have three separate Entries (a Part A and one Part B for each site). Alternatively the Data User could have one Entry consisting of a single Part A combined with three Parts B; for example, Part B (purpose for which personal data are used at Inverness), Part B (purpose at Birmingham) and Part B (purpose at Penzance).

3.2.10 However, what if the Penzance and Inverness branches carried out the **same** data processing function? The Data User could reflect that situation through a single Register Entry, and have a combination of a Part A and one Part B (purpose for which personal data are used at Penzance and Inverness) with a second part B for the Birmingham operation. Alternatively, the Data User could decide to have two separate Register Entries: a Part A and one Part B to describe the personal data used at Penzance and Inverness, the other Entry consisting of a Part A and a Part B for the personal data used at Birmingham.

3.2.11 In addition, the Registration format also allows a Part B to be associated with a particular data processing function. For example, suppose the Inverness branch performs Personnel Administration and Stock Control, whereas the Birmingham branch just performs Stock Control. Thus, instead of a Part B (purpose at Inverness) and a Part B (purpose at Birmingham) which are particularised in terms of geographic location, it is possible to have a Part B (Stock Control data processing) and a Part B (Personnel Administration data processing), where the latter are expressed in terms of the Data User's activity.

3.2.12 In these ways, a Part A or a Part B can relate to various aspects of the Data User's organisation. Note that if a Part A is completed to describe a Data User's activities at Inverness, **all** Parts B that are associated with that Part A must describe purposes that are carried out at Inverness (this is because the Part A describes the Data User at Inverness and will be associated with one or more purposes described in Parts B). However, if a Part B is described in terms of an activity that takes place in Inverness, then that Part B relates solely to Inverness whilst another Part B may describe a personal data activity in Birmingham: both Parts B may then be combined with one Part A which describes the Data User in general terms.

3.2.13 In large Data Users, data processing activities are often described in terms of organisational structure. For example, if a Local Authority has 13 departments, of which one department has four distinct computer applications each using personal data, it is possible to assign a Part A to that department, and one Part B to each application or section within that department (see paragraph 3.4.14 below).

3.2.14 At first reading (and perhaps even thereafter!) all these options may seem to provide a recipe for confusion. However, once it is grasped how a Part A or Part B can reflect function, organisation or location, it is up to the Data Protection Officer to employ this facility to ensure that the Registration clearly and accurately reflects how the Data User utilises personal data.

3.3 The Part A form

3.3.1 The Part A form is the easiest to complete. On the top right hand corner of the first page is an Application Number which will be used later when completing every Part B associated with that Part A. The first page will consist of a declaration which will be signed, when the Application is complete, by the 'responsible person' designated by the Data User or Computer Bureau. The person who signs the declaration will have to have formal authority from the Data User to do so, and in many cases will be the Data Protection Officer. On the bottom right hand corner of the first page there is a box to be completed by Data Users, stating how many Parts B are associated with that Part A. Thus the first page of Part A is the last section of the Application to be completed!

3.3.2 There are eight questions in Part A, and all Data Users must complete A1, A2, A7 and A8; questions A3 to A6 are optional. A Computer Bureau need only complete A1, A2 and A7. Failure to complete one of the mandatory questions will hold up the Application for Registration. An optional question can be recognised via the use of the verb 'may' or 'wish'. All mandatory questions can be found in Section 4 of the Act, and the Registrar has added the others to increase the clarity of the Registration process.

3.3.3 A1 asks whether the organisation is a Data User and Computer Bureau, or only a Computer Bureau or Data User. Many organisations will need to tick the first category because, even if they had not recognised this aspect, they in fact operate a bureau service when they provide computing facilities to other Data Users. Conversely, many Computer Bureaux will also be Data Users, as they will control the contents and use of personal data about their customers or staff.

3.3.4 A2 asks for the Data User's full name and address. This is the complete and formal address of the legal entity that 'holds' the personal data (ie controls the contents of the data and causes them to be processed). For companies, this means their full name and address as found in the Register of Companies, whereas partnerships and self-employed people should enter their usual place of work. Abbreviations of names should not be used, unless they are the Data User's formal name. All formal communications from the Registrar will come to this address. Note that Data Users are identifiable legal entities, so that departments or sections within a Data User cannot use A2 (they can only be specified in A6, see paragraph 3.3.8 below).

3.3.5 A3 asks for a contact name and address. This is to allow the Registrar, should any query arise, to contact the person who has filled in the form on behalf of the Data User. Consequently, A3 will generally specify the Data Protection Officer or whoever was directly responsible for completing the application. Using A3 will ensure that some problems can be dealt with quickly; however, not all communications from the Registrar come to the A3 address (see above) and Data Protection Officers should ensure that any post sent to the A2 address is forwarded immediately.

3.3.6 In A4, companies must provide their Company Registration Number as it appears in the Register of Companies. Public Authorities do not have these numbers.

3.3.7 In A5, a Data User may provide additional names that are more familiar to the public. For example the abbreviation IBM, TUC and DSS are much more widely known and used than the formal organisational name (eg Department of Social Security). It is also useful to include in A5 any previous names of the Data User, especially if there has been a recent merger or a structural change. All these names are shown, together with the full current name, in the Registration particulars made available to the public, and help Data Subjects to recognise the identity of the Data User.

3.3.8 A6 is the section which allows the Data User to assign the Part A (ie the whole Register Entry), to a particular sub-division or department of the organisation, for example, Data User X (Inverness Division) or Data User Y (Social Services Department). If A6 is used in this fashion then all associated Parts B will describe data processing of Data User X (Inverness Division) or Data User Y (Social Services Department) etc. Note that a subsidiary company cannot use A6 if it is a separate legal entity; such a subsidiary must register separately as an independent Data User.

3.3.9 A7 asks whether you wish to register for one, two or three years. As the Registration fee is the same in each case, there is little advantage in registering for the shorter periods. To leave A7 blank implies a Registration period of three years.

3.3.10 A8 defines the contact point for Data Subject Access and provides, as well as space for free text, boxes marked A2 and A3. If the box marked A2 is ticked, then the contact point will be the formal address of the Data User. Those Data Users who wish to centralise Subject Access (say, via the Data Protection Officer) should tick box A3. Ticking A2 and A3 means that Subject Access can be via either address. In addition the Data User can designate any number of different Subject Access addresses within the form, or use a general description such as 'any branch office'.

3.3.11 However, if neither of the boxes A2 and A3 is designated here, at least one formal address must be given in A8, so that Data Subjects can be certain that their request for Subject Access has been properly served on the Data User; the Registrar will refuse the application if no address is specified. A word of warning: even though one or more Subject Access addresses have been provided, Data Subjects are under no obligation to use them.

3.4 The Part B form

3.4.1 Part B of the form looks formidable, but looks can be deceiving. However, **before ticking (or otherwise clearly marking) anything in a Part B**, a Data User should closely examine the relevant section in the Registrar's 'NOTES' booklet to ensure that the consequences of ticking a box, or not, have been fully understood. Some of these consequences, particularly those that pertain to the various 'non-disclosure exemptions' in the Act, are by no means obvious and require careful consideration before the Application is dispatched (for one example see paragraphs 3.4.23 and 3.4.24 below).

3.4.2 The Part B form has, in fact, been designed for easy completion; it uses codes and lists of categories, some of which are described in greater detail in the 'NOTES' booklet. The particulars required define Standard Purposes (or purposes described in free text), Data Subjects, Data Classes, Disclosures, Sources and Overseas Transfers (ie the information collected in the census). Note that the term 'purpose' (eg as used in some of the Data Protection Principles) will be interpreted as comprising **all** the particulars registered under that purpose, and not simply the description of a purpose as found in the 'NOTES' booklet.

3.4.3 In essence, the relevant codes have to be selected, starting with the codes in the list of Standard Purposes, and then the codes that describe, in general terms, the other particulars. These are then ticked on the Part B. As will be seen, if there is no adequate code it is possible, and often highly desirable, to describe the activity in free text, although this is likely to prove unnecessary in the majority of cases.

3.4.4 The primary question the Data User must ask when completing B.1 (Purpose) is 'what use is made of the personal data?'. Having performed a census, the Data Protection Officer will have a list of activities which can be matched with the list of Standard Purposes in the 'NOTES' (there are also 'Full descriptions', on pages 15 to 38 of the 'NOTES', which illustrate typical activities associated with each Purpose).

3.4.5 Hopefully, it will be possible to match the activities revealed by the census with Standard Purposes described in the 'NOTES', especially since the Registrar strongly recommends this course. If this proves feasible, then the Code for the Standard Purpose is transcribed to Section B.1 of the form; the title of the Standard Purpose also has to be entered, in the space available ('Method 1'), and acts as a check on the choice of Code. A separate Part B must be completed for each Standard Purpose.

3.4.6 This matching of activities to Standard Purposes will, in general, be straightforward. However, in some cases there will be an activity which, at first sight, could easily fit into one or more Standard Purposes. Where this problem arises, the question to be asked is 'which Standard Purpose is closest to the activity?'. Remember: the list of activities provided by the Registrar is not exhaustive; it is meant to illustrate the Standard Purpose, and act as a guide to the best choice.

3.4.7 For example, suppose management keeps a file of personal data which concern complaints that arise during the progress of building work on a property. Should these personal data be registered under 'P020 Property Management' or under 'P012 Ancillary and Support Functions' whose 'Typical activities' include 'complaints and claims from the general public'? The choice of Standard Purpose would depend on an assessment of how much effort is spent on these complaints, and whether such effort is an established, discrete part of the building work programme. The more incidental to the programme, the better the choice of Standard Purpose P012.

3.4.8 This means of course that there is always the possibility of choosing the 'wrong' Standard Purpose. However, there is nothing illegal in this unless the Standard Purpose has been chosen deliberately to mislead, or the form has been completed in a negligent fashion. If there is a problem which causes the Registrar to investigate the Data User, the likely outcome will be either that the Data User can justify the original choice of Standard Purpose, or that the Data User will be advised to change the Standard Purpose. Consequently where the choice has proved to be a problem, it may be prudent to record the reasons for selecting the particular Standard Purpose (eg in the minutes of a formal Data Protection meeting).

3.4.9 Standard Purpose P012 is unique in that it acts as a 'catch-all' Purpose that **supports a main activity** (ie P012 should **not** be used to register a main activity). The list of illustrative descriptions is wide: it includes maintaining internal directories, computer-assisted teaching, electronic mail facilities, complaints, demonstration of systems that use personal data, and testing programs that use personal data. This Standard Purpose is also used to register those personal data that support administration across a Department or Data User as a whole.

3.4.10 Care should also be taken not to confuse an external disclosure (that has to be registered) with an internal (within the Data User) disclosure (which may require Registration of a new purpose). For example, one Department may routinely obtain a printed copy of another Department's personal data, or the second Department may have on-line read-only access. Thus one Department may use a name and address for billing (P008 Purchase/Supplier Administration) whilst another Department accesses the personal data for Direct Marketing (a different Standard Purpose, P004, requiring a separate Part B). If these names and addresses are sold to a mail order company, then a Part B describing a new Standard Purpose, P018 'Trading in Personal Data', will need to form part of the Registration.

3.4.11 Life can be difficult: what happens if an activity revealed by the census can not be associated with a Standard Purpose (ie it is simply not of the same kind as any of the other activities for which Standard Purposes have proved adequate)? In that case, the Purpose can be described in the Data User's own words, at the foot of Section B.1 ('Method 2'). It is very rare that Data Users find this necessary. Since 'Applications containing text will be closely scrutinised by the Registrar and are more likely to require further clarification' ('NOTES', page 7), Data Users should only use Method 2 as a last resort.

3.4.12 Some Standard Purposes are ticked with an asterisk; this means that the Data User **MUST** add further details of the Purpose in the two-line space provided (P012 is an example of such a Standard Purpose). The descriptions of these Standard Purposes in the 'NOTES' give some indication of how the Registrar wants the Purpose amplified (a common mistake is to put these details in the four-line space).

3.4.13 As noted in paragraphs 3.2.9 to 3.2.14, the Data User can opt in a Part B to qualify a Purpose by a particular function or location, eg Housing Management (rent collection) or Personnel Administration (at Inverness). The four-line space in 'Method 1' is provided for this (a common mistake is to put this amplification into the two-line space). This option helps large Data Users to clarify the Registration particulars, and make them more relevant to specific sections of the organisation.

3.4.14 For example, a Housing Department in a large Local Authority had three major schemes that could come under Standard Purpose 'P021: Housing Management'. Two schemes were associated with rent collection on a weekly or monthly basis, and the third with tenants wishing to change rented accommodation. The choice, therefore, was between merging all three schemes under one P021 Part B, or submitting three P021 Parts B, using the four-line space to specify 'weekly rent collection', 'monthly rent collection' and 'tenants mobility'. The latter was preferred, since it not only increased the clarity of the Housing Department Entries, but would also be of help to a Data Subject inspecting the Register. Staff also benefit, as it is easy to appreciate which Part B belongs to what part, or activity, of the Data User.

3.4.15 The first half of Section B.2 describes Data Subjects (page 2 of the Part B form) and requires answers to the questions 'Who are the **primary** Data Subjects?' and 'What is the **main** relationship between Data Subject and Data User?'. For example, suppose a Data User keeps personal data to rent houses to 'Tenants' **all** of whom are 'Students', then both these categories should be ticked because the category 'Students' adds 'significantly to the description' (see page 8 of the 'NOTES'). If, however, the houses are rented to anybody, only 'Tenants' should be indicated; the fact that some (or even most) of the tenants may also be students (or any other category) should not be indicated on the form. The additional qualifications 'Current', 'Past' and 'Potential' should be added, as appropriate (eg if future tenants are offered accommodation, and their details stored until accommodation becomes available, then 'Potential Tenants' should be ticked; if details of previous tenants are kept for accounting purposes then 'Past Tenants' should be ticked).

3.4.16 If details concerning tenants who have left are only retained until they can be deleted by the monthly update, then 'Past Tenants' should not be ticked, even though the data reside on file for some time. This is because the Data User does not intend to process the data with respect to 'Past Tenants'. In brief, ticking a box indicates that the Data User has a reason for processing personal data concerning the chosen 'Data Subject Type'.

3.4.17 In the second half of Section B.2, Data Classes (page 3 of the form) have to be assigned to **all** data fields associated with the personal data. The 'NOTES' assist in this task, by listing 'Example Data Items' to illustrate the standard descriptions which appear on the form. For example, Data Class C011 ('Personal details') is expanded as 'Age, sex, date of birth, place of birth, nationality, legal status'. Even if a data field is not illustrated directly in the 'Example Data Items', the most appropriate Data Class can usually be chosen; if not, a free text description can be used in the three-line space at the foot of page 3.

3.4.18 Avoid the urge to tick a multitude of boxes (a common problem). For example, suppose a Library maintains a list of Club Secretaries - and those clubs include political clubs, gay clubs, pressure groups, etc. This **does not mean** that C121

(Political party membership); C115 (Sexual life), etc should be ticked. The primary aspect of the Data Class is 'Secretaries of Clubs', and it is secondary what the nature of the club is (note also that information that relates to types of club is not personal data). In this example the correct choice would be C037 (Membership of voluntary or charitable bodies). Consequently, if the problem seems to be that 'the data could be in this Class, or in this Class, or in this Class ... etc', the chances are that the primary Data Class has not been evaluated properly. Finally, do not be afraid of defining your own Data Class. If the choices of Data Class are becoming uncomfortable, defining your own Class may be the easiest solution to the problem.

3.4.19 The choice of Data Classes and of Data Subjects acts as a check on the Standard Purpose chosen for B.1. For example, if the Data Classes are weighted to Employment Details, the Data Subject Type should have an 'employment' perception and the Standard Purpose should have some relationship to an 'employment' function. If many Data Subject types are ticked, this suggests that the primary relationship may not have been properly defined, and that some extra thought is required.

3.4.20 Section B.3 (page 4 of the form) requires the answer to the question 'What is the nature or description of the Source or Disclosure?'. All Sources and Disclosures with Code numbers from D101 to D208 inclusive reflect both a description and a relationship, for example D101 to D112 are Sources and Disclosures directly associated with the Data Subjects, whereas D201 to D208 have this relationship with the Data User. All Codes from D301 to D381 inclusive consist of a 'General Description' of organisations or individuals, including Central and Local Government Departments, public bodies, private agencies, professions, etc. Those marked with an asterisk will require further details in the five-line space at the foot of page 5; the 'NOTES' give some indication of what is required.

3.4.21 The relationship between the Data User and the reason behind the Source or Disclosure is vital. For example, suppose information is obtained from the Home Office about a prospective employee of the Data User. Does that mean that box D307 ('Home Office') should be marked as a source? If the general purpose is to obtain a reference from a Data Subject's previous employer then D104 ('Employers - past, present or prospective') should be ticked even though the previous employer was the Home Office. If, however, information is routinely obtained from the Home Office, say to confirm the nationality of relevant prospective employees, then D307 is the correct choice. In some cases, it might be correct to tick D104 and D307; it all depends on the procedure involved. Note that by ticking a box, a Data User is by inference capable of justifying the statement 'I collect information from X (or disclose personal data to X) because ...'.

3.4.22 As noted before, do not be afraid of using free text. For example, when the Greater London Council was being abolished, successor bodies could obtain personal data from the Council. At the time, these successor bodies could be certain Government Departments, Health Authorities, various Quangos and Trusts and even some Companies, and to mark all these on every Register Entry could appear strange to say the least. The solution to this was to register the disclosure 'D382 Potential or actual successor bodies of the Greater London Council'. Welfare agencies, who often have to share personal data, may find that to describe sources and disclosures in this way could clarify their Register Entries.

3.4.23 Caution should be exercised when ticking Disclosures to ensure that there is no confusion over the many 'non-disclosure' exemptions (see Chapter 3, Section 3.2.7 for details). For example, should personal data about an employee who is sick, which are then sent to the DSS, be marked as a D305 disclosure? The answer is: 'it depends on what is sent, and why'.

3.4.24 Section 34(5)(a) of the Act states that personal data required to be disclosed 'by or under any enactment' are exempt from the 'non-disclosure' provisions. This means that there is no need to register those disclosures that the Data User is obliged to make by law, which in turn means - no tick for D305 as regards those data that **have** to be sent. If, however, personal data beyond those required for statutory purposes are disclosed, a D305 tick is essential.

3.4.25 Section B.4 (page 6 of the form) requires a list of those countries to which it is intended to transfer personal data. Note that the Channel Islands, Isle of Man and UK Embassies abroad are 'Overseas' in this context, and that a transfer abroad implies a Disclosure which has to be marked in B.3. Since, by virtue of Section 4(3)(e) of the Act, a transfer involves 'data' (information recorded in a form in which it can be processed), transfers **only** take place if the information is in machine readable form (ie transferred by electronic means).

3.4.26 Sections B.2, B.3 and B.4 have to be completed for every Purpose B.1. When all Parts B associated with a Part A have been completed, a 'responsible person' (see paragraph 3.3.1) acting for the Data User should sign the declaration on the first page of Part A, and enter the number of Parts B at the foot of this page. It is important to check that the 'Application Number' in the top right corner of page 1 of the Part A is transcribed to the same position on Page 1 of **every** Part B associated with that Part A.

3.5 Conclusion: general points and a Registration Map

3.5.1 The Application for Registration will consist of at least one Part A and one Part B (the former with the signed declaration from the Data User that the application form is 'correct and complete'), and a Registration fee of £75 for each Part A. These papers can conveniently be sent by means of the return envelope which the Registrar has provided (a stamp is required) and if sent by recorded delivery (highly recommended)

Figure 1 – A SAMPLE REGISTRATION MAP

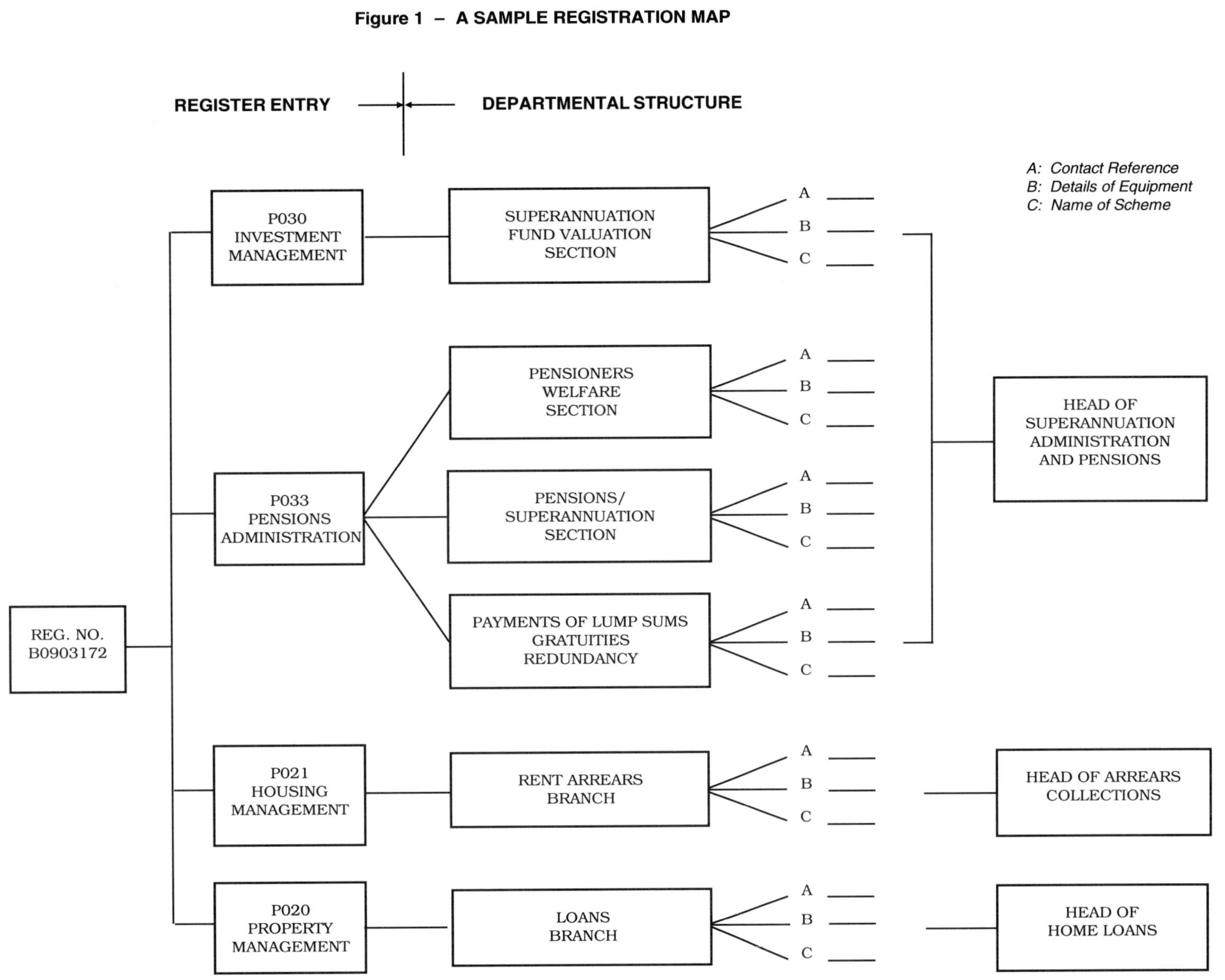

are considered to have been received by the Registrar from the moment of dispatch. In this way, the activities covered by an Application are legalised at the earliest possible date (as is any subsequent amendment sent in this way), unless and until the Registrar says otherwise. Applications for Registration have been known to go astray, so a copy should be kept.

3.5.2 Ticking boxes can be too easy: the warning to Data Users is that they are not embarking on a trivial exercise. Thus, where doubt exists as to 'what to do', Data Users should seek advice - and the first port of a call should be their representative body or Trade Association. In addition, the Registrar can offer advice over the telephone. It is advisable to check with the Registrar's Office beforehand if Data Users intend to employ free text descriptions in a Part B.

3.5.3 A useful record to help monitor Data Protection work is a 'Registration Map'. This shows, in diagrammatic form, the relationship between Register Entries, census and organisational structure (see Figure 1 on the previous page). In essence, each Register Entry and all Parts B associated with that Entry are listed, and linked to the names of the sections (or functions) within a department. Each such section is in turn linked to a contact or contacts (usually the census respondents), to important details of computing equipment used by the section (if appropriate) and to the name of the computer scheme found in the census (if necessary). If a particular Part B covers more than one section, then that Part B will be linked to several parts of the organisation (Figure 1, P033 shows this feature). A further link indicates where management responsibility lies for each section.

3.5.4 This simple tool can be very useful. Firstly, it assists consideration of whether the Register Entry structure is correct: in the example in Figure 1, it is likely that Housing Management and Property Management could usefully constitute a separate Entry. Secondly, it provides a basis for planning the work in relation to the Data Protection Principles and Subject Access.

3.5.5 Suppose, for example, a Subject Access request is received for the Register Entry displayed in figure 1. The map has details of who to contact and which mainframe and/or microcomputer files need to be searched. Responses from the contact(s) can be 'ticked off' as personal data are retrieved from the relevant section(s). Similarly, suppose the Data Protection Officer wishes to examine the procedures which govern compliance with the First Data Protection Principle in relation to this Entry; the work of making contacts, assessing progress, or interviewing staff can be documented on such a map in a systematic way. Note that the map can diagrammatically represent disclosures within the Data User.

3.5.6 In conclusion, it is worth the time and effort to get Register Entries as accurate as possible. It will then be easier to keep within the bounds of a Register Entry; it will be easier for Data Subjects to understand the Entries and, perhaps most important of all, it will be easier to train staff about how the Registration particulars affect their work. As a result, it will be easier to avoid problems with the law. A final reminder: it is a criminal offence to 'knowingly or recklessly' hold personal data which have not been registered, or to furnish the Registrar with a false or misleading application for Registration.

Chapter Three: Registration: Policies, Problems and Pitfalls

1. The current requirement and its critics

1.1 'The Registrar shall maintain a register of data users ...' (Part II, Section 4(1) of the Act). It cannot be denied that this short statement, qualified by the deceptively simple provisions for Registration which are contained in Section 4(3), creates a significant amount of additional work for many Data Users. Not surprisingly, the fact that this work has been imposed by an Act of Parliament, and **has to be done**, has been the cause of much criticism.

1.2 In practice, the Registrar has a degree of flexibility in the design of the Registration process which has been used to reduce the burden. Section 6(1) of the Act (which requires Data Users and Computer Bureaux to 'furnish the Registrar, in such form as he may require, with the particulars required to be included in the entry') and Section 7(3) (which permits 'acceptance by the Registrar of particulars expressed in general terms') allowed the Registrar to develop the current format. However, the Registrar is constrained, as a result of Section 4(3) of the Act, to ask for those specific details which Parliament concluded should be contained in the Entry.

1.3 The current Registration procedure was the outcome of a considerable amount of consultation and testing. Identification particulars of the applicant, and Registration as Data User, or as Data User and Computer Bureau, are entered on one form: the 'Part A'. The description of a Data User's activities is confined to the second form: the 'Part B'; each purpose for which a Data User holds personal data requires a separate Part B. Such a structure also satisfies the reduced Registration requirements of Computer Bureaux; since they do not control the contents and use of personal data they do not complete a Part B, only a Part A. To assist the process, the Registrar has provided a list of 70 'Standard Purposes', and extended descriptions of these Purposes, in his brown Booklet 'NOTES to help you apply for Registration' (from hereon referred to as the 'NOTES'). A Data User may have one or more Parts A, each associated with one or more Parts B; detailed guidance on the options involved is provided in the 'NOTES' (and in the rest of this Chapter).

1.4 The selected Standard Purpose (or, if absolutely necessary, a free text account of a purpose) is entered on page 1 of the Part B, and is described further on pages 2 to 6. These descriptions are entered by ticking standard categories (there is provision for free text additions or amplifications) and comprise **types** of Data Subjects, **classes** of personal data held about Data Subjects, **sources** from which the data may be obtained, **disclosures** that may be made, and **overseas transfers** of personal data outside the UK. To reduce the load further, the Registrar developed a simplified

Registration form (Form DPR.4) appropriate for 'small' Data Users (ie mainly small businesses). Once an activity is registered, the registered particulars are only lawful under the terms of the Data Protection Act; they do not legitimise the activity itself (eg registering personal data for blackmail purposes does not legitimise the act of blackmail, and a disclosure that transgresses another statute cannot be legitimised by registering that disclosure).

1.5 Despite a straightforward Registration process, there has been a continuous chorus of criticism, often spiced with a generous proportion of special pleading; much of this has been misconceived and has tended to involve generally unsubstantiated assertions of 'innumerable forms', 'bureaucratic nonsense' and the like. Similarly, pressure has grown for the omission of 'small' Data Users from the provisions of the Act; however, it is clearly not the number of a Data User's employees (or the Data User's turnover) that is crucial in this context but rather the number of Data Subjects whose personal data are held by that Data User, the nature of those personal data and how they are used. For example, a private detective agency may be a 'small' Data User, but the personal data could be particularly sensitive. And even if the number of Data Subjects about whom personal data are held is small, every Data Subject should be entitled to expect equal protection under the law.

1.6 Through such disparagement, positive aspects of the Registration process have tended to be ignored. Some of these aspects are quite distinct from the requirement from which Section 4 of the Act developed - for controllers of data to 'specify' their personal data holding, and to enable any person 'to establish the existence of an automated personal data file' (1981 Council of Europe Convention, Articles 5(b) and 8 (a)). Registration can actually be of significant value to Data Users, although many Data Users have failed to recognise, let alone act upon, this fact.

1.7 For instance, the organisational effort required to achieve a satisfactory Registration, and to keep it up to date, also provides a structure for evaluating the effectiveness and security of current procedures. This benefits not only efficiency, but also the prevention of fraud and sabotage across the whole spectrum of Data User activities. In many cases, this work has caused Data Users to critically examine the personal data held, and their uses and disclosures, for the first time. Also, the mere fact that a Data User has to compile, maintain and generally take responsibility for a signed public declaration tends to concentrate the mind wonderfully! Sometimes other important activities can be integrated with Data Protection work; for example, training courses that mention criminal offences under the Data Protection Act could easily include reference to such offences under the Computer Misuse Act or Copyright legislation.

1.8 It can also be argued that compared with quarterly VAT regulations, yearly Income Tax returns, monthly returns in relation to employment or sickness etc the 'bureaucratic load' of the Data Protection Act is by no means severe. For example, the average Data User has a single Register Entry involving a total of four forms (the Registrar's Third Report, June 1987) and pays a single fee covering a period of up to three years; changes in the Entry can be made at will and are free of charge.

1.9 Some Data Subjects have complained that 'The Register does not tell me who holds information about me or to whom it is disclosed'. They are disappointed that the compilation mainly identifies categories, types and classes of various kinds and does not hold the names of Data Subjects; similarly, with the exception of some Central Government Departments and information that may appear in free text form, that the Register does not contain the names of the sources of personal data or of those to whom the data are disclosed.

1.10 Another problem, from the viewpoint of the Data Subject, is that the format does not allow these details about the Data User's activities to be linked (eg one cannot deduce from an Entry which classes of personal data are held on which types of Data Subjects, or which classes of personal data are disclosed to whom). Such linking of the types of Data Subjects to the classes of personal data or to specific sources and disclosures would undoubtedly help Data Subjects; however, the increased complexity needed to resolve such ambiguities could further increase Data User resistance to Registration, and thus could be counter-productive as far as Data Subjects are concerned.

1.11 Thus a Register that attempted to eliminate such complaints would not only be some orders of magnitude larger than the one we now have but would also involve monitoring and updating on a prodigious scale; some Data Users have millions of Data Subjects on file. In fact, there is nothing in the 1981 Convention that advances such an aim. Article 8 of the Convention does not specifically require **any** Register to be created although, clearly, such a facility can assist with establishing 'the existence of an automated personal data file'.

1.12 Other significant ambiguities result from the non-disclosure exemptions of the Act which, as far as Registration is concerned, can be interpreted differently by different Data Users. The problems, advantages and disadvantages raised by these exemptions, in this context, are discussed in Section 3.2.7 below.

1.13 As to the future of Registration, the Registrar set out his views in his Fifth Report dated June 1989. His recommendations take account of responses to the May 1988 consultation document 'What are your views', and envisage a restricted Registration system, applicable only to certain types of Data User and/or certain kinds of data thought to be of special data protection interest. This remodelled system would be balanced by a significant, and perhaps controversial, increase in the supervisory and enforcement powers of the Registrar, coupled with the requirement for all Data Users to maintain, and provide on request, an up to date description, in general terms, of their activities which involve personal data.

1.14 Whilst some of these recommendations were largely incorporated in the Government's own review of the Registration process ('Review of the Data Protection Act: Report on Structure' prepared for the Government by an Interdepartmental Committee chaired by the Home Office), it should be noted that the Registrar told the Home Affairs Select Committee (HC 115, Session 1990-91) that he considered that both sets of recommendations 'seem likely to be overtaken by events in the European Community' (a reference to the European Directive on Data Protection which was published in December 1990). (Full details of all these initiatives can be found in Chapter 9, Sections 4 to 7).

1.15 Nevertheless, and despite adverse and often misinformed comments, a universal Registration process undoubtedly has merits; whether its current framework needs to be improved is a different issue. Since Data Subjects experience considerable difficulty in deriving useful information from the Register (even though a copy of any Data User's Registration is generally available, free of charge, from the Registrar), it is clear that changes can be anticipated. However, until Parliament passes the necessary amending legislation (possibly not for several years, if at all) the current Registration regime is the one that should be obeyed, understood and constructively used.

1.16 To assist comprehension of the remaining Sections of this Chapter, readers are recommended to have the 'NOTES' booklet and a copy of a Part A and B by their side.

2. Simple errors to avoid

2.1 It is quite common for applications for Registration to contain errors (as distinct from inaccurately described activities). If the Registrar discovered such errors, hopefully they were easily remedied - particularly if Section A3 (name and address of contact person in the Data User organisation) was completed. Such errors may have comprised simple misuse of the spaces provided for free text (eg 'further details' of an asterisked Standard Purpose were inserted in the 4-line space rather than in the 2-line space on page 1 of a Part B). In other cases essential information may have been omitted (eg as Source and/or Disclosure ticks to the right of the 5-line space on page 5, or an asterisked code number, where appropriate, in this space). Again, the number of Parts B may have been filled in incorrectly on page 1 of a Part A, and so on.

2.2 In fact, even more basic errors are the norm - in his Second Report (June 1986) the Registrar recorded 'Declaration not signed' and 'No subject access address given' in a list which totalled 8% of the applications received; over 2% did not even show the type of application (ie neither Data User nor Computer Bureau status was indicated).

2.3 The Registrar formally queried most applications which included Data Subject category S040 (Members of the public), and only accepted this in rare instances. The reason was plain - the use of this category conveyed that any individual, however unrelated to the Data User, could be randomly included in the activity concerned and this, in general, was unlikely to be the case. It was often possible to circumvent this problem by using the free text option to define Data Subjects more precisely (eg 'anyone who applies to run in the Marathon', or 'anyone contributing to the campaign fund' etc). Part B forms issued since June 1991 do not include category S040; a free text description now has to be given in appropriate cases.

2.4 A further query may arise whenever Data Users have ticked 'Worldwide (T999)' transfer of the data since, in due course, the Registrar may wish to exclude specific countries which do not have satisfactory data protection legislation; in some cases, the Data User may well find that likely overseas transfers can be defined more narrowly.

2.5 Even if the Registrar raised no query, factual errors in the current Entry may be discovered. Perhaps some ticks were in the wrong places, whether by accident, or through incorrect or incomplete census data, or just because there was insufficient understanding on the part of someone who should have thought more deeply or consulted more widely before putting pen to paper. Sources and Disclosures may have been entered in the 5-line space on page 5 of a Part B when they should, more correctly, have been associated with either the Data Subject or the Data User and, therefore, have been entered in the 2-line space on page 4. Probably not a matter for undue concern if no serious ambiguities arise. (All corrections can be made using Application Form DPR.2; see paragraph 4.1 below).

2.6 Suppose none of these errors apply but, on reflection, the Data Protection Officer has come to realise that the Registration particulars could be conveying wrong, or misleading, or just plain confusing information to Data Subjects, even if the forms were correctly completed. Has this possibility been considered, as well as the effect it might have on generating complaints or even Subject Access requests? After all, for a Data User, Registration fulfils three basic aims:

(a) it legalises, under the terms of the Data Protection Act (Sections 4 to 9), the Data User's holding of personal data and related activities as long as these activities are accurately reflected in the particulars registered;

(b) it demonstrates to staff the Data Protection framework within which the relevant work is to be done (ie the constraints which apply to each registered purpose and to the various activities involved in each purpose);

(c) it sends a message, reassuring or otherwise, to Data Subjects and to any others who may be interested enough to examine the Register.

2.7 Each of these three aspects imposes specific obligations on the Data User. Taking these in turn:

re(a): Register Entries must be kept up to date (see Section 4 of this Chapter);

re(b): staff (and management) must be trained to appreciate their obligations under the Act, and to be fully conversant with those Register Entries that are relevant to their work (see Chapter 6);

re(c): the Registration structure, and the Registration 'message', should be considered in the specific context of Subject Access (see Section 5 of this Chapter) and, more generally, in terms of Public Relations and maintaining the confidence of Data Subjects. These latter aspects are examined immediately below.

2.8 Parliament decided that Registration (namely the public declaration of what Data Users intend to do with personal data in their charge) has to be taken seriously; if Registration responsibilities are not carried out effectively (eg a Data User does not make a public declaration, or makes a declaration that does not represent the activities of the Data User) then criminal offences can be incurred (see Section 6 of this Chapter).

3. The Register Entry and the facts it conveys

3.1 Checking accuracy and structure

3.1.1 As soon as confirmation has been received from the Registrar that an application for Registration has been accepted, a continuing process of checking and, whenever necessary, amending each Register Entry begins for the Data User. The first task is to ensure that, in the Registrar's words, 'the entry accurately reflects your application' - since discrepancies between application details (of which a careful Data User will have kept a copy) and Register Entry details are by no means uncommon.

3.1.2 Depending on the length of time that has elapsed since the application was completed, it might be necessary to submit amendments. A regular review of activities involving personal data should, at any rate, have been instituted, together with appropriate procedures to ensure that, at any time, amendments to the Register Entries are not overlooked. But even if the Entries are, temporarily, correct it may well be advantageous to carry out a reappraisal based on the analysis outlined in Section 3.2 below.

3.1.3 The structure of Register Entries is important; it indicates to Data Subjects the boundaries which the Data User has imposed on requests for Subject Access. Section 21(3) of the Act states that '... a separate request must be made and a separate fee paid under this section in respect of the data to which each entry relates', and consequently each Access request relates to **one** Part A and **all** its associated Parts B (see Section 4 of the Act). Reassessment of, and amendments to the structure of a Data User's Registration in relation to Subject Access may be important if a fee is charged for Subject Access.

3.1.4 Section 21(3) of the Act is prefaced by the qualification 'In the case of a Data User having separate entries in the register in respect of data held for different purposes ...'. If you have concluded from this that a single request for Subject Access would therefore extend to **all** separate Entries which hold data for the **same purpose** (ie to any Parts B, with the same purpose, in your **other** Register Entries), then be reassured - it does not. A 'Part B purpose' is qualified by such other descriptions as the Part B contains (ie although the purpose is P001, P013 or whatever, it is 'different' to any other P001, P013 etc by virtue of the associated information in the rest of the Parts B). In other words, the **whole** of the Part B particulars (Purpose, Data Subject types, Data Classes, Sources, Disclosures and Overseas Transfers) defines the 'Purpose'.

3.2 The Entry and its message to Data Subjects

3.2.1 Even if the personal data processed by the Data User are limited in scope, a Part B description can hardly be described as 'user friendly', certainly not in the sense that it presents a clear and unambiguous picture of the Data User's activities.

3.2.2 The Registrar reserves the right to refuse an application for Registration if its complexity appears to frustrate Subject Access ('NOTES', page 2, fifth paragraph). However, whilst he also cautions against confusing the Data Subjects ('NOTES', page 7, third and final paragraphs) the 'NOTES' draw attention to several instances in which there clearly is potential for confusion.

3.2.3 In some instances, the confusion is inherent in the Registration format, and each Register Entry therefore contains appropriate 'health' warnings. Taking these instances in the sequence in which they appear in the 'NOTES', Register Entries should be checked against the points, detailed in Sections 3.2.4 to 3.2.9 below, which relate to specific sections of a Part B (note: we have adopted the Registrar's style by addressing the reader as 'you').

3.2.4 **Selection of Data Subject types** ('NOTES' page 8, fourth paragraph)

(a) Have you ticked more than one Data Subject type? If so, are they each 'primary' **and** separate, with any 'overlap', as indicated by the Registrar, fortuitous rather than fundamental? As an example, to explain these points, suppose two Data

Subject types, namely S006 (Claimants, beneficiaries, payees) and S022 (Tenants) were ticked - this could arise when the Part B in question combined two separate activities, each for the same purpose, and each involving one Data Subject type. Alternatively, there could be just one activity, involving these two Data Subject types for quite distinct reasons. As a third option, it could be that Claimants and Tenants were identified, say in relation to a computerised benefit scheme, because **all** Claimants were **also** Tenants, and this dual identification added, again as indicated by the Registrar, 'significantly to the description'. The trouble is that there is no way to distinguish these three options, and that the right decision would have been made in **every** case. If, however, both boxes were ticked in order to be helpful to Data Subjects, because the **majority** of the Claimants were, also, Tenants, then this would actually be misleading (since some Tenants who were **not** Claimants might believe they featured on the computer file). This type of problem is common and arises because although all Claimants are Tenants, not all Tenants are Claimants. Note that this confusion can also occur with the third option described above, if a Tenant, who is **not** a Claimant, endeavours to interpret the Entry which is specific to Data Subjects that are **both** Tenants and Claimants.

(b) Confusion as to what a Register Entry means would, thus, seem to be unavoidable, even in a simple case involving just two Data Subjects. How can a Data Subject draw the correct conclusion? What can you say to any Data Subjects who have made an effort to understand the particular use of personal data, or who may even have spent time and money on applying for Subject Access (and also **your** time and money on searches and replies), only to be told that they have been misinformed, and that the Register Entry does not relate to them?

(c) It is clear that such confusion could generate suspicions, let alone fruitless Subject Access requests, even if all is well legally speaking. As a consequence, if your Entries are sufficiently numerous or complex then a leaflet or Guide, to explain to Data Subjects how you use their personal data, might well repay (in Public Relations terms) the effort involved in its production. Such a Guide can also help staff understand the Register Entries that apply to their work.

(d) Did you remember to include in your Registration all personal data which, at first sight, relate only to **groups** of individuals (eg organisations, businesses, etc) but **could** include identifiable individuals (eg sole traders)?

(e) Similarly, are you processing information about job descriptions or staffing complements, which does not include the names of the job holders but from which, in certain cases, individuals can be identified (eg 'The Mayor', 'The Chair of Committee X', or even 'the tree surgeon in the Borough' if there is a tree surgeon complement of one)?

(f) Do you have any automatic data collection systems (eg logs which monitor individual use of entry cards, electronically controlled machinery, or electronic equipment such as telephones, photocopiers, fax machines and word processors; see the Registrar's Guideline 2, Section 13)?

(g) Lastly, have you discounted personal data from Registration on the grounds that there is no **capability** or **intention** to process with reference to the individuals involved. If so, you are walking a tightrope. Have you considered whether the system in question has, or will have, a free text retrieval capability? Would you never use this capability 'with a view to locating the information **about the individuals**' (see Guideline 2, page 24)? If the matter ever became the subject of legal dispute, might it not be difficult to disclaim 'intention' if there was 'capability'?

3.2.5 **Selection of Data Classes** ('NOTES' page 8, sixth paragraph)

(a) '... IT SHOULD NOT BE TAKEN THAT DATA IN EVERY CLASS LISTED ARE HELD ON EVERY DATA SUBJECT ...'. This part of the Registrar's 'Interpretations', found in each Register Entry, repeats in modified form the advice provided on page 8 of the 'NOTES'. It can, of course, not resolve the problems faced by a Data Subject in interpreting the Register Entry, nor any consequent difficulties faced by you - the Data User.

(b) Consider the same simple example (used in paragraph 3.2.4(a) above) involving S006 (Claimants, etc) and S022 (Tenants) and, say, Data Classes C001 (Personal identifiers), C061 (Current employment) and C113 (Disabilities, infirmities). Suppose a Tenant suspects that the Data User was misusing information under C113 or that the information might be incorrect (for example, because of some action taken by the Data User). The Tenant might then apply for Subject Access only to find that information about disabilities was held solely about Claimants. The result, as a consequence of the ambiguities of the Registration procedure, is similar to the situation described in 3.6.1(b) above: possible frustration, and a waste of time and money by both sides.

(c) To avoid the problems created by these ambiguities, you may wish to consider whether extra descriptions in the Entry in free text, which could be put forward via form DPR.2, might provide an answer. The Registrar's prior approval should be obtained for such amendments, particularly since they might not come under the allowed categories of 'additional refinement' or 'extra descriptions' of Data Classes. Should separate schemes be involved (eg housing allocations, weekly and quarterly rents, maintenance, etc), then the other Register Entry option available is submission of further Parts B. Finally, these matters could be resolved in an explanatory Guide or leaflet which describes the activities covered by the Entry in simple terms.

3.2.6 **Identification of Sources and Disclosures** ('NOTES' page 9, third paragraph)

(a) '... IT SHOULD NOT BE TAKEN THAT ... ALL ITEMS OF DATA HELD ARE OBTAINED FROM, (OR) DISCLOSED TO ... EVERY CATEGORY LISTED.'. This extract, again from the Register Entry 'Interpretations', closely resembles the comment on page 9 of the 'NOTES'. Even when this warning has been noted and fully appreciated by Data Subjects or others examining the Entry, there is much scope for confusion and misunderstanding in this Section of Part B since disclosures can, in some cases, be specially sensitive.

(b) For example, consider a computer system which holds both financial data and medical data, for disclosure to 'Building Societies' (D363) and 'Registered medical practitioners' (D353) respectively. Data Subjects could reasonably conclude, having examined the Register Entry, that the financial data are to be provided to doctors and the medical data to Building Societies. Indeed, it may take case law to decide whether the Data User (or an employee of the Data User) can do this - by mistake or intentionally (even, say, maliciously) and still remain immune from prosecution under the Act. At the moment it is by no means clear that the Third Principle, specifically its interpretation in Schedule 1 Part II of the Act can resolve this issue (see Chapter 4, paragraph 2.3.1(d)).

(c) As far as amending or improving a Registration is concerned, for the benefit both of Data Subjects and the Data User, some additional text, whether in the Register Entry or issued to enquirers in the form of an explanatory leaflet, might again be the only way.

3.2.7 **Disclosures exempt from Registration** ('NOTES' page 9, fourth paragraph)

(a) An exemption from the non-disclosure provisions means that the disclosure need not be registered (ie ticking the relevant box is optional). For each such provision the Act defines the strict conditions under which that exemption applies, for example if: 'the data subject ... has ... consented to the particular disclosure' (Section 34(6)(b) of the Act).

(b) Many Data Users have ignored non-disclosure exemptions and have ticked disclosures that occur in circumstances covered by such exemptions. Although in some cases this will have been done to help the Data Subject, by drawing attention to **all** likely disclosures, it is nevertheless a fact that the Registration of a disclosure to which a non-disclosure exemption applies could carry two additional and perhaps quite unwarranted messages:

(i) the Data User is not prepared, or able, to meet the conditions which would satisfy the non-disclosure exemption

(ii) the Data User wishes to disclose personal data outside the conditions specified by the non-disclosure exemption.

(c) The 'NOTES' draw attention to two non-disclosure exemptions - disclosures to the Data Subject to whom the data relate, and to employees of the Data User acting in **that** capacity (Sections 34(6)(a) and (c) of the Act). However, in the case of these two instances there are Disclosure boxes provided in the Part B form; the Registrar notes that there might be '... other circumstances in which disclosure to these categories is registrable' - but does not provide any examples of such circumstances. There are of course several other non-disclosure provisions (eg disclosures made with the consent of the Data Subject, or required by law, or for the purpose of law enforcement but only if not to disclose would be likely to prejudice that purpose) where you also need to consider the message that ticking a box could send to Data Subjects.

(d) So have you ticked either of these two Disclosure boxes D101: 'The Data Subjects themselves' and D203: 'Employees, agents' in any Part B and, if so, was this by design or by mistake? There clearly are situations in which a D101 Disclosure tick might be appropriate: namely when data about one or more Data Subjects are disclosed to one or more others or to all the Data Subjects concerned (eg distribution of mailing lists, which include personal data, to the Data Subjects; telling a group of disabled persons where other persons with the same disability live; notification of examination results to all the students examined, and further examples of this nature).

(e) As regards disclosures by a Data User to enable his employees to perform their duties, Guideline 6 (paragraph B.3.1) points out that these disclosures 'need not be shown' in the Register Entry but provides no further guidance. So it is important to appreciate that a D203 Disclosure tick allows (as far as the Act is concerned) your employees freely to obtain information they do **not** need for their work; this tick could, therefore, be interpreted as one that might protect the Data User, and careless employees, against the consequences of inadequate security and access procedures. In addition, a D203 tick may provide a defence under Section 1 of the Computer Misuse Act 1990 (the offence of unauthorised access to a computer or data); since a D203 tick implies that personal data can be disclosed to staff for unauthorised purposes, it can be argued that this authorises staff to obtain such personal data.

(f) Thus whilst it is relatively easy to decide whether D101 was ticked by design or by mistake, a D203 tick raises far more complex issues and should be carefully considered by Management in the light of possible Public Relations problems, advantages (should you omit the tick), risk analysis and the like.

(g) Other examples of non-disclosure exemptions also require detailed attention.

Firstly, did you examine the justification for registering **any** disclosure in the light of the exemption provided by the Data Subject's consent? Here there is a very clear message to the Data Subject, whether you intended it or not: a registered disclosure legalises that disclosure in cases where the Data Subject has **not** provided consent and, taking this further, effectively provides notice to the Data Subject that the disclosure may be made however strongly the Data Subject may object to this course. It follows that, unless you wish to 'send' this message via the Register Entry, you should not have ticked a disclosure to which the Data Subject has consented **or when you have reasonable grounds for believing this to be the case** (see Sections 34(6)(b) and (d) of the Act). Common examples of 'disclosure with consent' are the disclosure of an employee's salary level to an organisation (eg a Bank or Building Society) from whom that employee has requested a loan, the disclosure, to a trades union office, of personal data concerning members of that trades union, and so on.

(h) Have you ticked disclosures required by law ('by or under any enactment, by any rule of law or by the order of a court' - see Section 34(5)(a) of the Act)? Routine examples are certain disclosures (eg of earnings or other financial) information to the Inland Revenue (D301), and of information required by the DSS (D305). There are some 140 statutory provisions bearing on the disclosure of official information (Hansard, Written Answers, col 561 and 562, 21.1.87), and the report of the Review Committee on 'Banking Services: Law and Practice' (February 1989) lists 19 statutes which provide for disclosure of confidential information. A potentially contentious case, on which the Registrar has issued some guidance, is disclosure of data required for statutory audit. Here, the Registrar has pointed out that '... in many cases other information will be disclosed in the course of an audit ...' and has suggested that 'it would be wise to tick the appropriate box in Section B3'. However, in further comment he stated that clear advice could not be offered on this issue, and that 'an individual Data User must clearly strike a balance between relying on the non-disclosure exemptions and giving a potentially misleading impression ...'. Additionally, the provision of uncontrolled access to auditors can, in the public sector, be fraught with political problems.

(i) A positive approach, and one that avoids any confusion, is to take advantage of non-disclosure exemptions by **publicising** non-registration of particular disclosures - and thus to indicate that the conditions of exemption will be met in each and every case. These conditions impose, of course, significant obligations on the Data User, who has to maintain and monitor the strict (but no more than reasonable) controls which are necessary in order to prevent unauthorised disclosures. In the case of personnel information, for instance, disclosures are likely to be covered by agreements with staff representative bodies or with trades unions. Thus if the policy decision is taken only to disclose personnel personal data either with the consent of the employee or by or under any enactment, then no disclosures need to be registered.

(j) At the other end of the spectrum, there could be situations where such strict controls cannot be assured, or are unrealistic for any reason. In such cases, the Data User may wish to publicise (**or need to publicise**; see paragraph (p) below), and legitimise via the Register Entry, any disclosures that may occur in addition to those that are exempt from Registration. A possible disadvantage to this procedure is that queries, from Data Subjects, may be generated as a result.

(k) Have you ticked a disclosure under D341 (Police forces)? Here again, a decision should have been made on the **basis of policy** (see Chapter 7 for a discussion, concerning Section 28 of the Act, in relation to forming a policy), and also in full recognition of consequential procedures, such as monitoring and recording of disclosures, that reliance on the exemption in Section 28(3) should involve. A D341 tick signals that by no means all of these disclosures could justifiably be claimed as necessary to 'the prevention or detection of crime', or 'the apprehension or prosecution of offenders' (see Sections 28(1) and 28(3) of the Act). For example, suppose a Social Work department discusses personal data at case conferences in relation to missing children. One of the organisations present may be the Police Force, but the disclosure to the Police may not strictly be for a purpose mentioned in Section 28 (let alone evaluated, as reliance on the exemption requires, in the context of whether not disclosing the data would be likely to prejudice such a purpose). Consequently a D341 tick would be essential in registering this activity. However, this could give the impression that **any** personal data from the Social Work Department could be disclosed to the Police for a purpose not associated with law enforcement. Controversy and confusion over this issue can be avoided by fully explaining the D341 tick in a leaflet describing the Entry, or by a free text specification of the disclosure to cover **all** organisations that would be involved in these case conferences (eg the text 'D382 - any organisation involved in the tracing of individuals in emergency circumstances' would cover disclosures made for the purpose of locating missing persons). Placing text in an Entry under D382 may also simplify and clarify the number of source and disclosure ticks. For example, if disclosures concerning child abuse are to be made to appropriate organisations, then the text 'D382 - any organisation involved in the care of children thought to be at risk from sexual abuse' would be better than a plethora of ticks elsewhere.

(l) Police guidelines have been discussed in Parliament (Hansard, Col. 14, 21.4.86), where it was noted that civilians employed by Police Forces, as well as Police Officers, could be liable to prosecution under the Official Secrets Act 1911 (this is less likely with the replacement Official Secrets Act 1989), or under Section 5 of the Data Protection Act, for any breach of the Data User's Register Entry. The ACPO (Association of Chief Police Officers) Code of Practice for Police Computer Systems, issued in 1988, provides in Appendix B a 'Declaration form for Data

User' in which it is stipulated that enquiries are being made under Section 28(3) of the Data Protection Act.

(m) In relation to computer maintenance, did you tick D206 (Suppliers, providers of goods or services) as a disclosure, in **every** Part B you completed, to indicate disclosure for the purpose of system maintenance or repair (see Guideline 3, Section AX.7)? Alternatively, did you adopt the free text option (undoubtedly less confusing when there may be other good reasons for ticking D206), of 'Suppliers of computer hardware and software services', or some variant of this description? Many organisations considered that even this was not sufficiently rigorous, and used the following sentence in the free text space in the middle of page 4 of a Part B ('associated with the Data User'): 'Providers of computer hardware or software, strictly in order to maintain or restore the proper functioning of the system(s)'. One possible quick way of achieving this end is to submit a DPR.2 (a form used to make amendments to current Entries: see Section 4 below) to request 'Please add the disclosure 'Providers of computer hardware or software, strictly in order to maintain or restore the proper functioning of the system(s)' to all Parts B of this Entry'. An alternative is to submit a P012 ' Ancillary and Support Functions' Part B, in which the required amplified description of the Purpose is 'Testing of computer systems'; the Data Subjects are described in free text as 'any Data Subject registered under another Part B of this Entry'; the Data Classes as 'any Data Class registered under another Part B of this Entry'; the Sources are described as 'any Source registered under another Part B of this Entry'; whilst the **only** registered Disclosure is to 'Providers of computer hardware or software, strictly in order to maintain or restore the proper functioning of the system(s)'. It is unlikely that any overseas transfers are involved (but check Sections 3.2.8 and 3.2.9 below).

(n) If you consider that your payroll, pensions and accounts data are exempt from Registration by virtue of Section 32 of the Act, have you realised that such a D206 disclosure is likely to invalidate this exemption (see Guideline 3, page 31, and Guideline 6, Section A.5.7)? The same disclosure may also invalidate the exemption for Research and Statistics described in Section 33(6) of the Act.

(o) Careful consideration needs to be given as to whether any disclosure has been registered without prior close examination of all the relevant factors, implications and consequential impact on Data Subject attitudes and queries. Many Data Users could even find it advantageous, in appropriate circumstances, to seek Data Subject consent to disclosure, or otherwise to use the non-disclosure provisions to minimise the number of registrable disclosures and thereby eliminate many concerns of Data Subjects. A free text description, in every relevant Part B, could read: 'Disclosures to third parties are made only with the consent of the Data Subject, or if required by law'. Publicity to explain the empty disclosure boxes could then be on the following lines: 'We guarantee to take all reasonable steps to ensure that the only disclosures of your personal data, for this purpose, will be those that are made to yourself, or with your consent, or to our employees or agents strictly as required for their work, or...' etc etc (listing the conditions of any other appropriate exemptions).

(p) As shown in Chapter 4 (section 2.1.1), the First Data Protection Principle requires that **before** information about Data Subjects is collected, 'all the intended uses and **disclosures** are clear from the context in which the information is being supplied' (our emphasis; Guideline 4, paragraph 1.2). Clearly all such disclosures, except those subject to a non-disclosure exemption, will need to be registered. Thus compliance with the First Principle requires that all registered disclosures must be reflected in, or be compatible with, any statements made to individuals before the collection of personal information.

(q) All staff should be aware of the contents of the Register Entry, especially the disclosures that they are allowed to make. If the non-disclosure exemptions are used some disclosures may not be registered; it will, therefore, not be sufficient to rely on the detail contained in the Entry to alert staff to the authorised disclosures.

3.2.8 **Data transferred overseas by a Data User** ('NOTES' page 10, seventh paragraph)

(a) An overseas transfer is defined in terms of the transfer of personal data (Sections 4(3)(e), 5(2)(e) and 12 of the Act); this means that what is transferred has to satisfy the definitions found in Sections 1(2) and 1(3). Thus overseas transfers must be transfers of information in machine readable form (eg on disk, tape, via a network, satellite etc). In an era of portable computers, it might be the equipment that is transferred (eg taken to an international sales conference). In addition, with multi-national joint ventures becoming commonplace, it could be vital to consider the implications of Section 39. (Note: Appendix 6 addresses the problems associated with transborder data flow).

(b) Data Users should check the following:

(i) Are your networks or dial up lines connected to international exchanges? If so, how are these used with respect to personal data?

(ii) Did you discuss with senior managers and sales staff the personal data they take on international visits?

(iii) Did you check any collaborative projects involving overseas partners or locations, for example pan-European marketing initiatives in anticipation of the free market?

(iv) Have you checked that transfers have corresponding registered disclosures? (Note that in some instances it is possible to transfer personal data overseas without a disclosure; for example, managers who take overseas customer lists abroad on a portable computer might only use the personal data for their own purposes).

(v) Have you checked whether any personal data transferred could still be controlled from within the UK? If so, your organisation could be a Data User with respect to those data, but only if they are also used or intended to be used in the UK.

(vi) Have you checked whether you are providing services in relation to any personal data transferred into the UK? If so, your organisation could be a Data User or Computer Bureau with respect to those data.

(vii) If personal data are transferred abroad, do you need to take account of other countries' Data Protection legislation?

(viii) Are any of your computer maintenance contractors based outside the UK? Do they have terminal access into your systems?

3.2.9 **Data transferred overseas by a Computer Bureau** ('NOTES' page 10, seventh paragraph)

(a) If you use a Computer Bureau you should, in addition to the questions posed in Section 3.2.8 above, check the following:

(i) Did you make adequate enquiries of any Bureau you may use, and register such overseas transfers as may be involved in the Bureau's processing of your data?

(ii) Does the Bureau appreciate its responsibility to inform you of any relevant change in its working procedures, in case this requires you to register any additional overseas transfers? (Note that responsibilities of Computer Bureaux are covered in detail in Chapter 8).

(iii) Does the Bureau you use have communication links to specialist services (eg maintenance diagnostics) in other countries? For example, IBM's Remote Support Facility has been based in the Netherlands and this would require a T036 (Netherlands) tick in **your** Register Entry. Any other overseas transfer originated by the Bureau should, similarly, be noted in **your** Register Entry. Obviously, if the maintenance firm or the Bureau becomes a Data User with respect to these personal data, it will be responsible for registering any overseas transfer which it initiates. Finally, you may need to take account of other countries' Data Protection legislation in these circumstances.

(iv) If your organisation provides Bureau services with respect to personal data that are transferred abroad, or transferred into the UK, have you checked whether you need to take account of other countries' Data Protection legislation?

4. Amending or renewing a Register Entry: corrections; updates; new systems coming on-line

4.1 Form DPR.2 is supplied by the Registrar for 'Alteration or Removal of a Register Entry', and form DPR.3 for 'Renewal of a Register Entry'. As in the case of form DPR.1, which comprises Parts A and B of the Registration process, forms DPR.2 and DPR.3 are designated **'Application'** - for the Registrar to consider prior to formal acceptance. Such applications may be requested by the Registrar (for instance, through his query, referred to in paragraph 2.3 above, concerning use of the S040 Data Subject type). If the alterations are 'particularly complex', a new Part B, marked 'Alteration Only' should be submitted as well (see Note 9 of DPR.2). If the change involves a 'different legal person' (Note 8 of DPR.2), then DPR.2 should **not** be used since application must be made for that new Data User (enclosing the Registration fee). If implementation of an amendment is particularly urgent (eg because of a new system coming on-line, or to ensure that Subject Access is to the new structure of Register Entries), then the amendment should be sent by recorded delivery (when, according to Section 7(9) of the Act, the date of posting is the date of application). No fee is payable with a DPR.2.

4.2 When the copy of your Register Entry is sent you by the Registrar, as formal notification of its acceptance, a reference number for future use is also supplied, as well as one copy of form DPR.2. Prior to this, the reference number found on the Registration acknowledgement card can be used in any communication with the Registrar, including submission of urgent amendments to the Registration forms.

4.3 For most of the alterations discussed so far in this Chapter, and for minor changes to existing Entries (and certainly for removal of Entries) form DPR.2 will suffice. Registration of a new activity, however, is more likely to require a new Part B; certainly so when the activity is carried out for a purpose not previously registered. The Registrar suggests that a new Part B may be necessary to preserve clarity when a new activity differs significantly from one already registered, even though a new purpose is not involved. In the case of a new Part B there is a bias towards finding it a home within an existing Part A, rather than in a new Part A for which a new Registration fee would be needed (the only disadvantage to using an existing Part A would lie in Subject Access implications; see paragraph 3.1.3 of this Chapter).

4.4 There are two key requirements for dealing efficiently with the Registration of new activities which involve personal data:

(a) **maintaining a clear record** of what activities (as distinct from purposes) have been covered by the existing Registration. This involves a record which identifies each activity, a 'responsible' person to contact with respect to that activity, and details of the individual Registration parameters in those cases where a 'multiple-activity' Part B has been completed. This record, which can take the form of a structure diagram showing Departments, Register Entries, Parts B, Computer Systems and Liaison Officers, can be used to determine whether the application is to be for a new Part B or for amendment of an existing Part B;

(b) **receiving early warning**, from management, of any new activities whilst these are in the planning stage (a suitable reference to the Data Protection Act, in every Standards Manual, Development Methodology and Procedure Manual, would help to achieve this). At this point, not only can Data Protection aspects be taken into consideration (this may, in extreme cases, include re-evaluation of whether a computer-based or manual system is the best solution) but sufficient time should then also be available to prepare and despatch the necessary forms **before** the date when the system is required to go on-line;

(c) **receiving early warning**, from management, of any reorganisations, or company acquisitions (eg via a takeover).

4.5 Remember, any activity must be covered by the Registration at the time it begins to **process** personal data; this could well be some time before the system goes 'live'.

5. Amending a Register Entry: the basic structure

5.1 If your Registration proved to be a substantial task, then the odds are that it involved a considerable number of Parts B, distributed between, say, from five to fifty or more Parts A. The number of Parts A and Parts B will have been determined by considerations that are likely to include one, or a mixture of, the following:

(a) reflecting the organisational structure (eg by relating each Part A to a particular sub-division, location etc, using Section A6);

(b) allowing for a complexity of computer systems (eg by having more than one Part A for each such sub-division);

(c) placing emphasis primarily on activities or systems (eg by grouping the Parts B in accordance with such a relationship, using the 4-line space on page 1 of a Part B);

(d) structuring the Parts A specifically with Subject Access in mind, to ease the task of providing Subject Access. This structure could be determined by location, purpose, number of Data Subjects about whom information is held, likely frequency of Access requests, sensitivity of the personal data, special problems concerning identification of Data Subjects, and any other relevant issues which impinge on the organisation's proposed Subject Access arrangements. Note that if no fee is charged for Subject Access, the Subject Access considerations which relate to the structure of the Register Entries are irrelevant;

(e) describing to the public, in as clear a manner as the format allows, all activities which involve the processing of personal data.

5.2 Whatever the considerations (and it has been known that, due to staff changes, no one knows why a particular structure was adopted), it is worthwhile to review the Register Entries, particularly in the context of (d) and (e) above. If Subject Access was a determining consideration, or the overriding consideration, in structuring the Registration forms, it is now clear (in the light of the very few Subject Access requests that have been received) that for the vast majority of large Data Users a reduction in the numbers of Parts A can be considered, subject to the demands of clarity and of Public Relations.

6. Criminal offences associated with Registration

6.1 Sections 5 and 6 of the Act establish two distinct categories of offences with respect to Registration; the two types are:

(a) offences against which no defence can be offered (ie offences of strict liability, where ignorance of the law is no excuse);

(b) offences against which the defence of 'this was not done knowingly or recklessly' (eg deliberately, maliciously) can be offered.

6.2 Offences of strict liability can occur when:

(a) any Data User holds 'personal data without being registered or without having applied for registration' (Section 5(1) of the Act). Most prosecutions to date have related to this offence;

(b) a registered Data User or Computer Bureau fails to keep the registered address up to date.

6.3 Offences against which the defence of 'this was not done knowingly or recklessly' can be offered occur when:

(a) a registered Data User holds personal data 'of any description' that are not described in the Data User's Register Entry;

(b) an unregistered Computer Bureau provides services with respect to personal data;

(c) anyone (eg Data User, agent of the Data User, or employee of the Data User) provides false or misleading information on an application for Registration or for alteration of a Register Entry;

(d) any registered Data User, agent of the Data User, or employee of the Data User uses, obtains, discloses or transfers personal data other than described in the Register Entry

(e) any Computer Bureau, agent of the Computer Bureau, or employee of the Computer Bureau discloses personal data without the authority of the Data User.

6.4 Note that Section 20 of the Act extends the liability for any offence committed, under the Act, by a body corporate, to 'any director, manager, secretary or similar officer of the body corporate or any person who was purporting to act in any such capacity', if that offence 'is proved to have been committed with the consent or connivance of or to be attributable to any neglect' on their part.

6.5 The Registrar has powers to prosecute the above offences and can, through Section 36(2), follow up a complaint from a Data Subject which concerns a possible breach of a Principle. It is therefore possible that what starts off as a polite enquiry from the Registrar leads to a close scrutiny of the particulars registered under a specific Entry. As soon as this becomes a distinct possibility, it is generally advisable to seek legal advice as to the best course of action.

Chapter Four: The Data Protection Principles

1. General

1.1 The eight Principles are set out in Schedule 1, Part I of the Act; Schedule 1, Part II shows how they are to be interpreted (the Fourth and Sixth Principles excepted). Part II also draws attention to the limited role of the First and Sixth Principles in the specific case of personal data used for historical, statistical or research purposes.

1.2 The Principles are fundamental to the Act. Their development can be traced through the 'Younger Committee' (1972), the 'Lindop Committee' (1978) and the 1980 OECD Guidelines; the version which appears in the Act was finalised in response to Articles 4 to 11 inclusive of the 1981 Council of Europe Convention ('the Convention') 'for the protection of individuals with regard to automatic processing of personal data'. These Articles are quoted in full below (for the text of the Principles in the Act, see Section 2 of this Chapter). Note that Article 11 specifically permits a Party to the Convention to grant Data Subjects 'a wider measure of protection than that stipulated in this convention' - a point worth bearing in mind whenever the provisions of the Act are being implemented in practice.

1.3 **'Basic principles for data protection'** (from the text of the 1981 Council of Europe Convention)

'4 Duties of the Parties

1. Each Party shall take the necessary measures in its domestic law to give effect to the basic principles for data protection set out in this chapter.

2. These measures shall be taken at the latest at the time of entry into force of this convention in respect of that Party.

5 Quality of data

Personal data undergoing automatic processing shall be:

(a) obtained and processed fairly and lawfully;

(b) stored for specified and legitimate purposes and not used in a way incompatible with those purposes;

(c) adequate, relevant and not excessive in relation to the purposes for which they are stored;

(d) accurate and, where necessary, kept up to date;

(e) preserved in a form which permits identification of the data subjects for no longer than is required for the purpose for which those data are stored.

6 Special categories of data

Personal data revealing racial origin, political opinions or religious or other beliefs, as well as personal data concerning health or sexual life, may not be processed automatically unless domestic law provides appropriate safeguards. The same shall apply to personal data relating to criminal convictions.

7 Data security

Appropriate security measures shall be taken for the protection of personal data stored in automated data files against accidental or unauthorised destruction or accidental loss as well as against unauthorised access, alteration or dissemination.

8 Additional safeguards for the data subject

Any person shall be enabled:

(a) to establish the existence of an automated personal data file, its main purposes, as well as the identity and habitual residence or principal place of business of the controller of the file;

(b) to obtain at reasonable intervals and without excessive delay or expense confirmation of whether personal data relating to him are stored in the automated data file as well as communication to him of such data in an intelligible form;

(c) to obtain, as the case may be, rectification or erasure of such data if these have been processed contrary to the provisions of domestic law giving effect to the basic principles set out in Articles 5 and 6 of this convention;

(d) to have a remedy if a request for confirmation or, as the case may be, communication, rectification or erasure as referred to in paragraphs (b) and (c) of this article is not complied with.

9 Exceptions and restrictions

1. No exception to the provisions of Articles 5, 6 and 8 of this convention

shall be allowed except within the limits defined in this article.

2. Derogation from the provisions of Articles 5, 6 and 8 of this convention shall be allowed when such derogation is provided for by the law of the Party and constitutes a necessary measure in a democratic society in the interests of:

(a) protecting State security, public safety, the monetary interests of the State or the suppression of criminal offences;

(b) protecting the data subject or the rights and freedoms of others.

3. Restrictions on the exercise of the rights specified in Article 8, paragraphs (b),(c) and (d), may be provided by law with respect to automated personal data files used for statistics or for scientific research purposes when there is obviously no risk of an infringement of the privacy of the data subjects.

10 Sanctions and remedies

Each Party undertakes to establish appropriate sanctions and remedies for violations of provisions of domestic law giving effect to the basic principles for data protection set out in this chapter.

11 Extended protection

None of the provisions of this chapter shall be interpreted as limiting or otherwise affecting the possibility for a Party to grant data subjects a wider measure of protection than that stipulated in this convention.'

1.4 The Principles thus set the standards against which the activities of Data Users may be judged - notably by the Registrar who may enforce their observance. Data Users should, therefore, regularly audit their procedures, not only to ensure that the Principles are being complied with, but also so that reasonable efforts towards such compliance can be demonstrated. To assist this process, a sample of questions basic to such an audit (taken from in-depth 'Procedural Reviews' which are carried out by Information Protection and Management Consultants, Hoskyns Group plc) is provided, in this Chapter, for each Principle.

1.5 In accordance with Article 6 of the Convention, any Principle, or its Interpretation, may be modified or supplemented by the Secretary of State (see Sections 2(3) and 2(4) of the Act) '... for the purpose of providing additional safeguards ...' in relation to certain particularly sensitive personal data (racial origin; political opinions; religious or other beliefs; physical or mental health; sexual life; criminal convictions).

Relevant Orders would have to be laid before Parliament and approved by a resolution of each House of Parliament; no such Orders have been laid to date.

1.6 It is worth noting here that whilst the Principles provide the basis for coherent and comprehensive safeguards for Data Subjects, these safeguards are additional to a number of existing legal remedies. For instance, there are contracts which prohibit unauthorised disclosures (eg contracts with employees or agents, with companies that have access to data for the purpose of maintaining or repairing computer systems or software, and contracts covering similar circumstances where confidentiality has to be maintained). If a person is owed a duty of care, an action for negligence can be instituted; similarly, in the case of published information, there could be an action for defamation (unless the disclosure is privileged). Action can also be taken for breach of copyright or for breach of confidence. Obviously, the Data Protection Act may overlap with any Freedom of Information legislation.

1.7 Some of the requirements of the Principles are met by other current legislation. For example, information relating to creditworthiness is already protected by the Consumer Credit Act 1974. Under this legislation the requirements of the Seventh Principle (see paragraph 2.7 below) are met, since a person can obtain access to all relevant information on the files of a credit reference agency. The 1974 Act takes precedence (see Chapter 7, paragraph 9.2.5), and provides a larger entitlement than the Data Protection Act, since the sources of the information must also be revealed.

1.8 By means of the Principles, the Data Protection Act establishes data processing standards to meet:

(a) the fears of Data Subjects that privacy could be threatened by the use of computers for data collection, correlation, matching, searching, and transmission (the last being of particular importance as regards transborder flow of data, which may well take place merely because cheap rates are available elsewhere for processing at night);

(b) the fears of Data Users that public concern over such privacy issues could impede co-ordination of government, production, marketing, financial and management information;

(c) fears that other parties to the Convention could discriminate against the UK, as regards transborder flow of data, should the UK's data protection practices be considered to be in breach of the terms of the Convention.

1.9 It should be stressed that some of the requirements of the Principles could be achieved in other ways, and reference has already been made to the current debate on the future of Registration (see Chapter 3, paragraph 1.13). This and other relevant topics are discussed in more detail in Chapter 9, Sections 4 to 7. Finally, it is useful to remind Data Users and Computer Bureaux that they may need to take note of the equivalent of the Data Protection Principles in the legislation of other countries.

2. The Principles: their Interpretations; practical examples; Procedural Review questions

Note: All Principles apply to personal data held by Data Users. The Eighth Principle alone also applies to Computer Bureaux which provide services that relate to such data. Each Principle is illustrated with examples of practical problems; these are followed by a checklist of 'Procedural Review' questions.

2.1 The First Principle:

'The information to be contained in personal data shall be obtained, and personal data shall be processed, fairly and lawfully.'

Interpretation:

'(1) Subject to sub-paragraph (2) below, in determining whether information was obtained fairly regard shall be had to the method by which it was obtained, including in particular whether any person from whom it was obtained was deceived or misled as to the purpose or purposes for which it is to be held, used or disclosed.

(2) Information shall in any event be treated as obtained fairly if it is obtained from a person who -

(a) is authorised by or under any enactment to supply it; or

(b) is required to supply it by or under any enactment or by any convention or other instrument imposing an international obligation on the United Kingdom;

and in determining whether information was obtained fairly there shall be disregarded any disclosure of the information which is authorised or required by or under any enactment or required by any such convention or other instrument as aforesaid.'

2.1.1 Comment: Fair obtaining

(a) The Principle addresses two separate activities - the obtaining of relevant information, and its processing. The 'Interpretation' only gives guidance on 'Fair obtaining', and contrasts the evaluation of how to achieve this with an account of the circumstances under which, 'in any event', such evaluation becomes irrelevant (eg if 'any enactment' is involved).

(b) The importance of this Principle, in the Registrar's view, could already be gauged from the first edition of his Guideline 4 (March 1987) in which it received more space than any other Principle. August 1988 saw the issue of the controversial 'Guidance Note 19' on 'Fair Obtaining - Notification' (reference GN19-RPJ-8/88) which drew attention to several onerous obligations which, in the Registrar's view, this Principle imposes on Data Users.

(c) For instance, Guidance Note 19 (GN19) stresses that the issue to be decided is not the intention of a Data User, but if the obtaining is unfair 'whether intentionally or not'; that obtaining information fairly would require 'the knowledge and ability of the individual from whom it is being obtained' to be taken into account (eg what is 'fair' for one individual might not be considered 'fair' for 'an individual of lower than average knowledge or ability'); and that individuals cannot be deemed to know the contents of a Data User's Register Entry (eg the purpose or purposes for which the Data User may wish to process personal data). A further problem was created for many Data Users through the Registrar's view that the source of the information had to receive adequate notification, concerning the personal data and their use, **'Before'** providing the information concerned; in summary, that notification should be given 'clearly, simply, honestly and fully'.

(d) The Registrar, in his 'Revised List of Guidance Notes' dated June 1989, has drawn attention to the fact that 'GN19 has now been incorporated in Guideline 4, The Data Protection Principles' (February 1989 edition). Whilst, not surprisingly, the First Principle again occupies by far the most space in this Guideline, and the text does adopt the same approach as GN19, it is fair to say that abridging some issues has also reduced their impact - for instance, there is no reference to 'an individual of lower that average knowledge or ability', and the word **'Before'** has disappeared, as has the phrase 'clearly, simply, honestly and fully'.

(e) Further clarification was provided in 1990. In notes supplied by the Registrar to seminars on 'Data Protection Guidance for Direct Marketing', he summarised his views on when it is appropriate to provide an 'opt-out' (eg when the source of the information is asked to tick a box to indicate that something **should not** happen to personal data) or an 'opt-in' (eg when the source is asked to tick a box to indicate **consent** for something to happen). He states that:

> 'The principle underlying 'fair obtaining' is that sources of information should be aware of how the information they give is to be used. A source (often an individual), can then chose whether or not to provide the

information, or put some sort of limitation on its use. There may be situations where individuals do not have this choice - such as when they are applying for connection to a public utility. In such circumstances, in order to ensure that the information is fairly obtained, individuals should be given the opportunity to opt-out of any secondary uses of their data for direct marketing purposes.

If a data user chooses not to tell his sources about a secondary direct marketing use which he has in mind (such as the sale or exchange of mailing lists), when the information is obtained; then the information will only have been fairly obtained for the primary or obvious purpose (which would include further marketing by the data user himself). Before it could be used for any secondary purpose, it would be necessary to 'fairly obtain' it a second time, by gaining positive consent of the data subject (asking them to opt-in). This necessity can of course by avoided by making all the intended uses clear at the time the information is first collected.'

(f) Given this stress on 'Fair obtaining', Section (2) of the Principle's Interpretation (see paragraph 2.1 above) can come as something of a shock; the phrase 'in any event' might well permit deception of the individual in appropriate circumstances. The force of this derogation from a 'fair' approach can be illustrated by extending the two scenarios which the Registrar outlines in paragraph 1.5 of Guideline 4. In the first, a Community Charges Registration Officer acquires, by statute, a list of names and addresses; in the second, an employer discloses, by statute, information to the Inland Revenue which employees have supplied about themselves. Taking these lawful instances further, it could **still** be 'fair' for agents of a CCRO to canvass a housing estate (in which tenants are known to oppose the Community Charge) and obtain names and addresses by pretending that these were required for a petition **against** the Charge; in the second instance, an employee could be assured that the information would be kept confidential when, in fact, the employer had no such intention as far as the Inland Revenue was concerned. Although the above scenarios are theoretically possible, it is to be hoped that anyone empowered by Parliament to use such a derogation from the First Principle will not then abuse these powers. In his Fifth Report (June 1989; Part B, paragraph 118) the Registrar argues that 'this complete exemption for those acting under statutory authority is too sweeping and may licence practices which on their merits would be unacceptable in other circumstances'.

(g) Similarly, Section 28(4) of the Act removes the powers of the Registrar to enforce the First Principle in any case in which the application of those provisions to the data would be likely to prejudice the prevention or detection of crime, or the apprehension or prosecution of offenders, or the assessment or collection of any tax or duty. Thus the Police would **not** have to obtain information fairly if (and **only** if, in each particular case concerned) they would thereby prejudice a criminal investigation (see also Chapter 7, Section 3.2). For instance, it would be absurd for an undercover detective, on being given a list of gang-members destined for a Police computer, to be challenged on the grounds that the information had been unfairly obtained because a statement about the Officer's intentions had not been given!

2.1.2 Comment: Fair Processing

(a) 'Fairness' needs to be judged, on its merits, in each particular case, 'by reference to the purpose of the processing, the nature of the processing itself and to its consequences for the individual affected by it' (Guideline 4, paragraph 1.9). The example given by the Registrar (also in paragraph 1.9) is that:

> '... it would be unfair for a data user to process personal data with the result that unsolicited marketing material is sent to an individual who has informed the data user that he does not wish to receive such material.'

(b) As regards 'unsolicited marketing material' (eg Direct Mail, sometimes described as 'Junk Mail'), in many cases a Data Subject is likely to contact the relevant Data User (if identifiable) with a request on the lines of 'Please take me off your mailing list'. It is worth noting, therefore, that 'A data subject has no right to have personal data deleted merely because he would prefer that the data user should not keep that information about him' (Guideline 4, paragraph 7.3) and that the Data User's obligation in this instance is confined to cessation of the specific **processing** that is bringing about the 'unfair' consequences. Note again that it is **holding** which is permitted but not any **unfair processing**, and in relation to Mailing Lists, the Registrar writes 'When registered, the personal data may continue to be held whether or not the individual objects' (Guideline 6, paragraph A.7.4). Note that this implies that any other processing (other than mailing lists) of the same personal data remains lawful, under the Act, as long as it is covered by the Data User's Registration and has not been declared unfair by the Registrar.

(c) The Registrar's Guidance Note 9 on 'Implications of the Data Protection Act for Direct Marketing/Direct Mailing' (reference GN9-NSW-9/88) clarifies the roles and data protection obligations of the five kinds of parties who may be involved in this activity (List Owner; List Broker; Client Advertiser; Advertising Agency; Mailing House or Computer Bureau). The List Owner controls the use of the list, and will have acquired or generated its contents, having registered standard Purposes P013 (Customer/Client Administration) and/or P004 (Marketing and Selling). If the List Owner wishes to be free to disclose the list to third parties (whether for payment or otherwise) then P018 (Trading in Personal Information) will also have to be registered; appropriate disclosure categories are D381 (Traders in personal data) if recipients are List Brokers, and/or D382 (other organisations or individuals) if disclosure is to one or more specific end-users (note that these would have to be described in more detail). The Registrar stresses that even if no personal data are disclosed, ie if the List Owner mails material, from a third party, for the purposes of that third party 'however occasionally or incidentally', then P018 needs to be registered. Additionally, he advises that if the data themselves are not disclosed to a third party, this can be indicated, in free text, on the relevant Part B Form; this point could prove crucial in maintaining the confidence of Data Subjects.

(d) Of the other four parties listed, only 'Mailing house or Computer Bureau' **must** register under the Act (as a Computer Bureau) if they process the personal data on behalf of others; the activities of List Brokers, Client Advertisers and Advertising Agencies do not, if limited to the descriptions mentioned above, require Registration (because these bodies do not control the contents and use of personal data or provide processing services).

(e) Attention should also be drawn to the 'Mailing Preference Service', an organisation 'supported by the Post Office' and by 'the majority of leading firms in this country which do business by mail' (all quotes in this paragraph are from a leaflet issued by the Service). Application can be made to the Service either for 'more offers by mail' (a list of 8 topics, including 'Home', 'Sport' etc, is provided) or for no 'Direct Mail from the participating members of the Mailing Preferences Service' to be sent. The leaflet draws attention to the fact that the latter request cannot affect mailings 'by firms who hold your name as a customer (or as an agent)', or mailings 'derived from telephone or town directories' (see also Chapter 5, paragraphs 3.3.16 to 3.3.20).

(f) Paragraph 7 of the Interpretations to the Principles (in Schedule 1 Part II of the Act) takes account of those instances in which the value of personal data, for historical, statistical or research purposes, was not (or could not be) appreciated at the time the information was obtained. Paragraph 7 states that:

> 'Where personal data are held for historical, statistical or research purposes and not used in such a way that damage or distress is, or is likely to be, caused to any Data Subject' ... 'the information contained in the data shall not be regarded for the purposes of the first principle as obtained unfairly by reason only that its use for any such purposes was not disclosed when it was obtained'.

Note that this exception applies even when these purposes **were** known, but were not revealed, at the time the information was collected. The exception does **not** apply if the Data User already has it in mind to disclose the information, for these purposes, to a third party.

(g) The Registrar has also taken enforcement action to prevent a breach of the First Principle by consumer credit agencies. Because this action is the culmination of a dispute that has been simmering for four years, the complex details and latest developments relating to credit referencing have been combined in Appendix 1, under the heading 'An insight into 'fair' processing'.

2.1.3 Some further examples of potential problems for the Data User:

(a) Have personal data been obtained for one purpose and also been used for another? This could be very common within a group of companies where one Data User's customer base is used by another Data User for marketing purposes. For example, have data collected for grants made to students found their way to, say, credit card companies or sales representatives? Could it be argued that these disclosures were not revealed to the providers of the information (whether the Data Subjects themselves, ie the students, or other individuals providing information about the Data Subjects)?

(b) Could information sources claim that they were 'deceived or misled' because the heading to a form gave the wrong impression? A typical instance would be a form headed 'Application for Housing' or similar, which, in the absence of any indication to the contrary, an applicant could reasonably expect to be used solely for a 'Housing Management' purpose. Nevertheless, since it is quite common for an applicant to provide information on ethnic origin on such a form, this information may well be transferred to another Department, eg for processing under a Personnel or Public Relations purpose; similarly, other information from the form could well be used for the 'Marketing and Selling' purpose in relation to 'Right to Buy' aspects.

(c) In an example reported in Computer Talk (04.08.86), a Local Authority job interview panel obtained information concerning an applicant's rent arrears with that Authority. Such an internal disclosure is lawful only if the separate purposes involved (in this case 'Personnel/Employee Administration' and 'Housing Management') have been registered; as regards the First Principle, the attention of tenants should have been drawn to the fact that rent information might be disclosed to the Personnel Department of the Authority, in appropriate cases. The relevant internal disclosures might also be registered (even though there is no legal requirement to do so) since this would improve the only description of the activity concerned which is actually in the public domain.

(d) Could information sources claim that unfair, unjust or improper means were used to induce them to provide the personal data? Note that it is 'unfair pressure' and 'unjustified threats' to which the Registrar refers in paragraph 1.1 of Guideline 4. It may well be perfectly fair to point out to Data Subjects that if they decide not to provide certain information, eg by filling in a form, then the service to which the form refers would, as a consequence, not be provided. By contrast, an example of unfair threats, which resulted in much adverse publicity, and extra work, for the majority of Community Charges Registration Officers, was contained in those Community Charge Canvass Forms which did not distinguish between questions that **had** to be answered, by law, and questions that were optional. To illustrate the problems this caused, the following written undertaking was provided, to the Registrar, by the CCRO of Trafford Metropolitan Borough Council:

> 'that no further copies of the canvass form which was the subject of the complaint would be distributed;
>
> that any form used in future would be such as to ensure that information obtained by its use would be obtained in compliance with the Data Protection Principles;
>
> that no information relating to relationships obtained by use of the previous form was now held as personal data nor would be so held in the future;
>
> that no information relating to dates of commencement of residence obtained by the use of the previous form was held as personal data, and that no such information relating to dates of commencement of residence before 31 March 1990 would be held as personal data;
>
> that information objected to by the Registrar and contained in the completed forms but held manually would not be released to the Borough Council in its capacity as charging authority.'

(e) If any of the above, or equivalent, situations apply, can procedures be instituted to resolve the problems? Forms that the public fills in may need to be redesigned, so that they 'clearly, simply, honestly and fully' draw attention to all the purposes for which any or all of the information requested may be used. New instructions may also need to be issued to staff who conduct surveys. Note that it is insufficient to rely on the fact that the Register Entry is in the public domain, as paragraph 1.3, Guideline 4 states that:

> 'The law does not assume that individuals know the contents of the Data Protection Register. The Registrar considers the circumstances in which it would be sufficient simply to tell the individual that the information he or she is being asked to supply may be held, used or disclosed as

described in the data user's register entry to be extremely limited.'

(f) The Registrar sees Codes of Practice (see Chapter 5) as having a role in relation to the First Principle as he 'expects Codes of Practice developed by groups of data users to encourage the provision of helpful explanations to individuals' (paragraph 1.3, Guideline 4).

(g) Any disclosure that is subject to a non-disclosure provision will not be subject to the First Principle, as Section 26(3) removes the Registrar's power to enforce **any** Principle (**but only** if the conditions that surround the non-disclosure provision have been applied). Thus any disclosure of personal data outside these conditions would not be protected from the Registrar's powers. For example, any personal data disclosed to a Government Department which are additional to those specified as required by statute, would be fully subject to the First Principle.

(h) Note that disclosures that are registered are those that the Data User intends to make. Consequently, there is a link between registered disclosures and the explanations provided, under the First Principle, to the sources of the personal data.

2.1.4 **Some Procedural Review questions**:

(a) From whom are the personal data obtained? Are the data solicited, unsolicited or anonymous?

(b) How are they obtained? By telephone? By individual contact? From replies to advertisements? In confidence?

(c) Are markers needed to identify the sources of information? Was unfair pressure used to collect information?

(d) How are people advised, at the time the information is obtained, of the various purposes, uses or disclosures involved?

(e) How are statutory limitations to obtain personal data checked?

(f) Do forms need to be redesigned? Do staff need to be trained in the proper techniques of collecting personal data?

(g) Is the processing of personal data fair? Does the processing discriminate against certain types of Data Subject?

(h) How are procedures to obtain information monitored?

2.2 **The Second Principle**:

'Personal data shall be held only for one or more specified and lawful purposes.'

Interpretation:

'Personal data shall not be treated as held for a specified purpose unless that purpose is described in particulars registered under this Act in relation to the data.'

2.2.1 **Comment**:

(a) The text of this Principle (together with that of the Third Principle) is modelled on Article 5(b) of the Convention (see paragraph 1.3 above) and, similarly, on paragraph 9 of the OECD Guidelines. The latter is more detailed in that it provides for the purposes to be 'specified not later than at the time of data collection' (a point reiterated in GN19; see paragraph 2.1.1(c) above).

(b) The Interpretation in the Act makes it clear that what matters are the 'particulars registered', and not any description elsewhere which may also define the purpose. Thus even if a purpose is described elsewhere in greater detail, or with greater clarity than is required (or permitted) by the Registration format (for example, in a Code of Practice or publicly available Guide), it is the registered particulars that will count in a Court of Law. It is for this reason that Registration is by no means a trivial event, quite apart from the fact that it is a legal obligation.

(c) These aspects clearly place much responsibility on the design of the Registration process - notably, in relation to this Principle, on the permitted use of 'Standard Purpose' titles, as well as on their 'Full descriptions'. These descriptions are provided on pages 15 to 38 of the Registrar's 'NOTES to help you apply for Registration' which, the Registrar states, 'are not intended to be comprehensive or exhaustive' ('NOTES', page 12). Indeed, the 'NOTES' further stress that a selected Standard Purpose should be the one that 'most closely' describes the relevant use of personal data and that further details should only be given if the standard description 'is misleading in some way'. It can be seen that there is scope for the Data User's purpose to diverge significantly from the description, and also that Data Subjects, or even a Court of Law, might not necessarily agree with a Data User's view that the Standard Purpose quoted in a Part B provides an adequate indication of the particular activity involved.

(d) Checking and validating the Registration, to ensure that it is correct and remains so (see Chapter 3, Sections 3 to 5) will go a long way towards satisfying this Principle, at least as far as **specifying** the purpose is concerned. It should be noted that Registration does not, in itself, make a purpose (or other registered particulars) lawful with respect to other legislation; this is an especially important consideration in the public sector (see also paragraph 2.3.1(d)).

(e) In Guideline 4, paragraph 2.1 the Registrar states that 'as well as being registered, purposes must of course be lawful'. Registration only makes a purpose lawful with respect to the Act, it cannot guarantee that the purpose itself is lawful (eg registration of personal data used for blackmail purposes does not make blackmail lawful.)

(f) Note that if personal data are to be used for more than one purpose, there may be a need with respect to the First Principle to inform sources, **before** the personal information is collected, about the other uses .

2.2.2 **Some Procedural Review questions**:

(a) If a Standard Purpose has been chosen, does it adequately describe why the personal data are held?

(b) Are further details required to fully define the purpose(s)? Has a Census been carried out? If so, how representative is the Census? Has the Census covered **all** personal data processed on behalf of the Data User (eg by a Computer Bureau?)

(c) How are the various purposes and uses of personal data monitored, to ensure that they are lawful at all times?

(d) Who is responsible for Registration?

(e) How is a new purpose notified to the person responsible for Registration?

(f) How are the particulars contained in the Register Entries kept up to date?

(g) Do staff know which Register Entries relate to their work, what these Entries contain, and how these Entries affect their day-to-day activities? Do the Entries relate to the Data User's organisational structure in a meaningful way (eg can they assist staff to recognise which Register Entries relate to their work)?

(h) When are audits carried out to check the accuracy of each Entry?

(i) Do sources of personal information need to be informed about the Data User's registered purposes?

2.3 **The Third Principle**:

'Personal data held for any purpose or purposes shall not be used or disclosed in any manner incompatible with that purpose or those purposes.'

Interpretation:

'Personal data shall not be treated as used or disclosed in contravention of this principle unless -

(a) used otherwise than for a purpose of a description registered under this Act in relation to the data; or

(b) disclosed otherwise than to a person of a description so registered.'

2.3.1 **Comment**:

(a) As stated in paragraph 2.2.1(a) above, this Principle is derived from provisions contained in the Convention and in the OECD Guidelines. The Interpretation of the Principle introduces, additionally, the requirement to **describe** disclosures within the Registration particulars (as provided for under Section 4(3)(d) of the Act; note that Section 4(3)(c) of the Act extends these obligations even further, to include a description of the **sources** from whom the information is obtained).

(b) To meet the requirements of this Principle in practice, **all levels** of staff will have to be trained to recognise authorised disclosures, and that a new disclosure (or source) may need a prior change to the Register Entry. Guidance will be required on how to deal with enquiries from, on behalf of, or about Data Subjects, with enquiries from the Police, Inland Revenue and other prosecuting agencies, and with enquiries in emergency situations. Personal data should never be disclosed unless the disclosee has been identified as authorised to receive the personal data; where necessary, a proper record of the disclosure should be taken. Telephone enquiries may present difficulties in this context if staff are put under pressure to disclose personal data; training and guidance on how to deal with such awkward situations is essential.

(c) Data Users may find it necessary to keep a record of disclosures (despite the fact that arguments to make this mandatory were not accepted by the Government) so that compliance with this Principle can be demonstrated - if necessary, in Court. Note that even a disclosure which is within the registered particulars could be judged to be ultra vires (ie to contravene **other** legislation; see paragraph 2.2.1(d) above). For example, a Community Charges Registration Officer may have registered a disclosure, for this purpose, under 'Housing department D322', in order to cover the circumstances in which such a department is asked to confirm details of a specific individual (since communication with a source may involve a disclosure of personal data held by a CCRO). However, if, instead, the disclosure is, say, for a Housing Benefits purpose, a legal challenge might ensue since the Local Government Finance Act 1988, and the Regulations made under it, do not authorise the use of Community Charge information for any purpose other than the Community Charge.

(d) The Interpretation of this Principle specifies what is **not** a contravention rather than what **is** a contravention. If a disclosure is registered there **cannot** be a contravention of the Third Principle; however if a disclosure is unregistered there **can** be a contravention of this Principle. The important consequence of the use of this negative in the Interpretation is that an unregistered disclosure does not **automatically** contravene the Principle, and this accounts for the words in Guideline 4, paragraph 3.3 where the Registrar states that 'Whether a use or disclosure is compatible with a registered purpose will be a question of fact for the Registrar to consider.' However, this position may be confused by the first sentence of paragraph 3.3 which states that 'Disclosures may be made or data used for a purpose not described in a data user's register entry.' It is important to realise that the word 'may' is here **not** being used in the permissive sense (ie this can be done), but rather to illustrate a possibility (ie this might occur) - since knowingly or recklessly using or disclosing personal data other than described in the Register Entry could be a criminal offence.

(e) The Interpretation creates two problems with Section 23 of the Act, and can encourage Data Users to register more disclosures than may be strictly necessary. The problems arise as:

(i) the purposes for which the data are used, and any disclosures, are deemed lawful (under the Act) if covered by the Registration particulars. Many of the registered purposes and disclosures in a Part B are broadly defined and, through their use, a Data User can authorise several disclosures that are not intended. For example, most Data Users disclose specific personal data to specific suppliers, and consequently register a D206 disclosure ('Suppliers, providers of goods or services'). The D206 disclosure tick would, however, legitimise such disclosures to **any** supplier associated with the Data User, and make it difficult for a Data Subject to obtain compensation for damage caused. This situation is even worse if a D203 disclosure is registered, as this legitimises disclosures to employees for purposes **not** associated with their work functions (see Chapter 3, paragraph 3.2.7(e)).

(ii) an ambiguity seems present in Section 23(2) of the Act as it excludes the possibility of claiming compensation, by reason of unauthorised disclosure or access, if the disclosure is to any person or persons so registered. However, whilst it can be presumed that the registered disclosure referred to would have to be one that is specified within the **relevant** Register Entry (and in the **one** relevant Part B within that Entry, if the Entry contains several Parts B), the words used in 23(2) are '... falling within a description ... in an entry in the register relating to that data user'. The use of the phrase 'an entry' (rather than 'the entry' or 'the relevant' entry) raises the spectre of any disclosure being 'lawful' with respect to **any** purpose, so long as the disclosure is registered in **any** Part B, associated with **any** Part A. As a result, it may be questioned whether the Registration format is consistent with the provision of Article 5(b) of the Convention (see paragraph 1.3 above).

(f) In Guideline 4, paragraph 2.1 the Registrar states that 'as well as being registered, purposes must of course be lawful'. Since the Standard Purpose registered in a Part B will be qualified by the disclosures registered in the same Part B, all disclosures too must be lawful. Thus the fact that a disclosure is registered with respect to the Act does not in itself legitimise that disclosure; a general point which has had particular impact in the public sector. For example, with respect to the Community Charge, the legislation identifies the few organisations and the limited number of circumstances in which personal information used for Community Charges Registers can be disclosed. Thus, registration of a disclosure to an organisation (or in circumstances) **not** specified by these Acts could not legitimise such disclosure of Community Charge personal data; consequently the disclosure could be challenged as being unlawful.

(g) Note that if personal data are being disclosed to more than one organisation, there may be a need with respect to the First Principle to inform sources about all these disclosures **before** the personal information is collected. Disclosures made within the Data User are not registered; however, such disclosures should be traced to check whether they subsequently become external (ie need to be registered) or whether they support any new uses of data which need to be registered.

2.3.2 **Some Procedural Review questions**:

(a) Have all necessary disclosures been indicated in each Register Entry? Are all registered disclosures compatible with established procedures, Codes of Practice, and statutory limitations?

(b) How accurate is the Census in relation to disclosures? Have all disclosures made within the Data User been traced? Does an audit or compliance check need to be carried out?

(c) How are the various disclosures of personal data monitored, to ensure that they are lawful at all times?

(d) How is a new disclosure category notified to the person responsible for Registration?

(e) What steps are taken to ensure that personal data can safely be disclosed?

(f) Are staff aware of disclosures permitted, or required, by statute? Are staff aware of disclosures prohibited by statute?

(g) Are staff trained to cope with difficult (eg aggressive) enquiries involving the disclosure of personal data?

(h) Do staff know in particular what the permitted disclosures are?

(i) Are staff aware of all the non-disclosure exemptions (and their limitations) that may apply?

(j) Is there a policy on sensitive disclosures (eg to the Police)?

(k) Do sources of personal information need to be informed about the Data User's registered disclosures?

2.4 The Fourth Principle

> 'Personal data held for any purpose or proposes shall be adequate, relevant and not excessive in relation to that purpose or those purposes.'

2.4.1 Comment:

(a) No Interpretation of this Principle is provided in the Act, and consequently a breach of the Principle can only be assessed with respect to purpose (ie the particulars registered). For example, what a Data User (eg a private detective agency) might deem to be relevant personal data with respect to a particular purpose, might be deemed irrelevant when viewed from the standpoint of the Data Subject (eg the person under investigation). It is pertinent to conclude that applying 'adequate' and 'relevant' not only to the data, but equally to how the Data Subject is affected by the way these data are used and disclosed, might have provided additional safeguards.

(b) In determining whether personal data conform to this Principle, it is well to recall the comment concerning Data Classes in Part B of the Registration forms. By marking a box, Data Users are indicating that a Data Class is 'to be held for the

Purpose described' (ie is relevant to the specified purpose). Thus, the Data User should be able to answer the questions: 'Why has box Cxyz been ticked in relation to this purpose?', or 'What justification, in relation to this purpose, have I for holding data in Class Cxyz?'. In particular, where a Data Class consists of a free text field, management should be able to check the quality of the data stored in the field, to ensure they satisfy the criteria for 'relevance'.

(c) Defining the meaning of 'adequate, relevant and not excessive' can ultimately become a matter for the Registrar (also for the Tribunal, and the Courts). Whilst the definition of these terms will vary according to the situation, adequacy will, clearly, be established by the **minimum** amount of information which is necessary for the purpose. Inadequate data can also cause problems. For example, on an application for credit, credit reference agencies may use the postcode as a factor in determining creditworthiness. The assumption is that a 'poor' address, or an adverse credit rating of third parties who live at the same or at a similar address, implies that the applicant is a poor risk. Public Utility companies may, similarly, demand deposits whose size is based on the area in which a customer lives. In both these cases use is made of information not directly related to the financial resources of the applicant, and this may be deemed inadequate for the purpose of awarding credit or determining the size of deposit. The practice may also be considered 'unfair processing' of information about applicants (ie a contravention of the First Principle).

(d) Note that there is a link between the Fourth and First Principles. For example, holding personal data on 'relationships' and on 'dates of commencement of residence before 31 March 1990' (see paragraph 2.1.3(d) above) was deemed excessive in the context of the statutory purpose of compiling and maintaining the Community Charges Register and, therefore, in breach of the Fourth Principle as well as the First.

(e) There is also a link between the Fourth and the Fifth or Sixth Principles. If personal data are inadequate for the purpose, this might be because they are inaccurate, whilst if they are held for too long, they may through time become inadequate.

(f) It appears that optical disks that contain the image of documents containing personal information could potentially cause havoc with this Principle. The technology, which provides a very convenient method of storing documents invites, through that very convenience, a method of storing personal data that is excessive for the purpose. For example, an individual claiming a benefit might write a letter containing completely irrelevant personal information. If that letter is stored on optical disk, that irrelevant personal information could easily become irrelevant personal data. Consequently, users of such systems will need to consider very carefully how such documents are to be retrieved, and if retrieved through the use of an index, how such documents are indexed.

2.4.2 **Some Procedural Review questions**:

(a) Have the terms 'adequate, relevant, not excessive' been defined in relation to the purpose(s) for which the personal data are used?

(b) Can the reason for holding every data field be justified?

(c) Is any data field outside the scope of the registered purpose? Is any data field outside relevant limitations imposed by statute? Have all the necessary Data Classes been indicated in the relevant Register Entry?

(d) How accurate is the Census in relation to Data Classes? Does an audit or compliance check need to be carried out?

(e) How is a new Data Class notified to the person responsible for Registration?

(f) Are any data held merely because 'they could be useful'?

(g) Are the data sampled, at intervals, to check their relevance?

(h) Are there procedures to remove irrelevant and/or excessive personal data?

(i) How is the Fourth Principle integrated into the methodology for the design or modification of software?

2.5 **The Fifth Principle**:

'Personal data shall be accurate and, where necessary, kept up to date.'

Interpretation:

'Any question whether or not personal data are accurate shall be determined as for the purposes of section 22 of this Act but, in the case of such data as are mentioned in subsection (2) of that section, this principle shall not be regarded as having been contravened by reason of any inaccuracy in the information there mentioned if the requirements specified in that subsection have been complied with.'

2.5.1 **Comment**:

(a) Section 22 of the Act, referred to in the Interpretation, excludes compensation for damage suffered by reason of inaccuracy (defined as 'incorrect or misleading as to any matter of fact') in cases where the data are accurately recorded and indicate whether the source was a third party or the Data Subject. In addition, if the Data Subject has described the data as incorrect or misleading, compensation is excluded if there is an indication in the data to that effect (more detailed guidance on this topic is provided in Guideline 5, paragraph 3.6).

(b) Personal data received from third parties or Data Subjects should, therefore, be marked as such where practicable, as should personal data whose accuracy has been challenged by Data Subjects. These procedures are likely to be difficult to incorporate into existing computer schemes, but could be designed into new ones.

(c) Whilst a Data User is not **required** to check the accuracy of information provided by a third party (or, for that matter, by a Data Subject), a Data User can reasonably be expected to take **some** steps towards verification, if circumstances permit. However, the Principle clearly places an obligation on a Data User to take all reasonable steps to ensure that the information is **entered** accurately; this means establishing proper quality controls and validating data input.

(d) Especially where sensitive data collections are concerned, it is important to ensure that proper procedures have been established to record a third party source of the information. For example, the statement 'Mr X beats his baby', if provided by, say, Mr Y or the DSS, could be recorded as 'Mr Y says Mr X beats his baby', or 'The DSS have information that Mr X beats his baby'. Note that, to exclude having to pay compensation for any damage caused by the personal data, the marker to indicate a third party source has to be used in all circumstances in which the personal data are used.

(e) Consideration should be given to sampling techniques to check the accuracy of a Data User's personal data on a random basis. Assessment of the information provided by such sampling should form part of each data audit (eg a Procedural Review). This sampling may be especially important when free text comments about Data Subjects form part of the personal data.

(f) Accuracy, particularly in the case of information that needs updating at regular intervals, can of course be crucial in a variety of contexts, of which obvious examples are creditworthiness and entitlement to benefits. Management must therefore ensure proper quality controls, and resourcing, in relation to routine updating.

(g) Care must be taken when some action is dependent on accuracy of the data; for example, a decision to withdraw a service or take legal proceedings. An instance reported in 'Computing' (21.11.85) involved a Local Authority. It was stated that a pensioner was notified that he would, in view of £12.22 rent arrears, not be eligible for allocation of a Council home nearer his daughter, and that this resulted in his suicide. It was then claimed (though denied by the Council) that, through a programming error, the Council's computer had failed to record the fact that the arrears had, in fact, been cleared.

(h) Note that the accuracy provisions of the Act in relation to compensation do not apply to opinions that are properly recorded (eg that include the source of the opinion), since opinions are not facts. However, if the opinion can be shown to be based on error or to be inappropriate (or inadequate: Fourth Principle), then the opinion may have to be deleted. Recording the sources of opinions also prevents opinions from being interpreted as facts; for example, so that 'Mr X thinks Joe Bloggs is ...' is not confused with 'Joe Bloggs is ...'.

(i) Note also that the provisions in Section 24(3) allow potentially damaging information to remain on file indefinitely (even if damage has been suffered, a Court is not **obliged** to order erasure).

2.5.2 **Some Procedural Review questions:**

(a) Is there a marker to indicate whether the source of the personal data is a third party or the Data Subject?

(b) How are data input and verified (eg are personal data derived from application forms sampled and checked against the information provided on the form in order to assess data input as a whole)? Are other checks for accuracy necessary? Are source documents retained?

(c) Do the Data User's activities include punitive actions in relation to Data Subjects (eg deny benefit, withdraw credit)? If so, are special accuracy checks carried out prior to taking such action?

(d) How often are accuracy checks carried out?

(e) Is there a provision for a Data Subject to indicate any disagreement about the accuracy of personal data held?

(f) Are such disagreements, or agreed corrections, notified to all those within the Data User who have received the original data? Should disclosees in other organisations receive such notification?

(g) What procedures allow rectification or erasure of personal data, in compliance with requests from Data Subjects and/or Court Orders?

(h) Are there procedures to determine whether the data require updating and, if so, at what intervals?

(i) How sensitive are the data? What degree of damage could be caused due to their inaccuracy? Are opinions recorded by the Data User capable of substantiation? Is the source of each opinion identifiable?

2.6 **The Sixth Principle**:

'Personal data held for any purpose or purposes shall not be kept for longer than is necessary for that purpose or those purposes.'

2.6.1 **Comment**:

(a) Like the Fourth Principle there is no Interpretation of the Sixth Principle as such, and in similar fashion to the Fourth Principle, no account can be taken of the effect on the Data Subject of the retention of personal data by a Data User. The lack of an interpretation could cause circumstances whereby personal data can be retained for the purpose, even though their retention causes problems for the individual. In the specific instance 'Where personal data are held for historical, statistical or research purposes and not used in such a way that damage or distress is, or is likely to be, caused to any data subject', Schedule 1 Part II, paragraph 7 of the Act states: 'the data may, notwithstanding the sixth principle, be kept indefinitely'.

(b) Defining the length of time appropriate to storage of data kept for a particular purpose will be a matter for the Data User in the first instance. Whilst different organisations can adopt widely different standards for the periods over which particular types of personal data are retained, the periods should in no instance exceed what is legally defensible. In assessing this, Data Users will need to take into account any generally accepted standards and procedures, and in particular any relevant Code of Practice.

(c) To demonstrate compliance with the Principle, a Data User may have to provide evidence of periodic reviews of the data held, in which the data are critically examined to establish whether they need to be retained further. This applies particularly if there is a statutory duty to hold personal data for a period of years (see (d) below), since it could be argued that keeping these data for longer contravenes this Principle. In summary, Data Users must be prepared to justify, in each case, the length of time for which particular data are held.

(d) It should not be overlooked that if retention of the data is a consequence of a statutory duty (eg for certain financial or personnel data), then the **ability** to recover the data must also be retained, irrespective of any changes to hardware and software which the Data User may implement.

(e) In the majority of cases archived data are in fact 'held', as defined in Section 1(5) of the Act, since data are usually archived 'in the form in which they have been or are intended to be processed' (Section 1(5)(c) of the Act), eg on disk, or after a disk to tape transfer. Even if the data have been converted into **another** form, they would still be held if the intention was for the data to be 'further so processed on a subsequent occasion' (Section 1(5)(c) of the Act). Justifying a claim that there was no such intention (ie that the data are not held, and hence not covered by the Act) could, in practice, prove very difficult, since the decision to archive might itself be taken as providing evidence that subsequent processing was intended (see also Chapter 7, paragraph 9.2.9). In short, why keep information in machine-readable form (note that this description will include printed material, if suitable scanning or OCR technology is available) if further processing is **not** intended? And if there **is** no intention to process the information, then why has it not been deleted?

(f) There is a link to the Fourth, Fifth and Eighth Principles. To the Fourth and Fifth, since personal data that have aged are potentially inadequate or inaccurate; to the Eighth, since the disposal of personal data that are no longer required has to be carried out in a secure manner.

(g) As with the Fourth Principle, it appears that optical disks containing images of documents containing personal information could potentially cause havoc with this Principle. Users of such systems will need to consider very carefully how such documents can be purged, or failing that, how such documents can no longer be retrieved when they are of no further use.

2.6.2 **Some Procedural Review questions**:

(a) How often are personal data reviewed, to establish whether they are still required for their purpose(s)?

(b) Are there any legal requirements for keeping personal data for a certain length of time?

(c) Are there procedures to record when the personal data were obtained?

(d) In what circumstances would personal data be purged?

(e) Are personal data archived or kept for historical or statistical purposes?

(f) Are these data reviewed periodically to determine if continued archiving is necessary?

(g) Are these data reviewed periodically to determine if appropriate hardware and software for their processing is available?

(h) Are there secure procedures for disposing of those personal data that are no longer required?

2.7 The Seventh Principle

'An individual shall be entitled -

(a) at reasonable intervals and without undue delay or expense -

(i) to be informed by any Data User whether he holds personal data of which that individual is the subject; and

(ii) to access to any such data held by a Data User; and

(b) where appropriate, to have such data corrected or erased.'

Interpretation:

'(1) Paragraph (a) of this principle shall not be construed as conferring any rights inconsistent with section 21 of this Act.

(2) In determining whether access to personal data is sought at reasonable intervals regard shall be had to the nature of the data, the purpose for which the data are held and the frequency with which the data are altered.

(3) The correction or erasure of personal data is appropriate only where necessary for ensuring compliance with the other data protection principles.'

2.7.1 This Principle establishes the right of Subject Access, a major provision of the Act which is covered in detail in Chapter 4(A). For completeness, and as provided for the other Principles, relevant Procedural Review questions are listed below.

2.7.2 **Some Procedural Review questions**:

(a) Are there any existing procedures whereby Data Subjects can have access to their data?

(b) What are the procedures for verifying the identity of Data Subjects?

(c) How easy is it to locate the personal data to which Subject Access is requested?

(d) Who is responsible for 'weeding' the personal data?

(e) Do the personal data include information which identifies another individual? If yes, what is the procedure for deciding whether the option of deleting this information is to be taken up, or whether that individual's consent for the disclosure is first to be requested?

(f) Is there any information that describes the intentions of the Data User towards the Data Subject? Is the option of withholding this information to be taken up?

(g) Are there any personal data that contain other information which might be exempt from Subject Access?

(h) Are there any particular difficulties in providing access to data held on micros or in archive?

(i) Are there any Codes or other terms that require explanation to make them intelligible to the Data Subject?

(j) Is there a procedure for monitoring compliance with Subject Access to ensure that the data are released within the prescribed 40 days?

(k) What procedures allow rectification or erasure of personal data, in compliance with requests from Data Subjects and/or Court Orders?

(l) Do the Subject Access procedures take account of possible Public Relations benefits?

2.8 The Eighth Principle

'Appropriate security measures shall be taken against unauthorised access to, or alteration, disclosure or destruction of, personal data and against accidental loss or destruction of personal data.'

Interpretation:

'Regard shall be had -

(a) to the nature of the personal data and the harm that would result from such access, alteration, disclosure, loss or destruction as are mentioned in this principle; and

(b) to the place where the personal data are stored, to security measures programmed into the relevant equipment and to measures taken for ensuring the reliability of staff having access to the data.'

Note: **All Principles** apply to personal data held by Data Users.

The **Eighth Principle** alone also applies to Computer Bureaux which provide services that relate to such data.

2.8.1 **Comment**:

(a) Section 23(1) of the Act establishes the rights which a Data Subject can seek to enforce against a Data User or Computer Bureau, following a breach of this Principle; Section 23(3) states that taking 'such care as in all the circumstances was reasonably required' can be cited as a defence in any such action. Section 23(2) of the Act removes these same rights in those cases where the disclosure or access has been described, by the Data User, in 'an entry in the register' (see paragraph 2.3.1(e) of this Chapter).

(b) Section 23(1)(b) of the Act shows that there will be no entitlement to compensation in those cases where personal data are destroyed **with** the authority of the Data User (or any relevant Computer Bureau). At first sight this appears to be yet another nail in the coffin of the Data Subject, since it implies that destruction of personal data which is authorised with the intention of causing harm would not be actionable. However, in cases where authorised destruction in some way conflicts with a duty of care, with good practice or legal requirements (eg where medical or other records of long-term value are destroyed), redress may well be available.

(c) The Principle is widely cast. Satisfying the requirement to examine the 'nature of the personal data' and the 'harm that would result' from a security breach, means that the Data User will generally need to assess the sensitivity of the personal data and the risk of their exposure. The fact that existing measures against unauthorised access, or alteration etc have to be taken into account requires the Data User to institute or examine procedures to prevent such access, alteration etc from occurring. The reference to 'accidental loss or destruction' raises the question of disaster recovery, whilst reference to the 'security measures programmed' implies the need to examine access control and password security. Finally, reference to 'the reliability of staff' not only has implications for staff vetting, but also asks the Data User whether staff have been sufficiently trained to operate equipment or to process personal data.

(d) Data protection aspects of security are dealt with in Chapter 8.

2.8.2 Some Procedural Review questions:

(a) **Physical security**

- Are the locations of all equipment, on which personal data are held or accessed, known to management?
- How is access to these locations safeguarded?

(b) **Software security**

- How is access to equipment, programs and personal data restricted to appropriate staff?
- How are the magnetic media used, stored and disposed of?
- How sensitive are the data?
- What are the networking implications?
- How is the security software supervised?
- How is password security maintained?
- How are the access controls supervised?
- How regularly are access and usage monitored?
- Are security copies of programs and data taken?
- Is there a recovery plan to cover situations when processing is impossible?

(c) **Printed matter** (input, output, documentation etc)

- Where are the documents stored?
- How is output distributed?
- How is output disposed of?
- Where is the documentation kept?
- How is access to documentation controlled?

(d) **Contingency planning**

- Are data sets adequately backed up in a secure location?
- What procedures (including manual office procedures) are there to ensure recovery from fire, flood and other disasters?
- What procedures (including manual office procedures) are there to cover lesser accidents such as loss of personal data, unavailability of equipment or network, corruption of personal data etc?

(e) **Staff awareness**

- What precautions are taken to prevent accidental disclosures?
- Are staff aware of security issues, and what training and guidelines have they received?
- Who is responsible for security of the personal data?
- Do all staff know who is responsible for security?
- How and when are security procedures reviewed?

(f) **Staff reliability**

- How is staff integrity evaluated prior to any activity that involves access to personal data?
- Are staff properly trained to process personal data?

(g) **Contracts**

- Do the conditions of service embody a statement that informs staff of their responsibilities towards personal data held by the Data User?
- Do contractors, external agents or consultants have in their contract with the Data User a written obligation towards the requirements of the Data Protection Act?

3. The role of Auditors in ensuring compliance with the Principles

3.1 Auditors have a general duty to ensure the probity of financial systems, and to measure the efficiency and effectiveness of all activities and of management. In relation to Data Protection, the Auditor will want to ensure that the Data User's procedures comply with the law, and that managers are able to maintain compliance in future.

3.2 In particular, the Auditor will be concerned with the Data User's Registration, to ensure that it accurately reflects the use of personal data and that all appropriate staff are aware of the Register Entries relevant to their work (Sections 5, 15 and 20 of the Act). In addition, the Auditor will want to be satisfied that the Data User can organise a defence with respect to compensation (Sections 22 and 23), and can deal with enquiries from the Data Protection Registrar in relation to the Principles. Where Computer Bureau services are provided, the Auditor may wish to check the requirements of the contract with the Bureau's clients. Finally, the Auditor will want to ensure that procedures relating to all Data Protection Principles, particularly with respect to data accuracy and security, are supported by the management process, and that staff have been instructed to alert management to any changes that are required.

3.3 In practice, therefore, the Auditor will monitor independently how the Data User copes with the obligations imposed by each Data Protection Principle. In many cases, the Auditor will want to investigate problem areas and examine relevant documentation.

3.4 It should be noted that an Auditor's status in exercising these functions can vary - for instance, the Auditor can be an employee of the Data User, or an independent consultant, or an official having a statutory duty to perform with respect to the Data User. Such status can itself have a bearing on how disclosures to the Auditor are treated in the Data User's Registration, notably since, in many cases, the disclosures could be covered by a non-disclosure exemption and therefore not required to be registered.

3.5 Appendix 3 is devoted to the role of the Auditor in checking compliance with the Data Protection Principles.

3.6 **Checklist of audit issues**

(a) Is there a Data Protection Policy?

(b) What is the reporting structure that supports and reviews the Policy and its effectiveness?

(c) Is that Policy sufficiently resourced?

(d) Are data protection procedures formally documented and reviewed by management (eg records of changes, or minutes of meetings, that could assist in a defence to an action under the Act)?

(e) What is management's awareness of the Act in general?

(f) How are Data Protection problems resolved and timetabled for action?

(g) How effective is the Data User's procedure for maintaining a comprehensive and up to date census of personal data?

(h) Do contractual relationships between Data User, Computer Bureau, contract staff etc specify Data Protection requirements?

(i) How does management recognise particularly 'sensitive' personal data that may require a special procedure?

(j) Are the Principles taken into account during system design, during the development of methodologies, and before the purchase of hardware or software?

(k) Are staff adequately trained in the necessary procedures?

(l) Has the Data User any special statutory powers (eg Environmental Health, Electoral Register, Community Charge) in relation to the obtaining and disclosing of personal data and, if so, is there satisfactory proof as to whether these powers are exercised properly?

(m) Does any international use of personal data need to be considered? Could more than one Data Protection legislation become involved?

4. The role of the Registrar in ensuring compliance with the Principles

4.1 Section 36(1) of the Act places a duty on the Registrar to promote observance of the Principles. Section 36(2) requires him to consider any complaint of substance which relates to contravention of any of the Principles or of any provision in the Act.

4.2 Sections 10, 11 and 12 of the Act provide the Registrar with powers to enforce compliance with any of the Principles through the issue of Supervisory Notices: respectively Enforcement Notices, De-registration Notices and Transfer Prohibition Notices. The Registrar can also institute Court proceedings for the fifteen new criminal offences established under the Act (note that civil remedies are available to Data Subjects in the pursuance of their new rights under the Act, eg the right of access to their personal data, the right of compensation for damage caused by inaccurate data etc).

4.3 A Data User or Computer Bureau served with a Supervisory Notice can appeal to the Data Protection Tribunal, and the time specified by the Registrar for compliance with the Notice must allow for this procedure to take effect. Should the Registrar decide that enforcement is a matter of urgency, the specified time can be shortened to a minimum of 7 days, and an appeal to the Tribunal, in this eventuality, can be decided by the Tribunal's Chairman or a Deputy Chairman. An appeal from a decision by the Tribunal can be made to the Courts, on a point of law.

4.4 In cases where the Registrar suspects that the Principles are being (or have been) contravened, the Registrar may also apply to a circuit judge for a warrant to enter and search premises, and he may also seize evidence with the backing of a warrant.

4.5 However, the Registrar has expressed the view (Fifth Report, Section B2.4) that his powers of inspection and seizure are, in practice, ineffective. He also argues that significant enhancements of his supervisory powers, in general, would be essential if his recommendations to reduce the scope of Registration, under the Act, are adopted (see also Chapter 9, Section 6).

5. Prospects for change

5.1 Whilst this Chapter is primarily concerned with procedures to ensure compliance with each Data Protection Principle, it would be wrong not to acknowledge the impact of some of the changes that are likely within the next decade (ie when Parliament has returned to the Act, and when the European Commission's Directive on Data Protection has been adopted: see Chapter 9 for comprehensive comment). However, although there could be major changes in emphasis, these will not change the substance of the Data Protection Principles as such; consequently the main thrust of the Procedural Review questions will remain. The most likely scenario is that Data Users might, additionally:

(a) have to apply the Review questions to those manual files that are structured in a way that facilitates the retrieval of personal information (**Note**: this is not as big a step as it seems, since the definition of data already extends to manual files through technology that can scan, store and index such files)

(b) in relation to the First Principle and personal data held in the **public sector**, have to take more care to ensure that uses and disclosures of personal data are strictly limited to those sanctioned by statute

(c) in relation to the First Principle and personal data held in the **private sector**, have to give more emphasis to obtaining (and retaining) the consent of the Data

Subject, having first provided fuller details as to the likely uses and disclosures of personal data

(d) have to accept that Data Subjects will have additional levers of control over how the personal data are collected, used and disclosed by the Data User.

5.2 The Directive aside, the most likely change in the UK will be to the Registration structure. The 'bureaucratic' forms may change (ie less detail may need to be registered and more personal data may not be subject to Registration); however, the effort to comply with the Second and Third Principles will remain. In addition, the fact that certain details may not have to be registered **does not mean** that information about such details will not need to be collected. For example, a Census **will still be needed** since specified information (known as a 'specification') that describes purposes, sources, disclosures, overseas transfers and the items of data held **will** have to be made available to the Data Subject, and such information could also be vital to demonstrate to a Court that certain personal data did **not** have to be registered. Staff who currently need to be aware of the Registration particulars will still need to know about the authorised methods of using, collecting and disclosing personal data. Thus, in practice, **some** of the Review questions in relation to the Second and Third Principles will change slightly in their emphasis (ie others stay the same) and become:

(a) If a purpose has to be registered, does it adequately describe why the personal data are held?

(b) Have the details been collected that demonstrate that a purpose need not be registered? Are they in the correct form as specified by the Registrar or by legislation? Has a Census been carried out to check whether this is the case? If so, how representative is the Census? Has the Census covered **all** personal data processed on behalf of the Data User (eg by a Computer Bureau)?

(c) Who is responsible for Registration and for collecting the information required for the specification?

(d) How are the various purposes and uses of personal data monitored, to ensure that they are lawful at all times?

(e) How is a new purpose notified to the person responsible for Registration or for the specification?

(f) How are the particulars contained in the Register Entries or the specification kept up to date?

(g) Do the Register Entries relate to the Data User's organisational structure?

(h) Do staff know which Register Entries relate to their work, what these Entries contain, and how these Entries (or the specification) affect their day-to-day activities?

(i) How and when should auditing checks in relation to the accuracy of the Entries or the specification be carried out by the Data User?

5.3 Other changes to anticipate are:

(a) that disclosure logs may be necessary in some cases, so that those who have received inaccurate personal data can be contacted

(b) that the security of personal data will become a more important issue both to Data Users and Data Subjects

(c) that the Registrar will have stronger powers of intervention (this means that the Data User's defences will need to be more formally established, and documentary evidence more robust)

(d) that there will be increased emphasis on the Council of Europe Recommendations and on the importance of Codes of Practice and Cross-sectoral Guidelines (see Chapter 5 for a discussion of those currently available).

Chapter Four(A): Subject Access

1. The legal basis

1.1 The Seventh Data Protection Principle provides the foundation for the whole framework of rights through which Data Subjects can access their personal data, at reasonable frequencies and without undue expense, and take action which may lead to correction or erasure of the data. The Subject Access provisions (exemptions apart) take **precedence** over 'any enactment or rule of law' which prohibits or restricts the disclosure of information (Section 26(4) of the Act).

1.2 The Principle (together with its Interpretation) generally reflects the text of Article 8 of the Council of Europe Convention and Paragraph 13 of the OECD Guidelines. The Act diverges from the OECD provisions in two instances:

(a) OECD Paragraph 13 makes no reference to the frequency with which data may be requested, but Section 21(8) of the Act identifies 'unreasonable ... frequency';

(b) OECD Subparagraph 13(c) notes the right for a Data Subject to be given the reasons for which a request is denied, and 'to be able to challenge such a denial'; there is no such provision in the Act.

1.3 The Principle is given effect through the provisions found in Section 21 of the Act, through the Registrar's powers (Section 36) to ensure compliance with all the Principles (via Enforcement and De-registration Notices if necessary - see Section 10 of the Act), and through Court action following an application by the Data Subject (see Sections 24 and 25).

1.4 Subject Access exemptions apart, a Data User has to comply with a valid request for Subject Access within forty days; to do otherwise is to break the law. It should not be overlooked, though, that Data Users are free to take the initiative (under Section 34(6)(a) of the Act) to disclose their own personal data to Data Subjects without reference to these provisions.

2. Experience of Subject Access

2.1 Few hard facts are available, but it is clear that the general public (as distinct from employees of some Data Users) has made little use of these new rights, and Data Users' worries about their ability to cope with the procedure have, in the vast majority of cases, proved unfounded.

2.2 Data Users have each received, on average, no more than one or two Subject Access requests. However, the Registrar has pointed out that, from his point of view, this represents a very significant total. Extrapolated from the figures (up to May 1988) given in his 5th Annual Report (dated June 1989), this total could now be well in excess of 300,000, with some 50,000 requests involving subsequent remedial action by the Data Users concerned.

2.3 Two notable exceptions are the Ministry of Defence, over 20,000 of whose employees have received information under the Subject Access provisions (even this represents no more than 0.15% per annum of the eligible total, which encompasses the Armed Forces), and the Driver Vehicle Licensing Authority in Swansea that has had over 17,000 Subject Access enquiries. Whilst employees are sure to feature prominently in the 300,000 total mentioned above, even this class of Data Subjects has, clearly, generally exhibited little interest (although in many cases this can be attributed to the fact that a proportion of Data Users routinely discloses the relevant information).

2.4 The Registrar has issued no De-registration Notices in relation to Subject Access. An Enforcement Notice, for failure to give information in response to an Access request, was served on the Halifax Building Society on 1.2.89. The Society has appealed to the Data Protection Tribunal which is due to consider the appeal towards the end of 1991.

3. Subject Access: general considerations

3.1 Subject Access may only be the beginning of a long process, particularly if it leads the Data Subject to assert that one or more of the Principles have been contravened. For example, following Access there may be a complaint to the Registrar that the personal data are inaccurate (Fifth Principle), coupled with a demand for correction of the data or even for their erasure; a claim that damage has been caused by such personal data could result in an action for compensation. The Data User could be accused of providing false particulars in the relevant Register Entry (Second and Third Principles), or of holding redundant information (Sixth Principle). Carelessly recorded, or out of context personal data may breach the Fourth Principle. In contentious cases, Data Subjects may apply to the Courts for redress.

3.2 Subject Access is easy to understand as a concept. In simple terms, Data Subjects are entitled, on making a Subject Access request and after payment of the appropriate fee, to a copy of all their own personal data within the single Register Entry to which a request has to relate, and to an explanation of any codes or data which are not intelligible. The Data User has to be satisfied that the Data Subject has been correctly identified, and may ask the Data Subject for additional information, if this is reasonably required to locate the personal data, before proceeding with the request. Note that there is no **obligation** for the Data Subject to enclose the fee with the request, as long as payment is made during the forty day period.

3.3 One major benefit, for Data Users and Data Subjects alike, derives from the fact that the right of Subject Access is a powerful tool for achieving, and then maintaining, data integrity. In some instances (eg where employees, customers or clients of the Data User are concerned), it will additionally foster good public relations to release, at regular intervals, their personal data to these Data Subjects, for checking and correction as may be necessary. As outlined in paragraph 3.1 above, the Data Subject's view of the accuracy of the data can have far-reaching consequences and the Data User should interpret these rights constructively.

3.4 In practice, a Data Subject faces many problems. For example:

(a) The Data User is entitled to charge a fee (currently set at a maximum of £10) for Access to each Register Entry. A Data Subject may, therefore (in the case of a Data User who charges for Access and whose activities are at all complex), need to pay a significant sum in order to ensure that all relevant data will be revealed (see also Chapter 3, paragraph 5.1).

(b) The Data User is entitled to help from a Data Subject to locate the personal data, and to identify the Data Subject as the true Data Subject (Section 21(4) of the Act). How specific will the Data Subject have to be, to ensure that Access cannot 'reasonably' be refused?

(c) The whole gamut of exemptions of personal data from Subject Access (national security, crime and taxation, judicial appointments, financial services, certain health and social work records, etc) may generate suspicions that personal data are being withheld unnecessarily.

(d) In the case where a Data User has decided that an exemption from Subject Access applies, the Data Subject **might** be informed that 'there are personal data, but they are exempt'. More likely, the comment would be on the lines that 'under the provisions of the Act, herewith a nil return' (or an equivalent ambiguous statement), or even 'there are no data', thus giving rise to further suspicions (see also Chapter 7, paragraph 3.2.24).

(e) The option (granted by Section 21(4)(b) of the Act) of withholding personal data that can identify a third party may lead to Subject Access refusal on the grounds, say, that the data could indicate their source. How is the Data Subject to know what data are actually held, let alone what reliance can be placed on their accuracy?

(f) The Data Subject may suspect that the data have been changed or deleted as a result of an Access request (an unlawful procedure), when in fact such amendments may have been the result of routine processing during the forty day period (permitted via Section 21(7) of the Act).

3.5 In addition, there are many obstacles which Data Subjects will have to overcome in relation to the accuracy of personal data. These obstacles can be summarised as follows:

(a) The data will only be deemed inaccurate if 'incorrect or misleading as to any matter of fact' (Section 22(4) of the Act); this can be difficult to prove.

(b) The data may be designated as 'an accurate record of what someone else said' (Government spokesman, Standing Committee, Sixth Sitting) and those data, of course, may be completely incorrect.

(c) If the data indicate third party origin and/or Data Subject objection then the Data Subject cannot claim compensation for any damage suffered by reason of the inaccuracy of the data (Section 22(2)).

(d) Any record of the Data User's intentions in respect of the Data Subject may be excluded (Section 1(3)). A Data User might deliberately frame an 'opinion' as an 'intention' (in some cases this is easily done) in order to evade Subject Access on the grounds that the information is not personal data.

(e) The Registrar's powers do not extend to data, shown to have been held by a Data User prior to 11 May 1986, however inaccurate they may be (Section 42(5)); a Data Subject may have to take Court action to achieve amendment of such data.

(f) Data Subjects have no right of appeal to the Data Protection Tribunal, should they be dissatisfied with the Registrar's action (or inaction).

(g) Should Data Subjects have to go to litigation to achieve their objective, they could find previously favourable rulings made by the Tribunal being overturned by the Courts (which are superior to the Tribunal).

(h) Since Codes of Practice have no legal standing under the Act, a Data Subject cannot rely on their provisions being enforceable against a Data User.

3.6 In summary, to ensure compliance with the Seventh Data Protection Principle, Data Users should appreciate how a Data Subject could view the process. The Registrar's Guidelines, notably Guideline 5 and Part C of Guideline 6, provide a useful introduction to these problems and to other Subject Access issues, and point the way to at least some solutions. The remainder of this Chapter develops that guidance in relation to those practical and organisational problems which Data Users may find perplexing - assuming they have become aware of them despite the low number of Access requests!

4. Subject Access: detailed procedures

4.1 Receiving a Subject Access request

4.1.1 In each Register Entry, a Data User has to specify 'one or more addresses for the receipt of requests from data subjects for access to the data' (Section 4(3)(f) of the Act, and Section A8 of Part A of the 'Application for Registration'). A Data User may thus be faced with a multiplicity of options, eg:

(a) specifying a single address (perhaps that of the Data Protection Officer) for all Register Entries;

(b) specifying more than one address (but the same set of addresses throughout) for each Register Entry;

(c) specifying a different address (or addresses) for each Register Entry, or for some of the Register Entries.

4.1.2 Most Data Users select option (a). This simple solution may be by choice - eg because a single address is deemed a necessary adjunct to a centralised approach (which, in turn, facilitates consistency of Subject Access procedures throughout the organisation). Alternatively, the Data User may, of course, have only one address (and no sub-divisions to which requests might, otherwise, be routed directly). Many large Data Users, though, delegate to each branch, department, etc the duty to satisfy relevant Access requests.

4.1.3 An organisation which has offices located over a wide geographical area may also retain a centralised approach, even if it takes the view that a single reception point for Access requests would cause unwarranted difficulties to Data Subjects. In this case, the various addresses quoted in the Entries will act merely as post-boxes for forwarding Subject Access mail to the central point.

4.1.4 These offices can also play a significant Subject Access (and Public Relations) role even **before** a request is received. Posters to publicise Data Subjects' rights could be prominently displayed; handouts (or computer terminals) could provide a programmed guide to the Access procedure and to the Data User's Register Entries; designated public liaison officers and multi-lingual staff could be available to assist in cases of difficulty. Distributing information about the Data User's activities can increase the confidence of Data Subjects in the way the Data User deals with sensitive information, and in some cases would remove the grounds for the Subject

Access request. Allaying the suspicions of ratepayers, customers, etc can promote interest in the services provided and, in general, reap financial and Public Relations benefits.

4.1.5 The minimum Subject Access function of such an office is acceptance of 'a request in writing' and dealing with 'payment of such fee (not exceeding the prescribed maximum)' as the Data User may require (Section 21(2) of the Act). This will be coupled with keeping formal records of requests received and, if appropriate, of replies sent out. Beyond this minimum, a Data User's approach will be determined largely by the facilities that can reasonably be provided, and by the view the Data User takes of responsibilities towards Data Subjects.

4.1.6 It should not be overlooked that satisfying Subject Access could, on occasion, prove to be very expensive (see 4.4.11 below); some Data Users may, therefore, limit their publicity to the absolute minimum, and hope to receive a minimum number of requests.

4.1.7 A word of warning! Although the Register Entry does contain one or more addresses for Subject Access, a Data Subject need not use any of them - Section 21(2) of the Act defines the Data Subject's obligation as, merely, a 'request in writing' to the Data User. Consequently, staff should at least be aware that any 'stray' Subject Access requests should be forwarded for action. From the Data Subject's point of view, use of an unregistered address could make it more likely that the request would be overlooked, and more difficult to prove that the request was issued (unless recorded delivery was used, or a receipt obtained for delivery by hand). Equally, without some proof that the request has been received by the Data User, the Courts and the Registrar may find it difficult to use their powers of enforcement on the Data Subject's behalf.

4.1.8 The Data Subject may, initially, write to the Data User in a general way (eg 'I have heard about the Data Protection Act and would like to know what information you have about me'). If there is no clear reference to the Act, the nature of the request or how best to provide the information will first have to be determined (see paragraph 4.2.3 below). However, once a Subject Access request has been properly identified, a precise and well documented path has to be followed.

4.1.9 The first response of the Data User to a Subject Access request which provides insufficient information should be to send the Data Subject guidance (see below) on how to clarify what the Data Subject wants, what further information, if any, is needed to locate the personal data, and what identification criteria have to be satisfied before the personal data can be released. These requirements may differ for different activities of the Data User, and some Data Users have found it convenient to prepare an application form on which such information can be entered. If the Data Subject, or representative, arrives in person, one or more of these forms, as appropriate, can be handed over (note that any person who applies for Subject Access on behalf of another individual must have written authorisation for this process; see also Chapter 7, paragraph 4.6.2(a) in relation to a Data Subject who cannot apply by reason of mental disorder).

4.1.10 If the Data User has more than one Register Entry, the application form or covering letter should request the Data Subject to identify the Entry or Entries to which Subject Access is required. Only when Access requirements have been precisely defined, can the formal Access procedure begin. Consequently, a Data User will find it useful to compile a Register Entries list (including Registration Numbers) which can be sent to Data Subjects. The information provided should include a brief description of the purposes, or activities, that are covered by each Entry, and the information that the Data User needs to locate the data and identify the Data Subject.

4.1.11 As mentioned in Chapter 3, paragraph 5.1(d), if a Data User has a 'no charge' policy it is irrelevant whether there are one or more Register Entries; a list of Data User activities, involving personal data, is all that is needed to provide Data Subjects with the required options.

4.1.12 Data Subjects should be notified as soon as possible (and certainly within 40 days; see Guideline 5, paragraph 2.22) if the information they have provided is incomplete or requires further validation. Note that it is not until any necessary additional information has been received by the Data User (see also Sections 4.3, 4.4 and 4.5 below) that the formal 40 day period, which the Act grants for fulfilment of the Access request, actually begins!

4.1.13 Since the time factor is of crucial importance throughout the Subject Access procedure, all correspondence and communications with Data Subjects should be filed and dated as appropriate.

4.1.14 The following forms to assist Subject Access are derived from those produced by LAMSAC (Data Subject Access Vol. 2 - Application Forms). Forms of this type can be used **once it is clear to which Register Entry or Entries the Data Subject seeks Access**. They comprise a standard letter (which includes a paragraph for use only if **more** information can justifiably be requested to identify the Data Subject and/or to assist with locating the personal data) and a Subject Access Application for **each** Register Entry to which Access is requested. If there is a 'no charge' policy, the references to 'Registration Number' can be replaced by 'Purpose' or Activity'. The letters and forms assume that the further information outlined in paragraph 4.1.10 will be sent with the following letter and Subject Access form.

4.1.15 Letter to the Applicant in response to a Subject Access enquiry

(**Note**: dotted lines to be completed by the Data User for each Register Entry; sentences marked with a * may have to be deleted depending on the circumstances of a the Access request in question. For example, if the Data User does not charge a fee the fifth paragraph is not needed; if the Data Subject has already provided the information the Data User needs (see paragraph 4.1.10 above), the letter serves as an acknowledgement that the Access request has been received).

Registration Number .... **Date**..........................

Dear

Thank you for your communication dated .... in which you exercise your right of Subject Access under the Data Protection Act. *We enclose a Subject Access form for you to complete.

*Before we can satisfy our obligations under this Act it is necessary for us to obtain from you further information identifying you as the subject of the personal data, and to help us in locating the data. For this purpose, could you please provide .... to identify yourself as the Data Subject, and .... to help us locate the data you seek.

*If you are acting on the Data Subject's behalf please enclose your authority for doing so.

As required by the Act, we shall provide you with a copy of your personal data within forty days; please contact us if your personal data do not arrive in good time. *We can only begin to service your request following our receipt of the additional information identified above.

*The appropriate fee is £........... (state amount up to the £10 maximum per Entry); please note that your Application will lapse if the fee is not received within the forty day period.

If you have any queries, please do not hesitate to contact us, when we shall do our best to assist you.

Yours sincerely,

4.1.16 DATA PROTECTION ACT 1984: SUBJECT ACCESS APPLICATION

To enable this Data User to deal promptly with this request for Subject Access and to satisfy the legal requirements to ensure the identity of Data Subjects and locate the personal data, please complete the following in BLOCK CAPITALS:

1. **Registration Number** ....

   Data Subject's full name ....
   (include below **any former names**, if appropriate)

   Address of Data Subject ....

   ....

   ....

   ....

   Post Code .... **Tel.No**......................

2. Agents of the Data Subject: Please complete this section if you are seeking access to personal data that relate to another Data Subject. Please note that you **must** provide proof of your entitlement to act on the Data Subject's behalf.

   Agent's full name ....

   Address of Agent ....

   ....

   ....

   ....

   ....

   Post Code .... **Tel.No**......................

3. **Data Subject Access requirements** *(please delete as appropriate)

In response to your letter dated, I enclose/am sending* a fee of £ for the Subject Access request.

I enclose the information requested in your letter*

(a) to help locate the personal data I seek*

(b) to confirm my identity as the Data Subject/confirm my entitlement to act on the Data Subject's behalf*

Signed .... Date ....

Note: we shall send the personal data to the Data Subject's address unless the contrary is indicated.

4. **FOR OFFICIAL USE ONLY**

Enquiry No. ....

Date request received ....

Date identity confirmed.............................. by ....

Date locating information received ....

Date authorisation of Agent confirmed .... by....................

Date of 40 day period start......................... end...........................

Data extracted .... from .... system, by ....

Data extracted .... from .... system, by ....

Data extracted .... from .... system, by...............

Fee paid by Cheque No. .... by cash .... on date........

Date if fee returned ....

Date of completion of Subject Access request ....

Name of Officer responsible for completion......................................

Signature of Officer ....

4.1.17 A copy of **all** the relevant personal data should be filed with this form. If any personal data have been exempted by the Data User, then the grounds for the exemption should be clearly stated, and a copy of the personal data sent to the Data Subject should additionally be filed.

4.1.18 Finally, note that a policy has to be developed to establish the criteria for refusing Subject Access, whether on the grounds of 'unreasonable' frequency or for any other reason (see Section 21(8) of the Act). As far as frequency is concerned, the context of the particular data in question will be decisive here, notably how often the data change, and how significant these changes are.

4.2 Identification of the type of enquiry

4.2.1 Most organisations have well-established procedures for satisfying routine requests for information. Appropriate modification of such procedures allows decisions to be reached as to whether an enquiry has to be dealt with formally, under the provisions of the Data Protection Act (or under any other legislation that provides for disclosure of information), or whether the particular data involved can be made available through some alternative means.

4.2.2 For example, almost everybody makes enquiries to a shop, bank, building society or Council office, where the nature of the enquiry is 'Have you a record of my purchase?' or 'How much is in my account?' or 'Have you received a cheque?'. Obviously, such requests will continue to be dealt with immediately, and not via the formal Subject Access procedures which can cost the Data Subject £10 and take up to 40 days to produce the answer! In other cases that already involve a fee, Data Subjects might want the cheapest option, which may or may not be Subject Access; for example, where a charge is made for producing documentary evidence, should the Data Subject lose the original copies. Birth, death and marriage certificates, planning applications, improvement grants, examination marks and similar documents (should they be defined as personal data) may fall into this category. Where such documents currently cost **more** than £10 to obtain, Data Subjects may request evidence contained in the document via Subject Access, and Data Users need to determine if this poses particular problems.

4.2.3 Staff dealing with enquiries for personal data therefore have to be trained to recognise requests for information which should not follow the Subject Access procedure. The following sequence of instructions is suggested:

(1) Does the applicant have a right to the information requested, **without** recourse to the Data Protection Act? If so:

either (a) advise the applicant of the correct procedure to be followed;

or (b) advise the applicant that you are dealing with the enquiry (but without recourse to the provisions of the Act) by following the procedure laid down for these enquiries.

In **both cases**, any Subject Access fee sent by the applicant by mistake should be returned with the comment:

either (a) that no fee is involved;

or (b) that the required fee (eg for replacement documents) will be advised in due course;

or (c) that an invoice for the correct fee is enclosed.

(2) If Subject Access is the agreed procedure, but the applicant has not identified the appropriate Register Entry, purpose or activity, provide the applicant with the necessary information (see paragraphs 4.1.10 and 4.1.11 above).

(3) When a Subject Access Application form has been received, and if the Subject Access provisions apply:

(a) check that the correct fee was enclosed, or note that a fee remains to be paid before the personal data are released to the Data Subject (the Act does not stipulate that the fee has to accompany the Application form);

(b) confirm the identity of the Data Subject using the criteria established for this purpose as appropriate to the data being requested;

(c) if appropriate, confirm the applicant's authority to act as Agent on behalf of the Data Subject;

(d) check that any additional information that has reasonably been requested to locate the data has been provided;

(e) complete relevant parts of Section 4 of the Subject Access Application form.

(4) If there is any problem with the Subject Access Application form (eg if insufficient additional information has been provided), write immediately to the Data Subject or Agent to seek clarification.

4.2.4 The requirements of (3) above are discussed further below.

4.3 Identification of the Data Subject

4.3.1 Identification requirements can vary widely, depending not only on the sensitivity of the data but also on whether the Data Subject wishes to collect the data in person, or whether identification is by means of information received via a Subject Access Application form. Whilst account needs to be taken of the damage the personal data can do if released to the wrong person, the identification procedure should not, in general, be onerous, or oppressive, or differ significantly from normal practice (if precedent exists) for the same or similar type of information.

4.3.2 In many cases it will be possible, through examination of the activity described in the Register Entry, to strengthen the identification criteria by asking Data Subjects for information which only they are likely to know. For instance where there is, or was, a relationship between the Data User and the Data Subject, this itself can provide evidence of identity (eg if the Data Subject is an employee or ratepayer, customer or client etc there may be some key number, account reference or other relevant information to prove this). Where the data are collected in person, photographs and signatures can be compared (eg passport, driving licence, credit card etc); in some circumstances, a birth certificate or other official document will be needed. For much information, a signed declaration by the applicant will suffice, coupled with confirmation of the address to which the personal data are to be sent. Similar considerations will apply when Data Subjects authorise other persons to act on their behalf.

4.3.3 It should also be noted that, in cases where minors are involved, there is an underlying principle of law (in England, Wales and Northern Ireland) which defines the right of a minor to be an applicant for Subject Access (in Scotland, girls over the age of 12 and boys over the age of 14 are entitled to Subject Access rights). As the Law Commission emphasised in its report on 'Family Law, Review of Child Law, Guardianship and Custody (No 172, 25th July 1988, paragraph 2.6), the concept of 'parental responsibility', as demonstrated by the Gillick case, 'must also vary with the age and maturity of the child and the circumstances of each individual case'. In other words, parental right yields to the child's right to make its own decisions when the child reaches a sufficient understanding and intelligence to be capable of making up its own mind on the matter requiring decision.

4.3.4 It is the Data User who has to judge the child's understanding and intelligence, and it is obvious that care has to be exercised when Access is sought, by a minor, to sensitive personal data. Data Users should take care that any test they propose is modest and does not discriminate unfairly. For example, the filling in of an application form may not be a simple matter for a minor who is dislexic or has English as a second language. Note that Data Users should not provide a child's personal data to a parent if they suspect the parent's motives; Subject Access on behalf of a child should be in the child's interests (see the Children's Act 1989, which begins by stressing that 'the child's welfare shall be the court's paramount consideration').

4.3.5 Remember that partnerships can cause Subject Access problems - particularly failed or failing partnerships! For example, one spouse in a failed marriage may be trying to locate the other (possibly with the intention of causing bodily harm), or to obtain financial information to which he/she is no longer entitled. To ensure that such difficult cases are dealt with properly, the officer dealing with the request must fully appreciate the importance of correct identification of the Data Subject, and have received training to cope with this problem.

4.3.6 Care will have to be exercised if two people (usually father-son or mother-daughter) with the same or similar name are known to be living at the same address.

4.4 Fee charged by the Data User

4.4.1 In his Third Report (June 1987), the Data Protection Registrar commented that 'research shows that a majority of individuals agree that a small charge would be reasonable. However the charge which these individuals might find acceptable appears to lie in the range of £3-£5' (for a single Subject Access request). Nevertheless, Government determined a maximum of £10 per Register Entry. Experience to date (Fifth Report, June 1989, Section A7(h)) indicates that under half of Data Users charge a fee. Whilst some of these charge less than £10, the Registrar's research identified as a problem area 'the deterrent effect of the fee, especially in relation to multiple entries'.

4.4.2 It is likely that many organisations charge a fee principally to discourage irresponsible applications, though clearly this policy may, in practice, discourage applications as a whole. Some organisations set a fee, but take account of the applicant's financial circumstances. One option is to waive the fee for personal data that are easy to obtain, and to charge for those that involve more effort. Further options include waiving the fee for one application (or some greater number of applications) from one Data Subject in any one year.

4.4.3 A policy to charge a Subject Access fee brings with it all the problems of handling small sums of money, and it is often more expensive (in staff overheads) to charge a fee than to waive it. For example, an invoice may have to be sent, a record of the payment has to be made, and provision has to be made for dealing with postal orders, 'bounced' cheques, etc. Even those Data Users who have decided not to charge have to decide whether to accept, and then reimburse, those payments that may nevertheless be received - an expensive task involving significant overheads. There also has to be provision for the occasional cash transaction.

4.4.4 Data Users who follow 'Freedom of Information' or 'open files' policies should consider their position very carefully. Subject Access, as defined by Section 21 of the Act, is a legal procedure which includes the right of access to material that could be very difficult to recover (eg previous years transactions); which has to be carefully documented in view of its legal implications; which has to be provided on a tight timetable (forty days); and which could be requested in furtherance of a dispute with the Data User!

4.4.5 How then can a Data User implement such policies, knowing that a zero charge could result in a high proportion of requests for Access each of which encompasses **all** Register Entries? This can be an alarming prospect for large organisations (even though some activities or purposes can often be eliminated from consideration once the relationship of the Data Subject to the Data User has been established). Options to mitigate the difficulties inherent in this situation are, therefore, examined below.

4.4.6 Section 34(6) of the Act says that 'personal data are exempt from the non-disclosure provisions' (ie from Registration) if 'the disclosure is to the data subject or a person acting on his behalf'. Thus, any Data Subject's personal data can be given to that Data Subject so long as the Data User identifies the Data Subject properly. Such disclosures are **not defined as Subject Access** and are common occurrences (see paragraph 4.2.2 above).

4.4.7 A Data User who has an 'open files' policy can, therefore, release personal data free of charge to any Data Subject via Section 34(6) (and can base this practice on reasonable conditions to reduce the cost of the procedure; see below). Any Data Subject who wishes to follow the formal Subject Access procedure could then be asked to pay a fee. Note that although an 'open files' policy will already be subject to proper identification procedures, these may well need to be strengthened, and additional information may be needed to help locate the data, as under Subject Access proper.

4.4.8 The options can, thus, be summarised as follows:

either (a) via Section 34(6) of the Act, Data Subjects can be granted free access to personal data (and also to their information held on manual files) so long as they are prepared to allow the Data User to satisfy their request within available resources, and to trust the Data User not to take an unreasonable length of time to satisfy such requests;

or (b) via Section 21, Data Subjects, if they are in a hurry, or do not trust the Data User's undertaking in (a) above, or want a copy of their personal data as defined by the provisions of the Act, can follow the formal Subject Access procedure for a fee of up to £10 per Register Entry.

4.4.9 If a zero fee, 'open files' policy is followed it will be important for the Data User to advertise this fact, and to stress:

(a) that the request will be subject to the Data User's current resources and ability to provide the information, and therefore dependent on the demands made on those resources, and that, despite these problems, the request will be satisfied as quickly and efficiently as possible;

(b) that by this route the Data Subject will receive more information than via Subject Access, as the 'open files' policy relates to manual files as well;

(c) that if Data Subjects wish to request formal Subject Access, they are free to do so, but that this procedure will involve a fee of up to £10 per Register Entry;

(d) that under both procedures routine updating, as allowed by Section 21(7) of the Act, may take place, up to the time of release of the information. 'Open files' data may, therefore, differ from 'Subject Access' data, depending on when any updating took place.

4.4.10 Finally, a warning: Data Users who decide to set a fee for Subject Access, whether at the £10 maximum or less, should not overlook the fact that Data Subjects will then be seeking 'value for money'; not only will Data Subjects insist that all the personal data to which they are entitled are released, but it may be more difficult to convince Data Subjects that this has, indeed, been done - archives and all.

4.4.11 Unless Data Users are prepared to be reasonably helpful in satisfying a Data Subject's suspicions, they could quickly become embroiled in acrimonious correspondence, certainly with the Data Subject and, possibly, with the Registrar (particularly if complaints mount up). They would then be obliged, in their own interests, to check and re-check internal disclosures (in case new computer files containing personal data have been established and overlooked in the Subject Access search), uncategorised information (concerning employees, say, who firmly believe something vital is being kept hidden from them), justification for exemptions, how the data were weeded and so on. All in all, an expensive process, and certainly not within a £10 budget!

4.5 Information reasonably required to locate the data

4.5.1 This information is quite distinct from the information required to identify the Data Subject. For example, provision of a surname and its initials may suffice to locate all the personal data relating to that particular name, but on its own is generally not adequate for identification purposes. Note that a Data User is not entitled to request information to locate the data unless it can be claimed that the initial information already provided by the Data Subject is insufficient, that the additional information will significantly help the Data User to locate the data, and that the Data Subject can reasonably be expected to be in possession of that additional information.

4.5.2 Even then, there may well be some personal data whose location **was** adequately identified by that initial information, and if the same information also satisfied the criteria for identifying the Data Subject then **these data will have to be released within forty days** (with the rest to follow within forty days of receipt of the additional information required to locate the further personal data).

4.5.3 Here, clearly, are the seeds for much dispute, and conflict, between opposing viewpoints of Data Users and Data Subjects which, in some instances, may have to be resolved by the Courts. Can Data Subjects claim that their name and a Registration number is adequate information in some, or even all, cases to locate the personal data? Can (or should) the Data Subject's response be employed by the Data User to limit the searches within a Register Entry to those areas, interests, systems or activities which the Data Subject has indicated? If so, could the Data Subject claim to have been misled by a form which invites indications of such areas, interests, etc? In turn, could the Data Subject's response (or Data User's interpretation of that response) effectively mislead the Data User into overlooking files containing personal data and, thereby, into contravening the Seventh Principle?

4.5.4 For example, a Data User may ask simple questions like: 'Where and when did you work with this organisation?' or 'Which school or schools did you attend?', with the intention of limiting searches to files covering particular branches, or periods, or schools. In such a case the Data User would need to be confident that no relevant data existed outside these limits, ie that no personal data had been extracted, or copied to another file within the Data User organisation, and then processed further within the scope of the Register Entry. As far as schools or other educational establishments are concerned, these could well be linked by a computer network, either now or in the future, and this could facilitate the transfer of personal data. Thus in the situation of a Data User who routinely copied data, processed only at one location, to computer files at other locations, a Subject Access request would necessitate a search of the files at **every** location covered by the Register Entry. This would be the only way of making **certain** that no new personal data had, in fact, been generated which have to be released, in their own right, under the Subject Access provisions.

4.6 Identifying and obtaining personal data held by the Data User

4.6.1 To assist with the retrieval of all relevant personal data, it is essential to maintain a Registration Map (see Chapter 2, Section 3.5) or equivalent record, and to ensure that this record is kept updated at all times. The person responsible for dealing with the Subject Access request (usually the Data Protection Officer for the Data User, or a departmental officer) consults the Map, informs all sections, departments etc covered by a Register Entry that personal data relating to a named individual are required, and then monitors response (note that the Map should list all the computers which may store personal data).

4.6.2 In some cases, particularly in larger Data User organisations, discussions with the Computer Centre may be required. This is because many schemes, applications, programs etc on mainframes have not been designed with Subject Access in mind, and special programs may need to be written to retrieve the relevant personal data. However, all new programs that process personal data should be designed to cope with the implications of Subject Access.

4.6.3 The Computer Centre should be asked the following questions in respect of each computer scheme, application etc, to assist with the design of any new software:

(a) Does the scheme incorporate software which facilitates Data Subject Access to personal data? Does this facility include retrieval of any personal data that are archived?

(b) What information could be requested to verify the identity of Data Subjects? Is there any information likely to be known only to a Data Subject?

(c) What information is reasonably required to assist in locating the personal data (or a subset of the data) to which Subject Access is required?

(d) Does any special program need to be written to retrieve personal data belonging to a Data Subject?

(e) How easy would it be to allow Subject Access to archived data (or to other data such as history files associated with the scheme) and would special routines need to be written to retrieve such data?

(f) How will codes or technical terms in the copy of the personal data be explained to a Data Subject?

(g) How easy would it be to allow rectification or erasure of personal data?

(h) Can a random sample of an individual's personal data be provided to test Subject Access procedures?

4.6.4 More detailed questions may follow, once answers have been received:

(a) Does the Data Subject's record contain any personal data that identify another living individual? (these need not be revealed to the Data Subject).

(b) Are there any personal data in the record that describe the intentions of the Data User towards the Data Subject? (these need not be revealed to the Data Subject).

(c) Are there any personal data in the record that contain other information which might be exempt from Subject Access? Data that relate to the following circumstances may be exempt: prevention of crime; taxation purposes; judicial appointments; legal professional privilege; statistics or research; back-up; credit reference; data incriminating the Data User; health or social work; disclosures prohibited by law; financial regulatory activities (see Chapter 7 for detailed comment).

4.6.5 The fact that archived personal data may have to be retrieved should never be overlooked, and it may be appropriate for the officer dealing with the Access request to check that this has been done. A further check, since a Data User is allowed to do routine processing or updates whilst servicing a request, would be for the officer to ensure that the personal data have not been amended **because** a Data Subject has asked for them - this is prohibited by Section 21(7) of the Act.

4.6.6 When the officer asks for personal data from departments, it is best to do so in writing, requesting a reply in, say, two or three weeks at most. If after this time nothing has materialised, appropriate action at management level may become necessary to meet the forty day deadline.

4.7 Preparing the personal data for dispatch

4.7.1 The following Data Subjects' rights established by the Subject Access provisions of the Act are considered below:

(a) the right to be informed whether personal data are held;

(b) the right to receive a copy of one's own personal data;

(c) the right to have that copy explained in terms that are intelligible.

4.7.2 These rights create a number of issues for the Data User. In the first instance, although perhaps an academic point, it should not be overlooked that if a Data Subject just asks the question in writing whether relevant personal data are held, the Data User must treat this request as a request for a **copy** of the personal data (see Section 21(2) of the Act) unless the Data Subject clearly indicates otherwise.

4.7.3 More significant, in practice, is the Registrar's view that 'A data user must always reply to a subject access request', even if there are no personal data or if they are wholly covered by one of the Subject Access exemptions (Guideline 5, paragraph 2.8). However, it should be noted that in Guidance Note 13 (ref GN13-FGBA-10/87) the Registrar refers to the fact that 'The contrary view has been expressed by others' and that it might need the Tribunal or the Courts to resolve the disagreement. Furthermore, it is always possible that the Data Subject receives no reply because the request has been addressed to someone who holds no data of any kind, ie who is not a Data User as defined by the Act and who, therefore, is under no legal obligation to reply to such an enquiry.

4.7.4 By definition, personal data include 'any expression of opinion about the individual', but exclude 'any indication of the intentions of the Data User in respect of that individual' (see Section 1(3) of the Act). Data recorded in the form of 'intentions' (eg 'I am not going to give Joe Bloggs credit') are, therefore, not personal data as far as the Act is concerned and Data Subjects' rights cannot apply. Although at first glance this seems a major loophole, in practice any Data User who deliberately and consistently structures information to exploit this definition, and thereby to avoid Subject Access, can expect to be brought before the Courts (note that the equivalent opinion 'I believe Joe Bloggs is not creditworthy' **is** personal data).

4.7.5 A Data User must consider how to determine whether a Subject Access exemption applies, and should be prepared to justify to the Courts or Registrar why an exemption pertains to the personal data (see the discussion of all the Subject Access exemptions in Chapter 7).

4.7.6 If some or all of the personal data are subject to an exemption, and the Data User decides that the exemption needs to be exercised, there is the problem of what to tell the Data Subject. In rare cases, merely revealing the fact that personal data have been exempted could, in itself, indicate their nature, and thus negate the intended effect of the exemption (eg by alerting a criminal to the fact that an investigation is proceeding; by causing serious harm to an ill person). Exemptions from the Subject Access provisions therefore also exempt the right to know **whether** personal data are held (see Section 26(2)(a) of the Act) and permit the Data User to employ a neutral statement with which to preface the personal data (or lack of data), eg 'Herewith a copy of the personal data to which you are entitled'. Care has to be taken not to use such a statement solely in the case of exempted data, since it could then again be inferred that the personal data are held (for a more detailed discussion of this issue see Chapter 7, paragraphs 3.2.18 to 3.2.27).

4.7.7 Any personal data that relate to another individual, or identify another individual as the source of the personal data, can be withheld from Subject Access unless that other individual has consented to have these personal data disclosed. Note that the Act in Section 21(4)(b) says 'individual' rather than 'person'; consequently, any record of the type 'the DSS says that Joe Bloggs is ...' will have to be released with 'the DSS' named as the source. However, if the record says 'Fred Smith says Joe Bloggs is ... ', then, 'Fred Smith' being an individual, his name need not be divulged. In this latter case, Joe Bloggs could obtain 'X says Joe Bloggs is ...' via Subject Access and 'X' would be explained as the source of the data.

4.7.8 Note that the Data User is not **compelled**, by the Act, to withhold third party personal data; the decision is one for the Data User to take in the light of the particular circumstances involved. Nor is the Data User under any compulsion to seek the authority of those other individuals to allow their personal data to be released. Where partnerships (see paragraph 4.3.5 above) are involved, care should be taken if only one partner requests formal Subject Access. It may then be best to contact the other partner or, in the covering letter that goes out with the Subject Access Application form, to ask for explicit permission from the other partner.

4.7.9 Although most Data Users will not identify the source of the information, there is one significant grey area. What if the Data Subject can use the personal data to **infer** the source, ie the identity of another individual? For example, it may be that certain personal data, relating to a person's previous employment, could only come from the previous employer who may, thus, be identifiable from the context. Is it legitimate to refuse Access to these personal data?

4.7.10 The answer, according to the Registrar, could well be 'no'. The Data User must give the maximum amount of information possible, and

> 'Information should not be withheld under this provision merely because the data user suspects that the data subject may be able to guess the other individual's identity. The provision applies only where anyone lacking the data subject's special knowledge could reasonably be expected to identify the other individual from the information' (Guideline 5, paragraph 2.25).

4.7.11 In plain English this means that, for Access to be refused, **anybody** should be able to look at the information to be sent to the Data Subject and say 'X is the source'. Often, however, it is **only** the Data Subject's special knowledge that allows the source to be deduced.

4.7.12 For example, suppose the personal data were 'Fred Smith of Acme Ltd says Joe Bloggs is a ...', and further suppose that Joe Bloggs has only met Fred Smith of Acme Ltd. Depending on the circumstances, it is likely that Joe Bloggs could identify Fred Smith as the source if he receives, via Subject Access 'X of Acme Ltd says Joe Bloggs is a ...'. However, from the viewpoint of the 'person in the street' the data would not reveal Fred Smith's identity, since that person would not know that Joe Bloggs had only met certain Acme Ltd staff. Nevertheless, if the Data User has reasonable grounds for believing, in this example or in others, that the source of the personal data may come to serious harm as the result of Subject Access, then the Data User should withhold the identifying data and, if the Data Subject complains to the Registrar or to the Courts, be prepared to justify the action taken. Section 21(8) of the Act allows the Court **not** to make an order compelling the Data User to provide Subject Access 'if it considers that it would in all the circumstances be unreasonable to do so, whether because of the frequency with which the applicant has made requests to the data user under those provisions or **for any other reason**' (our emphasis). Note: Chapter 7, paragraphs 4.3.5 to 4.3.7 and 4.4.10 outline when such action, in relation to Social Work and Health personal data, could be legitimate).

4.7.13 Wherever possible, it is clearly advisable to record in the personal data the individual sources of those personal data. Not only will this assist any weeding process with respect to information identifying other individuals, but this procedure will also go some way towards satisfying the accuracy provisions in Section 22 of the Act ('Compensation for inaccuracy').

4.7.14 In conclusion, the Data User's procedures must cover all the eventualities under which Data Subjects receive only an edited version of their personal data, whether because a particular Subject Access exemption has been applied, or because data which identify other individuals have been removed.

4.7.15 After assembling all the personal data that the Data Subject will actually receive, the only remaining problem is to explain all 'terms which are not intelligible' (Section 21(1) of the Act). This includes identification of computer codes, and explanations of abbreviated items, technical terms and the like, to the extent that these become 'intelligible to people unconnected with the data user' (Registrar's Guideline 5, paragraph 2.10). Note that this admits of the possibility that Data Subjects may have to turn to experts in the particular field, for a full assessment of the meaning or accuracy of the data. To avoid confusion, the personal data may need to be related to a particular activity, eg 'these are the personal data held for purpose X'.

4.7.16 The copy of the personal data provided under the Subject Access provisions need not be a photocopy of the record, or a computer printout. In many cases, it will be best to incorporate the personal data into a prepared document which can explain the data items fully, within their context and use, to the Data Subject. Where a Subject Access exemption applies, or personal data relating to another individual have been removed, it is important to copy the Data Subject's personal data onto a separate piece of paper. If the information is merely 'blotted out', the number of blank spaces in the copy sent to the Data Subject may allow some or all of the missing information to be deduced.

4.7.17 When the copy of the personal data is sent to the Data Subject, it is useful to include a covering letter stating that the request has now been satisfied, and inviting the Data Subject to make any observations as to the personal data. Having signed and completed the 'Date of completion of Subject Access request' part of the Application form (see Section 4.1.16), the officer coordinating the Access request should file, with the Application form, a copy of the personal data sent to the Data Subject, in case there are subsequent developments. After that, all the Data User can do is to wait and see whether the personal data generate yet **further** problems.

5. Challenges from the Data Subject

5.1 If Data Subjects **are not satisfied** with the information provided in response to the Subject Access request, they may

(a) complain to the Data User;

(b) complain to the Data Protection Registrar;

(c) complain to the Courts.

5.2 The form these complaints take will vary. Complaints to the Data User are likely to concern whether the Data User has properly fulfilled the Subject Access provisions, or arise because the Data Subject seeks further information on, or modification of, personal data held by the Data User. Complaints to the Data Protection Registrar are likely to refer to contravention of particular Data Protection Principles, particularly the Fifth Principle in relation to accuracy, the Fourth in relation to the relevance of the data to the purpose, or the Seventh in relation to Subject Access, correction or erasure of personal data. Complaints to the Courts are most likely to occur when a Data Subject, via Subject Access, has come to realise that damage suffered could well be related to contravention of a Principle.

5.3 In essence, all three routes of complaint are likely to generate the same questions: 'Was the Data User acting properly?', 'Were the data correct?' or 'What can be done to redress the situation?'. This redress can take the form of the Data User changing procedures, or compensating the Data Subject, or rectifying or erasing personal data. In extreme cases, the Registrar or the Courts may **force** the Data User to take one or more of these steps.

5.4 A prudent Data User will, therefore, establish formal, documented, procedures that will:

(a) deal with follow up enquiries by the Data Subject, after Subject Access;

(b) allow for the correction of personal data;

(c) allow for further verification of personal data if received from a third party;

(d) allow for the erasure of personal data;

(e) allow for actions based on incorrect personal data to be reversed (if possible);

(f) allow for disclosures of incorrect personal data to be recognised, and for disclosees to be advised of the correct data (if possible);

(g) where necessary, allow for a sound defence by the Data User to be presented to the Data Protection Registrar or to the Courts;

(h) ensure that, where appropriate, the views of the legal officer are obtained.

5.5 All these procedures can be presented in a positive light, and promoted in the covering letters to Data Subjects (following Subject Access; see paragraph 4.7.17 above) as a way of increasing confidence in the services provided by the Data User. For example, a simple statement 'Please let me know if any corrections to the data are required' may work wonders. Data Subjects who know what remedial actions Data Users intend, are not likely to take further steps unless the matter is serious.

5.6 According to a survey carried out by the Data Protection Registrar (Third Annual Report), over 93% of people interviewed expected the right of correction of data to be enforced, and within this percentage there are bound to be Data Subjects who are prepared to push the law to its limits; consequently, it may be wise to yield to the inevitable and to be prepared not only for eventualities (a) to (f) above, but also to keep formal records to assist a defence, as in (g) and (h).

5.7 If, following Subject Access, the Data Subject replies to the coordinating officer and offers corrections to the data, and these corrections concern information originally provided by the Data Subject, then they should be incorporated in the personal data immediately (assuming the identification of the Data Subject is still valid!). Once this has been done, it would be good practice (and good Public Relations) to notify the Data Subject, preferably enclosing a copy of the revised data.

5.8 If the correction is to personal data whose origin is the Data User or a Third Party, or which were originally verified by the Data User or Third Party (by some formal process or the provision of documentary evidence), then the situation is not so straightforward. There will need to be an intermediate stage whereby formal processes are repeated to verify what the Data Subject claims. The correction is made if, and only if, this verification is validated, and the Data Subject is then notified as before. Both the Third Party and anyone within the Data User organisation who has received the original data should be informed of the corrected information. Wherever possible, any other disclosee(s) should also be informed.

5.9 The implications of informing external and internal disclosees can be quite daunting. Firstly, the task may be quite impractical unless a disclosure log is kept. Although the Act does not specifically demand that disclosees should be alerted to corrections, it is good practice to keep such a log for certain collections of personal data, and any new software should contain provision for the log.

5.10 Secondly, the Data User has to know wherever the personal data reside within the organisation, since a Data Subject will expect **all** future employment of these data, by the Data User, to involve the new, accurate, information. As long as a census has been taken which explicitly demanded a record of internal disclosures, then it is relatively simple to inform the relevant disclosees. In addition, the increasing use of Data Dictionaries may help to update personal data comprehensively throughout the organisation.

5.11 Finally, failure to solve the problem of incorporating corrected data is, of course, a breach of the Fifth Data Protection Principle and could also lead to problems with Section 22 of the Act.

5.12 In some instances, a Third Party source of information may not be contactable. If this is the case, and where the data are incapable of being verified, there is no option but to accept (or note in the data) the Data Subject's correction. To keep and use, without qualification, personal data that cannot be verified and have been challenged, is just asking for trouble (see also paragraph 5.18).

5.13 Note that a structured 'correction procedure' outlined above cannot be applied to opinions. An opinion accurately recorded (including its source) is, by definition, factually correct - the source **holds** that particular opinion. All that a Data User can do with challenged opinions is either to leave them in the personal data (together with a record of the challenge) or to delete them. However, a Court may order the correction or erasure of an opinion which appears to be based on information that has been shown to be inaccurate (see Section 24(1) of the Act).

5.14 'Caring agencies' who deal with sensitive data about a Data Subject's circumstances are likely to find it especially difficult to cope with the issue of opinions, since they may often encounter opinions that are not substantiated. Subject Access may well force such agencies to look again at their recording techniques.

5.15 For example, consider the record of an opinion which consists solely of: 'When I last visited Joe Bloggs, I thought he was aggressive'. This might be vital information to have; the next home visitor may be attacked! However, in reality, such personal data must be deleted, or properly augmented, on three counts. Firstly - who is the holder of the opinion? As far as the record is concerned, it could be anybody; it might be somebody with a grudge against the Data Subject. Secondly, what does 'last visited' mean; yesterday or ten years ago? The entry is 'timeless' and its direct relevance to current information is difficult to ascertain. Finally, what does 'aggressive' mean? It could be anything from 'shouting' to 'threatening with a knife'. Not only does the absence of any context preclude evaluation of the relevance of the opinion, but if the source cannot be identified then the qualifications of that person, eg as a judge of 'aggression', cannot be determined.

5.16 In short, leaving such an opinion on file could lead to problems. The Data User must employ procedures which ensure that, wherever feasible, records of opinions and the like are related to factual events, identify the holder of the opinion and contain the date of entry of the personal data into the record. Only by these means can any challenge from the Data Subject be dealt with in a proper manner.

5.17 In some cases, the Third Party or the relevant person in the Data User organisation will say that the correction offered by the Data Subject is invalid. If this view is accepted by the Data User, and the personal data are not amended, they should be annotated with a code or marker to the effect that the Data Subject disputes the record, and future use of that record should only be with this code or marker. As before, it would be good practice to advise disclosee(s) of the dispute, but this may prove difficult without a disclosure log.

5.18 Alternatively, the Data User would have to decide whether the continued use of these challenged data was likely to cause damage. If yes, a decision should be taken whether to correct or delete the data, as appropriate, even though the use of the marker would protect the Data User against an award of compensation (Section 22(2)(b) of the Act).

5.19 If there is little risk of causing damage, the Data User could decide to retain the personal data. Nevertheless, the Data Subject might complain to the Registrar or to the Courts, asking for the correction or erasure to be enforced, and this may in turn require management to justify its course of action. The outcome will then be determined through legal argument.

5.20 If a complaint by the Data Subject, or legal action, begins to look a possibility, it might be useful for a Data User to seek the Registrar's advice, to see if the issues can be resolved by negotiation. In these circumstances, it may be important to seek legal advice to protect the Data User's interests.

5.21 In summary, dealing with complaints from Data Subjects and informing them of the outcome is not simple. The salient points of the data correction process are summarised below:

(a) **Source of personal data: Data Subject**

No verification possible - accept the correction.

Original data were verified - accept the correction only if the correction is verified.

(b) **Source of personal data: Third Party**

Accept a verified correction from the Data Subject.

Accept an unverified correction only if agreed by the Source.

Note The verification process need not identify the Source to the Data Subject, unless the Source has agreed to this.

(c) **Source of personal data: Data User**

Accept a Data Subject's correction, subject to any validation procedure employed by the Data User.

Advise internal disclosees of any accepted correction.

Advise internal disclosees of any challenges to the accuracy of the data, if the correction has not been accepted.

Advise external disclosees of any accepted correction, if at all possible.

5.22 Where contentious or sensitive personal data are involved, always date them, identify their origin, substantiate their content where this is feasible, and maintain a disclosure log in appropriate cases.

Chapter Four(B): Case Studies

1. First Principle: fair obtaining and fair processing

1.1 Case histories

1.1.1 Case A

In the early 1980s the authors of this book heard rumours from a Housing Department of a Local Authority that a financial services company carried out a survey of employment within a Council estate. Those interviewees who said they were in employment subsequently received information from the company advising them of their right to buy their council home, and offering the company's mortgage facilities (one of IPMC's case studies; also The Guardian, 31.3.90).

1.1.2 Case B

'An order form used by a shop, which had a section for customers to enter their names, address and telephone numbers ... needed to be completed only if home delivery was required. Many customers completed this section, even when they were taking goods away at the time of purchase' (Case 8, 5th Report of the Data Protection Registrar, June 1989).

1.1.3 Case C

'A Home Counties comprehensive school is offering a pioneering package to employers in an attempt to seek commercial sponsorship.... The school has issued a brochure saying that it will give investors the names of all those going to university or college' (from The Sunday Correspondent, 25.9.89).

1.1.4 Case D

'Electoral Registers, which include details of who lives with whom, are sold by some Councils often for more than £2,000 a time, on computer disk. Other Councils charge around £2 per 1,000 names. The lists are then used by mail order firms to target likely customers. Some Councils even provide special lists, such as of single women living in a certain area' (from The Daily News, 17.4.87).

1.2 Discussion

1.2.1 The starting point for Cases A and B is the Data Protection Registrar's advice on the application of the First Principle, found in Guideline 4, paragraph 1.9 and in Guidance Note 19 (ref. GN19-RPJ-8/88). GN19 states that:

> '**BEFORE** a source gives information the data user must have ensured that the source has been informed as set out below.
>
> A data user cannot fulfil his obligation to obtain fairly by simply offering an explanation after the source has given the information.
>
> The source should be told:-
>
> what information it is intended will actually become personal data;
>
> by whom it will be held (that is the identity of any relevant registered data user);
>
> who else will be able to use it, (this can be described either by a name or by a general description);
>
> how it will be used.
>
> The source must not be misled and it should not be implied that any particular item of information is necessary to establish a relationship or effect a transaction if this is not the case. Where different pieces of information are being obtained for different uses or for different data users the obtainer should explain clearly which information is requested for which use and which user.'

1.2.2 With respect to Case A, a 'survey of employment' clearly does not alert people who provide personal details to the fact that their personal data will be used to market mortgage facilities. Omitting the latter purpose means that these individuals were misled (ie tricked), and this is a clear breach of the First Principle. However, the more difficult aspects of the Case concern whether explanations that are 'economical with the truth', or that leave facts to be inferred, can also be misleading. The Director General of the Office of Fair Trading (The Guardian 31.3.90) has warned credit brokers against this 'undesirable activity' connected with the sale of council houses.

1.2.3 In Guideline 4, paragraph 1.1 the Data Protection Registrar gives a further indication that the Data User who takes a passive approach to explaining the purpose(s) for which information is being obtained risks breaching the Principle. If the Data User omits to provide an explanation, the test of whether or not the First Principle was breached could rest on whether the individual providing the information was 'under the impression that the information would be kept confidential by the data user' and whether that impression was 'justified by the circumstances and did the data user intend to preserve that confidence'. In paragraph 1.2 the Registrar states that some active steps need to be taken and that passivity, by itself, is insufficient: 'the duty to obtain information fairly requires steps to be taken' to make the individual providing the information 'aware of the true position'.

1.2.4 In Case B, the argument concerns the need to provide information: clearly the name, address and telephone number are required to deliver an item (the name and address to deliver; the telephone number in case the delivery plans change). However, there is no requirement to collect these items of personal data if the goods are taken home by the customer.

1.2.5 If the shop intends to use the information for a direct marketing purpose, and does not reveal this to the customer, a breach of the First Principle occurs. Just as in Case A, the items of personal data are obtained for two distinct purposes: in this instance for home delivery and marketing. Consequently both purposes must be declared to the Data Subject at the outset. If the name and address were to be disclosed to other mail-order companies (ie the shop has registered the purpose 'Trading in Personal Information'), then this would also have to be declared to the customer.

1.2.6 Case B was resolved by the organisation concerned agreeing to redesign the order forms to include the statement that the information on the forms would be used for mailing purposes, and that customer details only needed to be completed if home delivery was required.

1.2.7 To meet widespread criticism of the 'junk mail' problem, the Mailing Preference Service (MPS), to which many (but not all) mail order companies belong, has a procedure which allows Data Subjects to remove their names from the lists of **all** the member companies. There are problems: for example, the person who sent the offending advertising material may not belong to a member company of MPS, or the organisation that bought a list of names and addresses may simply have obtained a collection of sticky labels (ie the organisation does not hold personal data), or a Data Subject may wish to receive some types of mail but not others. However, MPS can be seen as a step in the right direction to stop a major source of irritation to the public (for more detail see Chapter 4, paragraph 2.1.2(e)).

1.2.8 Case C raises the issue of unfair processing. What happens when Data User X wakes up one morning and says "I have collected personal data for purpose X; I could now use those data for purpose Y, or disclose the data to Z". The problem is "do I need to inform my sources of information about the new purpose Y or new disclosee Z?".

1.2.9 Whilst the answer to this question is "NO", such a Data User nevertheless needs to take care. Guideline 4, paragraph 1.9 states that 'fairness will need to be judged by reference to the purpose of the processing, the nature of the processing itself, and to its consequences for the individual affected by it'. So, for example, 'it would be unfair for a Data User to process an automated mailing list with the result that advertising material is sent to an individual who has informed the Data User that he does not wish to receive such material' (Guideline 4, paragraph 1.6). Thus, with respect to Case C, although the school may not have breached the First Principle, the school may do so on a subsequent occasion if a pupil has formally asked for that particular use of the pupil's personal data to cease.

1.2.10 In Case C, there is a further issue that could come into play: whether the school is legally entitled to sell the names of pupils in return for sponsorship. Even if there is no conflict in law, if the school is answerable to some ruling body then the latter could take a different view of the school's remit (eg for state schools the Local Education Authority may have a policy that can override the school's initiative).

1.2.11 In Case C, the Education Authority spokesperson indicated that Authority's policy was that names and addresses were used only for educational purposes and only disclosed for other purposes with parental consent. In these circumstances, any other use of personal data by the school would probably not be covered by the Data User's Register Entry, and therefore could be unlawful under Section 5(1) of the Act. Any disclosure made 'knowingly or recklessly' in deliberate contravention of the Authority's Registration particulars could lead to criminal charges under Section 5(5).

1.2.12 Case C, and certainly Case D, are also affected by the statutory duties to maintain, respectively, the School Register and the Electoral Register; they enter the legal morass of problems which is highlighted by the Cases associated with Community Charge (see Section 2 of this Chapter). The requirement in law to collect information means that 'in any event' the information is obtained fairly since, as defined in the Interpretation of the First Data Protection Principle

> 'Information shall in any event be treated as obtained fairly if it is obtained from a person who -
>
> (a) is authorised by or under any enactment to supply it; or
>
> (b) is required to supply it by or under any enactment or by any convention or other instrument imposing an international obligation on the United Kingdom;
>
> and in determining whether information was obtained fairly there shall be disregarded any disclosure of the information which is authorised or

required by or under any enactment or required by any such convention or other instrument as aforesaid.'

1.2.13 Case D highlights an activity that has long been a source of public controversy. Back in the 1970s the Younger Committee, set up to examine 'Privacy', carried out a survey. They asked a random selection of people whether they were in favour of a list (placed in the public library and freely available for inspection) which contained the addresses of properties coupled with the names of the people who lived there. To the Committee's surprise, 35% of those questioned said that they would object to this invasion of privacy, and that there should be a law against it - it was clear that they did not appreciate that the description applied to the Electoral Register!

1.2.14 In 1986 (and again in 1990) Parliament approved a Statutory Instrument, under the terms of Schedule 4, Section 87 of the the Representation of the People Act (1985), to allow the sale of Electoral Registers. Section 34(5) of the Data Protection Act 1984 permits such disclosures to go ahead without being registered, as the subsection states:

> 'Personal data are exempt from the non-disclosure provisions in any case in which the disclosure is made ... under any enactment.'

1.2.15 Thus, with respect to the Data Protection Act, Data Users who obtain the Electoral Register for use with their personal data must specify it as a Source of personal data in their relevant Register Entry, whilst the Electoral Registration Officers (who are the relevant Data Users responsible for the compilation of the Register) need not specify the disclosure of these data in their Entry nor inform the Data Subjects that the disclosure takes place (because the disclosure of personal data from the Register is sanctioned by law and is subject to the non-disclosure provision described in Section 34(5)).

1.2.16 The Government argues that, since the Electoral Register must be widely distributed for electoral and political purposes, there is no practical way of restricting its use for other purposes. The list of voters has to be a public document in order to help prevent electoral fraud and, once in the public domain, its use for other purposes without the knowledge or consent of the voter becomes inevitable. The sale of the Electoral Register is merely formal recognition of this position and, at least, brings in some money. When asked in Parliament (Hansard, 5.5.87) why the Secretary of State for the Home Office was unwilling to change the electoral registration form to inform voters that their names and addresses may be sold without reference to them, or to give individual voters the option of not having their name and address sold to other organisations, the then Minister, Mr Douglas Hogg, replied:

> 'It is of overriding importance to ensure that the Electoral Register is as complete as possible. A warning notice might discourage people from

registering'.

1.2.17 The Government has, however, indicated (Hansard 26.1.90) that it will review certain aspects of the sale of the Electoral Register, should there be a problem in protecting those at risk (eg women who have suffered violence from their partner, senior Civil Servants, Police and Military Officers, MPs, Ministers who may be subject to terrorist attack etc may all be put at risk if their name and address could easily be found by consulting the Register).

1.2.18 Whilst individuals at risk are also protected under Community Charge legislation, which allows their omission from the 'Extract' of the Community Charges Register which is in the public domain, the arguments in favour of selling have **not** been repeated in the Community Charge instance. In England and Wales the legislation forbids not only the sale but also the copying of names and addresses from the Extract (although 'inspection' is permitted), whilst in Scotland a high charge has been imposed (£1 per name and address sold) although copying in writing is free. Whether these legal and financial hurdles are likely to have any practical effect, eg to prevent the compilation of Community Charge based mailing lists, must remain in some doubt.

2. First, Third and Fourth Principles: statutory powers

2.1 Case histories

2.1.1 Case A

> 'The degree of chaos over poll tax registration became clear yesterday when Eric Howe, the Data Protection Registrar, revealed he has approved forms issued by only 37 of 403 councils in England and Wales. Mr. Howe has asked 304 local authorities to justify questions they have asked ... ' (from The Independent, 4.8.89).

2.1.2 Case B

> 'Schools may be required to release parents' names and addresses to poll tax officers despite Department of Education and Science assurances that registers would be used only for education purposes' (from The Independent, 24.3.89).

2.2 Discussion

2.2.1 The Community Charge offers a classic case study of the problems that surround the exercising of statutory powers with respect to the collection and use of personal data. These problems are exacerbated as the Charge is not universally popular, with the result that not only the powers and their limitations, but also the resultant processing of personal data come under the closest of public scrutiny.

2.2.2 When statutory powers are employed, both the discloser and the recipient must be aware of the how the powers to obtain and disclose personal data are circumscribed, and what implications arise as a result of the dispensations from the First Data Protection Principle (ie the information to be contained within personal data is always deemed to have been obtained 'fairly') and the Third Principle (ie the personal data can be disclosed via the non-disclosure exemption). It is crucial, therefore, to keep within the scope of these dispensations, since otherwise the personal data obtained or disclosed will fall within the full ambit of the Data Protection Act. So, with respect to Community Charge, the personal data obtained or disclosed by a Community Charges Registration Officer (CCRO) must conform with the CCRO's powers as defined in the Community Charge legislation and its supporting statutory Regulations; a failure of procedure, a mistaken judgement, or a lack of recognition on the limitations placed on the exercise of these powers, may mean that an action could be illegal.

2.2.3 In Case A objections were raised, for instance, to the inclusion of questions, in the Community Charge Canvass form, on the 'Relationship' of residents in a property. This and similar questions appeared in the forms sent out by certain Local Authorities (eg Trafford Metropolitan Borough Council) and were covered by the general comment that the information was 'required by law' and that 'a civil penalty may be imposed' if no information, or incorrect information, was supplied.

2.2.4 The grounds for the objections to the collection of these data were founded on the fact that the functions associated with Community Charge are split between two separate legal entities: the CCRO who has the duty of compiling and maintaining the Register, and the Charging Authority who has the duty to collect the money. Consequently, as the question concerning 'Relationship' has no part to play in compiling a list of names, addresses and dates of residence (the CCRO's principal aim), it is unfair for a CCRO to collect 'relationship' details by exercising statutory powers (or by implying that such powers apply). Thus it was argued that the First Data Protection Principle had been breached in these cases (eg 'unfair pressure' or 'unjustified threats' had been used to obtain the information; see the Data Protection Registrar's Guideline 4, paragraph 1.1).

2.2.5 Note that the collection of 'Relationship' data can be fully justified, in specific instances, by the other legal entity, the Charging Authority; for example in the case of married or cohabiting couples, where one partner can be held responsible for the Community Charge not paid by the other. However, this information is only needed when a Charge has been levied **and** has not been paid, **and** after a liability order has been made against the defaulting chargepayer. So, even here, care needs to be taken;

if personal data on 'Relationship' are held for those chargepayers who have no Community Charge debt, this could be claimed to be 'excessive in relation to that purpose', ie in breach of the Fourth Principle.

2.2.6 As a result of the objections, the CCRO of Trafford Metropolitan Borough Council (and other CCROs) gave written undertakings to the Data Protection Registrar that 'Relationships' information would not be held as personal data. The assurance given by Trafford, for example, included:

> 'that no further copies of the canvass form which was the subject of the complaint would be distributed;
>
> that any form used in future would be such as to ensure that information obtained by its use would be obtained in compliance with the Data Protection Principles;
>
> that no information relating to relationships obtained by use of the previous form was now held as personal data nor would be so held in the future;
>
> that no information relating to dates of commencement of residence obtained by the use of the previous form was held as personal data, and that no such information relating to dates of commencement of residence before 31 March 1990 would be held as personal data;
>
> that information objected to by the Registrar and contained in the completed forms but held manually would not be released to the Borough Council in its capacity as charging authority.'

2.2.7 In addition to the Trafford case, the Data Protection Registrar sent letters to over 200 CCROs during December 1989, indicating that unless the CCRO deleted certain items of personal data (which were demanded on Community Charge Canvass Forms but should not have been), formal action on breach of the Data Protection Principles would follow. Most CCROs responded positively, but in April 1990 the Registrar issued 9 Enforcement Notices (which specify the action required to comply with one or more Principles) and 13 Refusal Notices (rejecting applications for Registration because these were likely to contravene one or more Principles); four of the CCROs appealed to the Data Protection Tribunal which later in the year decided in the Registrar's favour in each case.

2.2.8 Case B highlights concern about a CCRO's ability to obtain information from school registers; the question here was not the names and addresses that the CCRO hoped to obtain, but whether a CCRO had the power to obtain information from a particular organisation. Following public controversy, the Department of Education and Science (in a letter dated 2.5.89 addressed to the Association of County Councils) issued advice to Local Education Authorities (LEAs) that showed how the use of a CCRO's powers balances on a knife edge; any slip and the CCRO gets cut!

2.2.9 The letter stated that the CCRO can only obtain the required information about parents and guardians from a Local Education Authority if the latter has already obtained it, from the school, for other purposes (eg for consulting parents about the school); the CCRO has no legal power with respect to a school. The relevant text is quoted in full below; it directs attention to the care that needs to be taken. The advice is:

> 'The understanding of the Department and that of the Department of the Environment is that the 'possession or control' of the school admission register rests with school governors and that the LEA may not lawfully make extracts from the register except for the purposes of the Education Acts. Where however the LEA possesses extracts from a register, obtained lawfully, this information is deemed to be in its possession and thus available to CCROs on demand. CCROs are not empowered to demand information other than from precepting or charging authorities; they may not approach schools directly. LEAs are not empowered to make extracts from a register solely for the purpose of providing information for CCROs and governors would be justified in withholding permission for the making of extracts in these circumstances.'

2.2.10 Following such advice is difficult and requires formal procedures that ensure that the letter of the law is being meticulously followed. The advice is an object lesson in alerting any organisation that exercises statutory powers to the need to examine the 'small print'. This is especially true if the legislation is controversial, as is the case with almost everything that concerns the collection, use and disclosure of personal data associated with the Community Charge - a significant number of Data Subjects are antagonistic and looking for errors in procedure. In these circumstances, it is very easy for a complaint to the Registrar under Section 36(2) of the Data Protection Act to turn any minor mistake over procedure into maximum public embarrassment.

2.2.11 Whenever statutory powers are used to obtain information, public attention can easily focus on the proper use of such powers, and on its precise limitations. Consequently all such demands for information to be contained within personal data must be in writing. The person receiving such a request should be able to identify:

(a) the identity of the body exercising the powers,

(b) the statute involved and any Regulation or Statutory Instrument that supports the use of the powers,

(c) precisely what information has to be provided and how every item falls within the scope prescribed by statute,

(d) the timescale for a reply.

2.2.12 If the above are not specified, then the demand could be interpreted as including information that is outside the statutory powers (ie subject to the procedures specified in 2.2.13 below). Failure of either party (ie the person obtaining or the person disclosing) to keep formal records that statutory powers were involved will make it difficult to show that the powers were exercised properly.

2.2.13 Of course, it is open to individuals to provide additional information, voluntarily, in excess of that which has been demanded. If the discloser is a Data User, it is crucial to appreciate that the additional information will not be covered by the non-disclosure exemption, and that it will therefore be necessary to adhere to the Data Protection Registrar's advice on the application of the First Principle (see the extract from Guidance Note 19 quoted in paragraph 1.2.1 above); the disclosure will also have to be registered.

2.2.14 A further problem facing Data Users that collect information via statutory powers is that the processing of personal data, obtained in breach of the First Data Protection Principle, will then also breach the Fourth Data Protection Principle even if the personal data have been given voluntarily (whether by the Data Subjects themselves or by another source). For example, a CCRO might ask all chargepayers to provide their Date of Birth, on the grounds that it would be useful to identify pensioners so that they can be treated more carefully or sympathetically by the authorities. However justified (or reasonable) collecting the Date of Birth might be (and there **are** circumstances in which holding the Date of Birth is necessary for the Community Charge to function properly), it still can be claimed that this particular request, which is not provided for by statute, exceeds the statutory function of the CCRO (which is to compile and maintain the Register of chargepayers). To hold personal data without statutory backing, as would be the case when the Date of Birth is held in order to identify who is a pensioner, would therefore be excessive to the CCRO's purpose, and would thus constitute a breach of the Fourth Data Protection Principle.

3. Second and Third Principles: unlawful use or disclosure

3.1 Case histories

3.1.1 Case A

British Petroleum ran a 'BP Lucky Numbers' competition in 1985. If drivers found their vehicle registration number displayed in the garage where they were buying petrol, then they won a prize. It transpired that certain Police

Officers used the Vehicle Index of the Police National Computer (PNC), which identifies the name and address of the vehicle owner when given a registration number, to contact the vehicle owner and to offer, in return for payment, to reveal the address of the garage so that the prize could be claimed (from The Sun, 1.5.85).

3.1.2 Case B

An Asian family moving from one part of London to another was met by a crowd of 'white power' racists. Information concerning the move was held by the Local Authority (one of IPMC's case-studies).

3.1.3 Case C

A man inquired about a vacancy advertised in a Job Centre. On telephoning the prospective employer, he was only asked to provide his full name and to declare which newspaper he read. At the interview, it transpired that the employer had obtained details about the prospective employee's frail and sick parents, the Social Work services they received, and information about the employee's medical condition (from a Thames TV News item in 1984).

3.1.4 Case D

The Cabinet Office is examining whether the Security Service used the premium bond system ERNIE to pay its freelance agents (from The Times, 26.2.90).

3.2 Discussion

3.2.1 Case A was investigated by the Police Complaints Board and a report (HC425) was submitted to Parliament in July 1986. The report's recommendations are analogous to those which the Registrar could enforce to ensure compliance with the Data Protection Principles (see the procedures accepted by Trafford MBC when in breach of the First Data Protection Principle; paragraph 2.2.6 above). In this case, the Police Complaints Board considered that the following guidelines should form the basis of instructions to each Police Force:

(i) 'access to personal data held on the PNC must be permitted only for purposes necessary for the efficient discharge of bona fide police duties, and personal or private use must be strictly forbidden;

(ii) it is essential to secure the integrity of the PNC. To achieve this, relevant transactions must be subject to monitoring and validation by random sampling; validation must reach the actual reason for a transaction being originated;

(iii) accurate records of transactions must be made which identify the persons responsible for initiating and handling a request for information;

(iv) all officers who may have cause to access the PNC must be directed and reminded from time to time that PNC records are confidential, that such information must not be disclosed to unauthorised persons and that abuse of the system will render them liable to disciplinary or statutory sanctions;

(v) since originators may be called upon to justify their transactions possibly weeks or months after the event, they should make a record of sufficient detail to refresh their memories in order to avoid unwarranted suspicion of malpractice;

(vi) officers who receive requests for information from any person which would necessitate access to the PNC must satisfy themselves that the purpose can properly be regarded as a genuine police matter before responding to such requests.'

3.2.2 Internal disciplinary proceedings were taken in twelve Forces and several Officers resigned as a result of the enquiry. The Officers were lucky to escape prosecution under Section 2 of the Official Secrets Act 1911 which was in force at that time (in 1985 the relevant provisions in Section 5(5) of the Data Protection Act were not in force), as they had signed a declaration which warned them of the consequences of unauthorised disclosures in the following terms:

> 'I understand also that I am liable to be prosecuted if I publish without official sanction any information I may acquire in the course of my tenure of an official appointment (unless it has already officially been made public)'.

3.2.3 Nevertheless, the list below given in reply to a Parliamentary Question (Hansard 15.12.86) provides further examples of those who took the risk despite signing the above undertaking, and were caught and prosecuted:

(a) a civilian Police employee who offered confidential information from the Police National Computer to a burglar alarm company

(b) a solicitor, alleged to have offered money to a Police Officer to disclose criminal intelligence information in relation to a client, who was charged with corruption and offences under Section 2

(c) a clerk, employed in a local DHSS office, who imparted personal information about claims made by the husband of a local councillor to an agent of a rival political party (the clerk pleaded guilty at Crown Court, and was sentenced to three months imprisonment suspended for 12 months)

(d) two Police Officers who were alleged to have obtained information about criminal records for unauthorised supply to a security consultant

(e) a journalist who was alleged to have obtained a copy of police intelligence records relating to a known criminal

(f) two Police Officers who were alleged to have made unauthorised supply of information, obtained from the Police National Computer, about vehicle registration and criminal records.

3.2.4 Although this list relates only to unauthorised use or disclosure of personal data held by Government or the Police, it demonstrates:

(a) that the temptations for staff to disclose or use personal data for unauthorised purposes can be great if the rewards are significant, and

(b) that in a wide variety of circumstances, the Data User did not have procedures to guarantee that personal data would be used or disclosed only for authorised purposes. It would be foolish to assume that such problems do not also concern sensitive or confidential personal data held by other Data Users.

3.2.5 In the circumstances of Case B, a member of staff could have been prosecuted, under the Data Protection Act, in the way Civil Servants can be prosecuted under the Official Secrets Act 1989 (eg, in the latter instance, for unauthorised disclosures of classified data, or for disclosures that impair the investigation of crime). If a sympathiser of the racist group was employed by the Local Authority and disclosed personal data to the group in order to help organise intimidation of individuals of a particular ethnic origin, under what circumstances could the Local Authority be sure that this kind of damaging disclosure of personal data could be punished by the criminal law?

3.2.6 Firstly, it is important for employers to include a 'duty of confidentiality' clause in the terms of employment of all employees. To ensure that such a declaration is prominent in the employee's mind, this can be reinforced by a specific reference to confidentiality in induction courses; if appropriate, a 'duty of confidentiality' clause could be signed separately, as is the undertaking with respect to the Official Secrets Act (see paragraph 3.2.3 above). Secondly, an important part of this process is to ensure that all employees are trained to be aware of the constraints on uses, disclosures, sources, personal data descriptions etc that are formalised through the

Data User's Registration. Finally, employees should be left in no doubt that the employer takes a breach of confidentiality as a serious issue that could lead to disciplinary action, dismissal, or, in extreme cases, criminal prosecution by the relevant authorities. If these actions are carried out thoroughly, it could only be through a deliberate act that an employee would use, collect or disclose any personal data for a purpose that was not officially sanctioned.

3.2.7 If staff are not told formally of the limitations or constraints placed on them by the Data Protection Act, a prosecution against an individual employee is likely to fail. For example, it would be difficult to prove to a Court that a member of staff disclosed 'knowingly or recklessly' (as in Section 5(5) of the Data Protection Act) if the range of authorised disclosures is not known to staff. It even may be difficult to dismiss an employee, as it could be argued that it is unfair to dismiss a person who, through the neglect of the management, was left unaware of employee responsibilities. In such cases, where procedures fail badly, with serious consequences, it could be argued (via Section 20(1) of the Act) that individual managers were to blame (since the consequences were 'attributable to ... neglect') and that one or more managers, as well as the Data User, were 'liable to be proceeded against and punished accordingly'.

3.2.8 Note that Section 23 of the Act implies that in all cases of unauthorised disclosure (irrespective of the circumstances), a claim for compensation for the damage caused by that disclosure could be made against the Data User (ie against the employer, and not against the employee). Such actions could well be successful since, if staff were unaware of their responsibilities towards personal data, or if the senior managers had not been mindful to train their staff in correct procedures, it would be difficult to for the Data User to claim, via Section 23(3), that 'reasonable' care had been taken to protect the personal data. In summary, if managers take the risk and staff are not trained in their responsibilities under the Act, it could be the former who commit the criminal offence, and the employer (the Data User) who pays any damages.

3.2.9 Case C provides a study of how publicity can reduce public confidence in an organisation if personal data, originally collected to assist with the provision of benefits and social services, are then disclosed to an employer for the purpose of vetting an applicant for work. As the Thames TV News program was watched by about 3 million people and since, at that time, the unemployment rate was approximately 10%, there could have been around a quarter of a million clients of the benefits service watching, and being shown how their personal data, which they had provided in order to claim benefits, could be used by employers to assess their employment prospects. (The program's reporters discovered that a member of DHSS staff was paid to provide information; the member of staff was dismissed). Clearly, such an unauthorised disclosure of personal data can jeopardise public trust; if it happened in the private sector, it could threaten the company's customer base.

3.2.10 Case D is an extreme example where the Data Protection Act, at first sight, does not apply to a 'new' use of personal data (the implied manipulation of 'random' numbers in such a way that specific winning premium bonds are selected and attributed to certain secret agents appears to be a complex means of processing personal data for payroll purposes!). According to Section 27 of the Data Protection Act, personal data used for the purpose of safeguarding national security are exempt from Part II of the Act (Registration and Registrar's powers) and Sections 21-24 (Rights of Data Subjects). However, a complaint can be made to the Courts (under Section 25(2): to determine whether a Subject Access exemption was properly applied); to the Data Protection Registrar (under Section 36(2) this could result in a Court case to test whether the use of the personal data should have been registered: if the Minister does not sign a certificate as specified by Section 27(2) then the use of the personal data for payment purposes via ERNIE would be unlawful); or to the Security Service Commission (established under the Security Service Act 1989: if an individual has suffered damage as a result of the operations of the Security Service). Thus, even in circumstances where it appears that the Data Protection Act may be of limited application, especially when exemptions apply (in this case in the sensitive situation of national security), there are still ways in which Data Protection issues can be raised in the Courts or through the Registrar to test whether the use of an exemption by a Data User is justified.

3.2.11 In his Fifth Report (June 1989), the Data Protection Registrar reported the successful prosecution of 8 Data Users for non-registration. These low figures were stated to be due to the Registrar's 'fairly gentle policy' under which 'those prosecuted have generally been advised to register and failed to do so before prosecution proceeding are started' (page 15, Fifth Report). This policy was to change as far as Data Users who needed to renew a Register Entry, and failed to do so, were concerned; in the next paragraph the Registrar forecast his 'intention to commence prosecution proceedings against such data users as they are discovered' (in his Sixth and Seventh Reports, such prosecutions totalled 19 and 11 respectively). The Registrar also referred in his Fifth Report to the first prosecution of a Data User for acting outside the terms of the Register Entry; this resulted in fines of £2,000 plus £900 costs in November 1989 (Sixth Report); three such prosecutions were brought in the year ending May 1991 (Seventh Report).

4. Third Principle: unlawful disclosure

4.1 Case histories

4.1.1 Case A

A Local Authority used personal data, collected for purposes associated with Council rents, for a purpose associated with employment with the

Authority. At the end of an interview for a job as a Rent Arrears Officer, the applicant who was also a tenant of the Council was asked what she thought of her own rent arrears of £180 (from Computer Talk, 4.8.86).

4.1.2 Case B

'Britain's newest trade union will sign its thousandth member at Heathrow airport tomorrow amid a flurry of writs and solicitors letters.' The story relates to an entire committee of a branch of a Union resigning and using the Union's mailing list to contact all branch members asking them to join the new Union (from The Sunday Times, 26.3.90).

4.1.3 Cases C

(a) A complaint had been made to the Data Protection Registrar, following a press release from the Labour Party stating that some Councillors of the Scottish National Party had paid their Community Charge. It had been alleged that personal data held by Lothian Regional Council 'somehow' leaked (from the Local Government Chronicle, 24.11.89).

(b) Despite the Honourable Member's traditional rant against the Community Charge, he should be congratulated in registering his second home in the London Borough which has one of the lowest charges in the capital (the gist of an exchange, Hansard, Col 916, 21.2.90).

(c) A row has blown up over allegations that Leeds city councillors have access to sensitive data through a micro linked to a personal computer (from Computer News, 28.05.87).

4.1.4 Case D

The Inland Revenue disclosed personal data, relating to the tax affairs of strikers employed by Thamesdown District Council, to the Wiltshire Police. NALGO and Dale Campbell-Savours MP took up the case, with the result that the employees concerned received a letter of apology from the then Chancellor, Nigel Lawson MP (from Computer Talk, 6.11.89).

4.1.5 Case E

A wife badly beaten by her husband was taken, by ambulance, unconscious to hospital. The husband phoned round the hospitals in the District to discover her whereabouts, came to the ward and assaulted her again. (An incident vouched for by one of our course delegates).

4.2 **Discussion**

4.2.1 All disclosures described above are subject to the provisions of the Third Data Protection Principle, which states:

> 'Personal data held for any purpose or purposes shall not be used or disclosed in any manner incompatible with that purpose or those purposes'.
>
> In particular, the Interpretation of this Principle explains that:
>
> 'Personal data shall not be treated as used or disclosed in contravention of this principle unless -
>
> (a) used otherwise than for a purpose of a description registered under this Act in relation to the data; or
>
> (b) disclosed otherwise than to a person of a description so registered.'

4.2.2 To summarise:

(a) a disclosure is lawful if it is registered,

(b) a purpose is lawful if it is registered,

and in Case A, the personal data were used for two purposes:

(a) Personnel/Employee Administration (P001), and

(b) Housing Management (P021).

> **Note:** the word 'lawful' applies with respect to the terms of the Data Protection Act, and **not** necessarily with respect to any other legislation. The fact that a use or disclosure of personal data is registered does not make that use or disclosure lawful in every circumstance (eg registering personal data used for a blackmail purpose does not legitimise blackmail).

4.2.3 The Case concerns the legal aspects and procedures which surround the use of personal data obtained for one purpose (in relation to rents), and then disclosed to another part of the Data User for another purpose (in relation to staff recruitment). In fact **both purposes were registered**, so there was no legal problem as regards the Third Principle (if only one purpose had been registered (eg P021 but not P001), then there would have been a contravention of the Registration particulars, a criminal offence if done 'knowingly or recklessly').

4.2.4 A further issue in relation to this Case is whether the disclosure from one part of a Data User to another part can in any way breach the Third Principle. The Registrar's Guideline 6, paragraph B.3.1 clarifies the conditions that permit such disclosures: 'Disclosures by a data user to his employees or agents are exempt if the disclosure is made to enable them to perform their duties as employees or agents. Disclosures of this sort do not need to be shown in the data user's register entry'. Since the Departments of a Local Authority are not legally distinct (they jointly comprise the Data User) and the disclosure was to enable employees to perform their duties, registration of such disclosures between the Housing and Personnel Departments was not necessary.

4.2.5 An interesting aspect of Case A, as far as the Data Subject is concerned, is whether there was an infringement of the First Data Protection Principle. The Interpretation of this Principle in Schedule 1 Part II of the Act states that:

> '... in determining whether information was obtained fairly regard shall be had to the method by which it was obtained, including in particular whether any person from whom it was obtained was deceived or misled as to the purpose or purposes for which it is to be held, used or disclosed'.

4.2.6 Thus, if the Authority wishes to use tenants' 'Housing Management' personal data when such individuals apply for a job with the Authority, then this latter use should be referred to on the relevant 'Housing Management' forms (eg those that deal with rents), and explained to Data Subjects as part of the recruitment process. For example, job application forms could state 'If you are a tenant, the Authority reserves the right to examine tenancy records held by the Authority'. As a result of these considerations, and although the disclosure did not **have** to be registered, the Registrar requested the Local Authority to clarify and publicise the procedure in the relevant Register Entry.

4.2.7 Lastly it can also be argued that rent arrears should have no bearing on employment prospects, and that there is therefore no good reason for a Personnel Department to hold this information under Purpose P001 (ie a breach of the Fourth Principle). This issue is less clear cut, and hinges on whether 'being in rent arrears' can be equated with 'dishonesty', 'likely to be dishonest' or 'a security risk'. Even if the information itself is judged to be relevant, and not excessive to the Purpose, the fact is that the opposite view of rent arrears can also be defended; ie somebody who understands the problems of being in rent arrears could be well qualified to help the Authority, and tenants in arrears, to improve procedures for the collection of arrears. Additionally, an apparently 'honest' tenant, employed by the Authority, could decide to amend the system so as to escape paying rent, or be so 'sympathetic' to people in rent arrears as to amend their payment records in their favour.

4.2.8 Analysis of Case B depends on **when** the mailing list was used, for this determines whether or not there has been a lawful disclosure. For example if the Committee, **before** resigning, used the mailing list of branch members to inform members of the reasons for their intended action, then it is very likely that their action would be compatible with their functions as branch officials of the Union from which they were about to resign. If, however, the Committee resigned, and then a week later an ex-member of the Committee entered Union offices to secure a copy of the mailing list, then it can be argued that the disclosure of the personal data to an ex-union member was unauthorised.

4.2.9 There is a further aspect of the latter situation. Under the terms of the Eighth Data Protection Principle, the Union, as the Data User in this Case, is obliged to take appropriate security measures to protect the personal data from unauthorised access and unauthorised disclosure. If an ex-member of the Union can easily access personal data held by the Union, this is a clear breach of those security obligations. So whilst the individual who took a copy of the mailing list might be guilty of theft, or of damage following trespass, the Data Protection Act would bear on the Union for having lax security procedures. In addition, if damage was caused to a union member by the unauthorised disclosure, then compensation might have to be paid by the Union.

4.2.10 As shown with Cases C, the temptation to use or disclose personal data in order to cause embarrassment can be quite high, especially if there is a political context (note that in Case C(b) it is possible that information was obtained from a source that is publicly available: eg telephone directory, Electoral Register or the Extract of the Community Charges Register). Often such uses or disclosures result from a member of staff, or other person who has access to the personal data, making the 'connection' (eg a strong supporter of public health care is found to have a partner who uses private health care; vociferous opponents of a change to the secondary education system send their children to private schools; a public figure calls for a non-payment campaign and, in private, makes arrangements to pay).

4.2.11 Staff (this includes Councillors, Governors, Members of public sector Boards etc) need to be aware that such temptations should be resisted, as staff are the recipients of personal data (in the context of Section 34(6)(c) of the Data Protection Act) only in order to perform their official functions, eg for work purposes. As a result, any disclosure of personal data that is not for such a function would be unauthorised. Although elected members of public bodies may also have other obligations that allow a wider remit (eg investigating a complaint from a constituent), these circumstances should not be interpreted as providing a 'roving commission' that allows 'access to everything'; usually there are formal and established procedures to allow access to personal data (for details see Chapter 6, Section 3.4). Consequently, whilst in Case C(c) there are no legal restrictions to bar such Councillors from obtaining personal data via their own personal computer, there would clearly have to be stringent access controls to impose limits on such a practice.

Whether the use of such computers is prudent (there is a high risk that the Eighth Data Protection Principle can be breached when personal data are accessed in an insecure home environment) poses a further Data Protection problem.

4.2.12 Case D demonstrates the thin line that exists between disclosures that may be subject to the non-disclosure provisions (eg are authorised by statute), and an unauthorised disclosure. In this case, whether the disclosure to the Police was unauthorised will depend on whether the Police were ticked as a disclosure in the relevant Register Entry (a D341 Disclosure) or, if not, whether Section 28(3) of the Data Protection Act applied.

4.2.13 If a D341 Disclosure to the Police **has** been registered for any particular purpose, this ensures that the Third Data Protection Principle is not breached irrespective of which personal data, held for this purpose, are disclosed to the Police (note, however, that if Data Subjects have not been alerted to this then the Data User could be accused of contravening the First Principle). If a D341 Disclosure has **not** been registered, the issue depends on whether the disclosure was for 'the prevention or detection of crime; the apprehension or prosecution of offenders; or the assessment or collection of any tax or duty', and whether it could justifiably be claimed that not disclosing the data 'would be likely to prejudice' any of these matters. Given that an industrial dispute with a Local Authority is not a crime, attention would focus on the internal procedures used by the Inland Revenue's management to ensure that the disclosure was for 'the prevention or detection of crime; the apprehension or prosecution of offenders'. For example, did the Revenue keep records of the circumstances surrounding the disclosure; if so, what was recorded?

4.2.14 If the procedures that allow disclosures to the Police via Section 28(3) are inadequate, there are grounds for asserting that this non-disclosure exemption does not apply. Thus, without formal records, there is no means of demonstrating (if necessary to a Court) that a disclosure of personal data was for one of the purposes specified in Section 28 of the Act. As a result, if the disclosure was also not indicated in the Register Entry, and was made in full knowledge of these circumstances, then the Data User or the specific employee concerned would be liable to prosecution. In the worst case (say the unauthorised disclosure led to the arrest or detention of an individual, who in turn lost employment, or a contract, or some business etc), this could result in damages being awarded by a Court, against the Data User, under Section 23 of the Act.

4.2.15 Case E relates to a telephone disclosure which led to a harrowing event; if ever there was a story that preached caution when being helpful over the phone, it is this one. Surprisingly, however, there is a good chance that the disclosure would not be punished by the Courts. This is because the Data User (in this case a Health Authority) would very likely have registered a disclosure of this nature in order to inform close relatives about the location, or the condition of the patient. In this event, the Data User would have a defence under Section 23(2) of the Act, as the disclosure appears in a Register Entry. Furthermore, if the disclosure did not appear in the Entry, the Health Authority could claim (although subject to the considerations below) that in normal circumstances it had 'reasonable grounds' for believing that a disclosure to a worried husband would have the consent of his wife (see Section 34(6)(d)).

4.2.16 Disclosures of personal data during a telephone call present one of the most difficult areas of judgement. To be totally uncooperative and withhold all personal data could frustrate callers who have genuine problems, and exacerbate an already difficult situation; to be too helpful could result in serious damage to customers and clients whose personal data should be protected. It is the Data User's duty to achieve the difficult balance between these options, and to train staff to be aware that before information is provided to a caller, that caller has to be properly identified. If there is any doubt over identification, there should be no disclosure of personal data. Many Data Users (including some banks) have decided that the only safe option is not to disclose any personal data (eg about customer accounts) over the telephone.

4.2.17 In the Hospital case, the staff on the central switchboard usually have access to a list of all patients who have been admitted. The computer system could have a data field to indicate that a patient's details were not to be disclosed to callers, in which case the system would not display the patient's personal data on the list. Reception staff, on receipt of a request for information concerning a patient not on the list, should be trained to take the details of the caller (eg name and telephone number), and to pass them on to an administrator who could evaluate the situation (eg discover whether the patient was in hospital and, if so, to ascertain the patient's wishes). Patients could be asked, during the routine admission procedure, whether they wished their presence in the Hospital to be disclosed (eg some patients in certain specialist wards might want the fact that they were in hospital to be kept confidential). Those who were unconscious on admission could have the data field completed, as appropriate, following an assessment of how their injuries were obtained (but always with the emphasis on 'when in doubt, do not disclose'). Thus following a traffic accident it could be assumed that consent would be given (to allow details to be disclosed to distressed relatives), whilst following a deliberate and violent attack on an individual, where the attack could be repeated (as in the case of attempted murder), it would be wiser to assume that consent would be withheld. The field could be changed when the patient had sufficiently recovered to take a decision. Although this procedure is not perfect with respect to unconscious patients, its objective is to obtain, wherever possible, the Data Subject's consent to the disclosure of personal data that relate to their health.

5. Fourth Principle: adequacy and relevance

5.1 Case histories

5.1.1 Case A

'A word processor operator has been made to feel like a criminal by a shop chain and their computerised financial snoopers. When Mrs X of Redhill in Surrey decided to buy a three-piece suite at a store in Croydon she applied for a charge card, but was informed by the chain that she was not creditworthy and her application had been refused. 'I was stunned', she says, 'my bank account was clear and neither I nor my husband have ever been in debt'.

She complained to the shop and was told that credit applications were checked by a firm in Nottingham, a leading direct mail company, and that she was entitled by law to see a print-out of the information on her - which she did. 'From the print-out, the only reason I'd been refused credit was the fact that the people who had lived in our house before us had had a county court judgement against them'. I was very upset, I began to worry that I'd be refused credit everywhere', says Mrs X.' (from Computer Talk, 11.5.87).

5.1.2 Case B

'The Commission on Racial Equality is to launch an investigation into discrimination against blacks at one of Britain's leading medical schools, it was disclosed yesterday. The inquiry follows the Guardian's disclosure last month that the school was using a computer program which deliberately downgraded non-white applicants.

Two of its consultants (named in the Article) ran applications through the computer and found that being a non-Caucasian female lowered the applicant's ranking for interview by up to 20 points - probably enough to reject a candidate who would have been accepted on academic performance alone. The program was designed to mimic the decisions of the selection committee, which it replaced' (from The Guardian, 30.1.87).

5.1.3 Cases C

(a) 'When Mr. X, a resident of east London, sought the assistance of police in the departure terminal at Heathrow Airport, he received an unexpected response. He was arrested and locked up for three and a half hours. Mr. X was released - without apology, he says - and told it was a case of mistaken identity. Meanwhile his estranged wife, on whom he was attempting to enforce a court order, successfully flew his children out of the country' (from The Observer, 5.1.87).

(b) Mr. Y from Marlborough and Mr. Y from Somerset don't just have their names in common. They are both the same age, have brown hair, moustaches and are almost the same height. But one was wanted for motoring offences; the other wasn't and Police picked up the wrong man. It led to the Mr. Y from Marleborough losing his job, his savings and his car before being cleared of the charges by magistrates (from the Sunday Times, 10.1.88).

5.1.4 Case D

Early Day Motion 996 laid before Parliament in July 1988 drew attention to a British Gas policy of 'plussing up' customers estimated bills to an extreme, so that the formula used by British Gas to estimate bills was causing major distress.

5.1.5 Case E

Staff involved with delivering goods for a major company used a code BOD as a warning to 'Beware of the Dog'. The field was used to alert van drivers to be on guard should they deliver to a specific address. Unfortunately, a code BOB, ('Beware of Bastard') became the shorthand for 'awkward customers' (one of IPMC case studies).

5.2 Discussion

5.2.1 In all these cases there are procedural problems for management to solve. The grounds for complaint would be supplied by the Act's Fourth Data Protection Principle, which stipulates that the personal data shall be adequate, relevant and not excessive in the context of the purpose in question.

5.2.2 The denial of credit based solely on a person's address, as specified in Case A, is not the only data protection problem. For example, the Registrar's Fourth and Fifth Reports quoted the following instances which resulted in refusal of credit: records of houses in a road being out of date; the address of an individual with a record of debt having been incorrectly entered with the result that a person living at that address was refused credit; 'Walk' addresses had been confused with 'Lane' addresses; the credit details related to a stepson who had left his stepmother's address five years earlier. All these examples raise a fundamental query: whether information that relates to one person's address, circumstances or status can be relevant in determining the credit rating of another individual.

5.2.3 The result is an issue that the Registrar has taken very seriously; in fact early mention of credit referencing as a data protection problem appears in relation to a National Credit Register in his Third Report (June 1987, page 5). By May 1988 (five months after his powers to investigate substantial complaints came into effect) the Registrar was so concerned that he called a meeting of representatives of the Credit Industry to attempt to sort out the problems (Fourth Report, pages 5-9, give a comprehensive exposition of his concerns). The following year (Fifth Report, covering 1988/89) confirmed the trend; approximately 400 of the complaints during that period (35% of the total number of complaints) were about credit referencing. Although the Registrar indicated in the Fifth Report that the Industry had made some 'positive proposals', an impasse had been reached; he wrote that 'the industry takes the view that the way in which they process third party information is fair: I take the view it is not' (pages 6-8). Armed with advice from 'leading counsel' and the tacit support of the Office of Fair Trading (Fourth Report, page 6), he served Preliminary Notices on the four Credit Referencing Agencies in June 1990 (Sixth Report, page 6), by which time the number of complaints had risen to 450 per year (17% of the total number of complaints received). Formal Enforcement Notices were served by the Registrar in August that year, to take effect by 1st January 1993 (Appendix 1 contains comprehensive details of this data protection saga).

5.2.4 Case B relates to a recruitment procedure that was swayed by data on race and sex, and sends a warning in relation to any computer system that scores an individual's potential and then suggests the decision to be taken. With more and more expert systems becoming available (eg in relation to the care of patients) it is of fundamental importance in each case to ensure that, in relation to the purpose involved, the personal data processed are not only adequate but also relevant.

5.2.5 Evaluation of Cases C (a) and (b) depends on whether inadequate personal data were used to identify the individuals. Clearly the Police have a duty to act on suspicion, and to use all the information at their disposal. However, given the protestations of innocence by the innocent parties in both cases, the question arises as to whether the information used to identify them as guilty of offences was complete, or whether further details should have been checked much earlier, and certainly before arrests were effected. In both cases compensation for the damage suffered could only be considered (via Section 22(4) of the Act) if the personal data were judged to be inaccurate, or 'misleading as to any matter of fact' (eg because they were not adequate for correct identification).

5.2.6 Case D involves the extent to which it is proper to extrapolate from accurate personal data. According to the Motion laid before Parliament, a person's gas bill was estimated from previous consumption; if the personal data used in the algorithm are accurate, how far can the extrapolated result be relied upon to represent future consumption adequately?

5.2.7 Every model is only as good as the assumptions from which it is derived. For example, if winter temperatures are average, then it is safe to assume that gas consumption will be likewise. However if, as happened in the UK during the 1980s, extremes of cold and mildness were experienced during successive winters, then the safe tolerances of the underlying assumptions in the model can be exceeded.

5.2.8 If a model generates personal data under extreme conditions, the results could breach three Data Protection Principles: the First on the grounds that the model is processing personal data for predictive purposes in a way that is unfair to the individual; the Fourth on the grounds that the personal data are inadequate for use in the particular model; and the Fifth on the grounds that the personal data are inaccurate (and require updating).

5.2.9 Case E is an example of how irrelevant and/or excessive personal data can creep in, perhaps initially simply to amuse staff, or through the desire of staff 'to get their own back'. Whatever the temptation, staff should never pervert a valid and relevant warning code as the warning may then not be heeded. This assumes that the company can justify why BOD was entered in the first place, for example by having recorded when and where the incident involving the dog took place, the address where the incident took place, the identity of the particular delivery driver and the breed of dog. Codes that can be categorised as offensive can lead to breaches of the Fifth Principle (see the analysis of Case C in paragraphs 6.1.3, 6.2.8 and 6.2.9 below). Wherever possible, the design of database software, especially when codes are being entered, should always validate the code against a list of possible codes authorised for use in specific circumstances.

6. Fifth Principle: accuracy

6.1 Case histories

6.1.1 Case A

> 'Britain's new breast cancer screening programme - aimed at saving 2,000 lives a year - could be at risk because of low take-up in some city areas. Thousands of letters inviting women to have breast X-rays for the early detection of cancer are being sent to the wrong address, experts said last week'. A consultant radiologist said 'Almost a third of letters we send out go to patients who have moved' (from The Observer, 2.7.89).

6.1.2 Case B

> 'Worried hospital doctors sent a call to a Computer Company's bosses last week with this grim warning: 'Fix our computers before someone dies'. The

mercy plea follows months of complaints and letters from angry doctors who have been waiting over a year to get the £300,000 system working' (from Datalink, 23.3.87). Two years later, the same newspaper reported a comment by a pathology consultant to the effect that the medical computer, once dubbed a potential 'patient killer', was 'working better than it was before but we still have repeated ups and downs with it' (from Datalink, 30.1.89).

6.1.3 Case C

A London-based systems engineer, returning from Los Angeles, saw the VDU screen when he inquired about some lost luggage belonging to his fiancee. He noticed that it contained details about all the comments he had made, such as 'Pax (passenger) said do something constructive', 'Pax hung up phone', 'Pax obnoxious' and requested the full information. This request was denied and, when Subject Access was invoked, he was informed the information had been deleted (from Computing, 12.1.89).

6.1.4 Cases D

(a) Professor X, the distinguished scientist 'whose tragic death was reported in the Sun last Monday, spoke cheerfully enough to the Guardian yesterday'. The story revolves around how an obituary announcement of the death of Professor X was the result of a case of mistaken identity (from The Guardian, 10.6.89).

(b) Following the European elections, a computer was instructed to change 'each occurrence of the word Poll, into Turnout'. As a result, a successful candidate in the elections was printed 'as Ms A J Turnoutack, rather than Ms A J Pollack' (from The Guardian, 21.6.89).

(c) A database of crimes got mixed up with the personal data associated with traffic offences, with the result that around 41,000 Parisians received, instead of details of their traffic offences, summonses with respect to extortion, drug trafficking and prostitution (from The Guardian, 6.9.89).

6.1.5 Case E

'I am told that the director general of the Security Service of the day regularly advises an incoming Prime Minister... there was the rather hilarious case when he was advised not to continue the ministerial career of the Rt. Hon. Member for Plymouth, Devonport (Dr Owen). This turned out to be a confusion between a David Owen and a Will Owen' (from Hansard, col 189, 17.1.89).

6.1.6 Case F

Inaccurate and incomplete police computer files on defendants' previous convictions are forcing London Courts to make bail and sentencing decisions on the basis of wrong information (from The Guardian, 23.4.88). Defendants are being sentenced on the basis of criminal records which are in a 'terrifying state of inaccuracy', the Commons Home Affairs Committee was told last night. A former senior Crown prosecutor said 'criminal records are not being kept up to date ... which cannot be in the interests of justice' (from the Times, 22.2.90).

6.1.7 Cases G

(a) Because of insufficient computer space, the price changes were recorded as whole numbers only and the decimal places were not carried forward. Pensioners will be compensated for rather more than the actual loss that they have suffered (the reason for an error in the calculation of the old-age pension, from Hansard, col 1382, 18.12.87).

(b) Mrs X was prescribed one radiation treatment for cancer in 1982, but through human error she was given a second course which resulted in an overdose (from The Guardian, 29.3.90).

6.2 **Discussion**

6.2.1 The background to Case A includes the fact that, in the UK, every year, approximately 28,000 women will discover that they have cancer of the breast or cervix. In 1985, the mortality figures for England and Wales, published by the Government, showed that 13,500 women died of breast cancer and just under 2,000 women died of cancer of the cervix. The results of several medical research programmes in Europe show that the mortality rate for breast cancer can be reduced by 35%, and that of cervical cancer by 91%, if early diagnosis of the pre-cancerous state can be made. In UK terms, a well-organised scheme which can remind women to visit their doctor for a smear test, or to attend a breast screening centre for a simple examination, could save nearly 7,000 lives a year.

6.2.2 Consequently, the Government started the process of setting up a computerised call or recall system, in every District Health Authority, by March 1988. The essential specification of a recall system for both screening programmes is quite simple: it has to identify and categorise patients, send the patient a letter to encourage her to go for an appointment, monitor whether the appointment is kept and send a reminder letter if it is not, and be capable of keeping statistics for management purposes to show the take-up of the service.

6.2.3 As indicated in the Case history there is a problem with keeping addresses up to date, and the Data Protection Act should encourage more rigorous procedures to improve the accuracy of addresses. The reason for this is that, depending on the circumstances, an inaccurate address could make a Health Authority vulnerable to claims for damages under Section 22 of the Act.

6.2.4 For example, suppose a woman notifies a General Practitioner of a change of address and subsequently does not receive an invitation for cervical cancer screening, and suppose also that a cancerous state develops. In such a case, where it is medically proven that the prognosis for the successful treatment of cervical cancer in its pre-cancerous state is excellent, the only defence against damages would be to demonstrate that the Health Authority 'had taken such care as in all the circumstances was reasonably required to ensure the accuracy of the data at the material time' (Section 22(3) of The Act). If a Court is satisfied that the procedures for passing that new address from the GP to the recall scheme were unreliable, then the Court may determine that there is an entitlement to damages. Because of the differing mortality rate, this argument may not be so clear cut with respect to breast cancer.

6.2.5 With respect to Case B, a catalogue of lost records and mixed-up files led doctors to use manual methods for rushing vital blood test results to surgeons, and laboratory staff refused to use the system for fear that patients' lives could be lost if its software was ever relied upon. A senior consultant (named in the 1987 Article) said: 'If we used this system it could endanger patient care very seriously. It's scandalous - patients' lives are at risk yet no one has bothered to turn up here despite promises they would repair the system.' The remarks, two years later, by another consultant that he was still unhappy with the system can hardly inspire confidence.

6.2.6 This Case highlights the vulnerability of Data Users if they are deemed to have sanctioned the prolonged use of inaccurate personal data. For example, Section 22(3) of the Act states:

> 'In proceedings brought against any person by virtue of this section it shall be a defence to prove that he had taken such care as in all the circumstances was reasonably required to ensure the accuracy of the data at the material time.'

6.2.7 Mounting such a defence is going to prove difficult if, in a particular situation, doctors have for a period of years gone on public record to say 'continued use could endanger patient care' or the equivalent. The moral is: if a deficiency in a procedure is brought to a Data User's attention, management needs to assess the risks and priorities involved, decide what needs to be done, and act accordingly.

6.2.8 Case C raises a number of issues with respect to personal data that constitute opinions about Data Subjects. In summary, the facts which substantiate the opinions should also be recorded; the relevance of the opinions, at the material times, should be clear; and the sources of the opinions should be known.

6.2.9 Case C draws attention to several potential breaches of the Data Protection Principles. These relate to: (a) accurately recording what the customer said (Fifth Principle); (b) relevance of the recorded personal data to the problem reported by the passenger, and whether these data are excessive in this context (Fourth Principle); (c) the length of time for which the personal data relating to the enquiry will be retained (Sixth Principle); (d) the effect on customer-client relations following the disclosure of personal data under the Subject Access provisions (Seventh Principle). The Case shows that even when a Data Subject has demonstrated irritation or aggression, a complaint to the Data Protection Registrar might well carry weight with respect to several Principles.

6.2.10 Bad publicity, even if jokingly presented, as in all the Cases D, is not helpful in establishing a public image of professionalism or competence. Obituary information (Case D(a)) is now regularly maintained as personal data by the media, with the result that Subject Access becomes a possibility. If such personal data are inaccurately attributed to a **living** individual, and cause damage when published, then compensation can be claimed via Section 22 of the Act (by the living Data Subject, but not by the relatives of the deceased, as Section 22(1) says that the individual who suffers damage has to be 'the subject of personal data', and Section 1(3) defines personal data as 'information which relates to a living individual'). The unauthorised disclosure of personal data (ie printing an obituary notice) could lead to damages via Section 23. Cases D(b) and (c) show how inadequately defined instructions, whose consequences were overlooked (eg changing all occurrences of Poll to Turnout; mixing up two databases, perhaps because they have similar names and structure) can have the effect of making personal data inaccurate.

6.2.11 If, as in Case E, the personal data are held by the Security Service, Section 27 of the Data Protection Act can remove any claim for compensation, although it is possible that the Security Service Commission, established by the Security Service Act 1989, could help redress any problem. Note, however, the further damage that such errors can cause; they provide ammunition for detractors (eg 'if the Service has problems with information relating to an MP, how accurate are the personal data which relate to lesser mortals'), and can lead to loss of confidence by supporters.

6.2.12 All these issues seem to come together in Case F. The newspaper reports point to major problems with the accuracy of criminal records, and to the consequent damage to Data Subjects affected by the Criminal Justice system (eg the inability to get bail); there is nothing more serious than to deny a person their liberty. At a time when the Criminal Justice system is under review, inability to keep personal data accurate just adds to the problems facing the Police. It is clear that if a Data Subject can prove damage (eg having lost a job because of inaccurate criminal personal data), then there would be a strong case for compensation under the Act. Even when damage is not caused, the Registrar can intervene in respect of the Fifth Principle.

6.2.13 Cases G(a) and (b) provide a timely reminder that the design of hardware and software is an important component in maintaining the integrity and accuracy of personal data, and that the Data Protection Act can cover personal data held on a variety of electronic equipment. Thus programs or electronic equipment which degrade personal data will become subject to Section 22, with the result that the Data User could find the relevant quality assurance controls and design procedures being tested in a Court. If there are no formal records of software design quality checks, or of the standard performance parameters of the electronic equipment, it could prove difficult to establish the defence of having acted with 'such care as in all the circumstances was reasonably required'.

6.2.14 If Case G(a) proved serious enough to be debated in Court, the argument could focus on whether it was reasonable to use integer variables for pension calculations. As most computer trainees know (usually from bitter experience), the result of any integer arithmetic is limited by a maximum possible integer value (eg 2^n-1 where n, depending on the make of computer, is usually 16, 32, 48 or 64). Since integer division results in the loss of decimal places, it could be claimed in Court that the inevitable round-off errors should have been avoided during the design of the software. If the equipment involved in Case G(b) actually processed personal data, it could be argued that the data entry procedures (ie those setting up the patient's radiation dose) were not rigorous enough to maintain the accuracy of personal data (ie the accuracy of the patient's radiation dose). In addition, in both Cases, there could be grounds for examining whether the use of equipment or program with inaccurate personal data constituted 'unfair processing' in breach of the First Principle.

7. Fourth and Fifth Principles: vetting

7.1 Case histories

7.1.1 Case A

A woman applied for a special fostering programme in a Scottish Authority, who then checked her application against Police records. The Police provided information relating to minor offences, committed 40 years earlier by someone who had the same name and 'appeared to be identical' with the woman. Unfortunately, the Scottish Authority failed to check the validity of these old records. In fact, the applicant had been misidentified, and wanted to claim compensation from the Police on the grounds that the personal data they had disclosed were inaccurate. The Police took the view that the personal data were accurate insofar that they applied to somebody else, although not to the woman concerned (from The Guardian, 8.10.86).

7.1.2 Case B

'Over 115,000 personal records held on police computer files have been checked in the 18 months since local authorities were given wider powers to vet people applying for jobs in child care' (from Computer Weekly, 17.3.88).

7.1.3 Case C

Controls designed to prevent convicted abusers from working with children are leading to people being refused jobs because of minor, irrelevant offences. In one case a part-time worker lost her job following the disclosure of a conviction for growing a cannabis plant thirteen years ago; another case referred to an Oxford undergraduate who lost a temporary maths teaching post due to a caution for criminal damage over a schoolboy prank; and a man lost a job as a bus driver when a conviction in 1969 for importuning became known (from The Guardian, 26.9.88).

7.2 Discussion

7.2.1 With respect to Case A, the outcome as regards compensation can be summarised thus:

(a) there is no possible claim for compensation under the Data Protection Act against the Scottish Authority;

(b) there is no possible claim for compensation under the Data Protection Act against the Police.

7.2.2 The Authority is 'in the clear' because it did not 'hold' personal data on the woman or cause them to be 'processed'; it received information on paper about a woman with the same name. The Authority was, therefore, not a Data User with respect to the personal data, but merely the recipient of information extracted from personal data held by the Police. Even if the Authority did transfer the personal data to a personnel system, then as long as the Authority had accurately recorded the data, together with a marker that identified the data as having been received from a third party (in accordance with the defence outlined in Section 22(2)(a) of the Act), the entitlement to compensation would not apply.

7.2.3 Neither was the Police liable to pay compensation because:

(a) if the applicant was 'damaged', this occurred before the Act's relevant provisions took effect;

(b) the applicant might not have been 'damaged' although undoubtedly she suffered distress. Damage has to be something tangible which can be assessed by a Court;

(c) the Police maintained that it was reasonable to expect the Authority to check the information with the job applicant, to ensure that a mistake was not being made;

(d) there is a strong case for regarding the data as being accurate (with respect to another individual of the same name).

7.2.4 Re (d) above, the legal argument contends that the personal data are accurate but that they have been misapplied via wrong identification, and that this is not equivalent to the use of personal data which are factually inaccurate. Note that Section 22(1) of the Act states that damage must be suffered 'by reason of the inaccuracy of the data'. Hence the relevant question for a Court in assessing whether compensation could be awarded would be: 'Can the mistaken application of accurate personal data make the data inaccurate?'.

7.2.5 The Police had, in fact, provided the information with the disclaimer that Mrs X, whose details were drawn from Police records, 'appeared to be identical with' the Mrs X who was applying to the Authority; this wording should have alerted the Authority to the need to check the identity of the applicant before making use of the information. The Police could thus argue that, under the circumstances, they themselves had acted reasonably.

7.2.6 In summary, what the Authority did was to ask the Police 'Have you a Mrs X on file?', to which the Police replied 'Yes we have a Mrs X on file: here are the details which seem to correspond with your request'. Improvements that could be made in this situation are for the Police to emphasise more strongly that the information might relate to somebody else, and for the Authority to implement procedures to ensure that the data relate to the relevant person.

7.2.7 Case B and Case C show that whilst vetting is necessary for the protection of children, it is also necessary to exercise any vetting sensitively. Following the errors that occurred, the relevant Home Office Circular was amended (HOC 102/88), to include safeguards and procedures designed to mitigate some of the effects of the disclosure of Police records. The Circular suggests that:

(a) the nature of the job should be evaluated: is there one-to-one contact with young children? is the position supervised? is the position an isolated one? is there regular contact with children? are the children particularly vulnerable?

(b) the relevance of the conviction should be evaluated: what is the nature of the conviction? what is the nature of the appointment? when did the offence occur? what was the frequency of the offence?

7.2.8 In addition, the Circular suggests that vetting should be open; for example if there is a disagreement between the vetting and the information provided by the prospective employee 'the local authority **must** discuss the discrepancy with the person before reaching a decision to appoint' (paragraph 19 of HOC 102/88). To minimise the number of people checked against police records, the Circular states that 'requests for checking must not therefore be made when interview short lists are being drawn up, but only when the final candidate has been selected and in respect of that candidate alone' (paragraph 10). Finally, on appointment the 'information should be destroyed' (paragraph 20: if the information was retained as personal data, there would be a breach the Fourth Data Protection Principle), and only 'a senior nominated officer' (paragraph 22) should be responsible for making requests to Police Forces.

8. Sixth Principle: retaining personal data

8.1 Case histories

8.1.1 Case A

'The Metropolitan police turned down an application for a clerical job from a man (aged 37) who worked for them as a groundsman partly because he stole £1 when he was a 13-year-old schoolboy, an industrial tribunal in London heard yesterday' (from The Guardian, 31.7.85).

8.1.2 Case B

Harry Cohen MP in a debate on computer records reported the case of a 'man stopped by the police, who were able to discover that he had stolen a bottle of milk 22 years earlier when he was a teenager' (from Hansard, 20.2.87).

8.1.3 Case C

'A Private has been remanded in custody suspected of deserting from the British Army no less than 20 years ago - thanks to the vigilance of the Police National Computer which holds a file of 50,000 wanted and missing persons. The length of time that a wanted person is held on the computer files 'varies with the circumstances', said a spokesman for New Scotland Yard, 'but generally we keep them on file until they would be about 75 years old' (from Datalink, 28.7.78).

8.1.4 Case D

'The Data Protection Registrar has upheld a complaint from Brighton Borough Council that personal data collected for the Conservative Party Conference in October 1988 was obtained unfairly. ...However, the data collected by Sussex Police will not be destroyed. It will be made available to police forces covering other conference venues and may be stored on computer for a 'prolonged period' (from a press release, Brighton Borough Council, 26.5.89).

8.2 **Discussion**

8.2.1 In relation to the length of time Police records are kept, the Minister told Parliament (Hansard, 20.2.87):

'There are different criteria for different types of offence. I will deal first with the criteria for recordable offences - those offences which can lead to a sentence of imprisonment. The criteria for those offences provide that records will normally be weeded, where offenders have not been prosecuted for an offence of this kind for 20 years since their last conviction, whatever the number of convictions before that. There are exceptions to this 20-year rule, where retaining information on offenders seems justifiable, for example to help in the investigation of major crime. Records are not, therefore, deleted if they include evidence of mental illness; indecency; offences of homicide; and custodial sentences of more than six months. I must stress that records which are kept in this way are, of course, confidential like other police records, and access to them is limited in the same way.'

8.2.2 The Minister continued:

'The police have concluded, on the basis of their operational experience, that they need to keep a record of an individual for 20 years after his or her last conviction for a recordable offence. They consider that many offenders may well commit further offences during that 20-year period, particularly if the first offence was committed early in life, and that that information needs to be readily available to them - I stress, available to the police, not anybody else - during the whole of that time. But the revised criteria recognised public concern that an individual should not be prejudiced by youthful misdemeanour. Under the previous criteria, no records of anyone under 40 were weeded, irrespective of the length of time since that offender had been convicted. Now, the criteria provide that the record of an offender is normally to be removed after 20 years irrespective of his or her age'.

8.2.3 Note that the Minister does not rely on a statutory duty to justify the Police keeping records for particular lengths of time, but cities reasons based on the Police's operational experience. The latter can be challenged by the Registrar, if cases like the ones mentioned above are found, and since Cases A and B are outside the 20 year rule, the Registrar could order the data's deletion from active files. Clearly advice that might have applied in the late 1970s (as exemplified by Case C) is now incorrect; the Police, in common with all Data Users, have to be prepared to defend how long personal data are held.

8.2.4 Case D calls for a very difficult balancing act. It is important, bearing in mind the bomb outrage at Brighton which almost killed several Cabinet Ministers, that the Police obtain information (and retain it for many years) on individuals who do not necessarily have criminal records, in order to secure a Conference Centre, issue I.D. cards, vet conference and hotel staff, supervise conference events and perhaps identify those who may be planning a similar attack. On the other hand, the situation cannot provide carte-blanche to allow the Police the unrestricted collection, use and retention of personal data on individuals who visit, or plan to visit a town, on the grounds that for three days a year it plays host to a political party conference.

8.2.5 When the Registrar investigated a complaint from the Council, he dealt with concern in relation to four Principles:

(a) the First Principle: on the grounds that the personal data were collected without adequate explanation to Data Subjects, notably without alerting them to the fact that the personal data would be disclosed to other Police Forces on the conference circuit (the provisions in Section 28(4), which provide the Police with a dispensation from the First Principle, only apply to personal data used for the purpose of prevention or detection of crime etc if a test of prejudice can be satisfied, ie if explanations to Data Subjects would prejudice conference safety in this instance);

(b) the Fourth Principle: concerning which the Registrar was advised that the Police had already substantially reduced the amount of information they needed to collect;

(c) the Sixth Principle: relating to the length of time the personal data were retained, which the Registrar would be discussing further with a view to agreeing specified retention periods and criteria for the deletion of the personal data;

(d) the Eighth Principle: regarding appropriate security for the conference data, with which the Registrar expressed general satisfaction, whilst pointing out that he would seek to ensure, through further consultation with the Forces concerned, that access controls and levels of authorisation would be wholly consistent with each other in the future (as well as with the full, written, explanations to each interviewee which he was recommending in order to ensure compliance with the First Principle).

8.2.6 In summary, if circumstances are special then the personal data involved should similarly be treated as special. If the purpose is to guard against terrorist attack, it is reasonable to expect that the personal data would not be processed for purposes other than policing a conference, and that the personal data would not be integrated into other, more routine, Police information systems. It is also reasonable to expect that only authorised officers, who have a bona-fide function with respect to policing a conference, would use the personal data. Thus the problems surrounding this collection of personal data could be mitigated by enhanced procedures for authorised access, disclosure, and alteration (ie strengthened procedures with respect to the Eighth Data Protection Principle).

9. Seventh Principle: subject access, deletion and correction

9.1 Case histories

9.1.1 Cases A

(a) The complainant made Subject Access requests to two Health Authorities. One Authority provided a copy of the personal data whilst the other claimed the Subject Access exemption for Health personal data (Case 4, Section A3, Data Protection Registrar's Fifth Report).

(b) The complainant made a Subject Access request to a University. The Data Subject sent three letters in all, but the University claimed only to have received one letter. In another Case, a Local Authority failed to respond to a request. In both Cases, the Data Subject complained that the 40 day limit had been exceeded (Cases 5 and 6, Section A3, Data Protection Registrar's Fifth Report).

9.1.2 Case B

The Data Protection Act is being abused by employers who are using it to check up on the background of prospective employees (from Computing, 21.7.88). Of the 165 Subject Access requests made to Lancashire Constabulary the majority were made by taxi drivers on the insistence of Local Authorities who were using the personal data to vet whether taxi drivers had a criminal record, before allowing them a hackney-carriage or private hire licence (from Computing, 1.12.88).

9.1.3 Cases C

(a) A complainant was refused credit in a store. Following an Access request, she discovered that the reason why she did not receive credit was because her estranged husband had defaulted on loan repayments some 5 years ago, and was still recorded as living at her home address (one of IPMC's case studies).

(b) A complainant made a request to see her credit reference file when she was refused a bank loan. She discovered that the file contained a judgement entered against her stepson in 1987, even though the stepson had left her home three years earlier (Case 3, Section A3, Data Protection Registrar's Fifth Report).

9.1.4 Case D

'We see no reason why employers should be unable to use the services of organisations that compile information that may be helpful when selecting suitable employees' (a Minister's view of the vetting of employees using information on manual files; Employment Bill, Official Report of Standing Committee D, col 113, 20.2.90).

9.2 **Discussion**

9.2.1 Cases A(a) and (b) demonstrate the importance of keeping full copies of all correspondence and of keeping the documentary records which relate to each Subject Access request. The reason for this is simple: they may be needed to show the Data Protection Registrar (and possibly the Courts under Section 25(2) of the Data Protection Act) how the Data User complied with the request. If the Data Subject who complains can provide copies of repeated correspondence, but the Data User has no record of its receipt, this fact alone suggests that the Data User's procedures for dealing with Subject Access are at fault.

9.2.2 All Subject Access requests should be seen as part of a potentially larger legal process, which **begins** with the provision, by the Data User, of a certified copy of personal data to the Data Subject. Retaining a copy of all the information provided to the Data Subject will therefore be vital, as the individual may prove to have a grievance against the Data User, and may be using the Subject Access request as only the first planned step in seeking redress.

9.2.3 Formal record keeping is especially important if a Subject Access exemption is being relied upon. A complaint to the Registrar that a breach of the Seventh Principle has taken place, could be the consequence of the Data Subject expecting, and not receiving, a specific item of personal data (or even merely a ploy to put the Data User on the defensive). The Data User could then have to provide evidence on how any decision to withhold personal data was reached (or to defend the method through which all relevant personal data were identified). Thus in Case A(a) attention would focus on how one Health Authority concluded that to proceed with the Subject Access request was likely to cause serious harm to the health of the Data Subject (via the terms of the exemption in Statutory Instrument 1987 No. 1903; see Chapter 7, Section 4.4). In other words, if the Data User faces investigation as to why the exemption was applied, the absence of records of how that decision was taken could constitute an insuperable handicap.

9.2.4 Case B outlines how the right of Subject Access can be exercised in a perverse but perfectly legitimate way: Data Subjects have to exercise the right of Access not on behalf of themselves, but on behalf of a third party to whom they are beholden (in this Case an employer who may hire them or a Local Authority who controls the issuing of taxi licences). No doubt there are strong arguments for the validity of the process: security firms may want to confirm that they are not hiring a person with a criminal record, whilst Local Authorities will, for instance, want to protect women passengers by not providing convicted sex offenders with taxi licences.

9.2.5 However justifiable the cause (and the practice is extendable to many other instances (eg access to Social Services records before providing a bank loan, insurance, employment etc), the Data Protection Registrar has condemned this abuse of the right of Subject Access in his Fifth Report (Review, Section B 2.8). Stating that 'I do not believe this is a proper use of the Act', the Registrar recommended that the procedure 'should be prohibited with a criminal sanction' and called for Parliament to specifically legislate in those areas where criminal records require verification as a condition of employment or for the granting of a licence.

9.2.6 In Guidance Note 21 ('The use of the Subject Access provisions of the Data Protection Act to check the criminal records of applicants for jobs or licences'), the Registrar raises several problems. For example, the spirit of the Rehabilitation of Offenders Act may be broken, as a Subject Access request to a Police computer may reveal details of offences that are spent under the terms of that Act (see paragraph 8.2.1 above which shows that Police keep personal data for about 20 years). In addition, the vetting procedure itself could be unfair to the individual, as there is generally no right to be involved if the personal data are interpreted in a way detrimental to the Data Subject (in contrast to those procedures that apply when individuals are vetted for employment that involves contact with young children; see paragraph 7.2.8 above).

9.2.7 The Registrar has also indicated that the vetting process could be misleading, as the details of some convictions may not be personal data and hence not available via Subject Access (ie they are held on microfiche or manual files), or the Police may withhold personal data in accordance with Section 28(1) of the Data Protection Act (as prejudicial to 'the prevention or detection of crime; the apprehension or prosecution of offenders'). Thus the absence of manual information or some personal data could lead to a false sense of security, especially as the Police may find it necessary to withhold certain details about a Data Subject who they believe is about to commit a crime.

9.2.8 Cases C(a) and (b) illustrate the potential minefield that a Data User can enter following the release of personal data. In both instances, Data Subjects were denied credit because of personal data which actually related to the activity of an estranged partner or family member (ie another Data Subject). Note that via Section 34(3) of the Data Protection Act these Access requests for personal data consisting of credit information would have been treated as requests made under Section 158 of the Consumer Credit Act 1974.

9.2.9 As such circumstances can revive private and even traumatic events (and give one estranged partner leverage over the other), it is not surprising to discover that, according to the Registrar's Seventh Report that for the year ending May 1991, 31% of all complaints he received related in some way to consumer credit (see paragraph 5.2.3 of this Chapter for further statistics).

9.2.10 It is the Seventh Principle which provides Data Subjects with the right to have relevant personal data corrected or erased 'for ensuring compliance with the other data protection principles' (via the Interpretation of the Seventh Principle in Schedule 1 of the Act). As regards the First Principle, credit reference agencies and the Data Protection Registrar are in disagreement as to whether the processing of personal data about one individual, which relates the results of that processing to another individual, is 'fair'. (See Appendix 1 for the complete story of the enforcement action to date).

9.2.11 There are also potential breaches of other Data Protection Principles. Under the provisions of the Fourth Principle, are personal data about one Data Subject relevant to the purpose of giving credit to another Data Subject? Under the Sixth Principle, how long can personal data that relate to one Data Subject be retained for assessing the credit reference status of another Data Subject? There may be also grounds for complaint under the Fifth Data Protection Principle, as many credit reference agencies buy copies of the Electoral Register to enable them to link names with specific addresses. If the latest Electoral Register indicates the absence of the individual whose details are taken into account in 'scoring' the creditworthiness of the Data Subject, it can be argued that reliance on the previous Register constitutes failure to keep personal data up to date.

9.2.12 Case D brings in the topic of 'Blacklists', and the avoidance of Subject Access by keeping sensitive personal information in a form that cannot be processed automatically, and therefore outwith the provisions of the Data Protection Act. However, quite apart from any moral objections, it is prudent to point out that in the UK there is a continuing trend towards Subject Access to manual files (already achieved to a far wider degree in some other countries), and that access to social work, education and housing records, to medical health reports and to health records is a reality. As the European Commission have proposed a Directive on Data Protection that includes structured manual files (see Chapter 9, Section 4), it would be shortsighted in the extreme to design a personal information base on the assumption that access to personal information **of all kinds** will never happen.

9.2.13 Whilst the Minister addresses the argument whether it can be right for legislation to prohibit the seeking of advice on the type, character or reliability of an individual who is about to be employed, this argument to some extent misses the point. Legalising Subject Access to manual records need in no way restrict employers from using the information. What it would attempt to do, of course, is to ensure that any documentary information that an employer uses in making an assessment of an individual would be open to challenge, scrutiny, and possible correction.

10. Eighth Principle: security of personal data

10.1 Case histories

10.1.1 Case A : Untrained staff; no back-up

> 'Doctors have lost all their research work, including data on patients' illnesses, following a break-in at a Manchester hospital. Last week, thieves stole an IBM PC AT from the department of medicine in the research and teaching block at the hospital in Manchester. They took hard disks containing research data on gastro-enteritis and have so far failed to return them, despite an appeal by the doctors. Dr X, consultant physician in the department of medicine, commented: "Most of our data was on the hard disks and we hadn't got round to making back-up copies".' (from Computing, 25.6.87).

10.1.2 Case B : Unauthorised disclosure

'The Ministry of Defence has apparently fallen foul of the Data Protection Act - after a secondhand microcomputer containing personnel records of its staff was bought from a surplus store. An Oxford Polytechnic student bought the micro, previously used by the MOD's secret Royal Signals and Radar Establishment (RSRE), from a shop in Oxford for £45. It is reported that the machine's hard disk contained detailed information of the backgrounds, views and work of RSRE staff, and the machines were recently replaced and sold off in a public auction at Hereford - apparently without the hard disk-based files being wiped.' (from Computing, 26.3.87).

10.1.3 Case C : Poor security procedures

'A top-level blunder allowed a computer journalist to penetrate British Telecom's Prestel information system, a court was told yesterday. A secret identification code which allowed access to secret files was left unprotected within the computer system. It was alleged that he typed an experimental line of numbers, all twos, when the computer asked for a ten-digit identification (2222222222). It worked, and the computer then asked for a four-digit password. He typed 1234 which turned out to be a test account and gave access to the private Prestel telephone numbers.' (from The Times, 16.4.86).

10.1.4 Case D : Unauthorised access to data

'Office worker Miss X was pale and shaking as she put down the telephone. She was baffled by the bizarre conversation in which an anonymous caller had just revealed many personal details about her life which the 21-year-old Miss X thought no one knew. Her shock grew to terror over the next four months as she received up to 50 similar calls a day at home and at the computer manufacturing firm where she worked. The caller recited her social security number, her driving licence number, facts about her previous three jobs, where she rented furniture and how much she owed on a car loan. The caller even told her she was going to die.' (from the Sunday Express, 16.6.85).

10.1.5 Case E : Disposal of printout

'Police have arrested a 50-year-old former army warrant officer, now working in a hospital, after a series of rapes of women believed to have been selected from a hospital computer list.' (from The Times, 12.6.85).

10.1.6 Case F : Unauthorised alteration to data

'The Superintendent was in charge of a Midlands Police station, and clearly rather ill-liked by his staff. So one unusually inventive member of the plod entered the super's car registration as being stolen - accompanied by the legend: 'Suspect is known to impersonate a policeman, very convincingly'. He was apprehended by the wheeled arm of the law late one Friday night - just the time when his story would be difficult to check. Doubtless he played his part with considerable conviction for he enjoyed the compulsory hospitality of the local ratepayers as a result.' (from the New Scientist, 27.4.81).

10.1.7 Cases G : Accidental loss (lightning strikes twice!)

(a) 'So much for the old proverb that lightning can never strike twice. Hertfordshire County Council is living proof that it can ... A bolt of lightning created a massive surge in power causing its (a mini computer's) inside to blow up. Even the back-up devices got the melt-down treatment. ... three years ago ... lightning struck ...., blowing up some computer peripheral equipment.' (from Computing, 28.8.86).

(b) 'Lightning blacks out Garda system' (from Computing, 17.8.89).

(c) Lightning storms that hit the Yorkshire Electricity Board's computer centre resulted in hundreds of customers receiving reminders for bills they were never sent.' (from Computing, 25.8.88)

10.1.8 Case H : Bureau responsibilities

Three London Boroughs and one District Council have used 'Filipino labour' as a means to cut the cost of data input to Community Charge systems (from Computer Talk, 4.12.89).

10.1.9 Case I : Office cleanliness

According to a survey by a cleaning company 'In one case a malfunction was caused by pieces of a ham sandwich' (from Computer Weekly, 5.11.87).

10.1.10 Cases J : Insecure printouts

(a) 'Hundreds of confidential medical records were found dumped on a public rubbish tip in Norwich yesterday ... the records belonged to a consultant pathologist who died 10 years ago and concerned his private patients' (from The Times 18.8.87).

(b) 'Confidential documents, containing debt information on thousands of Edinburgh council house tenants, have been found scattered in city streets ... the firm did not have sufficient capacity in the plant and took it to another plant ... . It appeared that a bag had fallen from the lorry and burst' (from the Edinburgh Evening News, December 1987).

(c) Confidential data printouts belonging to Worthing Borough Council were allegedly found on a rubbish tip, even though the Council said that 'normally such computer papers are given to a disposal contractor' (from ITLG, February 1990).

10.1.11 Cases K : absence of security procedures

(a) Most companies contacted in a PC survey didn't know how to retrieve lost data, or whether their computers were hacker proof, and one in four did not take back-ups (from PC Week, 16.1.90).

(b) A survey for the 'Which Computer Show?' indicated that 17% of firms have been victims of hacking, yet 58% admitted that their computer systems were not protected against hackers (from The Guardian, 26.2.90).

10.2 **Discussion**

10.2.1 Each of the examples quoted above illustrates the contravention of one of the many facets of the Eighth Data Protection Principle. Such instances can result in:

(a) a complaint to the Data Protection Registrar and the subsequent serving of an Enforcement Notice; and

(b) a claim for compensation, by a Data Subject.

10.2.2 The Principle is very widely cast. It calls for 'appropriate security measures' (ie not too much and not too little) to be taken 'against unauthorised access to, or alteration, disclosure or destruction of, personal data' (note that the concept of 'unauthorised' means that Data Users, if a complaint is investigated by the Registrar, will be scrutinised as to their authorisation procedures), 'and against accidental loss or destruction of personal data' (ie how the Data User guards against, and recovers from, accidents may also be scrutinised).

10.2.3 The Interpretation of the Principle spells out further security concerns. 'Regard shall be had to the nature of the personal data and the harm that would result from such access, alteration, disclosure, loss or destruction' (ie Data Users are expected to anticipate what could happen to their personal data and to take appropriate countermeasures), 'and to the place where personal data are stored' (ie physical security), 'to security measures programmed into the relevant equipment' (ie controlling the access to data and equipment), 'and to measures taken for ensuring the reliability of staff having access to the data' (ie are staff properly trained; have they been vetted with respect to the data).

10.2.4 In the Cases described there has either been a security breach that resulted in disclosure of personal data to people not covered by a Register Entry, or a loss of data, or the alteration of data by unauthorised staff etc. In some of these Cases damage was caused to a Data Subject, who could claim compensation under Section 23(1) and, where damage did not occur, could complain to the Data Protection Registrar under Section 36(2).

10.2.5 In many of the above cases it could be difficult for the Data User to sustain the defence against compensation outlined in Section 23(3) of the Act. This states:

> 'In proceedings brought against any person by virtue of this section it shall be a defence to prove that he had taken such care as in all the circumstances was reasonably required to prevent the loss, destruction, disclosure or access in question.'

10.2.6 Where damage to a Data Subject did follow a breach of security, the Courts will decide the issue by examining whether it was reasonable to expect the Data User to have taken action to anticipate and prevent the problem that occurred. In judging this aspect, the Courts could examine whether the Data User acted responsibly towards the management of computer security, and what remedial actions followed any earlier breaches of security. For example, how does the Data User assign responsibility for dealing with computer security issues, who is responsible, and how is that responsibility devolved to other staff? It can be argued that whenever computer security has demonstrably been found wanting (eg a disk has been lost because of water damage; a hacker has been identified as having breached the access control system; a report that computer printout has been found on a rubbish tip has been submitted to management etc), the Data User should take immediate, visible and documented steps to prevent a repeat occurrence which might put at risk the personal data held.

10.2.7 Note that it will be difficult to establish a defence if the Data User does not keep documentary evidence of what was done to raise security standards, train management and staff, test procedures, implement policies etc. In summary, there is a lot of work involved and a great deal of detail to master (enough for another book on the subject!).

10.2.8 Even if damage does not occur (and the issue is not aired in Court), a complaint could be made to the Registrar that security of personal data cannot be guaranteed by the Data User. If the complaint is substantiated as a breach of the Eighth Principle, this could lead to enforcement action by the Registrar who could insist on specific security procedures to be set up. If, as is the Registrar's policy, details of the Enforcement Notice are made public, the damage done to the credibility, image and professional status of the Data User could be significant.

10.2.9 In Case A (failure to take a basic back-up copy), Case B (failure to delete personal data before selling obsolete computers) and Case C (failure to use safe passwords), the Data User's defence under Section 23(3) would be weakened, because clearly basic standards and procedures were not in place. For example, in Case C it could prove difficult to show reasonable care, when access to the system is protected by a ten-digit number whose digits are all the same, and by a password (1234) that is hardly complex. (These circumstances form part of the infamous Gold and Schifreen case which caused the Law Commission to produce its paper on Computer Misuse, and Michael Colvin MP to promote legislation to counteract Computer Misuse: somehow the inadequate password and access controls that Gold and Schifreen discovered have been forgotten). Case D (failure to prevent unauthorised access) is a more serious hacking incident which draws attention to an interesting aspect: although, under the anti-hacking legislation, the hacker could be committing a crime, under the Data Protection Act the Data User (who had insecure procedures that allowed the hacker onto the system) could end up paying the damages. In Case E (a breach in procedures for secure disposal of printout), the issue would depend on whether all reasonable precautions had been taken to ensure proper disposal, and whether staff had been trained to use these procedures. In Case F (failure to prevent unauthorised access to, or alteration of, personal data), the Superintendent could claim compensation because the personal data were inaccurate (Section 22(1)), and submit a substantial complaint to the Registrar under the Fifth Data Protection Principle.

10.2.10 In evaluating what 'was reasonably required', a Court will enquire about the steps the Data User could have taken, what steps the Data User had taken and, for comparison, what steps similar Data Users normally take in similar circumstances. Naturally, counsel for the plaintiff will endeavour to discover whether something similar had ever happened to the Data User before; if it had, this would weaken the defence against award of compensation, because the Court could take the view that the Data User had been negligent.

10.2.11 The same considerations apply to the Cases G (lightning strikes twice): a Court may take the view that to be struck by lightening once is unlucky, to be struck twice is unfortunate, but to be struck a third time and not to have taken appropriate precautions against the accidental loss of personal data is bordering on the negligent. Thus if the Data User had done nothing to protect the electricity supply against peaks or troughs in voltage, the Court might well ask 'How many times must lightning strike before the Data User takes notice?', and award compensation with respect to any claims from Data Subjects (note that the sending out of erroneous bills could set in motion procedures for debt recovery that may cause damage to an individual (and that the receipt of such bills alone has been known to cause physical damage to an individual in poor health), and that the production of inaccurate personal data could be actionable by the Data Subject under Section 22 of the Act, or by the Registrar under the Fifth Data Protection Principle).

10.2.12 Some of the Cases (as for instance Case H when an overseas bureau is used) present multiple security issues. As soon as an Authority processes the personal data by using the facilities of a Computer Bureau, it has additional concerns regarding the implications of the Data Protection Principles (eg it has to be satisfied with the Bureau's procedures that deal with the security of the particular personal data being processed, and with the reliability of the Bureau staff that have access to the personal data; it is responsible for any consequent changes to Registration under the Act, and for the accuracy of the personal data sent to, and received from, the Bureau; etc). Additionally, the use of an overseas Bureau could involve contractual problems that may have to be resolved under two jurisdictions. Checking some of these items is not easy from a distance of over 6,000 miles (or, for that matter, closer to home, as the article stated that 15,000 Community Charge Canvass forms returned by the Bureau were lost at Heathrow Airport!).

10.2.13 Case I (failure to dispose safely of a ham sandwich) is an example where poor office management (drinks near VDUs, plant pots on top of terminals, ash trays balanced on keyboards are other examples of this problem) is responsible for malfunctions that could corrupt personal data. Under the Eighth Principle, such malfunctions can concern 'the place where the personal data are stored' or 'the reliability of staff having access to the data'. Clearly management should have located equipment away from eating and smoking areas, whilst staff should have been trained (ie made reliable) so as not to 'eat, drink and be merry' in close proximity to computing equipment. If the malfunction resulted in inaccurate personal data or in the loss of personal data, compensation for damage could be sought from a Data User. In short, an expensive ham sandwich.

10.2.14 The three the Cases J (failure to dispose safely of printout) seem at first sight very similar; in practice, they raise some fundamentally different Data Protection problems.

10.2.15 Case J(a), assuming that the records were personal data, highlights 'who is responsible for security?', as generally in such circumstances two Data Users may be concerned. If personal data are held in a private capacity (eg by a doctor who takes on a private patient, or by a teacher who has a private pupil) the individual is the Data User responsible. Alternatively, the security breach could have arisen as part of that doctor's or teacher's employment in the public service (eg a doctor or a teacher who is authorised to take personal data or copies of personal data home), in which case the Data User responsible for ensuring that security is adequate would be the employer (note, however, that it is **control** of the personal data which is the deciding factor, via Section 1(5)(b) of the Act, and not **ownership** as such).

10.2.16 As an individual doctor can be employed in both a private and public capacity, there could be the need for procedures to link the two. For example, a patient may consult a doctor on a private basis and, on discovery that the course of treatment is too expensive, have recourse to treatment on the National Health Service. In this case, to ensure that personal data are up to date, there could be a need to disclose personal data, between the two Data Users, about the patient's medical condition (eg from the private consultant Data User to the Health Service Data User). Note that because two Data Users are involved, other differences may appear: eg a Health Authority may have liberal views on the application of the Subject Access exemption to Health personal data, whereas a private doctor may not, or vice versa.

10.2.17 As a Data User, the individual in private practice will need to conform with all eight Data Protection Principles. Thus, on retirement, the private practitioner should have:

(a) transferred the personal data to the patient's new doctor, or

(b) given the personal data to the patient, to pass on to the new doctor when chosen, or

(c) retained the personal data (if both the above options were impractical for any reason) with a view to transferring them to the new doctor (when appointed).

10.2.18 For a retired practitioner not to delete personal data, that related to the private practice, as soon as is practicable would not only breach the Sixth Principle, it could also constitute unfair processing (a breach of the First Principle), as the practitioner would be holding Health personal data on ex-patients. The breach of security that occurred when the personal data were disposed of in an insecure manner (probably dumped in the rubbish bin during a house clearance) not only could result in a breach of the Eighth Principle, but also could mean that compensation could be awarded against the deceased's estate (assuming a new Data User could be held responsible).

10.2.19 In Cases J(b) and (c), each Data User used a waste disposal company (which is therefore an agent of the Data User) to securely dispose of personal data. In the Edinburgh case, the disposal firm took the output, unknown to the Data User, to another company for disposal; it was during this journey that the personal data were accidentally 'scattered'. In Worthing, it was unclear how procedures broke down.

10.2.20 In both instances it is the Data User (the Local Authority) who is responsible for the security of the personal data, and it is the Data User (and not the agent) who could be liable for compensation under Section 23(1) of the Act. For example, a Court could decide that the Data User did not take sufficient care as to the choice of company who offered the secure disposal service (eg a 'fly-tipping' company was used), or that even though the Data User chose a reputable company, the former was negligent in specifying a disposal service that could not adequately protect the personal data, or that the Data User took no action to investigate whether there were problems with the service.

10.2.21 Consequently it is very important for a Data User to be satisfied as to the services offered by any agent who is to have access to the personal data; to monitor the performance of the agent to assess whether the Data User's instructions are being carried out; and to discontinue the contract if the services provided are unsatisfactory, or if required improvements to any service cannot be provided.

10.2.22 If the Courts or the Registrar become involved in an investigation, formal records of meetings between Data User and agent will be important evidence in establishing that the Data User was acting responsibly and with reasonable care. Finally, whenever agents are used, it is important that any contract should state that the agent will indemnify the Data User should the agent's action result in damages being awarded against the Data User.

10.2.23 Both the surveys mentioned in Cases K indicate considerable management complacency about basic security procedures. It seems an indefensible state of affairs that although nearly one fifth of the firms in question had suffered unauthorised access to data by a hacker, nearly two thirds admitted that their computer systems were left unprotected. Clearly, whilst a significant number of managers know that unauthorised access has taken place, they are at the same time not prepared to take countermeasures.

10.2.24 If such a situation was proved in Court, the consequences for the Data User could be severe. If a Data Subject (the second victim of the hacker who took advantage of the Data User's insecure computer system) is damaged through the unauthorised access to personal data, it would be the Data User (the first victim of the hacker), who would have to establish the 'reasonable care' defence. This could be difficult if the Data User was one of the 58% who have no anti-hacking strategy!

10.2.25 If damage to a Data Subject did not occur, there could still be a complaint to the Data Protection Registrar that the Eighth Data Protection Principle had been breached by the Data User. Thus even without the issue of compensation, the Data User could have very little to offer, to mitigate unfavorable publicity, should an investigation be started by the Registrar to determine whether appropriate measures were taken against unauthorised access.

10.2.26 It can even be argued that not to take basic precautions to prevent access to personal data by hackers, is passively to allow unauthorised disclosures of personal data by this means. Such a disclosure could be in a breach of the Data Protection Act via Section 5(5), as the personal data might be deemed to have been disclosed 'recklessly' by the Data User to the hacker (in contravention of the limits on disclosure set by the Register Entry). Section 20(1) of the Act might then apply, and the relevant manager(s) of the Data User could be prosecuted if the unauthorised disclosure was proved to be 'attributable to any neglect on the part of any director, manager, secretary or similar officer'. Thus although the hacker may be committing an offence under the Computer Misuse Act, it may still be possible for the Data User, and Data User employees, to be convicted of an offence under the Data Protection Act.

Chapter Five: Codes of Practice; Council of Europe Recommendations

1. Introduction: Codes of Practice and Data Protection

1.1 Background

1.1.1 Under Section 36 ('General duties of Registrar') the Data Protection Act states, in subsection (4):

> 'It shall be the duty of the Registrar, where he considers it appropriate to do so, to encourage trade associations or other bodies representing data users to prepare, and to disseminate to their members, codes of practice for guidance in complying with the data protection principles'.

1.1.2 Note that the Registrar's 'duty', in this context, is limited firstly by what he considers to be 'appropriate'; secondly by the fact that any action on his part is only 'to encourage'; and thirdly that the outcome of this initiative, even if issued by a trade association to its members (and with the Registrar's imprimatur), has a status no stronger than 'guidance'. It can be argued that Codes of Practice under the Data Protection Act have very little real authority.

1.1.3 By contrast, the Lindop Committee recommended in its Report Cmnd 7341) that the Data Protection Authority (equivalent to the Office of the Data Protection Registrar as now constituted) should draft Codes of Practice (paragraph 38.11), and that 'Codes of Practice should take the form of subsidiary legislation and acquire the force of law' (paragraph 38.15). The Committee also considered that 'The great majority of applications should be covered by a small number of Codes. Where an application belongs to a class of its own a special Code of Practice should be drafted for it.' (paragraph 38.12), and that 'Each Code of Practice should specify the data handling activities to which it applies and the measures to be taken by users to achieve the levels of compliance with the statutory principles judged necessary in that case' (paragraph 38.14).

1.1.4 The notion of statutory Codes of Practice (as defined by Lindop, and used elsewhere by Government, eg in relation to Trades Unions) is not without its critics, and an article by Robert Baldwin, lecturer in law at the London School of Economics, has outlined some well known problems (Guardian 30.5.88). He points out that the flexibility of Codes, which permits easier revision and which allows the use of language that is free of legal jargon whilst encouraging good practices and covering much detail, can in fact be used to weaken the democratic and parliamentary process: one of the attractions of Codes of Practice to Government is that 'Parliament does not have to be worried with (possibly controversial) details'.

1.1.5 For statutory Codes of Practice to have a foundation in law they must first have an origin within parliamentary procedures; usually those associated with Statutory Instruments. Whilst Statutory Instruments can be debated, the options before Parliament tend to be acceptance or rejection of the Instrument in its entirety. In addition, as Instruments tend to be the exercise of powers by Ministers, the support of Government means that they are usually accepted. If a serious error is discovered (eg by the Committee that checks the legality of the Instrument) the whole Instrument is withdrawn by Government. Baldwin stresses that this lack of Parliamentary scrutiny (compared with that of primary legislation which has three readings, a committee stage and a report stage, in both Houses of Parliament) can mean that the Codes may lack legitimacy in the eyes of the public.

1.1.6 An 'almost statutory' Code of Practice can be a half way house. For example, in the Report produced under the chairmanship of Professor Jack (Banking Services: Law and Practice, Report by the Review Committee, Cm 622), and in the subsequent White Paper (Banking Services: Law and Practice, Cm 1026), a Code of Practice was suggested as a means of strengthening the 'Tournier Rules'. These Rules govern bankers' duty of confidentiality and, in UK law, allow the disclosure of information: (a) when required by law; (b) where there is a public duty to disclose; (c) where the interests of the bank require disclosure, and (d) where the disclosure is made with the express or implied consent of the customer.

1.1.7 Jack argued that disclosures of: type (a) were excessive; type (b) were unnecessary; type (c) were too vague ('interests' could include numerous marketing initiatives to increase the uptake of credit); and type (d) needed amending so that express consent (ie the signature of the customer) had to be obtained in all other cases. The Government accepted the concerns about disclosures falling within types (c) and (d), and agreed the recommendation that the Code of Practice (a draft appears in both Cm 622 and Cm 1026) should require the customer's express consent to be sought in such circumstances. When finalised, the Code would be supported by the Bank of England and the Building Societies Commission (two statutory bodies) who would be responsible for gaining acceptance of the Code and for compliance with its terms and enforcement procedures (which have yet to be determined; a breach of the Code could lead to the involvement of the Banking or Building Societies Ombudsmen). Thus, unlike the 'voluntary' Codes of Practice produced under the Data Protection Act, this 'almost statutory' Code would be supported by supervision and enforcement procedures (and the active interest of Government).

1.1.8 Although voluntary guidance produced by professional associations, or Codes of Practice established by the Data Protection Act, may outline 'best practice', they do not have any Parliamentary authority, nor are they policed by the Data Protection Registrar. Since they are voluntary they have no legal status and can be ignored, and the lack of authority can downgrade their importance and significance to all those affected by the Code. Adherence to a Code does not mean that the Data User has complied with the Act although, obviously, if the Code is one that has been 'approved' by the Registrar, such adherence would be taken into account. When the 'voluntary versus statutory' issue was discussed at length by the Lindop Committee, it concluded that voluntary Codes were unacceptable because adherence to a Code could not be enforced.

1.2 Policy of the Registrar

1.2.1 The Registrar outlined the development of his policy towards Codes of Practice in two Guidance Notes (GN1 and GN6), respectively a 'Preliminary Policy Statement' dated September 1985, and a 'Second Explanatory Statement' dated August 1986.

1.2.2 **Preliminary Policy Statement** (Ref: GN1-EJH-9/85)

(a) In this Statement, the Registrar wrote that 'the development of voluntary Codes of Practice' will 'support the purposes of the Act by:

- assisting individuals in the exercise of their rights
- assisting computer users in meeting their obligations'.

(b) Regarding 'The Nature of Codes of Practice', the Statement noted:

'Codes of Practice will only be of value if they command the respect of those they are seeking to serve. In the case of the Data Protection Act, those to be served must primarily be the concerned individuals. Benefits to computer users will flow from assistance in applying the Data Protection Principles to their own practical situations. Adherence to good Codes of Practice will give a measure of the Data Users intention to meet and comply with the Data Protection Principles which can be taken account of by the Data Protection Registrar in cases of complaint or potential breaches of their obligations under the Act.

To command respect Codes of Practice must not simply paraphrase the Act or be exhortative - they must state clear practical actions which are to be followed. They must support the Act's objectives and requirements and not try to diminish or bypass them.

A Code of Practice might thus state:

- The individuals it is seeking to serve

- The rights of those individuals flowing from the Data Protection Principles
- The computer users who will find this Code of Practice to be pertinent
- The obligations which those computer users carry in respect of the Data Protection Principles
- The scope of this Code of Practice with regard to the rights and obligations
- The particular practices embodied in the Code; how they relate to the Data Protection Principles; how they can be incorporated in practical working operations within computer users
- How individuals can exercise any rights flowing from this Code of Practice
- How commitment to the Code of Practice is expressed
- The sanctions that may follow from a breach of the Code by a committed computer user
- Which computer users are committed to the Code of Practice

Codes of Practice will normally be backed by arrangements for periodical review, publicity, administration, advisory services (for individuals and computer users), monitoring and enforcement.'

(c) The Statement concluded:

'It is the Registrar's view that Codes of Practice, as outlined above, can be very beneficial to the operation of the Act. One of the priorities he has set for 1986 is to allocate senior staff resources to encourage their development.

The Registrar cannot give an assurance that adherence to a Code of Practice will in all cases or without qualification show that a Data User is complying with the Act. He will, however, take into account and give appropriate weight to compliance with recognised Codes of Practice in the event of a complaint or potential breach of the Data Protection Principles.'

1.2.3 **Second Explanatory Statement** (Ref: GN6-EJH-8/86)

(a) This Statement 'expands on the first in explaining what the Registrar means by

Codes of Practice in terms of their target audiences, content and structure; what he expects in the way of commitment to Codes; and what he proposes his own involvement will be in the development and adoption of Codes'.

(b) A key aspect of this Statement is the Registrar's view that a Code of Practice comprises one of three types of guidance, all of which may 'contribute to the promotion of Data Protection and to securing compliance with the Act'. The two other types, 'Cross-Sectoral Guidelines' and 'Operational Procedures', will, where appropriate, contain further detail.

(c) The Registrar suggests that these other types are a natural development from Codes of Practice. 'Cross Sectoral Guidelines will emerge in the form of technical or professional advice on Data Protection in relation to particular types of data, purposes, practices or equipment', and 'many organisation will need to develop internal Operational Procedures in order to apply a specific Code of Practice'. Operational procedures will deal 'with particular aspects of Data Protection as they relate to the work of specific groups of employees'. The Registrar views the three types of guidance 'as complementary rather than necessarily hierarchical or sequential', noting that Operational Procedures will normally be a matter for individual Data Users and, therefore, that his involvement in such Procedures will be limited.

(d) The Registrar's Office has also commented 'We obviously do not wish to discourage any Data User from adopting practices which are supportive of the Data Protection Principles, even if they go beyond the strict requirements of the Act itself.'.

(e) The Registrar's view of the Principles, set out in his Guidelines 4 and 5, can provide a foundation for appropriate sections of Codes of Practice. In the Statement, the Registrar noted that 'representative bodies may wish to discuss with the Registrar the appropriate scope and coverage of a Code of Practice, and any possible co-operation with other bodies covering similar or related organisations and areas of activity'.

1.3 Forewords to Codes of Practice

1.3.1 The Registrar uses a foreword to a Code of Practice to indicate that the Code has gone through some kind of official process with his office. This statement from the Registrar does not necessarily mean that the Code is wholly approved by him.

1.3.2 The forewords usually lay stress on compliance with the Principles (eg in the case of Direct Marketing and the First Principle, to a facility for individuals to suppress the receipt of unwanted mail; see also paragraph 3.3.2 below). The Registrar generally notes that he will take compliance with a Code as a positive factor in favour of Data Users who are accused of breaking any of the Principles, but that observance of a Code 'does not constitute an assurance that I will accept in all cases and without qualification that data users have complied with the Act'.

1.3.3 An important point, in the Registrar's view, is that Codes of Practice will change in the light of experience, and in consideration of 'the views of members of the public and their representative organisations'. Thus it is perfectly possible, following a particular event, to discover that adherence to an agreed Code of Practice by a Data User may still be insufficient to satisfy the Principles with respect to that event. So, for example, the Code of Practice developed by the Advertising Association has been published in a Second Edition, in which the Registrar's foreword stresses a disagreement with a significant aspect of the Code's recommendations.

1.4 Current activities

1.4.1 A number of Codes of Practice and Guidelines (not all with a Registrar's foreword) have already been prepared or are in draft. Examples in the Public Sector are the Department of Health's 'Code on Confidentiality of Personal Health Data' and the Department of Social Security's 'Access to Personal Social Services Records'; Local Authority Codes on 'Confidentiality/Security of Data on Ethnic Origin', on 'Extension of Data Protection to Manual Records', on 'Data Protection' in general, and on specific issues such as 'Data Protection and Personal Information', 'Social Services', 'Security of Computing Systems' and 'Data Subject Access'. Codes of Practice with forewords from the Registrar include those issued for Police Computer Systems (produced by the Association of Chief Police Officers) and for Employee Data (by the Institute of Personnel Management); the representative bodies involved with these 'approved' Codes of Practice are listed on the next page (copies of Codes of Practice are usually available, for a nominal fee, from the relevant Trade Association or representative body).

1.4.2 Codes of Practice have adopted a generally uniform structure. In addition to the foreword, which signifies the Registrar's involvement, the bulk of the Code, directly or indirectly, relates to implementation of the Data Protection Principles. In the case of the ABTA Code of Practice for Travel Agents, this takes the form of procedures and objectives that member travel agents will try to attain. Some other Codes, including the IPM Code on Employee Data, and the Code from the Advertising Association, are structured to address, in turn, compliance with each Data Protection Principle.

1.4.3 In his forewords, the Registrar has taken care to stress the points of the Code that he particularly welcomes. For example, in the first edition of the Advertising Association Code of Practice (1987), the Registrar said 'I particularly welcome the warranty provisions and the attention to be given to especially sensitive data'. In relation to the Police Computer Systems Code, he said that he particularly welcomed the undertaking 'to inform any third party to whom the inaccurate information may already have been disclosed'. He may also express reservations: as in the 'Code of Practice for Universities' where, in relation to an option for deleting examination marks from the computer, he states 'I find it disappointing that it should appear in an otherwise very positive document'; or disagreements: in the Advertising Association Code of Practice (1990), he states 'The Advertising Association's view of how this requirement can be met ... differs from my own'.

Codes of Practice Endorsed by the Data Protection Registrar

Advertising Association (on Direct Mail) (1987 and 1990)

Association of British Travel Agents (1987)

Association of Chief Police Officers, Scotland (1988)

Association of Chief Police Officers, England, Wales & Northern Ireland (1988)

Committee of Vice-Chancellors and Principals of the UK Universities (1987)

Community Charge (produced by the Department of Environment) (1989)

Computer Services Association (for Computer Bureaux) (1990)

NHS General Medical Practitioners (March 1991)

Institute of Personnel Management (April 1988)

National Computing Centre (on Security) (1989)

National Computing Centre (on Customer and Supplier Administration) (1989)

1.4.4 The effectiveness of Codes of Practice in protecting Data Subjects from irresponsible use of their personal data (and Data Users from acting irresponsibly) can only be judged in the long term, when the level of compliance with individual Codes has been assessed, and scrutinised in legal proceedings. One aspect which is likely to assume increasing significance is the use of Codes as a basis for data protection audit, especially as regards specific procedures that may be covered by a particular Code.

1.4.5 In the following pages, discussion of several important Codes of Practice is preceded by details of the corresponding Recommendation from the Council of Europe. These Recommendations are in part akin to 'Cross-Sectoral Guidelines' as defined by the Registrar (see paragraph 1.2.3(c) above), and are prepared by a Committee of experts on Data Protection under the authority of the European Committee on Legal Co-operation. The Recommendations, although not legally binding, have a heightened status given the fact that most European countries have ratified the Convention. It follows that the Recommendations should be regarded as establishing European-wide guidance and international standards with respect to Data Protection issues faced by a particular sector or related to particular types of data.

2. Employment records

2.1 Background

2.1.1 Trades unions and organisations that represent employees are concerned that information held in personnel systems, or obtained through systems that carry out surveillance or monitor performance at work, can, if not regulated by agreed procedures, be used for purposes detrimental to the interests of employees, and harmful to trades union activities. Similar concerns can arise as regards information derived from psychological testing (eg assessing the employee's or potential employee's response to stress, to establish suitability for a particular post); from the use of techniques involving devices such as lie detectors; or through extraneous disclosure of information divulged during counselling sessions (some employers offer staff professional help in relation to personal, drug or alcohol related problems).

2.1.2 Trades unions in the UK have addressed some of these problems on behalf of their members. A union representing technical staff (APEX), one of the banking unions (BIFU), and the union representing Local Government Clerical Officers (NALGO) all negotiated model agreements with some employers to limit the type of data to be collected for personnel systems, the purposes for which personnel data can be used, and the disclosures that are allowed. NALGO also held a national conference to discuss the negotiating stance to be taken by shop stewards before an employer registers any personal data under the terms of the Data Protection Act, and to discuss the possibilities that exist under the Act to extend an individual's rights. Another union (GMB) wrote to employers to request a copy of their proposed Registration forms, and also asked that disclosures to trades unions should be registered.

2.1.3 Trades unions are aware that for an organisation to implement the Data Protection Act it may need union co-operation, and that any failure in communication, or lack of co-operation, can lead to conflict and the disruption of data processing. For example, one public authority in South Yorkshire issued instructions to staff working in cramped conditions, in an open-plan office accessible to members of the public, that the Act made them individually responsible to keep any personal data secure. The worried staff involved their representative who, on observing the lack of filing cabinets and security locks, told staff not to handle any personal data until management had provided the bare essentials to maintain adequate security.

2.1.4 Many trades unions fear that unscrupulous employers will use automated equipment to collect personal information that could weaken trades unions and infringe the basic rights of their members. A report compiled by an international committee of trades union representatives, and presented to the Organisation for Economic Co-operation and Development (OECD) in 1985, raised problems that had been experienced by trades unions in member states. There were real fears that information from computer-controlled machines could, for example, be used to monitor rest times (some machines require the operator to state a reason for any pause), the numbers of corrections made by an employee, or the rate of key depressions per minute, and that such data would then be used to determine piece-rate wages or to identify the most cost-effective employees.

2.1.5 Systems of this kind can lead to increased monitoring of the performance and attendance records of employees. For example, the then Association of Scientific, Technical and Managerial Staffs (ASTMS, now part of the MSF Union) raised the issue of employers who use the number of words typed by a secretary, on a word processor, as a guide to efficiency. These activities may increase productivity, but the unions argue they do little for the working environment or to foster good employer-employee relations.

2.1.6 The report indicated that modern telephone monitoring systems, which automatically log the number dialled and the length of the call, are resented by many employees as an intrusion into their personal privacy. Although such systems provide valuable management data and restrict abuse, they can also be used for staff surveillance (eg to detect 'undesirable' contacts by staff) and to monitor any discontent in the workforce. One national newspaper used the automatic dialling log to identify (and then to dismiss) the reporter who had tipped off the BBC news desk of a dispute between the editor and the paper's proprietor.

2.1.7 Trades unions are aware that some employers in Europe have evaluated automated security systems, operated by security keys or passes, with a view to monitoring employee movement and, by inference, trades union activities and meetings. The report even mentions fears that electronic payment systems in company shops and canteens could be used to record social habits and consumer preferences of employees, and that the record that an employee bought several cans of beer at lunch-time could alert management to check that employee's performance in the afternoon.

2.2 Council of Europe Recommendation

2.2.1 In recognition of all these problems, the Council of Europe's recommendations on the 'Protection of personal data used for employment purposes' (Recommendation No. R(89)2 of the Committee of Ministers to Member States) places a moral obligation on these states to legislate in order to protect employees. A 'Recommendation' is not binding, but it is expected that states belonging to the Council of Europe should, in the words of the preamble, 'promote acceptance and implementation of the principles contained in the Recommendation by ensuring its wide circulation among representative bodies of both employers and employees'.

2.2.2 Under 'Scope and definitions', the text of the Recommendation defines 'employment purposes' as relating to recruitment, to fulfilment of employment contracts, to management and to planning and organisation of work. The principles also extend to the activities of employment agencies. The Recommendation does not apply where 'the protection of state security, public safety and the suppression of criminal offences' is involved. Further points stressed in this Section are that 'Manual processing of data should not be used by employers in order to avoid the principles contained in this Recommendation', and that the principles may be extended 'to manual processing in general'.

2.2.3 The Recommendation continues with several statements of good practice which amplify, in relation to employment purposes, the formal Data Protection Principles set out in the 1981 Council of Europe Convention (see Chapter 4, paragraph 1.3). These additional 'principles' (see the two paragraphs above) comprise a European Standard on data used for employment purposes, and it can be expected that they will be referred to by specialist Courts or Tribunals that deal with employment issues. In outline, and subject to the provisions of any relevant domestic law or practice, these principles establish that

(a) respect for the privacy and human dignity of employees calls for employers to safeguard the personal data collected for employment purposes

(b) employers should, in advance, 'fully inform or consult' their employees or their representatives about the collection and use of personal data by means of automated systems. The agreement of employees or their representatives should be sought before the introduction or adaptation of such systems (eg devices that monitor the movement or productivity of employees, including video surveillance, computer controlled security locks etc)

(c) the main source of personal data should be the individual employee, who should be informed 'when it is appropriate to consult sources outside the employment relationship'. With respect to recruitment the Recommendation uses stronger words: 'sources other than the individual may only be consulted with his consent or if he has been informed in advance of this possibility'

(d) any information should be relevant, and limited to the data necessary to fulfil the employment, career or recruitment function; and recourse to tests, analyses and similar procedures 'to assess the character or personality of the individual' should not take place without his consent

(e) all data should represent faithfully the employee's situation; judgmental data 'should be based on fair and honest evaluations and must not be insulting', and should not be stored or coded in a way that 'allow him to be characterised or profiled without his knowledge'. Employees should be able to contest any judgement

(f) personal data collected for employment purposes should not be used for other purposes. If the data are collected for a specific employment purpose and are to be used for another such purpose then 'adequate measures should be taken to avoid misinterpretation of the data in the different context'

(g) personal data may, in accordance with domestic law or practice, be communicated to employees representatives 'in so far as such data are necessary to allow them to represent the employees', or communicated to public bodies 'for their official functions only within the limits of employers' legal obligations'. Other communications with public bodies, unless authorised by law, must either be necessary for employment purposes and where the employees or their representatives are informed of the disclosure, or be made 'with the express and informed consent of the individual employee'

(h) special personal data (eg religious beliefs, political opinions, criminal convictions etc) should only be collected within the limits specified by domestic law, whilst health data (unless domestic law allows otherwise) should only be obtained from sources other than the employee with his express and informed consent. If the rules of medical confidentiality apply, the data should be stored separately (with enhanced security) by staff bound by these rules, and should only be disclosed to other staff 'if it is indispensable for decision making'

(i) information concerning personal data held by the employer should be made available to the employee or to his representative, or brought to his notice through other appropriate means, and employees should, on request, be able to access the data and seek corrections or erasure

(j) personal data should be deleted when no longer necessary for an employment purpose, or justified by 'the interests of a present or former employee' (eg personal data submitted for a job application should normally be deleted as soon as it is clear that an offer of employment will not be made).

2.3 The IPM Code of Practice on Employee Data

2.3.1 This Code, developed jointly by the Institute of Personnel Management and the National Computing Centre, is of particular importance as its subject matter is relevant to most organisations. The following description concentrates on those issues and recommendations, outlined by the Code, which are specific to employee records, and omits more general points which are covered elsewhere in this book.

2.3.2 The object of the Code is 'to give practical assistance to personnel administrators and others handling employee data in complying with the Act'. In the Code's foreword, the Registrar notes that he was pleased 'that it was produced in collaboration with the Confederation of British Industry and the Industrial Society'; the IPM Code thus has enhanced credibility and status because it is the product of more than one representative body. As such, it is well capable of setting professional standards, and of providing benchmarks to test and compare the procedures of employers.

2.3.3 The Code does not outline any further sanctions for non-compliance with the Principles, other than those established by the Act itself; for example, breach of the Code will not lead to action by the representative body. In the introductory comment to the Code, it is made clear that the Code is limited to providing guidance with respect to personal data used within the narrow framework of employee purposes: Standard Purposes P001 (Personnel/Employee Administration) and P002 (Work Planning and Management). Despite this narrow scope, closer inspection shows that the Code covers some aspects of personnel information held in non-automated form, and also advances other procedures (especially with reference to disclosures and to the obtaining of personal data) that strengthen individual rights beyond the provisions of the Data Protection Act.

2.3.4 In relation to the First Principle, the Code lists typical, reasonable, uses of personnel data. These include recruitment and references; administration of wages, pensions, salaries, benefits and deductions; work organisation (including the recording of time spent on work, and the scheduling of work); monitoring the use of equipment, plant, services and vehicles; compliance with employment, Health and Safety and other relevant legislation; and analysis for management purposes.

2.3.5 The Code specifies that 'Employees or potential employees should not be induced to provide information or led to believe that a failure to supply information might disadvantage them', and also that 'personnel administrators should be aware that they may be required to justify the collection of items of data' - a crucial point, given the diversity of information that may need to be collected.

2.3.6 The Code makes three strong recommendations concerning the First Principle. Personnel administrators should:

(a) 'not use data held about employees for other activities' (ie other than those that might reasonably be expected; see paragraph 2.3.4 above) 'without the knowledge and consent of the employee(s) concerned'. Note it is the use of the words '**and consent**' which strengthens employees' rights considerably if such data were used for marketing and selling. Mere 'knowledge' that the data were used for these other purposes would not satisfy the Code;

(b) 'adopt a clear policy on personnel data and communicate this to all employees and prospective employees', and consider very carefully whether this communication should include a statement 'that the information collected will be strictly confidential and used only for the purposes of personnel administration';

(c) only collect information that is required for 'legitimate business or legal reasons' ('legal reasons' can include statutory requirements to disclose personal data, eg to Government Departments).

2.3.7 With reference to the Second Principle, the Code again limits itself to Standard Purposes P001 and P002, and recommends that the exemption from registering payroll personal data is of such narrow scope that it should not be used.

2.3.8 Evaluation of the Third Principle is complicated by the number of 'non-disclosure exemptions' that can be used in relation to employee data. Dealing first with the list of these exemptions, the Code gives the following advice: 'Care should be taken when relying on any of the above', and for disclosures that are made under Section 28 of the Data Protection Act 'an employer would be advised to obtain appropriate written evidence' to satisfy the conditions of Section 28(3).

2.3.9 As regards registered disclosures, the Code includes the following specific recommendations to personnel administrators:

(a) 'in the interests of privacy, employee confidence and good employee relations, personnel administrators should seek to restrict the range of disclosures which are made without obtaining employee consent';

(b) 'seek, wherever possible, to obtain an employee's written consent, even if the disclosure in question has been registered' (note that this goes well beyond the Act's requirements), or 'advise employees of likely disclosures at the time data are collected' (the latter is also a consequence of the First Data Protection Principle);

(c) 'endeavour to restrict disclosures outside the organisation to those required by law' (again in excess of the Act's requirements).

2.3.10 The recommendations in the Code also extend to internal disclosures. The Code recommends that, within organisations, personnel administrators 'should have a clear policy to ensure that data about employees can be accessed only where there is a legitimate business need to know', and that there should be a policy to cover 'internal access to data'. There is, thus, an implication, although not expressed directly, that employees should know the scope of, and reasons for, all disclosures, whether internal, registered or statutory.

2.3.11 Under the Fourth Principle, the Code stresses the point that 'information which cannot be reasonably justified should not be gathered'. In a specific reference to manual files, the Code suggests that supplementary manual information 'will be pertinent to any assessment of the adequacy and relevance of the data', thus drawing attention to the importance of retaining documents, if need be as evidence in a court of law.

2.3.12 With reference to the Fifth Principle dealing with accuracy, the Code suggests several standard procedures; for example, 'reasonable checks on the accuracy of data provided by reference to original documentation or to third parties', and 'investigation of the cause of any errors detected and correction of the faulty data, software or procedures'. The Code states that the employer can assist accuracy 'by providing employees with copies of relevant, current data to be checked for accuracy, possibly at annual intervals'. Note that the emphasis on 'relevant and current data' means that the Code's suggested procedure is **not** a substitute for Subject Access; which entitles employees to request **all** their own personal data.

2.3.13 In relation to the Sixth Principle, the Code points out the importance of retaining personal data 'to meet subsequent legal or statutory claims'. It recommends that personnel administrators should consult Auditors with a view to developing 'a policy on how long and in what detail records will be held to meet statutory claims or legitimate business needs'. Personal data no longer needed should be deleted, and personal data retained for research or historical purposes should be made anonymous.

2.3.14 The Code proposes two major extensions to the standard procedures associated with the Seventh Principle. It suggests that 'In the interest of good employee relations', organisations should look favourably on requests to access manual files that contain information about employees, and that no fee should be charged to current employees 'making easily satisfied requests'. Waiving the fee, the Code points out, would benefit 'employee co-operation in maintaining accurate data'.

2.3.15 Note that by stipulating a condition of 'easily satisfied' the Code accepts that not all personal data can be furnished to employees easily and for no charge. For example, there might be severe technical and administrative problems to overcome in providing archived data within the scope of the definition in Section 1(5)(c) of the

Act. If employers find themselves in this position, the Code implies that any free provision of personal data needs to be accompanied by a statement which makes it clear to employees that:

(a) not all the personal data have been provided;

(b) the employee retains the right to specify the relevant Register Entry or Entries and to obtain (on payment of a fee or fees) **all** the relevant personal data (ie including those archived and not easily retrievable).

2.3.16 The Code reminds readers who claim the Payroll and Accounts exemption (Section 32 of the Act) that they are exempt from providing Subject Access so long as they adhere to the stringent conditions that relate to the exemption (but see paragraph 2.3.7 above). Even if the exemption applies, the Code suggests that Subject Access could be provided.

2.3.17 On the Eighth Data Protection Principle, the Code reminds personnel administrators that the security of personal data is also their concern. The Code states that they should 'ensure that there are policies and procedures laid down regarding physical and software security', and that 'supervisory responsibility' towards security 'should be clearly defined'. The Code notes that 'Sound induction and adequate training in the use of the system and associated procedures should be provided'.

2.3.18 The Code ends with a disclaimer, to the effect that 'although compliance with it may be evidence of good practice, it will not guarantee immunity from the sanctions of the Act'.

2.3.19 Single copies of the IPM Code (16 pages) can be obtained by sending an A5 sized, self-addressed stamped envelope to: Institute of Personnel Management, IPM House, Camp Road, Wimbledon, London SW19 4UW (Tel:081-946 9100).

3. Direct marketing

3.1 Background

3.1.1 The issues raised by this subject are both important and complex, so much so that its principal aspect, Direct Mail (or junk mail, depending on your viewpoint) has exercised most Data Protection Authorities within Europe: it usually generates more complaints than any other topic.

3.1.2 Two main conflicts need to be resolved:

(a) The more an organisation knows about a potential customer's preferences, choices, behaviour and spending patterns, thus ensuring that its marketing efforts are targeted at the people most likely to buy, the better the chance of a sale and the lower the promotional costs (and the less chance that individuals will be troubled with information that they don't want): however, the less privacy the individual has.

(b) To restrict the right of an organisation to communicate with an individual by letter raises the spectres of censorship and interception of correspondence: Article 10 of the Human Rights Convention states that 'Everyone has the right to freedom of expression' and that this right 'includes the freedom .... to impart information', whilst Article 8 deals with the 'right to respect for ... correspondence' and 'there shall be no interference by a public authority' with correspondence unless interception is for a specific purpose in the national interest (eg national security, policing matters etc).

3.2 Council of Europe Recommendation

3.2.1 The Council of Europe's policy on direct marketing (Recommendation No. R(85)20: 'Protection of personal data used for the purpose of direct marketing') is in some ways more extensive than the Registrar's controversial Guidance Note 19, and the Advertising Association's Code of Practice.

3.2.2 Although the Recommendation asserts that any person should be able to use data derived from previous relations with actual or prospective customers to form a marketing list, the collection of data from individuals who are not customers should 'be permissible for direct marketing purposes only on condition that this has been expressly stated at the time of collection'. Section 3.1 of the Recommendation also states that marketing lists can be made available to third parties 'provided that the data subject has been informed' of this possibility 'directly or by some other appropriate means at the time of the collection or at some later stage ... and unless he has objected'. The data disclosed to third parties should be limited: 'Unless the data subject has given his consent, the lists should not provide any information liable to infringe his privacy' (a reference, for example, to information on buying habits relating to certain goods and services.

3.2.3 The phrase 'at some later stage' in Section 3 of the Recommendation is at the root of fundamental disagreement between the Advertising Industry and the Registrar. The industry's view is that even though the Data User **knows**, at the time of collection, that it is intended to disclose the data for a different purpose, the consent of the Data Subject may be sought for such a disclosure **after** the collection of information, as long as the Data Subject is given an adequate opportunity to object at **that** stage (see paragraph 3.3.9 below). The Registrar, by contrast, is of the opinion that this practice is in contravention of the First Data Protection Principle, and that **intended** disclosures must always be brought to the attention of a Data Subject

before the information is collected, or **written consent** sought **after** collection (see paragraph 3.3.8 below).

3.2.4 The Recommendation suggests that in addition to the right of correction, any person whose name appears on a list should be able, where appropriate, either

(a) 'to refuse to allow data concerning him to be recorded on marketing lists', or

(b) 'to refuse to allow data contained in such lists to be transmitted to third parties', or

(c) 'unconditionally and on request to have such data erased or removed from several or all of the lists held by users.'

3.2.5 In addition, the Recommendation suggests four further obligations on list controllers. These are:

(a) 'controllers of marketing files should keep a record of all the users of their lists'

(b) any data subject should be able 'to identify the controller of the marketing file'

(c) 'The controller of the marketing file should ... notify users ... that the data subject has exercised his rights' (of refusal or removal of consent; see paragraph 3.2.4 above)' ... so that any necessary changes can be made to the lists'

(d) 'The goods and services offered and the messages transmitted should be presented in such a form and manner that the privacy of the address is not prejudiced' (eg inferences in relation to the individual's use of certain types of services can be made, if the nature of the service or a company's name is printed on the envelope).

3.2.6 It is clear that these rights and obligations can only be given effect if controllers of marketing lists keep a formal record of those individuals who do not want to appear on their lists. Thus if a controller buys in a new list, or sells a list to a user, the names and addresses of those who have already stated that they do not want to appear on such lists can be removed; without this record, these names and addresses would continue to reappear on the lists. In addition, there is an implication that list controllers should ensure that all list users take steps to alert the recipients of promotional material to their rights.

3.3 The Advertising Association Code of Practice

3.3.1 The 2nd Edition (June 1990) of the Advertising Association Code of Practice 'Covering the use of Personal Data for Advertising and Direct Marketing Purposes' is complemented by 'Recommended Standards of Practice in List and Database Management for Direct Marketing Purposes' (May 1990; the Standards have been in force since 1st July 1991).

3.3.2 This Code, together with the Standards, can thus be seen as the Advertising Industry's second attempt to put the Council of Europe's Recommendation into practice. However, the Foreword and the Preface to the Code are dominated, respectively, by the fundamentally differing viewpoints of the Data Protection Registrar and the Advertising Association, concerning the practical requirements of 'fair obtaining' in the First Data Protection Principle. Nevertheless, there is agreement on the implications of 'fair processing' of personal data with respect to the receipt of unwanted mail (one option being use of the Mailing Preference Service which allows Data Subjects to remove names and addresses from lists used by participants in this scheme), and there is much in the Code that exceeds the statutory requirements of the Data Protection Act.

3.3.3 In his Foreword, the Registrar sets out his view that 'when obtaining information for direct marketing purposes a data user should inform the person supplying the information as to whom the information is for, why the information is required and for what purposes the information will be used or disclosed. Armed with this information, that person can then decide whether to provide the information or not'. If this information is clear from the context of the transaction between the obtainer (usually a Data User but not necessarily so) and the provider, the Registrar states that 'no further explanations should be necessary'. However, if there are additional uses and disclosures, 'Then, the duty to obtain information fairly requires steps to be taken to make him aware of the true position'.

3.3.4 The disagreement between the Registrar and the Advertising Association concerns these 'steps' and when they should be taken, should a Data User wish to implement uses and disclosures which are 'significantly different' (Section 3.1.8 of the Code) to those already explained to the source of the personal information. Such 'intended uses, disclosures and users' (see the Registrar's Foreword) could arise in two circumstances: (a) when a Data User decides on an initiative that was not known at the time of collection of the information, or (b) when a Data User knows of that initiative before the collection of the information.

3.3.5 Consider Case(a), where a Data User, who has collected information fairly, subsequently has a bright idea to use or disclose personal data for a new purpose. In this case the Data User has no need to contact those who initially provided the information since, at the time the information was collected, the Data User had no intention to implement the new purpose. As its new features were not in the Data User's mind, it is hardly feasible for the law to insist that there is a duty to inform the original sources; it would however be good practice if this was feasible (eg if a Data User was in regular touch with those on a particular list). However, once the new 'uses, disclosures and users' are known, it would be encumbent on the Data User, in order to conform with the First Principle, to explain these new features to all future sources.

3.3.6 Consider Case(b), where a Data User knows of the other purpose, and the uses and disclosures involved, in advance of the collection of information, and is unable (or justifiably unwilling from a business point of view) to provide full details at the collection stage. For example, the Data User's main objective may be to sell a particular product through the kind of advertisement that encourages members of the public to write in, with the secondary objective the sale of the names and addresses of those who buy the product. As an effective advertisement in the media usually consists of the minimum number of words, it could detract from its success (and add to its cost) if additional words had to be used to fulfil Data Protection requirements.

3.3.7 Such commercial aspects are irrelevant to the Registrar: his view of the Act is that a Data User who intends to use or disclose personal data for a particular purpose or purposes has a duty so to inform the sources before collecting the information. However, as far as the Case (b) type of problem is concerned, the Registrar does offer one further option: for the Data User to contact those who have responded to the advertisement, and to seek their express consent to the other uses or disclosures. The Code does not adopt this 'opt-in' approach, and instead proposes that sources of information be contacted, in writing, with an 'opt-out' procedure. So when, for example, individuals respond to a sales advertisement, they will receive, with their purchase, a notice advising them of proposed new uses or disclosures, and giving them adequate opportunity to object (paragraph 3.1.9 of the Code; the Recommended Standards define 'at least 21 days' as being 'adequate' in this context).

3.3.8 In summary, the Registrar is bound by the provisions of the first Principle and its Interpretation, as embodied in the 1984 Act. There are three key points:

(a) contravention of a Principle is judged on the merits of each particular case, 'in relation to one individual' if appropriate (Guideline 4, paragraph 1.10)

(b) full notification of what information will become personal data, and who will use it and how, should be provided '**BEFORE** a source gives information' (Appendix, Guidance Note 19)

(c) in special circumstances, such as when the individual has no choice initially but to provide the information, and is subsequently informed of other intended uses, express consent to such uses may be required to ensure 'fairness'.

3.3.9 The Advertising Industry, by contrast:

(a) relies on paragraph 3.1 of the Appendix to the Council of Europe Recommendation R(85)20, which permits notification (of 'marketing lists to be made available to third parties for direct marketing purposes') not only 'at the time of collection' but also 'at some later stage' (Preface to the June 1990 Code of Practice)

(b) requires 'express consent' of the individual only to be 'considered' where 'sensitive information' (racial origin, etc, as listed in Section 2(3) of the Data Protection Act) is involved (Section I, A(iii) and B(vi) of the Recommended Standards)

(c) in all other cases concludes that once an individual has been provided with 'adequate opportunity to object' and has not done so then use for 'significantly different purposes' is permitted (Section I, B(ii) and (v) of the Recommended Standards).

3.3.10 The Preface to the Code draws attention to the 'freely acknowledged difference' between the Registrar and the Advertising Association, and concludes that 'the question will not be resolved until a case is decided by the Courts'. However, despite this currently irreconcilable difference, it needs to be recognised that the Second Edition of the Code shifts the Advertising Association's position considerably towards that of the Data Protection Registrar. For instance, the Preface notes that after 'vigorous debate', there has been a 'shift in emphasis away from reliance on register entry as the sole source of information for data subjects about data users' purposes and activities'. (This means that despite the fact that the Register Entry is in the public domain, the Association has now agreed that a Data Subject needs to be provided with other information, about the intended uses and disclosures of personal data, which is intelligible in its own right, and which, where appropriate, offers individual Data Subjects an 'opt out' choice).

3.3.11 The Code recommends list users to seek a formal warranty from the list supplier. Such a warranty should, in theory, require compliance with the Code; if a list supplier cannot provide the warranty, the Code implies that the list is suspect and should not be used. The warranty would seek assurance that the list supplier is registered as a Data User and has obtained personal data, contained in the list, fairly and lawfully as defined in the Code. This includes checks as to whether the supplier had informed the Data Subjects that their personal data would be disclosed in this way, whether the data had been 'cleaned' via the Mailing Preference Service, and whether deletions or corrections received from Data Subjects had been implemented.

3.3.12 In turn, a list supplier should seek a warranty from a prospective user of a list that any personal data disclosed by the supplier will only be used for those purposes authorised by the supplier; that the prospective user is registered under the Act for such authorised purposes; that no disclosure will be made to a third party unless formally authorised by the supplier, and that requests for access, correction and deletion will, 'when appropriate', be referred to the supplier. The Code does not define when appropriate'; however, the Recommended Standards (Section II, paragraphs B.2.(iii) and (iv)) specify that a list user, if so asked, 'is required to reveal the specific identity of the mailing list' (presumably the identity of the list owner) and also that the list owner does not have to be informed if an individual merely requests the suppression of mailings from the list user. **Corrections** advised to the list user must be transmitted to the list owner within 30 days (paragraph B.2.(vi)).

3.3.13 With respect to the Third Principle (which is usually satisfied if the uses or disclosures are registered), the Code states (in paragraph 3.3.1) that the Advertising Association will consider the Principle breached if the personal data are disclosed for a purpose that is 'so dissimilar to the purpose, or one of the purposes, for which they were originally held as to make it probable that harm to the data subject would result from that use' the Code defines harm as 'damage or distress that is material or substantial'; the use of the word 'distress' permits the inclusion of, for instance, the harm caused by acute embarrassment). Where 'harm of any kind is likely', the Code recommends that the disclosure should not take place unless Data Subjects have had the opportunity to opt-out. Thus mailing lists of groups that have specific interests or characteristics that make them vulnerable (eg lists that contain the addresses of individuals who own sporting guns, or who are disabled) could be covered by this provision, since disclosure would materially increase the risk of harm (in this case from burglary).

3.3.14 The notion of 'harm' is also raised in the discussion of the Fifth Principle, where the Code calls for Data Users to anticipate the harm that could arise if personal data were not updated. If Data Users form the view that the Data Subject would be harmed or treated differently by 'information being out of date', the Code calls for positive steps to seek information to make the personal data accurate. If Data Users cannot update these data to remove the risk of harm, then 'that part of any list should not be used or disclosed'.

3.3.15 To improve relations with Data Subjects, the Code outlines procedures (in paragraphs 3.7.5 to 3.7.9) which exceed the minimum requirements of the Act, eg it calls for Subject Access requests to be acknowledged within 10 days, indicating whether there will be a delay in fulfilling the request; Data Users should not normally 'avail themselves of the maximum period of 40 days'; and should a Data User and Data Subject disagree over the correction or erasure of personal data, the Data User should alert the Data Subject to the circumstances under which the Data Protection Registrar could investigate the complaint.

3.3.16 Finally, the Code (Part III) sets out a number of 'Additional Rules'. These pertain to adherence to certain other Codes (eg those relating to aspects of retailing practice); the use of the Mailing Preference Service to suppress unwanted communications in general, or the retention on file of the names of those who have objected to a specific mailing, so that their names can be removed from other lists the Data User may obtain; Data Users' obligations to reveal, if asked, the organisation who provided the personal data; and to the omission of 'references to age, economic status, education, purchasing behaviour, employments status, bereavement, marital status or children in the family, where such references would be likely to cause alarm, distress or legitimate offence to recipients'. Finally, there is a call for parties to 'comply with the warranty provisions'(see paragraphs 3.3.11 and 3.3.12 above).

3.3.17 In paragraph 2.7, the Code lists one of the Data User's key duties towards a Data Subject as being the 'recording and honouring' of objections to direct mail, 'whether received direct or via the Mailing Preference Service'. It is, therefore, relevant to discuss the Service in detail (see also Chapter 4, paragraph 2.1.2(e)). Individuals can register (free of charge) by sending their name and address and any variations of their name, status, initials and address (eg such as maiden names, common misspellings, titles etc) to the Mailing Preference Service, Freepost 22, London W1E 7EZ. Once registered, the Service will keep the name(s) and address(es) on file for five years; it is the individual's responsibility to renew registration or to notify any change of address. The correct postcode is extremely important to the Service.

3.3.18 Once registration is complete, the Service undertakes to advise those mailers who use the Service of an individual's wishes. However, this will not stop unaddressed leaflets, or other deliveries that do not use the post (eg free newspapers), mailings addressed to 'The Occupier', or mailings from organisations that do not use the Service (eg from local traders). In these cases, the Service advises direct contact with the company sending the mail.

3.3.19 The Service's offer to restrict Direct Mail is unqualified. Thus all mail from all users of the Service will be stopped: this can be particularly helpful if the addressee is deceased, as the distress caused to a surviving partner, or to relatives, will be reduced. But individuals who are keen to receive mail offers from only a few areas of interest, find that in order to receive less mail overall, they have to choose not to receive information even on their favoured topics.

3.3.20 On the other hand, the Service permits individuals to specify categories on which they would like to receive more mail. For example, the application form lists a number of topics (eg Travel, Children, Sport) where additional mailings would be welcomed by the recipient (though not to the exclusion of the other topics). It is perhaps a surprising aspect of the Service that it can increase mail selectively but offers only to restrict mail indiscriminately.

4. Police sector

4.1 Council of Europe Recommendation

4.1.1 Recommendation No. R (87) 15: 'Regulating the use of personal data in the police sector', establishes eight broadly based 'basic principles' deemed acceptable to the policing of European democracies. Although the Recommendation weaves a delicate path through the contentious issues which policing involves, some of its conclusions are controversial, with the result that when the Recommendation was adopted on 17th September 1987, some Member States of the Council of Europe, namely the Republic of Ireland, UK, Germany and Switzerland, indicated that they might wish to derogate from all or some of its provisions.

4.1.2 For example, paragraph 2.2 of the principles states that when data concerning individuals have been collected and stored without their knowledge, the Police should, when the data are no longer required for a policing function, either delete the data or inform the individuals, where practicable, that the data are held. Paragraph 44 of the relevant 'Explanatory Memorandum' recognises that this could prove difficult to implement in certain cases (eg following the policing of public order events when mass surveillance methods have been employed) and draws attention to the force of the phrase 'where practicable', in this context. The UK Government reserved the right to derogate from this recommendation, and also from the implications of paragraph 2.4 of the principles, which states that the collection of some sensitive personal data (akin to those specified in Section 2(3) of the Data Protection Act, and including membership of particular 'movements or organisations which are not prescribed by law', 'should be prohibited' except when 'absolutely necessary for the purposes of a particular enquiry'.

4.1.3 With respect to the the accuracy and relevance of data, paragraph 3.2 of the principles requires that 'categories of data stored should be distinguished in accordance with their degree of accuracy or reliability', and draws attention to the importance of identifying facts as distinct from 'opinions or personal assessments'.

4.1.4 In paragraph 1.3 of the principles, the Council of Europe calls for advance consultation with the supervisory authority (in the UK this is the Data Protection Registrar) over policing applications, that use personal data, 'which may possibly pose problems for the application of the Recommendation' (more detail is provided in paragraph 35 of the Explanatory Memorandum). This is strengthened in paragraph 5.6 of the principles with a recommendation to seek 'authorisation by the supervisory body' (unless there is 'clear legal provision') if files held for a different purpose (eg social security data) are to be linked together with police files 'for the purposes of enquiry into a particular offence'. Although the Police and Home Office do frequently consult with the Registrar and, if appropriate, follow the Registrar's advice, this is a long way from allowing the Registrar the power of veto over a particular interconnection of data.

4.1.5 With respect to the retention of data held on Police files, there is a clear difference in approach. Whereas Police practice in the UK (see the discussion on the ACPO Code of Practice below) emphasises specific time limits covering huge amounts of data (eg 3 years for all cautions), the Recommendation, in paragraph 7.1, stresses criteria based more on individual circumstances (eg 'an inquiry into a particular case; a final judicial decision, in particular an acquittal; rehabilatation; spent convictions; amnesties; the age of the data subject; particular categories of data').

4.1.6 The overall impression is that the Recommendation assumes a degree of formal involvement by the Data Protection Registrar with respect to the Police's personal data which is not provided by the UK's Data Protection Act. In addition to paragraph 5.6 quoted above, several other paragraphs which deal with disclosures from Police files call for 'the authorisation of the supervisory authority' as one of the checks to ensure that the procedure properly safeguards the Data Subject. Paragraph 7.2 of the principles suggests that storage periods for the different categories of personal data as well as 'regular checks on their quality should be established in agreement with the supervisory authority'. It could be that it is the absence of any legal duty to seek such agreements which lies behind the Registrar's reticent comments in the Foreword to the ACPO Code of Practice.

4.2 The ACPO Code of Practice

4.2.1 This 'Code of Practice for Police Computer Systems', first published in 1987 by the Association of Chief Police Officers (ACPO) on behalf of all 51 UK Constabularies, outlines several procedures that strengthen the Data Protection Principles. In his Foreword the Registrar particularly welcomes such aspects and points to 'the detailed guidelines for security and for monitoring and inspection', and to 'the recommendation not only to correct inaccurate information as soon as possible, but also to inform any third party to whom the inaccurate information may already have been disclosed'.

4.2.2 However, the Registrar in also very cautious, and in two paragraphs of the Foreword stresses that he wants to see how the Code's guidance 'is applied in practice'; a third paragraph refers to the needs for 'more detailed operating rules to make the Code a practical reality'. These statements should not be taken to mean that the Registrar suspects that the Code will not be applied by the Police, but more as recognition by the Registrar of the special data protection problems that surround all policing functions.

4.2.3 Caution is also necessary since each Constabulary is an independent Data User. Establishments vary from complements of several hundred officers and civilians to tens of thousands; Force boundaries are very different in size, whilst each Constabulary faces a different mix of policing problems (ranging from the policing of large, sparsely populated, rural areas to the contrasting requirements of policing the inner city). Consequently it is very difficult to establish standard procedures that apply, and that are relevant, to all Constabularies in all circumstances.

4.2.4 Yet it is these procedures which have to maintain the important and delicate balance between the need to invade privacy, in order to protect society from crime and misdemeanour, and the need to preserve privacy, in order to protect the quality of social interactions by maintaining the confidentiality of social, business and economic relationships. The Code of Practice should be seen as ACPO's attempt to strike that balance.

4.2.5 One important inference can be made from the fact that the Code of Practice uses the words 'records', 'personal data' and 'information' as almost interchangeable. This implies that the Police consider all information (whether on manual files, in notebooks, on video cameras, or stored on computer) as having to conform to the standards established by the Data Protection Act. In addition, many of the provisions of the Code provide a clear and public statement of Police procedure, and in several instances involve major extensions in sympathy with the spirit of that legislation.

4.2.6 With respect to the First Principle, the Code states that any civilian employee or Police Officer seeking information should 'make sure that the person from whom the information is requested knows the identity of the person making the request and the purpose for which the information is required'. Although this may be obvious in many circumstances (eg during a road traffic incident), the Code accepts that an individual Police Officer should always show proof of identity and provide such full explanations as may be necessary.

4.2.7 To clarify procedures for obtaining information through the non-disclosure provisions, a pro-forma designed to establish the formal and documentary requirements of Section 28(3) of the Data Protection Act is provided in Appendix B of the Code (see Chapter 7, paragraph 3.2.12). In addition, the individual Police Officer should 'make a suitable entry in his notebook' (these notebooks are usually retained by a Police Force for several years) and, in case of difficulty, involve a 'senior officer, say of Superintendent rank or above'. By making it Police procedure to proffer the necessary details (rather than wait to be asked), Data Users can be confident that the specific disclosures to the Police are in accordance with the non-disclosure provisions.

4.2.8 With respect to disclosures from Police computers, the Code re-inforces the requirement for all disclosures to be in accordance with Force instructions (these are a formal set of rules and guidelines), and stresses that disclosures made by the Police under the non-disclosure provisions (eg between Police Forces) should follow formal procedures, with the Chief Police Officer designating a Senior Officer to take the decision.

4.2.9 With respect to the Fourth and Fifth Principles, the Code stipulates several procedures to ensure that personal data are not inadequate, irrelevant or excessive. For example, 'Opinions should be clearly distinguishable from matters of fact', and officers who enter information on a computer 'must ensure that it is adequate, unambiguous and professionally worded'. In addition, the design of systems should be such as 'to ensure that only relevant information is obtained', and consideration needed to be given to the collection process through the design of interview procedures and forms. The Code states that the source of personal data should (whenever possible) be included as part of the data; steps should be taken 'to verify the information, if possible, with another source or, if reasonable, with the Data Subject'.

4.2.10 The Code goes further than is legally required by suggesting three innovations, with respect to these two Principles, once inaccurate information has been discovered. These are:

(a) 'passing the corrected information to any third party to whom the inaccurate information may have been disclosed'

(b) 'ensuring that any other consequences which may have arisen before the data was corrected have been acted upon to minimise the damage and distress'

(c) designating an Officer with the responsibility to perform 'random monitoring' to maintain compliance with both the Principles 'on a regular basis'.

4.2.11 The Sixth Principle pertaining to the retention of personal data provides special problems for the Police. For example, how long should Criminal Intelligence data be kept? Does the retention of criminal records of minor offences inhibit the ability to rehabilitate an individual with such a record? Will the requirement to destroy crime reports reduce the possibility that a convicted person can mount a successful appeal? How can the Police assess how long to retain information received, if the information relates to a potential crime which may not be committed at all?

4.2.12 As some criminal records ('reportable offences') have to be reported to a central National Identification Bureau, the rules of retention depend on the nature of the crime. For example, the Code states that with respect to reportable offences, 'currently the basic criteria are that records will be weeded where an offender has not been prosecuted for a reportable offence for 20 years since the last conviction'. However, the Code also states that records will not be deleted for offences 'where the aggregate sentence exceeds six months', 'where there is any trace of mental history' and where 'offences of indecency', or 'offences of homicide' are concerned.

4.2.13 The Code also sets out guidelines for the retention of other Police records. For example, with respect to non-reportable offences, the record should be retained for 10 years (unless there has been no further conviction recorded against the individual during this period), or when the subject has reached 70 years of age. Cautions should be deleted after 3 years (provided there has been no addition to the record); crime reports and major incident enquiries should be retained for 6 years (unless there is an appeal, or review pending) as should records relating to stolen or lost property, and road traffic accidents.

4.2.14 Even so, it can be anticipated that there are several areas where the Code will lead to controversy, even with respect to formal criminal records, especially as such records are increasingly used in vetting. For example, who assesses the 'trace of mental history' which allows records to be kept without time limit? Is there any distinction between the 'mental history' which followed the trauma of arrest, and the breakdown associated with a crime that followed a marital dispute? 'Offences of indecency', which are also not to be deleted, will include those committed by homosexuals; could this lead to allegations of discrimination?

4.2.15 In a section on Crime Intelligence (such records, according to the Lindop Committee on Data Protection, paragraph 8.05, are by their nature made up of information that is 'speculative, suppositional, hearsay and unverifiable') the Code states that 'it is not possible to lay down strict criteria for the removal of data'; thus it is possible for controversial and unsubstantiated data to be retained indefinitely.

4.2.16 The procedure laid down by the Code to overcome such problems states that 'it is essential that all criminal intelligence records be reviewed annually'. More generally, as regards all personal data, Police Forces should consider:

'(a) why are the data currently held?

(b) what purpose do the data now serve?

(c) are the data still relevant to the registered purposes?

(d) are the data up to date?

(e) how much credence can be placed on the source of the data and the data content?

(f) how useful is the information likely to be in the future?'.

4.2.17 Regarding the Seventh Data Protection Principle, the Code outlines the formal procedures that Chief Officers of Police must follow, especially as some of the personal data could be withheld from the Data Subject. For example, with respect to data that identify a third party, the Code goes beyond the requirement of the Act and recommends that 'the location where the omission occurs should be indicated by inserting a series of dots (...)' and that this 'should be explained to the Data Subject'. Access to personnel records should be provided to Police Officers and civilian employees once a year, if requested, free of charge.

4.2.18 To illustrate compliance with the Eighth Principle, the Code lays down over 50 different security procedures, many of which are standard and of general application. However, there are some noteworthy provisions to ensure that all staff are aware of the serious consequences (criminal offences could be involved) should data be abused, and of whether independent monitoring is actively taking place in order to detect abuse. For example, the Code calls for Forces, where possible, to keep a 'computer log ... of all transactions', to prohibit 'the use of home computers for police purposes or the use of police computers for unauthorised purposes', and to ensure that all civilian employees who access personal data held for policing purposes sign a declaration under the Official Secrets Act.

4.2.19 Finally, the Code stresses that responsibility for its implementation 'rests with the Chief Officer, who should appoint an officer of Assistant Chief Constable or equivalent to ensure that effect is given to the Code'. Whilst certain responsibilities can be delegated by this senior Police Officer, the Code calls for a monthly report, on all matters, to the Assistant Chief Constable.

5. Research and Statistics

5.1 Background

5.1.1 Several events in the UK have brought the disclosure of anonymous data, extracted from personal data, into the public eye; for example there have been suggestions that anonymous medical information, extracted from a patient's medical records, could be disclosed to private organisations for medical surveillance and market research, in return for the supply of 'free' computing equipment. New powers in the Local Government and Housing Act 1989 allow the relevant Secretary of State to introduce Regulations that would enable a Community Charges Registration Officer (CCRO) to disclose anonymised information from Community Charges Registers. Every 10 years, by means of the national Census, details of all individuals resident in the UK are collected, processed as personal data, and then disclosed in anonymised form, whilst market researchers are for ever seeking information as to changing lifestyles, in order to predict new consumer trends.

5.1.2 Is it safe to disclose anonymised data in these circumstances, when there is the potential to combine the data with data relating to millions of postcodes, disks full of names and addresses obtained from electoral registers, massive databases held by credit reference agencies, or comprehensive telephone directories that could soon be available on one Compact Disk? Could sets of anonymous data be combined to constitute personal data? If so, how does the disclosure relate to the Data Protection Act?

5.1.3 Section 1(9) of the Data Protection Act defines that a disclosure of personal data takes place if the Data User either discloses personal data, or discloses data plus other information which, when linked, identify the individual. So, for example, if a Data User discloses data relating to an address, plus a photocopy of part of an Electoral Register which links that address to one name, that would be a disclosure of personal data (note that the disclosure of the photocopy need not necessarily be at the same time as the disclosure of the data). If a Data User only discloses the data relating to the address, then that would be not be a disclosure of personal data. There are obvious areas that require legal clarification; for example, is a Data User who discloses address data, knowing that the recipient intends to inspect the Electoral Register to obtain the names, making a disclosure of personal data?

5.1.4 It is realistic to assume that disclosures of anonymous data will be subject to increasing controversy, especially if their origin is a high-profile or politically sensitive source (such as information contained within medical records). For example, it is very easy to imagine that, without proper care, a CCRO or Health Authority in a rural area could disclose statistical data, say on sufferers from Alzheimer's disease, which unwittingly includes sufficient detail to allow the identification of individual sufferers. Similarly, a particularly sensitive situation is created when a list of salaries and related addresses is disclosed to a person (eg a market researcher) who could then attempt, for direct marketing purposes, to relate an address to a particular individual.

5.1.5 This problem is especially acute with respect to the 1991 Census, and there is Parliamentary pressure to ensure that any disclosure of Census data for statistical purposes is not released with too narrow a threshold (eg too few postcodes) that could be used by the recipient of Census data to identify an individual, or used in order to 'red-line' a district (eg people with an address in postcode X do not get a service). Aware of these problems the OPCS, the Government Department responsible for the Census, has announced a doubling of the 1981 threshold, so that in 1991 the minimum threshold (below which statistics will not be disclosed) is 16 households and 50 people (Hansard, 15.1.90, col 86). Finally, the Census (Confidentiality) Act 1991 makes it an offence for any person to disclose personal census information without lawful authority.

5.2 Council of Europe Recommendation

5.2.1 The Council of Europe's policy on statistical data (Recommendation R(83)10: 'Protection of personal data used for scientific research and statistics') is very firm in its pronouncements. It calls for the privacy of individuals to 'be guaranteed' in any research project (paragraph 2.1) and in Section 3 requires persons furnishing information about themselves to 'be adequately informed about the nature of the project, its objectives and the name of the person or body for whom the research is carried out'. Individuals should be informed that they are not obliged to cooperate with the research project; should cooperation be withdrawn later, on the grounds that the original briefing on the nature of the project, etc, was inadequate, the individual can ask for the erasure of any data collected.

5.2.2 Unlike the UK Government's Code of Practice (see below), which does allow for a limited disclosure of information that identifies a statistical unit, the Recommendation unequivocally states that 'personal data obtained for research should not be used for any purpose other than research', and not even for 'another research project substantially different in its nature or objects from the first', without the consent of the persons concerned (Section 4). If 'it would be impracticable to obtain such consent by reason of the lapse of time or because of the large number of persons concerned', the data 'may be used in conformity with other safeguards laid down by domestic law'.

5.2.3 The Recommendation incorporates a statement which significantly extends the conditions of the Subject Access exemption defined by Section 33(6) of the Data Protection Act. Both texts permit the Subject Access provisions to be restricted (so long as the personal data are used for no other purpose, and results are not published in a form that identifies an individual), but the Recommendation attaches the additional condition of 'adequate security measures to ensure his privacy at every stage of the research project, including conservation of data for future use' (Appendix, paragraph 6.1).

5.2.4 This statement is far wider in its implications than the UK law's Eighth Data Protection Principle, as the Recommendation requires individual privacy to permeate all levels of any research project. For example, source documents containing raw personal information would not be protected by the Data Protection Act; the Recommendation implies that the researchers should ensure that such documents **are** protected.

5.2.5 The Recommendation, in contrast to Section 33(6) of the Data Protection Act, additionally allows the Subject Access exemption to be overruled in cases 'where in view of the nature of the research the individual can demonstrate a specific interest which deserves protection' (eg personal data relating to a limited trial of a new drug). This option is not catered for under the UK Act.

5.2.6 The Recommendation opts for 'consent' with respect to most of the actions that involve personal data, and seeks, as a prime objective, that the individual whose information is being processed should be kept fully informed; steps which are generally not obligatory with respect to personal data covered by the Data Protection Act. In addition, given the background of an increasing number of computerised research projects and public registers (eg the Electoral Register), the Recommendation calls for the governments of member states to encourage their respective research communities in the 'development of the principles and guidelines contained in this recommendation' (Appendix, paragraph 10.1). In view of these increasing concerns, it is somewhat alarming to discover that the UK has reserved the right not to apply the Recommendation as far as it relates to manually processed data.

5.3 The Government Statistical Service Code of Practice

5.3.1 The Code of Practice 'on the Handling of Data Obtained from Statistical Inquiries' (Cmnd 9270) was issued in 1984 (at the same time the Data Protection Act received Royal Assent and before the appointment of the Data Protection Registrar), and outlines the general principles that should apply to relevant research projects. Although the Code could not possibly have a Foreword from the Registrar, it does have authority as a statement of principle that has been laid before Parliament; it would be wise to consider this guidance as the minimum necessary when disclosing, using or obtaining statistical (or anonymised) data.

5.3.2 In its introductory section (paragraph 2) the Code states that 'it is important to reassure respondents to statistical inquiries that they can be confident the information they give is used only for statistical purposes, except under closely defined conditions, and is not published in a way which will allow information particular to an individual person or undertaking to be discovered unless permission for this has been given'. Although the Code does not enlarge on the types of 'closely defined conditions' which would allow the identity of the respondent to be divulged, one example would clearly be when a statutory duty to disclose has been imposed by another body (eg by order of a Court).

5.3.3 Parliament has been told that disclosures of information to the Police 'are the same as those for any organisation of bona fide researchers', and information 'about identifiable individuals is not transferred except in very limited circumstances' (Hansard 15.11.84, col 313). Thus the Code suggests that the Police would need statutory authority to obtain or seize information obtained during a survey or census (ie by warrant). If they obtained information that identifies an individual for a statistical purpose the Police would have to give the undertakings described below.

5.3.4 In the main body of the text, the Code outlines a comprehensive and firm commitment towards confidentiality for the Government Statistical Service. Paragraph 2 indicates that 'statistical inquiries are identified as such to the respondent, either on the forms to be completed, or by the interviewer. Respondents are informed when response to an inquiry is compulsory under statute'.

5.3.5 With respect to other **uses** of the 'statistical unit' (eg the household, the person, business etc), paragraph 4 states that 'information about identifiable statistical units is not used for other than statistical purposes or transferred to another department or outside organisation for such purposes unless:

- this is provided for by law and no undertakings have been given to the contrary; or
- in voluntary inquiries either the respondent was so informed when the information was collected, or has subsequently given consent in writing'.

5.3.6 Regarding **disclosure** to other departments of information about identifiable statistical units, the Code states (paragraph 5) that 'Information about identifiable statistical units is not transferred to another department for statistical purposes or to organisations and bona fide researchers outside government departments for statistical purposes, unless:

- this is provided for by law and no undertakings have been given to the contrary; or
- in voluntary inquiries either the respondent unit was so informed when the information was collected, or has subsequently given consent in writing; or
- prior written authorisation has been given by a minister in the department in possession of the information, and the transfer is not forbidden in law, and no undertakings have been given to the contrary'.

5.3.7 The obligations established by the Code's paragraphs 4 and 5, to the effect that 'no undertakings have been given to the contrary', and that 'consent in writing' is needed, together with the linking of several conditions by use of the word 'and' go well beyond the First Data Protection Principle's requirement not to deceive or mislead the respondent. Together they commit the Data User (or part of the Data User) to use the information for statistical purposes only, and to comply with strong limitations (both internal and external) on disclosures of information, concerning statistical units, unless consent for the disclosures is formally obtained or is allowed by law. Note that with respect to voluntary statistical inquiries, a respondent can decide whether or not to provide the information, once the range of disclosures has first been explained.

5.3.8 The Code does allow for the transfer of anonymous information about a statistical unit, but calls for 'all reasonable care' to be taken (paragraph 7) so that 'tables or analyses' are not published or generally made available if there is a risk that the statistical unit can be identified, 'unless the respondent concerned has given consent'. The Code specifically asks (paragraph 3) the Data User to seek formal assurance from recipients that they will 'apply the safeguards of this Code', which include confidentiality 'at all times'.

5.3.9 Despite the principles of good practice enunciated in the Code, the fact that it is voluntary (and thus can be ignored), coupled with the fact that the disclosure of anonymised or statistical data may escape the provisions of the Data Protection Act (see paragraphs 5.1.3 and 5.1.4 above), establishes a major loophole that gives rise to serious concern.

6. The CSA Code of Practice for Computer Bureaux

6.1 The Code of Practice 'for Computer Bureaux Services under the Data Protection Act 1984', produced by the Computing Services Association and the National Computing Centre in April 1990, is designed to help Computer Bureaux meet their requirements under the Act. Although there is little divergence from the points described by the Registrar in Guideline 8 (Summary for Computer Bureaux), the Code sets out computer security aspects in more detail (as is to be expected since, apart from Registration, the primary obligation of a Bureau is to meet the requirements of the Eighth Data Protection Principle). These recommendations are welcomed by the Registrar in his Foreword, with the proviso that Bureaux now 'develop their own detailed procedures'.

6.2 The Code's main objective is to alert Bureaux to the basic Registration requirements under the Act, and to outline areas where computer security procedures and staff training are required. For example, Bureaux are told in the Code: how and when to register; to obtain an assurance from clients that they are registered as Data Users; to seek 'written authority' for any disclosure of personal data; to forward to the client any request for Subject Access received by the Bureau. Much of the Code is devoted (like the Code of Practice for Police computer systems) to specific security measures that a Bureau should adopt, and Bureaux are advised not to handle any data that require a greater level of security than can be provided. The Code also attempts to stop unsafe practices: 'personal data should not be used for demonstrations to prospective clients. Such demonstrations should make use of non-identifiable data' and 'media belonging to a client ... should not be used for the processing of data not appropriate to the client'. (Note that it could be claimed that these extracts of the Code endorse the use of a client's anonymised data in demonstrations to another client, whilst the use of the phrase 'should not be used' may not be very effective!).

6.3 One disappointing aspect of the Code is that it encourages Bureaux to advise their Clients to register disclosure code D206 ('Suppliers of Goods or Services' to the Data User) and also to register each specific overseas transfer if the Bureau needs to send data media overseas for engineering repair. The Code thus fails to point out that it is possible to use free text descriptions in these instances, to add clarity to the Data User's Register Entry by explaining why the disclosure or transfer is taking place.

6.4 The Code also suggests that Computer Bureaux should be passive with respect to computer security issues facing their clients. Bureaux, according to the Code, should 'inform the data users what standard of security is in force' (section 9.8) and ask the Data User to 'inform them if any particularly sensitive data are to be handled'. Although it is clearly necessary to describe existing security standards to the Data User, the effect in practice could be to 'pass the buck' on security to the Data User. Thus if a Data User fails to assess a Bureau's security standards properly, or fails to appreciate the sensitivity of the personal data to be processed, or yields to pressure to cut costs, inadequate standards might be accepted. This section of the Code can thus imply that the Bureau should negotiate with clients on the following lines: "These are the Bureau's available security procedures; please choose what is appropriate to your personal data. If the choice proves to be inadequate for your work, we cannot be held responsible".

6.5 If a Bureau interprets the Code in this way there are several dangers ahead. Firstly, if the client uses the Bureau after being informed of the security position in these terms, the Bureau nevertheless still has a duty to assess 'the nature of the personal data' and to take appropriate security measures (Eighth Principle), even though it is the client who controls the data. Section 23(1) of the Act deals with compensation not only from a Data User but also from a Bureau, if the personal data are insecurely held, and allows a Court to decide whether the Bureau did not act responsibly towards security (ie is liable to pay compensation).

6.6 Financial pressures could also mean that the Bureau may not make available expensive and professional security advice that the client needs (after all security costs money, and the security costs added to a tender document could mean that the Bureau may not get the client's business; or, once a contract is signed, enhancing security could reduce profit margins). In summary, the advice to let the Client select the security standard gives the impression that it is aimed at protecting the position of Computer Bureaux from legal action by a Client, should the worst happen following a security breach, and that it is not wholly geared towards the overriding objective of securing the personal data. The fact that the Code does not suggest that Bureaux could offer an indemnity clause, in their contract with the Client, which undertakes to accept responsibility for a security lapse should the Bureau be at fault, reinforces this impression.

6.7 There is also scope for query in Section 6 of the Code ('Registration'). The word Bureau has a dual meaning under the Data Protection Act, where it is used both in a context familiar to the Computer Bureau service industry (defined in Section 1(6)(a) of the Act), covering, in the words of the Code, 'companies providing traditional computer bureau services to one or more clients', and also (Section 1(6)(b)) a person who, again in the words of the Code, 'although taking no active part in the processing, allows others to use computer equipment in his possession'. The Code thus quotes the advice provided by the Registrar (Guideline 2, paragraph 6.3) adding that 'Processing, as covered by this point, will be carried out by the staff of the data user rather than of the computer bureau'. However, the Code then concludes (Section 6, paragraph 6.7) that Computer Bureaux in this category 'need not be concerned with the question of whether their clients have registered'. This contradicts Section 2.7 of the Registrar's Guideline 8, which states that 'In cases where a person is a bureau solely because he allows others to use equipment in his possession for the processing of personal data, the bureau need only be concerned with whether its customers are registered data users'.

7. Other Council of Europe Recommendations

7.1 There are two Council of Europe Recommendations that cover very important fields but do not have corresponding UK Codes of Practice. They are 'Recommendation No. R(81)1 of the Committee of Ministers to Member States on Regulations for Automated Medical Data Banks', and Recommendation No. R(86)1 on the 'Protection of personal data used for social security purposes'.

7.2 As the Recommendation on medical databanks predates many data protection laws, its structure and jargon differ from the later sectoral Recommendations issued by the Council of Europe. Consequently, much of the advice relates to issues resolved generally in Data Protection laws (eg issues covered by Registration in the UK), and has also found expression in the UK's Subject Access Modification (Health) Order (S.I. 1987 No. 1903).

7.3 Some of the rules for governing access to medical data (Section 5 of the Recommendation) are in advance of the legal requirements of the UK Data Protection Act. However, the procedures are probably observed by most medical practitioners, and find expression in their Code of Practice (see paragraph 1.4.3 above). For example, an individual's medical data should only be disclosed to other medical professionals on a need to know basis, and medical data should not be communicated (unless permitted by the rules of medical professional secrecy) 'to persons or bodies outside the fields of medical care, public health or medical research' without 'the data subject's express and informed consent'. Medical data should not be used for another purpose unless in anonymised form, or unless the use is authorised (by the country's data protection regulatory body), or unless the different use 'is imposed by a provision of law'. In this last case, attention is drawn to the fact that 'national law or practice may impose an additional obligation to obtain consent of the data subject' (or, if the Data Subject is dead, to obtain consent of the deceased's family or physician). Finally, and indicating the extent by which the

Recommendation exceeds UK law, Section 6 demands that 'Measures should be taken to enable every person to know of the existence and content of the information about him held in a medical data bank'.

7.4 Recommendation No. R(86)1 Protection of personal data used for social security purposes' is relevant to Social Services, Advice Agencies and Benefit providers (eg Housing and Unemployment Benefits), and adopts objectives which resemble some of those in R(81)1 concerning medical databanks.

7.5 R(86)1 lays particular stress on obtaining the permission of Data Subjects for use of their information. For example, 'personal data of a sensitive nature may be obtained from other sources only with the informed and express consent of the person concerned or in accordance with other safeguards laid down by domestic law' (the UK reserved the right not to comply with this) and 'personal data should not be communicated outside the framework of social security ... except with the informed consent of the person concerned or in accordance with other guarantees laid down by domestic law' (Appendix, paragraphs 3.3 and 4.3 respectively).

7.6 In addition, paragraph 3.4 of the Recommendation calls for each Social Security institution to draw up a list, which is to be given adequate publicity, describing the personal data items stored, together with a description of the Data Subjects, the reasons why the data are held, to whom data are disclosed, and the categories of data so disclosed. This Recommendation is not satisfied by the UK Registration system, since this permits some disclosures made by Social Security agencies to be subject to the non-disclosure provisions, and hence not to be registered; the Registration particulars do not explain which items of personal data are disclosed to other bodies; and the words 'adequate publicity' may well impose a local initiative in this respect.

7.7 Regarding especially sensitive items of personal data, the Recommendation calls for personal data on racial origin, political opinions or religious or other beliefs not to be held 'unless absolutely necessary for the administration of a particular benefit' (paragraph 3.1). Finally, the Recommendation incorporates a sentence which could discourage the use of social security numbers as a unique personal identifier: such use 'should be accompanied by adequate safeguards provided for by domestic law' (UK derogation).

Chapter Six: Staff Training

1. Introduction

1.1 In any organisation that has a significant number of employees, staff training in Data Protection will involve at least three distinct categories of training, which can broadly be classified as:

(a) basic;

(b) specialist; and

(c) advanced.

1.2 Basic training should be provided, and repeated as necessary, for all staff, at **all** levels, who use personal data during the course of their work. Management has an obligation to ensure (see Section 20 of the Act) that all such staff are taught about their responsibilities under the Act, so that they can comply with their duties towards Data Users and Data Subjects alike. These aspects are dealt with in Section 2 of this Chapter.

1.3 Staff, whether in the public or the private sector, whose work demands expertise in the recording, processing or provision of particularly sensitive personal data, or who deal directly with members of the public, generally fall into category (b). Having received basic training designed to alert them to the problems, and to leave them with a constructive and sympathetic attitude towards the solutions, such staff will then require additional instruction on the specific aspects of, for instance, Social Services, Healthcare, Crime Prevention, Race Relations etc. Furthermore, counter staff and other employees in similar situations, such as those whose work involves responding to telephone enquiries, or who are engaged in Public Relations, also need specialist training. Computer professionals not only require alerting to the implications which the Act has for their specialist disciplines, but also need to receive training with respect to other legislation (eg the Computer Misuse Act 1990). Last but not least, it is vital to train managers, directors, councillors etc, and thereby also to gain their support for the resourcing of training programmes. Specialist training is dealt with in Section 3 of this Chapter.

1.4 An example of category (c) would be a 'departmental liaison team' or equivalent group, whose members need to have a detailed knowledge of the Act, and who should be capable of amending, or devising, procedures to comply with its provisions. Such a team may be headed by a full time Data Protection Officer. Training requirements to achieve this degree of proficiency are discussed in Section 4.

1.5 Quite apart from fulfilling legislative obligations, staff training in Data Protection, with its emphasis on principles of good practice, should aim to be not only cost-effective, but also to have a positive impact on work quality.

1.6 In addition to 'formal' sessions, there are many other ways of getting information to the staff. These include:

- Brief seminars to specialist clubs;
- Leaflets and posters;
- Articles in bulletins and news sheets; circulars;
- Stickers on output and on terminals;
- Returning discarded output that contains personal data, to those directly responsible for this lapse in security (or to the appropriate manager!);
- Messages of the day on computer systems;
- Messages on print-outs;
- Lunchtime presentations (for example, showing a video continuously in a canteen area or where staff congregate);
- Notice board displays;
- Induction courses;
- Contracts of employment.

1.7 When a written case is made for the purchase of equipment and software, a suitable reference to the Data Protection Act should appear in the paperwork, to alert managers to the requirements of the legislation. Similarly, the Data User's Standards and manuals which relate to programs or data should contain suitable references to the Data Protection Act.

1.8 To end on a practical and important note for trainers: take care to select a room which is suitable for the training course and, if possible, provide refreshments. Each hour of training deserves a break of about ten minutes, to give staff a chance to recover, to discuss immediate concerns with colleagues, and to prepare the queries which any good training session should generate. Even as lively a topic as Data Protection is not proof against dull training techniques!

2. Basic training for staff who use personal data

2.1 General

2.1.1 Staff who use personal data in their work will need to know the answers to the following questions:

Why is Data Protection important to my work? What are the particular problems I am likely to encounter? What are my legal responsibilities as an employee? How does Registration help to clarify these responsibilities? What are my risks of being prosecuted under the Act? How will my work patterns change as a result of this Act? Why do I have to keep personal data confidential and use them only for the purpose(s) of my work?

2.1.2 An adequate level of knowledge, at this stage, should be achievable in a 75 minutes training session, including 15 minutes allocated to questions (but excluding any training film or video).

2.1.3 Particular aspects of work can be emphasised even during basic training, but only if this is likely to interest a significant proportion of the audience. For example, if most of the staff present deal with telephone calls, some minutes can be spent discussing that issue. If the group consists of Social Workers, reference will need to be made to the Exemption Order under Section 29 of the Act, and to proper recording of personal data so as to ensure the accuracy and relevance of those data. In the case of computer users, extra stress can be laid on security problems. Clearly it is helpful to know the composition of the audience in advance and, if at all possible, to train as a group those staff who have similar functions or problems.

2.1.4 Press cuttings may also be distributed to illustrate data protection problems and to promote discussion; suitable stories (see Chapter 4(B)) regularly appear both in the national and trade press.

2.1.5 Several professionally made training videos are available; trade associations, professional bodies (or Hoskyns IPMC) can provide further details. Consideration can also be given to an in-house production, which has the added impact of relating the message to familiar surroundings and problems. A video will help to focus the training session, and can be particularly useful if the speaker is not used to leading a seminar, or is uncomfortable when speaking in public.

2.1.6 Participants in the seminar should be encouraged to raise problems they have come across outside work; for example worries concerning 'junk' mail, or relationships with officialdom that involved their own personal data. Not only does this break the ice, but it also demonstrates how Data Protection legislation can work to one's own advantage. Realisation of the harm that sloppy procedures can cause to oneself is the first step in improving procedures that relate to customers, clients, other employees etc.

2.1.7 Sections 2.2 and 2.3 provide, respectively

(a) the text of a 75 minute basic training seminar, which can also be used as a hand-out, and

(b) the text of a leaflet which contains the basic information that should be given to all staff who handle personal data during the course of their work.

2.2 **Text of a 75 minute basic training seminar**

2.2.1 The presenter should structure the seminar to achieve the following:

(a) Outline the need for data protection, using examples.

(b) Show how the Data Protection Act is a legal remedy.

(c) Explain the framework of rules which results from the Act.

(d) Show that employees as well as Data Users have responsibilities.

(e) Carefully explain criminal offences and compensation for damage caused.

(f) Show how Data Subjects (including employees) have new rights under the Act.

(g) Explain existing procedures and relevant Registration details; this helps employees to understand their responsibilities.

(h) Explain what data protection work has to be done (eg enhanced security), to ensure that employees are in sympathy with what is going to happen.

(i) Focus briefly on particular areas of interest to the audience (eg telephone calls, dealing with members of the public, social work records, housing records, etc).

(j) Summarise responsibilities, and repeat (e) quickly to ensure that the message has got through.

(k) Leave 15 minutes for questions.

2.2.2 The following text covers the contents of (a) to (f) above. Individual circumstances will determine the details of (g) to (i), which relate to the specific audience or organisation.

WHAT THE DATA PROTECTION ACT MEANS TO YOU

An example seminar for employees of a Data User

1. The Data Protection Act received the Royal Assent in 1984 and has been fully in force since November 1987. This legislation established certain rights in relation to the personal information held, about living individuals, in the files and databases of any computer. These new rights include the rights of individuals to obtain a copy of all the details about them stored on computer, and to have inaccurate data corrected or erased. Where appropriate, these individuals (defined as 'Data Subjects') can also seek redress, via the Civil Courts, for damage and for any distress caused through inaccuracy, unauthorised disclosure or destruction of their personal data.

2. The Act established a new public body (the Office of the Data Protection Registrar) to which organisations or individuals who control the contents and use of data ('Data Users') must provide a description of any personal data which they process, together with a description of the relevant purposes involved. These and other obligations for Data Users derive from eight internationally accepted 'Data Protection Principles' on which the Act is based, and which together define a code of good practice for the processing of personal data. To ensure compliance, the Act provides for criminal offences if these obligations are neglected. The rest of this brief account explains what duties and responsibilities are involved, and how they will affect you in your work environment.

3. The Act stems from the recognition that information is a powerful tool, particularly when the information contains personal data which are capable of being processed by computer in many different ways and for many different purposes. Misuse of this power can cause considerable damage or distress to those individuals whose data are recorded. Whilst this is especially true in the case of personal data of a very sensitive nature (eg details of an individual's financial affairs, health, school reports, family life, ethnic origin, sexual problems, living conditions and employment details), damage can also be caused when seemingly innocuous information falls into the wrong hands.

4. Proper procedures and good security for personal data are therefore important, and unfavorable publicity for the Data User can result if a complaint by a Data Subject receives newspaper or TV coverage. An instance of this occurred when a man from Walthamstow in London went into the local job centre and requested details of a job

displayed in the window. The clerk phoned the prospective employer who merely asked for the man's full name and which newspaper he read, and agreed an interview the next day. Following the interview the man complained to his MP, since the employer had, additionally, obtained many personal details about the applicant that were not relevant to the job on offer. For example, the employer knew about the length of time the man had been unemployed, details of his school records, and facts about the man's blind parents. Although the information in this case was leaked from the DHSS, personal data like these are also often stored in Social Work Departments of Local Authorities, where great care needs to be taken to prevent unauthorised disclosures.

5. Apparently 'non-sensitive' personal data can also cause considerable damage if they get into the wrong hands. Lists of customers, their addresses, and details of their purchases are now commonly held on computer, particularly where warranty periods, maintenance agreements and the like are concerned. In just one typical example of the misuse of personal data, a printout of such information fell into the hands of a burglar, who then used the list to steal particular makes of video recorders to order.

6. Many lists of commonplace commercial transactions would be very helpful to a criminal. For example, if criminals could somehow get hold of your holiday bookings via travel agents, or the time you cancel your milk or paper deliveries, they would know when your home was likely to be empty - valuable intelligence to have. Thus it is important to realise that any personal information you are entrusted with, however innocuous it appears to be, or however innocent or well meaning the reason why it is collected, can be used by others for completely different and possibly malicious purposes.

7. Two examples from the public sector demonstrate this simple point, and show how information, processed for perfectly good reasons, can be perverted by unscrupulous people. An Asian family moved from one Borough to another. Their details were stored on a Housing Mobility computer system, which assists council tenants to swap council dwellings. On the day of the move, the family was met at its new home by a hostile 'reception committee' of National Front supporters who had organised a demonstration against the move, and it seems likely that personal data processed to administer the move had been used to determine the time and place of the demonstration. This case also illustrates how sensitive just a name and address, in the wrong hands, can prove to be - particularly if the name, as is often

the case, indicates ethnic origin or religion.

8. The Times of 12 July 1985 carried a small news item. It said 'French police have arrested a 50 year old former army warrant officer, now working in a hospital, after a series of rapes of women believed to have been selected from a hospital computer list'. Thus personal data which contained the addresses of patients awaiting hospital treatment, were used to select the victims.

9. Data Protection legislation allows redress in all the circumstances outlined above. For example, under the United Kingdom Act, if it could be shown to the satisfaction of a Court that the hospital in the rape case had not taken all reasonable steps to dispose of computer listings securely, and that the rapist's access to the information was unauthorised, then the victims of these attacks could claim damages from the relevant health authority. Similarly, if the 'reception committee' caused damage to someone in the Asian family, and the latter could prove that this was due to unauthorised disclosure of their personal data, and if the Local Authority in question had not taken all reasonable steps to prevent that disclosure, then the person or persons damaged would have a good chance of obtaining compensation from that Local Authority.

10. Although the Data Protection Act allows for compensation to be obtained, via the Civil Courts, **only** from Data Users, individual employees **as well as** Data Users can also be punished by the Criminal Courts and end up with a criminal record. For example, in the case of the Asian family, an employee who **deliberately** disclosed personal data to assist the 'reception committee' would be risking prosecution under the Act. Similarly, in the Walthamstow example, if a DHSS official had disclosed the additional personal data to the employer, that official would be risking criminal prosecution under the Act.

11. It can be seen that everybody and every organisation that processes personal data must take positive action to ensure compliance with the law. Data Users have to take steps to avoid claims for compensation in Civil Courts, and Data Users as well as their employees must take measures to ensure that they do not fall foul of the criminal law. This means that within each Data User organisation the responsibilities for the personal data that are processed must be clearly defined.

12. The boundary between legality and illegality is defined by the Registration process. Every Data User who processes personal data

must provide details of those personal data to the Data Protection Registrar (a kind of data protection Ombudsman, who can also investigate and prosecute offenders) for inclusion in a public Register. These details are based on descriptions of **all** the purposes for which personal data are used. For each registered purpose, a description of **all** the types of individuals who are the subjects of personal data and of **all** the classes of their personal data, a description of **all** the sources and disclosures of the personal data, and a description of **all** overseas transfers (if personal data are sent abroad) must also be provided.

13. All Data Users must ensure that any processing of personal data is covered by a Register Entry. Once registered, the Register Entries define the boundary between what is acceptable and legal (under the Data Protection Act, though challenges under other legislation are not ruled out) and what is unacceptable and illegal. For example, Data Users will be committing a criminal offence if they 'knowingly or recklessly' **hold** personal data (ie control the contents and use of the data) for an unregistered purpose, or 'knowingly or recklessly' disclose personal data to, or obtain personal data from, unregistered categories of individuals or organisations. Thus every operation on the personal data performed by the Data User must be described or covered by a Register Entry, otherwise the Data User is risking prosecution for a criminal offence.

14. However, this framework is binding on employees too. If an employee 'knowingly or recklessly' discloses, obtains, or processes personal data that are not covered by a Register Entry then the employee can be committing a criminal offence. As far as senior management is concerned, if an offence has been committed, by a Data User organisation, with the 'consent or connivance' of a Director, manager or similar employee, or through 'neglect' on the part of such an employee, then that employee is also guilty of that offence.

15. Note that there are legal definitions of 'knowingly' (ie with intent); or 'recklessly' (ie as in reckless driving); or 'consent' (ie in agreement with the dubious course of action); or 'connivance' (ie tacit consent); or 'neglect' (ie as in well-publicised 'neglect of duty' cases involving children at risk). The legal meanings of these words do not include nuances such as 'accidental, mishap, unintentional, fluke, unlucky' etc but each involves an element of 'deliberate'. Thus an employee who deliberately disclosed personal data about the Asian family to the 'reception committee', or a DHSS official who similarly made an unauthorised disclosure of personal data (see paragraphs 4-10

inclusive), was risking a criminal offence.

16. Employees should also note that they become Data Users in their own right if they process personal data unofficially on their employer's equipment. For instance, the secretary of a 'Friends of the Hospital' association, who has access to the hospital computer for work purposes, may decide to use these facilities to process the Association's financial records. Since the personal data are held by the employee (and not the employer), the employee is the Data User. If the employee has not registered as a Data User, an offence of strict liability, against which no defence can be offered, is committed. Although it is the decision of the Director of Public Prosecutions or the Registrar to initiate criminal proceedings, employees should be aware of the risks that they take in these circumstances. What would happen, for example, if such 'harmless' information fell into the wrong hands and an individual suffered damage? Who would pay any compensation for the damage caused?

17. Although criminal prosecution of employees (and Data Users) will not usually follow the accidents that do occur in real life, Data Users (**not** their employees) are not only liable to pay compensation to Data Subjects for damage caused by unauthorised alteration, disclosure or destruction of personal data, but also for damage caused by accidental loss or destruction of personal data. Compensation can also be claimed by a Data Subject who suffers damage by reason of inaccurate personal data. In these cases, a Civil Court would consider whether the Data User took all reasonable steps to prevent the accident from happening, or to maintain the accuracy of personal data. If, in the Court's view, the Data User fails such tests then the Court would assess the damage and award appropriate compensation.

18. In addition to the responsibilities of Data Users described so far, there are other aspects of the eight Data Protection Principles which govern the ways in which personal data are processed. For example, the First Data Protection Principle states that all personal data should be obtained and processed in a fair and lawful manner. Thus each Data Subject has to be made aware of the reasons why their personal data are being collected, and be given an opportunity to have specific processing activities investigated, by the Registrar, on the grounds that the consequences of such processing, for the individual concerned, are 'unfair'. This obviously has a particular bearing on those employees involved in designing forms for use by the public, or who perform survey work.

19. Other Principles state that personal data should be adequate, relevant and not excessive in relation to the purpose in question, and should be accurate, kept up to date (where necessary) and kept for no longer than necessary. In addition, personal data should only be held for specified purposes, and not used or disclosed in any manner incompatible with those purposes (these provisions form the basis of the Registration requirements). Data Subjects have the right to obtain a copy of their own personal data (following a written request). Last but by no means least, the eighth Principle deals comprehensively with the Data User's obligation to maintain appropriate security. As can be seen, to meet the Registration requirements, to avoid civil suits for compensation, to alert staff to the criminal offences **and** to comply with the Data Protection Principles means that the complete spectrum of data processing activities has to be under review at at all times.

20. Most large Data Users (eg organisations) have appointed a person responsible for carrying out this work. An ongoing component of this activity is to update or modify the Register Entries, and thus to define the legal framework which they constitute. From time to time employees may need to be asked by the Data Protection Officer to describe the personal data in their care, why the data are collected, under what conditions they are disclosed and, in general, to explain their use of the personal data. All this is necessary to ensure accurate Registration, and to allow a realistic assessment of the security risks.

21. As a consequence of such assessments, changes in working practices may follow. There could be new practices to safeguard both the employees' and the Data User's interests when personal data are processed. Employees may be told about a new security procedure, or asked to follow strict instructions when handling a telephone enquiry, or to seek approval when taking personal data to work on at home. The way personal data are collected may be changed, or employees may be asked to obtain further information to ensure the accuracy of personal data. Training courses may have to be attended so that these changes can be explained, and to provide a forum for questions about the responsibilities that employees now have.

22. No doubt some changes to procedure will be irritating, or will seem to be bureaucratic or inefficient. However, the whole purpose of the legislation is to protect the individual whose personal data are processed, and to ensure that, to the best of everybody's ability, the highest data processing standards are adopted and followed. After all, if you were the man from Walthamstow whose intimate family circumstances were disclosed to a prospective employer, or a woman

whose name on a hospital list had such horrifying consequences, or a member of the Asian family who received the hostile reception, you would be the first to complain at any lapse in those standards. Now, with the Data Protection Act, the Courts could be on your side.

2.3 Text of a leaflet for employees

WHAT DOES THE DATA PROTECTION ACT MEAN TO ME?

The Data Protection Act affects everyone, since it controls the use of all personal information that is processed by computers. Somewhere there is bound to be personal information, which identifies you, stored on a computer or most likely on a series of computers. For example, details about you will be associated with your pay, your health, your education, your home, your driving licence and your gas or electricity supply.

Information of this nature is personal data, and any individual or organisation that processes personal data must conform to the Data Protection Act. The law says that they must register the reasons why they process personal data, and obey a set of Data Protection Principles. In addition, the law says that an organisation's employees have particular responsibilities for those personal data.

WHAT ARE MY RESPONSIBILITIES AS AN EMPLOYEE?

As an employee you may handle personal data during the course of your work. You may, for example, receive a computer printed form that contains personal details, use a computer or terminal to display personal information, or you may be involved in a survey that collects personal data to be processed by computer. Of course, if you are handling personal data you are in a position of trust. The Act says that you could be held legally responsible for the safe handling of those data. **Personal data must only be used to assist you to carry out your work; they must not be given to people who have no need to see them.**

There is nothing sinister in all this. After all, you would not give your own personal data to 'just anybody' or deliberately leave data where others could use them without your approval or authority.

If this presents a problem or if you have any doubts about what your responsibilities are, please seek guidance from your Data Protection Officer, Union representative, line manager or personnel division.

WHAT ARE MY RIGHTS AS AN INDIVIDUAL?

In most cases, the Act allows you to:

- obtain a copy of personal data that relate to yourself;
- have any inaccuracy erased or corrected.

You can also obtain compensation for any damage or distress caused because your personal data have been lost, are inaccurate or have been disclosed for an unauthorised purpose.

These rights apply to everybody whose personal data are processed on computers.

WHAT SHOULD YOUR EMPLOYER DO?

An employer's first priority is to comply with the law and to inform staff that they can in some cases be held responsible if any personal data are improperly disclosed or collected. A responsible employer should:

- be quite open about the reasons why there is a need to collect personal data;
- ensure that any personal data collected are relevant, adequate and not excessive, accurate and held for no longer than necessary;
- ensure that personal data are only used for the purposes registered under the Act;
- ensure the security of the personal data held;
- ensure easy access to personal data so that the individuals whose personal data are processed can check the data to see whether everything is satisfactory.

As can be imagined, some changes in working habits may follow. There could be new procedures that will be introduced to safeguard both your own and the organisation's interests when personal data are processed. You may be told about a new security procedure, or asked to follow strict instructions when you handle a telephone enquiry, or to seek approval before you take personal data to work on at home. The ways you collect personal data may be amended or you may be asked to collect further information to ensure the accuracy of personal data. You may attend training courses which will explain these modifications and your new responsibilities. **All these changes depend on you for their success**.

The Act is somewhat limited and some employers may wish to enter more fully into the spirit of Data Protection and extend its provisions. For example, the Act permits the use of many exemptions and, in most cases, excludes information not stored on computers.

3. Specialist training

3.1 **Emphasis on computer security** (1 hour)

3.1.1 The following aspects should be included (to allow discussion of special problem areas, or of specific interest to the audience, eg for Computer Centre staff):

(a) physical security (rooms, locks, cupboards);

(b) software security (passwords, access rights);

(c) operational security (operators, central programmers);

(d) access to data by staff (counter staff, print-out, telephone calls);

(e) contract staff and engineers (any new procedures);

(f) new administrative procedures (staff leaving, equipment purchase, defining responsibilities of staff etc);

(g) review of all operations of the Computer Centre;

(h) disposal of waste output;

(i) office security (problems with open plan) ;

(j) staff liaison (discuss what is happening to improve security);

(k) any new initiatives on security matters (see Chapter 8);

(l) any relevant Codes of Practice or Procedures Manuals;

(m) Conditions of Employment (eg they usually contain a confidentiality clause);

(n) offences created by the Computer Misuse Act 1990, and the implications of a breach of copyright should unauthorised copies of software be taken.

3.1.2 It is particularly important to stress that Section 23(3) of the Act states that 'In proceedings brought against any person by virtue of this section it shall be a defence to prove **that he had taken such care as in all the circumstances was reasonably required** to prevent the loss, destruction, disclosure or access in question' (our emphasis).

3.2 **Emphasis on program design and data accuracy** (1 hour)

3.2.1 Suitable for systems designers, applications programmers and similar specialist groups. The following aspects should be included :

(a) how the Data Protection Principles affect the design of programs, how modifications to programs could help constitute a defence under the Act and how those defences are defined;

(b) what are accurate personal data, the use of markers, the difficulties in incorporating markers, what is a 'matter of fact';

(c) an overview of design considerations, better use of operating system facilities, when to liaise with the Data Protection Officer, consideration of the 'end-user', and the implications of Subject Access;

(d) data input and the importance of the validation process, internal checks and quality of data, free text fields for the use of contentious remarks and the problems these fields can create;

(e) design of applications programs in relation to Subject Access, data that are covered by Subject Access exemptions, the use of markers to state that the Data Subject has challenged the accuracy of those data, the choice of 'default' values;

(f) the importance of documentation and of checking manufacturers' software;

(g) essential procedures for authorisation and checking of modifications to applications programs;

(h) changes in operation which may require amendments to Register Entries;

(i) the need, if in doubt, to consult the Data Protection Officer.

3.3 **Emphasis on management responsibilities** (1 hour)

3.3.1 Management will need to know its legal responsibilities and to obtain an overview of what is being done in relation to data protection. The following aspects should be included:

(a) the legal implications which the Act has for staff, and what happens if the Data User does not conform to the Data Protection Principles;

(b) the need for data protection procedures and security policies. Go through each Data Protection Principle in turn to explain how each Principle works, and what questions are relevant to management (the 'Procedural Review' questions after each Principle in Chapter 4 define the major problem areas);

(c) managerial staff must ensure that the Register Entries properly represent their area of work (as part of the training session they can be asked to study the current Entries and to report any changes that need to be made);

(d) good Public Relations possibilities. Compliance with data protection procedures fosters:

- a good Data User press, and the confidence of Data Subjects,
- better liaison with staff, and
- the Data User's image as regards all Access to Information legislation;

(e) how you, the Data Protection Officer are dealing with problems, eg:

- management of the work,
- reporting structure to senior management,
- how the work schedule is being maintained,
- how conflicts are being resolved;

(f) what actions can be taken if data protection objectives are not met (ask for senior management support if you cannot answer this: compliance with the Act is a management process and a management responsibility);

(g) the timetable for action: commit yourself to firm report dates; this helps concentrate the minds of those you rely on for information, and makes it easier to obtain senior management support should this prove necessary.

3.3.2 Note that items (b) and (c) should form the bulk of the presentation.

3.4 **Responsibilities of Councillors or Board Members** (1 hour)

3.4.1 This section relates to politicians or political appointees who run certain public bodies (eg Local Authorities). Often the problem here is one of generating and maintaining interest within the limited time that is normally available. Emphasise that since Councillors have two distinct roles - as a board of management (ie as policy-making employees) and as representatives of their constituents, it follows that:

(a) as managers, they are bound by the Register Entries, as are all employees: Councillors cannot go 'fishing' for personal data that are outside the scope of their work;

(b) when they act on behalf of Data Subjects, they should make sure the Data Subjects appreciate that the latters' own personal data might need to be accessed;

(c) any constituency work (eg using the computerised Electoral Register) would **NOT** be covered by the Authority's Registration. Stress, in particular, the consequent implications for party workers, and for all political activities;

(d) within an Authority, each Council has a set of standard procedures through which Councillors can access personal data.

3.4.2 The common law principles concerning elected members were comprehensively reviewed by the House of Lords in 1983 (R.v. Birmingham City District Council). The judgement can be summarised as follows:

(a) An elected member, by virtue of his office, is entitled to have access to all documents in possession of the local authority as far as such access is reasonably necessary to enable him to perform his duties properly .

(b) A Councillor has no 'roving commission' in respect of local authority documents and mere curiosity is not a sufficient basis for access to information.

(c) In the case of a Committee of which the Councillor is a member, there is a presumption that the Councillor has good reason for access to all the information and documents which pertain to the functions of that particular Committee (note that in two subsequent cases (both in 1985) of R.v. Hackney London Borough Council, and R.v. Sheffield City Council, such access was generally, though not as an absolute right, extended to subcommittee papers even though the member sat only on the parent Committee).

(d) In the case of Committees of which the Councillor is not a member, he has no automatic right of access to material and has to demonstrate a 'need to know' to enable him properly to carry out his duties as a Councillor. Note that in R.v. Eden District Council (1987) a Councillor's interest in this respect was equated with the interests of the Council, whereas in the Hackney case referred to above the judge suggested that the 'need to know' could also be established in order to represent constituents through policies that **conflict** with those of the Council.

(e) The decision about whether a Councillor has good reason for access to the material of a Committee of which he is not a member is ultimately one to be taken by elected members themselves, but the local authority can delegate to officials the right to decide whether an application for access to material ought to be granted (subject, however, to the elected member having a right of appeal to his peers).

3.4.3 Consideration should be given to a voluntary Code of Practice on access to sensitive information. For example, the Code adopted by Lothian Region establishes that:

(a) sensitive information (eg information which has been received from the medical profession, from the Police etc) will not normally be divulged to any person, including an elected member;

(b) if an elected member wishes to obtain access to such information he is required to establish to the satisfaction of the Director of Department involved that he has a 'need to know';

(c) if a Director decides to make access available to sensitive information but the source of that information refuses to consent to the information being made available, then the Councillor will in such circumstances voluntarily relinquish his right of access.

3.5 Other specialist training requirements

(a) DATA PROTECTION ACT (Overview for management) ($\frac{1}{2}$ day)

Contents: Importance of the Data Protection Act to managers. The Data Protection Principles and their implications for management (use examples relevant to the attendees). Criminal offences and risks to the Data User that arise from the Act. Management structures to meet the Act's requirements. What use is made of personal data: relevant marketing, personnel and business uses of personal data. Staff training.

(b) NEW LEGISLATION AND PROSPECTS FOR THE FUTURE ($\frac{1}{2}$ day)

Contents: Data Protection: the European dimension, the Registrar's activities, Court and Tribunal decisions, and the likely changes in the future. 'Access to Personal Files': the current legislation, including Access via the Education Reform Act. 'Freedom of Information' and the Official Secrets Act. 'Access to Information': review of current legislation, political trends and developments.

(c) DATA SUBJECT ACCESS(Problems and procedures) ($\frac{1}{2}$ day)

Contents: Rights and obligations of Data Subjects and Data Users. Policies as they affect Data Subjects. The Register Entry 'message' to Data Subjects. Identifying the Data Subject. Locating the personal data: the pitfalls. Subject Access exemptions, and 'weeding' the personal data. Other aspects of the Data Protection Principles, in relation to Data Subjects. Access via other legislation.

(d) IMPLICATIONS FOR HEALTH AND SOCIAL WORK DATA ($\frac{1}{2}$ day)

Contents: Subject Access requirements of the Data Protection Act. The impact of the Exemption Orders under Section 29 of the Act. The importance of recording personal data properly; the accuracy provisions of the Act; sharing personal data in a 'multi-caring' environment. The impact of Codes of Practice on Health and Social Work data. The impact of 'Access to Personal Files' legislation and 'Freedom of Information' initiatives (eg the Access to Health Records Act 1990). The Access to Medical Reports Act 1988. Community Charge and NHS Trust aspects.

(e) IMPLICATIONS FOR EDUCATION RECORDS ($\frac{1}{2}$ day)

Contents: Subject Access requirements of the Data Protection Act. The impact of Sections 29 and 35 of the Act. The importance of recording personal data properly; the accuracy provisions of the Act. The impact of Codes of Practice. Access to Personal Files via the Education Reform Act. Sharing records with other departments. The problems of schools which provide for special educational needs. Schools as Data Users: Grant Maintained status, the Admissions Register and LMS implications; guidance from the Department of Education concerning the role of Head Teacher, School Governors and Education Authority. Community Charge aspects.

(f) IMPLICATIONS FOR HOUSING RECORDS ($\frac{1}{2}$ day)

Contents: Subject Access requirements of the Data Protection Act. The importance of recording Personal Data properly; the accuracy provisions of the Act. The impact of Codes of Practice. The impact of 'Access to Personal Files' legislation. Sharing records with Social Work, Health, Police and other Authorities. The relevance of structural changes to Housing management: HATs, Housing Associations, Tenants Associations. Relationship with the DSS. Community Charge aspects.

(g) IMPLICATIONS FOR THE POLICE, PROBATION SERVICES AND MAGISTRATES COURTS ($\frac{1}{2}$ day)

Contents: Rights and obligations of Data Subjects and Data Users. Policies as they affect Data Subjects. Subject Access requirements of the Data Protection Act. The impact of the Subject Access and non-disclosure exemptions under Section 28 of the Act. The importance of recording personal data properly; the accuracy provisions of the Act. The impact of Codes of Practice. Sharing records with Local Authority Departments. Official Secrets Act 1989.

(h) TRAINING IN COMPUTER SECURITY PROCEDURES (1 day minimum)

Contents: These will depend on the objectives of the Course, the level of detail that needs to be communicated, and the time that can be devoted to each topic. Subject areas include:

- **Security objectives**: management overview of necessary policies, procedures, structures and responsibilities. Security management. Risk management and analysis, performing a security review. Computer security and the law. Insurance cover.

- **Physical security**: computer centre, offices, data, equipment, specific locations (eg data preparation, network centres, public reception areas), operations, physical access, communications areas, staff, disaster recovery.

- **Software security**: management, personnel, access controls, passwords, encryption, authentication, integration into software design, checking changes to software, operating systems.

- **Network security**: LANs, WANs, dial up line security, encryption, authentication, hackers, access control, network management.

- **Micro security**: management responsibility, disk management, access control, major problem areas, computer viruses.

4. Advanced training

4.1 Introduction

4.1.1 If the Data User has appointed a Liaison Team, its members will require extended training. The schedule outlined below covers a total of about seven hours. Sections 4.2.1 to 4.2.4 inclusive provide a broad brush outline of what the Team needs to know (and include some overlap, and repetition, to hammer the points home); Sections 4.2.5 and 4.2.6 deal in detail with the work to be done.

4.1.2 Give the Team the Registrar's Guidelines (especially Guidelines 1 to 5) to skim before the course; stress that you want the members to have an overview of the Act.

4.1.3 The topics listed under each Section provide the framework of the course's content.

4.2 Training a Departmental Liaison Team / Data Protection Officer

4.2.1 **Getting to know the Act** (about 1 hour)

Note: It is very important to go through these topics carefully, and to spend sufficient time on them. If the Team members do not understand the definitions, **they will not be able to help you**. Refer to the Registrar's Guidelines for examples if you cannot provide them from your own work.

(a) **Definitions:**

- What are 'personal data'?
- When are personal data 'held'?
- What is 'processing', and how does it affect personal data?
- To what extent are output and source data covered by the word 'extract'?
- Special categories of processing (eg word processing).
- Who is a Data User, a Data Subject, a Computer Bureau?
- What is a 'disclosure'? (NB: the medium of disclosure includes printouts, letters, telephone calls, display on VDU screens etc).
- What is an 'overseas transfer' of personal data?

(b) **Understanding the Data Protection Principles**: how they apply. Discuss every Principle, and also the Interpretations in Schedule 1 Part II of the Act. This is an overview; come back to the detail later.

(c) **The Data Protection Officer:** how the Officer is responsible for the procedures to bring the Principles into effect. Outline the special categories of personal data to which some of these Principles do **not** apply.

4.2.2 **Other aspects of the Act** (First overview session of about 1 hour)

(a) **The Registration requirement**

An overview of legal aspects of Registration, with brief mention of the Registration forms and how the Data User's Registrations are organised and kept up to date.

(b) **Liabilities of staff** (both criminal and civil)

- Knowingly or recklessly obtaining, disclosing or transferring personal data in contravention of the Register Entry.
- Liability of Directors etc: consent, connivance or neglect (Section 20 of the Act).
- Stress that there must be no unauthorised use of a Data User's equipment for private purposes.
- Make sure **all these points are clearly understood**.

(c) **Data Subjects' rights:** defending the Data User

- How a Data Subject can use the Act (eg complain to the Registrar, use the Courts, Subject Access).
- Implications of the Data Protection Principles (eg fair obtaining, fair processing, accuracy, relevance and timeliness of personal data).
- Liaison with systems analysts about relevant programs and data to be built into new schemes.
- Importance of liaison with the end-users who work with personal data.

(d) **Exemptions** (select the relevant types)

- Common non-disclosure exemptions.

- Crime and Taxation (the Data User's policy).
- Health and Social Work (DSS Circulars and Orders).
- Various limited exemptions (eg payroll, pensions).
- Examination marks (impact of the exemption on educational institutions).
- Stress again that work taken home does not thereby become work for a domestic purpose (Section 33 (1) of the Act), and that the Data User's formal approval, both of the work to be done and of the security that can be provided, must be obtained before an employee takes work home.

(e) **Policing the Act and duties of the Registrar**

- To encourage Codes of Practice, consider complaints, establish Registration requirements and enforce Data Protection Principles.
- How the Tribunal, Registrar and Data User will relate to each other.
- Use of the Courts to determine case law, and of the Tribunal to supervise the use of the Registrar's powers.

4.2.3 **Work that needs to be done by a Departmental Liaison Officer** (Second overview session of about 1 hour).

(a) **Census checks** and keeping Registration up to date (you are going to deal with this in detail later). Procedures for complying with the First to Sixth Data Protection Principles.

(b) **Data Protection** (outline of the problem areas)

- Data Protection Principles in relation to the specific activities of management (eg mailshots, personnel).
- Data Protection Principles: checking that employees and agents follow procedures. policy towards compliance.
- Need for practical support (eg helplines and information centres can be a major source of unauthorised disclosures).
- Impact of changing working patterns arising from new procedures.
- Legal responsibilities of staff.

- Getting known, liked and noticed.

(c) **Subject Access** (Procedures for the Seventh Data Protection Principle)

- Identification of Data Subjects, locating the data.
- 40 days time limit.
- Consistency of approach within the Data User organisation.
- Option of removing data which identify another individual (3rd party).
- Disclosures to the Data Subject by procedures other than those associated with Subject Access.

(d) **Security Review** (the Eighth Data Protection Principle, including any Computer Bureau responsibility)

- Physical security (rooms, locks, cupboards).
- Software security (passwords, access rights).
- Operational security (operators, operating procedures).
- Applications (procedures for applications programs).
- Access to data by staff (counter staff, collection of printout, programmers).
- Contract staff and engineers.
- Procedures when staff leave or join.
- Management awareness of security issues.
- Open plan offices (staff co-operation important).
- Formal review (when is it taking place).
- Production of documentation for staff.
- Telephone or desk enquiries.

(e) **Liaison** (with Personnel Departments or Trades Unions)

- Changes in working patterns through new procedures.
- Access to staff records.
- Liabilities of staff (changes in conditions of employment).
- Work taken home by staff.

(f) **Liaison with Registrar** (keeping abreast with developments)

- Registrar's Guidelines, Guidance Notes.
- Queries to be answered.
- Case law and Tribunal decisions.
- Books and articles.
- Professional body is a useful contact (as is Hoskyns Information Protection and Management Consultants!).

(g) **Data Protection** (Training)

- Staff to appreciate the meaning of Data Protection.
- Staff to understand why all the questions are being asked.
- Staff to take care in completing Data Protection census forms.
- Staff to understand their legal responsibilities.
- Staff to alert the Data Protection Officer to any problems.

(h) **Staff awareness** (less formal approaches)

- Induction seminars.
- Leaflets, bulletins news sheets, and circulars.
- Stickers on output terminals, messages of the day.
- Abandoned output ostentatiously returned to owner.

- Lunchtime or notice board displays, posters.

4.2.4 **Compliance in your organisation** (about one hour)

(a) **Six key factors for success**

- Know the organisation's structure and functions.
- Know the key personnel.
- Know the Act and your responsibilities.
- Establish good liaison with the end-user community.
- Fit the Departmental Liaison Team into the plan of action.
- If necessary, get managerial backing to speed up progress.

(b) **Registration** (if appropriate)

- Go through every Section of each form.
- Explain every question briefly.
- Refer to the Registrar's booklet for amplification.
- Give an example (eg personnel system).
- Briefly refer to the problems of the Registration format, and identify the constructive options it allows.
- Describe the responsibilities of staff, at all levels, in maintaining up to date Register Entries.

(c) **Census**

- Periodically take a sample census of an existing scheme, activity or purpose, to establish how well (or badly) Registration is being kept up to date.
- Take a census of new applications.

(d) **Subject Access**

- Demonstrate how this is organised in practice.

- Describe any problems that may be, or have been, encountered.

(e) **Other Data Protection Principles** (how procedures in relation to each Principle are to be formulated, checked, renewed, managed etc).

(f) **Staff training** (programme to include new recruits).

(g) **How data protection works in practice** (how it links into the management structure adopted by your organisation).

4.2.5 **Departmental Liaison Officers** (advanced training for those who need to know that little bit extra: about three hours in total)

(a) **What is to be done?** Explain to the Departmental Liaison Team what they need to do **in detail** in relation to the Data Protection Principles, by expanding on the 1 hour presentation for management (see Section 3.3 above). The 'Procedural Review' questions listed in relation to each Principle in Chapter 4 provide the basis of this training session, which should also include the detail of the current action plan for implementing and strengthening Data Protection in the organisation.

(b) **What you should know:** a Departmental Liaison Officer should know

- How to implement the data protection policy of the organisation.
- How to assess the Register Entry format and the many pitfalls and ambiguities involved.
- How to assess a Data Subject's viewpoint of the Act and the implications this has for the Act and its pressure points.
- How to assess the impact of the legislation on a Data User's employees.
- How to implement the Data Protection Principles.
- How to establish and monitor practices and procedures for compliance and for maintaining good relations with Data Subjects.
- Subject Access policies and procedures, assessment of accuracy of personal data, procedures for security, for disclosures and for correcting errors in personal data.
- Exemptions and their implications (**all** relevant exemptions mentioned in Part III of the Act should be covered, with special emphasis on those of particular

relevance).

- Relevant Statutory Instruments and Parliamentary Orders, update on case law, Codes of Practice and Registrar's advice .

(c) **Problem solving**: stress that if Liaison Officers have any problem with their work, or are unsure what to do, or have any doubt whatsoever, they should err on the side of caution and discuss the problem with the Data Protection Officer (using established lines of communication, as appropriate).

(d) **Data Protection:** helping one's career prospects?

This is a good topic on which to end, since a Liaison Officer may have been 'volunteered' to this post. The fact that Liaison Officers must gain a detailed appreciation of, and involvement with, their Department's data processing will be a valuable asset to their prospects. The objective is to show that the work is not a dead end, but offers interesting possibilities of career development, for example in the following areas:

- Security advice and options.
- Procedures and Codes of Practice.
- Involvement in data processing activities; data accuracy and relevance.
- Freedom of Information aspects; access to manual records.
- Quality control (privatisation and external liaison; ensuring work is carried out to clients' specification).
- Computer audit and computer fraud.

Chapter Seven: Exemptions Understood

1. Introduction

1.1 This Chapter discusses the exemptions of personal data from some or all of the statutory provisions of the Act. The text of the exemptions is taken directly from Part IV of the Act.

1.2 Exemptions fall into four distinct categories, **none** of which has the effect of exempting personal data, as is still common parlance, 'from the whole of the Act', ie including the fundamental provisions of all the Data Protection Principles. However, since the first two editions (March 1987 and May 1988) of the Registrar's Guideline 6 used this phrase, it is not surprising that this impression has taken hold. In the third edition (February 1989) the phrase has been replaced by 'Exemptions from Parts II and III of the Act', but this description also has to be qualified since, as Guideline 6 notes in paragraph A.1.1, 'the courts may inspect the data if an individual applies to them suspecting that the data are not exempt' - a provision founded on Part III (Section 25) of the Act.

1.3 It is important to appreciate that even the exemption for 'National Security', which might be regarded as the prime activity to which the Act cannot effectively be applied, only exempts the relevant personal data from 'the provisions of Part II of this Act and of sections 21 to 24' - in exactly the same way as, for instance, the exemptions for 'Payroll, pensions and accounts purposes', 'Personal data held for domestic or recreational purposes', etc (see Guideline 6).

1.4 The Principles, however, are introduced in Part I of the Act (as applying to 'personal data held by Data Users'), and are set out in Schedule 1 of the Act. As a result it can be argued that whilst the personal data need not be registered, and the Registrar has no powers in respect of those data, and the relevant Data Subjects have no rights in respect of those data (all of these matters being implemented via Part II and Sections 21-24), there is no exemption from the Principles as such, insofar as their implementation can be effected outside the provisions of Parts II and III (Sections 21 - 24 are in the latter Part).

1.5 It follows that even where the Registrar's writ does not run, the Act implies that Data Users should implement procedures to satisfy relevant Data Protection Principles.

1.6 In Part B of the Registrar's Fifth Report (June 1989), the results of a detailed review of the Act are summarised. In agreement with a clear majority of responses to that consultation exercise, the Registrar recommended that 'There should be an enforceable duty on data users, with very few exemptions and regardless of whether they are registered or not, to comply with all eight Data Protection Principles' (paragraph 253 of the Review). Note that the key word here is 'enforceable'. It is to be hoped, therefore, that not only in theory, but also in practice, the view that the Act 'does not apply' will finally be buried in the not too distant future.

1.7 Apart from the exemptions which disarm Part II and Section 21-24 of the Act, there are exemptions under the non-disclosure provisions (which permit certain disclosures in addition to those that are specified in the Data User's Registration), exemptions from the Subject Access provisions as a whole, and exemptions which modify the right of Subject Access in respect of particular personal data.

1.8 Where a non-disclosure exemption applies, the Registrar cannot serve any notice on the Data User 'by reference to any data protection principle inconsistent with the disclosure in question' (Section 26(3)(b) of the Act). Damages may, however, be awarded against the Data User if the disclosure can be shown to be unauthorised (eg if the Data User cannot demonstrate that the exemption is valid, in which case the Registrar's powers also apply).

1.9 Note that exemptions **remove** obligations from Data Users, rather than impose them, ie Data Users are **not** obliged to make use of an exemption, even where circumstances would permit this. However, if a disclosure is to be made and the relevant non-disclosure exemption is **not used**, the disclosure will need to be registered. This means that procedures to satisfy the requirements of the First Data Protection Principle will have to be put in train (ie sources may have to be provided with prior information about the particular uses and disclosures).

1.10 A crucial point as regards an exemption from the Subject Access provisions, and which is often overlooked, is that any such exemption (via Section 26(2)(a) of the Act) abrogates the right of the relevant Data Subject 'to be informed by any data user whether the data held by him include personal data of which that individual is the data subject' (Section 21(1)). Hence in a case where all the relevant personal data are covered by this exemption, **no** indication **has** to be given in the reply, to that Data Subject, to the effect that the Data User actually holds personal data about that Data Subject (note that under the Irish legislation, for instance, this fact may have to be revealed).

1.11 Lastly, the provision that a person does not become a Data User if processing is 'performed only for preparing the text of documents' (Section 1(8) of the Act) is often regarded as an exemption, although it has its origin in the definitions set out in Part I of the Act. A dangerous misconception is that it is a 'Word Processor' exemption; however, the type of hardware used to prepare the text is immaterial in this context, and the facilities employed in the course of word processing commonly exceed the limits of 'any operation performed only for the purpose of preparing the text of documents'.

2. Section 27: National security

2.1 **Text of Section 27:**

(1) Personal data are exempt from the provisions of Part II of this Act and of sections 21 to 24 above if the exemption is required for the purpose of safeguarding national security.

(2) Any question whether the exemption mentioned in subsection (1) above is or at any time was required for the purpose there mentioned in respect of any personal data shall be determined by a Minister of the Crown; and a certificate signed by a Minister of the Crown certifying that the exemption is or at any time was so required shall be conclusive evidence of that fact.

(3) Personal data which are not exempt under subsection (1) above are exempt from the non-disclosure provisions in any case in which the disclosure of data is for the purpose of safeguarding national security.

(4) For the purposes of subsection (3) above a certificate signed by a Minister of the Crown certifying that personal data are or have been disclosed for the purpose mentioned in that subsection shall be conclusive evidence of that fact.

(5) A document purporting to be such a certificate as is mentioned in this section shall be received in evidence and deemed to be such a certificate unless the contrary is proved.

(6) The powers conferred by this section on a Minister of the Crown shall not be exercisable except by a Minister who is a member of the Cabinet or by the Attorney General or the Lord Advocate.

2.2 **Comment:**

2.2.1 Section 27 is all-embracing. If a Cabinet Minister signs a certificate to say that certain personal data need to be exempted for the purpose of safeguarding national security, then the data are exempt from Part II of the Act (Registrar's enforcement powers and Registration) and Sections 21-24 inclusive (redress via the Courts and Subject Access). Note that Section 27(5) reverses the normal burden of proof; the certificate would have to be proved 'false' before a Court could use its powers, under Section 25(2), to inspect the personal data.

2.2.2 As stressed in paragraph 1.4 above, the exemption does not extend to Part I of the Act, or to its Schedules. Consequently, the Security Service is still covered by the provisions of Section 2(2) of the Act which says that the Data Protection Principles apply to personal data held by Data Users. However, in this case the Registrar cannot, for example, follow up complaints from Data Subjects by use of his enforcement powers, as these are in Part II of the Act.

2.2.3 The functions of the Security Service are set out in Section 1 of the Security Service Act 1989, and include 'the protection of national security and, in particular, its protection against threats from espionage, terrorism and sabotage, from the activities of agents of foreign powers and from actions intended to overthrow or undermine parliamentary democracy by political, industrial or violent means'.

2.2.4 In relation to personal data, and particularly the scope of the personal data held, it is the interpretation of the words 'undermine parliamentary democracy by political, industrial or violent means' (especially the first two means in the list) that can create controversy.

2.2.5 Answers to Parliamentary Questions indicate how Section 27 works in practice:

(a) Whether personal data are properly exempt under Section 27 can be determined by **any** Cabinet Minister, the Attorney General or the Lord Advocate, who will sign a certificate to this effect (Hansard 25.2.85). Via this certificate, the Security Service can obtain, use or disclose personal data for any of its purposes without being affected by Part II and Sections 21-24 of the Act.

(b) The Data Protection Registrar is unaware of any certificate that is signed by a Cabinet Minister etc except when he accidentally finds out that a certificate has been issued. He has no knowledge of the scope of Security Service data processing (Hansard 17.12.84).

(c) The Home Secretary does not know whether any other Cabinet colleague has signed a certificate (Hansard 25.2.85). This contrasts with the position in relation to telephone tapping warrants, where only the Home Secretary or Foreign Secretary can sign warrants, and where the number of warrants issued is eventually published.

(d) Once a certificate has been signed by a Minister there is no need to renew that certificate when that Minister ceases to hold office, but the need for and scope of any such exemption will be kept under review (Hansard 25.2.85).

(e) There is no obligation for the Home Secretary to have any procedures that examine the security and accuracy of data stored on Security Service systems (Hansard 5.7.84).

(f) The Government refuses to say how many certificates have been issued under Section 27, because that would compromise national security (Hansard 20.11.86).

(g) The Government will not hold discussions with the Data Protection Registrar to produce a Code of Practice covering data held for the purpose of national security (Hansard 12.2.88) and can see no advantage in a Code of Practice in this area (Hansard 2.3.88). It is not necessary for the Registrar, in the exercise of his responsibilities under the Act, to have details on the number, scope and extent of the certificates that have been signed under Section 27 (Hansard 28.3.88).

2.2.6 It is clear that the non-disclosure exemption provided by Section 27(3) has no practical implications for the vast majority of Data Users. The Security Service is unlikely to ask a Data User for access to personal data on the grounds of safeguarding national security, since to expose this fact would almost inevitably compromise national security.

2.2.7 Even if a Data User suspects that national security is involved, eg where personal data are requested by a relevant organisation (MOD, Home Office etc) concerning an employee who is being vetted for work with sensitive information, the disclosure would have to be registered and the provisions of the First Principle complied with. However, if a vetting procedure is established by law, a non-disclosure exemption can be applied via Section 34(5)(a) of the Act.

2.2.8 In conclusion, it is pertinent to recall the words of the Lindop Committee on Data Protection whose report was largely disregarded by Government. The Committee recommended, 'in line with the best practice abroad', the establishment of a supervisory body in which there would be somebody with security clearance, so that the Security Service would be 'open to the healthy - and often constructive - criticism and debate which assures for many other public servants that they will not stray beyond their allotted functions' (Lindop: Sections 23.24 and 23.21 respectively). By comparison, all the Registrar can do is to lay a report before Parliament concerning Section 27, or attempt to agree a voluntary Code of Practice for guidance in complying with the Data Protection Principles.

3. Section 28: Crime and taxation

3.1 Text of Section 28:

(1) Personal data held for any of the following purposes -

(a) the prevention or detection of crime;

(b) the apprehension or prosecution of offenders; or

(c) the assessment or collection of any tax or duty;

are exempt from the subject access provisions in any case in which the application of those provisions to the data would be likely to prejudice any of the matters mentioned in this subsection.

(2) Personal data which -

(a) are held for the purpose of discharging statutory functions; and

(b) consist of information obtained for such a purpose from a person who had it in his possession for any of the purposes mentioned in subsection (1) above,

are exempt from the subject access provisions to the same extent as personal data held for any of the purposes mentioned in that subsection.

(3) Personal data are exempt from the non-disclosure provisions in any case in which -

(a) the disclosure is for any of the purposes mentioned in subsection (1) above; and

(b) the application of those provisions in relation to the disclosure would be likely to prejudice any of the matters mentioned in that subsection;

and in proceedings against any person for contravening a provision mentioned in section 26(3)(a) above it shall be a defence to prove that he had reasonable grounds for believing that failure to make the disclosure in question would have been likely to prejudice any of those matters.

(4) Personal data are exempt from the provisions of Part II of this Act conferring powers on the Registrar, to the extent to which they are exercisable by reference to the first data protection principle, in any case in which the application of those provisions to the data would be likely to prejudice any of the matters mentioned in subsection (1) above.

3.2 **Comment:**

3.2.1 Section 28 does not just involve the obvious: Police (who register Standard Purpose P057 'Policing') or Inland Revenue (who register Standard Purpose P042 'Assessment and Collection of Taxes & Other Revenue'), but any agency that has the legal power to prosecute offenders or to collect taxes; many public authorities have responsibilities to effect prosecutions (all these register Standard Purpose P058 'Crime Prevention & Prosecution of Offenders'). Community Charge, although commonly know as the Poll Tax, is not in fact a tax, and consequently Charging Authorities or CCROs cannot claim any exemption under Section 28. In special circumstances, the Section might apply to organisations that do not prosecute, but are asking for personal data to determine whether they have been a victim of crime; however, such circumstances are likely to be comparatively rare.

3.2.2 Standard Purpose P058 may need to be registered 'by the investigating departments of private organisations such as banks and major retailers' (see Note 3 on page 35 of the Registrar's 'NOTES to help you apply for Registration'); it may well not apply, for example, to private investigators or general investigations. Where P058 has been registered, it will be possible to argue that a Section 28 exemption could be used in appropriate circumstances; without such a Registration it could prove very difficult to justify reliance on these exemptions.

3.2.3 Section 28 provides for two exemptions: Subject Access and non-disclosure, both of which need to be given effect through formal procedures. The provisions of Section 26 of the Act (see paragraphs 1.8 to 1.10 above) establish that where a Subject Access exemption applies, the Registrar cannot exercise any of his powers by reference to paragraph (a) of the Seventh Data Protection Principle, whilst a non-disclosure exemption precludes an Enforcement Notice in relation to **any** Principle inconsistent with the disclosure in question. A Subject Access exemption therefore raises the intriguing prospect of the Registrar being able to enforce correction or erasure of personal data (paragraph (b) of the Seventh Principle), but not Access, to those data, by a Data Subject.

3.2.4 Section 28(1) outlines two conditions that must be met if Subject Access is to be denied. Firstly, the personal data **must be held** for a purpose specified in 28(1) (see paragraph 3.1 above) and, secondly, Subject Access must be 'likely to prejudice' those specific purposes. It is the Courts and/or the Data Protection Registrar who may have to judge whether Subject Access is 'likely to prejudice' a purpose mentioned in 28(1); however, it is the responsibility of the Data User, in the first instance, whether or not to apply the exemption to any or all of the personal data. Thus Data Users who exempt personal data must be prepared to justify their decision in relation to a purpose mentioned in 28(1). Note that Section 25(2) states that a Court may inspect the personal data covered by a Subject Access exemption (see paragraphs 3.2.18 to 3.2.27 below for details of the correct exemption procedure).

3.2.5 Section 28(2) ensures that Subject Access does not occur by the back door. Suppose a Data Subject complains to the Police Complaints Board (PCB) about a policing incident, and suppose the PCB investigates the complaint. Any personal data obtained by the PCB are for the purpose of investigating a complaint and not for the purposes under Section 28(1). If it were not for 28(2), Subject Access could then be possible to Police records by making a Subject Access request to the personal data collected by the PCB from the Police. Note that 28(2)(a) presents a further limitation:

any Data User claiming this exemption must have a statutory function to perform (eg the PCB has a statutory duty to investigate complaints against the Police).

3.2.6 Section 28(3) allows a Data User to disclose personal data, without the penalties associated with an unregistered disclosure, if the disclosure is for the purposes mentioned in 28(1) **and** if the Data User is satisfied that not disclosing the personal data would be likely to prejudice any of these purposes. For example, 28(3) could be used by a Public Health Inspector from one Local Authority to request some personal data from another Authority in relation to a possible prosecution under the Public Health laws. If the latter Authority makes the requested (unregistered) disclosure, and this action is challenged in Court, it will be a defence to show to the Court that these two criteria applied. Particularly where the purposes described in Section 28(1) are concerned, it is important to remember that **there is no compulsion on the Data User to disclose personal data** (see paragraph 1.9 above). It is also important to bear in mind that some disclosures to prosecuting agencies will need to be registered, for instance disclosures made during Social Work or probation case conferences will **not** be covered by Section 28 (see Chapter 3, paragraph 3.2.7(k)).

3.2.7 Section 28(4) means that the Registrar cannot exercise his powers (eg serve an Enforcement Notice) in relation to the First Data Protection Principle. Thus the Registrar has no powers to prevent the Police, Inland Revenue etc (see paragraph 3.2.1 above) from misleading people into giving information, if the application of these powers, in the specific instances concerned, would prejudice a purpose mentioned in 28(1).

3.2.8 All Data Users should have a procedure (and policy) to deal with the potentially controversial disclosures that come under this Section (see also Chapter 3, paragraph 3.2.7(h)). Within a Data User organisation, a consistent policy towards such disclosures can reduce political tension over the issue, reduce staff worries as to whether they have acted properly, and determine which staff can authorise such disclosures. Options available within the procedure are explored below in relation to the Police; they also apply to the many other organisations that have powers to prosecute or to collect taxes.

3.2.9 If a Data User keeps all disclosures to the Police within the scope of the non-disclosure exemption, these disclosures do not have to be registered (Section 26(3)(a) of the Act). Such disclosures may occur when the Police ask a Data User for personal data, or when the Data User initiates a disclosure of personal data to the Police. In both cases, if disclosures to the Police are not registered, the Data User who discloses the data should be able to demonstrate that the two criteria (relevant purpose and test of prejudice) were satisfied, to establish the defence set out in 28(3). The fact that a disclosure is unregistered does not imply that the disclosure should be 'kept secret'. Indeed the Data User could publicise the fact that, since no disclosure is marked under category 'Police forces D341', the only disclosures which the Data User permits are those which fully comply with the exemption.

3.2.10 Alternatively, the Data User is able to indicate a more open relationship with the Police by ticking D341, and thus dispensing with the need to adhere to the tightly defined terms of the non-disclosure exemption. At first sight, no problems seem likely when the Police have been registered as persons to whom disclosures may be made since, if this box is ticked, **all** disclosures to the Police are lawful under the Act, whether they are for a purpose mentioned in Section 28(1) or not. However, this option could result in enquiries or complaints from Data Subjects, in particular as to whether the 'fair obtaining' procedures of the First Data Protection Principle had been properly observed, and from organisations concerned with civil liberties, who may feel that the scope for disclosures is unjustifiably wide (since any Police employee could then expect a reply from any Data User employee to any question posed by the Police for any purpose). Depending on the Data User's registered purpose, and on the strength of the complaints, the Registrar could find such a situation appropriate for investigation.

3.2.11 'Reasonable grounds' to justify a disclosure under Section 28(3) should be established formally. Firstly, a Police Officer may have explained the circumstances of the matter being investigated and indicated why failure to disclose particular information was likely to have an adverse effect. Secondly, the Data User has to consider the nature of the request, for example whether the crime in question is 'sufficiently serious for the public interest to prevail' (this recommendation is one of several restrictions listed in Department of Health Circular LAC 88(17), which deals with the confidentiality of Social Services information). Section 116 of the Police and Criminal Evidence Act 1984 provides guidance on the nature of 'serious arrestable crime' which can be of use in this context.

3.2.12 In most cases, however, a Police Officer should be asked to sign a statement, in regard to the requested information, indicating that a failure to disclose the personal data would be likely to prejudice the Police in their investigations. Provision of such a signed statement would afford the necessary protection for the Data User, and many Police Forces have indicated that they are prepared to sign such a statement (a model form appears in the ACPO Code of Practice; see Chapter 3, paragraph 3.2.7(l) and Chapter 5, paragraph 4.2.7). Alternatively, a confidential note of the meeting with the Police, its date and outcome and who was present, could be made and circulated to attendees; this would help constitute a defence under Section 28(3).

3.2.13 A problem occurs if the Police are unwilling or unable to give sufficient detail to satisfy the Data User. For example, a Police Officer might say that some personal data will be used to 'prevent' crime in a general way. In these cases, Data Users should exercise their judgement, and remember that they are under no compulsion to disclose personal data. If the decision is taken to disclose personal data, a proper record of the disclosure should be taken as described above. If the decision is **not** to disclose, the Police should be informed of this in writing, with a copy to the Legal Department, in case there are legal consequences or the Police decide to invoke their statutory powers.

3.2.14 It is possible for a disclosure to the Police to be covered by the different non-disclosure provision found in Section 34(5)(a) of the Data Protection Act (see Chapter 3, paragraph 3.2.7(h)). For example, Section 20 of the Police and Criminal Evidence Act (1984) allows a Police Officer with a warrant to seize any computer data. To quote the legislation:

'20(1) Every power of seizure which is conferred by an enactment to which this section applies on a constable who has entered premises in the exercise of a power conferred by an enactment shall be construed as including a power to require any information contained in a computer and accessible from the premises to be produced in a form in which it can be taken away and in which it is visible and legible.'

3.2.15 The exemption from the non-disclosure provisions in Section 28 still applies if the Data User discovers a crime and involves the Police. For example, routine audit work may discover an irregularity that warrants investigation by the Police. When the evidence is disclosed to them in order to apprehend the culprit, it will be prudent to have a formal meeting and to take note of who was present, the nature of the irregularity and what personal data were disclosed.

3.2.16 In summary, there are three ways to legitimise disclosures of personal data to the Police: through registration of D341, through application of the non-disclosure provisions and, finally, in cases where there is a **legal duty** to disclose personal data. The first two leave the Data User free to act as policy may dictate, ie to **volunteer** personal data to the Police in appropriate circumstances; such a policy should consider the nature of the data, the mechanism by which the disclosure is managed, and the circumstances when the policy applies. With respect to the last option, the Data User is **obliged** to provide personal data and will therefore only need to check the validity of the obligation.

3.2.17 **Checklist for Action**: disclosures made by the Data User under Section 28(3) of the Act (ie box D341 **has not** been ticked)

(a) Form a coherent policy, for adoption at senior level, which describes the recipients of personal data relevant to this Section, and identifies those authorised groups within the Data User (eg Auditors) who might initiate disclosures of such data.

(b) Determine which of the Data User's senior staff can authorise the disclosures, and train these staff in the necessary **written** procedures. Emphasise to senior staff that there is **no compulsion to disclose**, and that they **must** satisfy themselves that the disclosure is for a purpose mentioned in Section 28, and that the circumstances justify disclosure, before agreeing to the release of the personal data.

(c) Instruct all staff that any request for disclosure of personal data under Section 28 must be referred to these senior staff.

(d) Review the number of requests for disclosures under Section 28 to see if changes in procedure are necessary.

(e) Check periodically that procedures are being followed, and that any written documentation concerning disclosures is kept secure.

(f) Emphasise that these procedures do not apply when disclosees (eg a hospital, or the Police) request personal data for 'emergency health' purposes as defined by Section 34(8) of the Act, or when disclosures are covered by the Data User's Registration.

3.2.18 Different problems can occur if a Data Subject requests Subject Access to personal data which a Data User considers should be exempt from Subject Access via Section 28(1). As outlined in paragraph 3.2.4 above, if the exemption is applied the Data User will have to be prepared to justify this stance to the Data Protection Registrar or the Courts or, under certain circumstances, give a copy of the personal data to the Courts (Section 25(2)). It is likely that a Data User applying this exemption will have registered personal data for a purpose in Section 28(1), using one of Standard Purposes P042, P057 or P058. Note that even if a Data User **has** registered P042 (which comprises 'Assessment and collection of taxes, duties, levies or other charges'; see page 31 of the Registrar 'NOTES'), the exemption can only be used if a 'tax or duty' is involved (eg for relevant Road Fund Licence personal data, but not for Community Charge personal data).

3.2.19 It is unlikely that **all** personal data relating to a specific Data Subject will be exempt from Subject Access - the exemption covers only those personal data whose disclosure to the Data Subject would 'prejudice' any of the issues mentioned in 28(1). This means that the Data Subject must be allowed Access to all those personal data that do **not** 'prejudice' those issues, as the following example should make clear.

3.2.20 Consider a Public Health database which includes a list of names and other identifying particulars, details of offences and vehicles used in suspected dumping of waste, and finally a description of the criminal convictions of the individuals concerned. Assume that the complete personal data held on Joe Bloggs by the Authority comprise: Joe Bloggs' description, details of yellow van, conviction details in Brighton, details of suspected offence in London.

3.2.21 Following a Subject Access request, Joe Bloggs is entitled to the identification particulars about himself and the details about his conviction in Brighton. This is because his description and details of previous convictions may well be matters of public record (read in Open Court, reported in the newspapers etc) and, even if not already fully reported, or known to Joe Bloggs, because they are not capable of being designated as prejudicial to one or more of the relevant purposes.

3.2.22 The details concerning the suspected offence in London may be withheld under Section 28(1) if it is clear that Access could prejudice a future prosecution. The details concerning the vehicle may also be withheld if they relate to these suspicions. However, if the details of the vehicle are only associated with the offence that had been committed in Brighton, then they would have to be released.

3.2.23 What happens if disclosing the information that **any** item of personal data is held by the Data User, would tip Joe Bloggs off that he is under suspicion or would otherwise prejudice a Data User's purpose under 28(1)? In this case, the Data User can withhold **that** information as well, so long as the application of the exemption can be justified (see paragraph 1.10 above).

3.2.24 What then to tell the Data Subject in such circumstances? Clearly, the reply cannot be of the form 'we are withholding data under the provisions of exemption ...', and would have to be phrased in a neutral way, for example 'These are the personal data to which you are entitled under the Subject Access provisions of Data Protection Act.' The Registrar has suggested 'I do not hold any personal data which I am required to reveal to you' if **all** the personal data are exempt from Subject Access (see Guideline 6, paragraph C.1.2 and Guideline 5, paragraph 2.8). However, if different replies are used in different situations, Data Subjects might then be able to draw conclusions prejudicial to a Section 28 purpose! It follows that the reply to a Data Subject when no personal data are held, or when all the data are being provided, should use **the same neutral format** as the reply to a Data Subject whose personal data are wholly or partly exempt.

3.2.25 A final problem which relates to Section 28(2). A Data User may receive personal data, covered by a Subject Access exemption under this Section, from another Data User (eg the transfer of data between two Police Forces). In such cases, procedures can ensure that the personal data are marked so that there is no risk that they are disclosed to the Data Subject by a 'back door' route. Note, however, that if such personal data were disclosed to Data Users who had no 'policing' status (eg to a Local Authority who invite Police to social work case conferences concerning child abuse), then the Authority could not apply the Subject Access provisions described in Section 28. (See also paragraph 4.3.14 where a similar problem is identified in relation to Social Work records).

3.2.26 **Checklist for Action**: holding personal data exempt from Subject Access under

Sections 28(1) and (2) of the Act

(a) Determine whether any personal data under these Sections are held, and be prepared to justify why the personal data are covered by an exemption; formal records will help to prove that the Data User acted reasonably and responsibly.

(b) If such personal are held, determine how to reply to a Data Subject without prejudicing a Section 28 purpose, and what data, if any, can be released.

(c) Inform recipients of 'Subject Access exempt' personal data about the exemption, so that 'back door' Access to the data can be prevented if legislation permits this.

(d) Ensure that personal data covered by a Subject Access exemption, and received from another organisation, are recognised so that 'back door' Access can be prevented if legislation permits this.

(e) Ensure that with respect to these personal data a P042, P057 or P058 Standard Purpose has been registered by the Data User.

3.2.27 Finally, note that the Home Secretary could make an Order under Section 2(3) of the Data Protection Act to modify or supplement the Data Protection Principles in relation to personal data concerning criminal convictions.

4. Section 29: Health and Social Work

4.1 Text of Section 29:

(1) The Secretary of State may by order exempt from the subject access provisions, or modify those provisions in relation to, personal data consisting of information as to the physical or mental health of the data subject.

(2) The Secretary of State may by order exempt from the subject access provisions, or modify those provisions in relation to, personal data of such other descriptions as may be specified in the order, being information -

(a) held by government departments or local authorities or by voluntary organisations or other bodies designated by or under the order; and

(b) appearing to him to be held for, or acquired in the course of, carrying out social work in relation to the data subject or other individuals;

but the Secretary of State shall not under this subsection confer any exemption or make any modification except so far as he considers that the application to the data of those provisions (or of those provisions without modification) would be likely to prejudice the carrying out of social work.

(3) An order under this section may make different provision in relation to data consisting of information of different descriptions.

4.2 Background

4.2.1 Section 29 allows the Secretary of State to modify (by Order, which has to be passed by both Houses of Parliament) the Subject Access provisions in relation to personal data which pertain to an individual's physical or mental health or to information used in relation to Social Work. Such personal data could be held by central government, local authority, health authority, voluntary organisation or other bodies specified in the Order and a single Order may include many restrictions of varying degrees of exemptions.

4.2.2 The background to Orders under this Section involves long-lasting controversies over the 'style' of care, and the status of professionals who exercise the care of individuals. Many professionals value the traditional secrecy pertaining to personal data in this sphere of work, and support broad exemptions from Subject Access. This is because they consider that Subject Access will reduce frankness in record keeping, alarm the patient or client unnecessarily, and be unintelligible or misunderstood unless scarce resources are diverted to explain to the Data Subject the complex terms used in the record.

4.2.3 Other professionals hold the reverse view. They consider that any method of checking the integrity and accuracy of records with clients will both reassure the client, or patient, increase the element of trust in the professional relationship and reduce paternalism. Social Workers in particular are generally sympathetic towards Subject Access, and prefer to open records to clients, whereas some parts of the medical profession have opposed this approach.

4.2.4 Differences of this kind had a bearing on the relevant Orders which the then Department of Health and Social Security (DHSS) prepared for the Home Office, and the definitions of Social Work personal data and Health personal data provided in these Orders, together with the definition of 'serious harm' (the principal grounds on which Access can be refused) are all fraught with legal complications.

4.2.5 The divergence in approach between Health and Social Work professionals finds expression in the wording of the Sections in the Act which describe the exemptions for Subject Access that relate to Health and to Social Work personal data. The Subject Access modification for Health personal data must relate to 'information as to the physical or mental health of the Data Subject'; for Social Work the modification only applies if Access would 'prejudice the carrying out of social work'. Thus the wording of any Order could allow Health personal data to be exempt from Subject Access even though Access would not prejudice the carrying out of health care; however, this option has not been pursued.

4.2.6 The problems of Subject Access in these fields are exacerbated by the way information is exchanged between professions. In the past, notes on a client would form an aide-memoire and were usually limited to the professional who compiled a paper file. Now, computer systems and a multi-agency approach to the provision of care allow for the collection and common use of large quantities of information by many professionals, some of whom might only meet the Data Subject sporadically, if at all.

4.2.7 In addition, within the public sector, Health and Social Work records are often used together. Highly sensitive aspects can be involved (eg information concerning AIDS sufferers which is disclosed to Education and Housing Authorities; information about child abuse which may be released to the Police; information concerning the psychiatric problems of patients, which may need to be disclosed to hospital administrators; information concerning the treatment of patients, needed by accounts staff for invoicing purposes). Consequently, extra care has to be taken to ensure that confidentiality is respected, and that Subject Access exemptions are properly applied across many organisations.

4.2.8 Specific difficulties in relation to a multi-agency approach to the provision of care include:

(a) How can a Data User involved in such work recognise whether personal data fall within an exemption Order? If the Data User's registered purpose is P062 ('Provision of Health Care') or P054 ('Social Services/Social Work') the decision may be easy to make, but how is this problem resolved if the personal data are used with another purpose, for instance, P022 ('Education and Training Administration')?

(b) What procedure is to be followed if a Data User receives, from another organisation, personal data which are provided in confidence (see paragraph 4.6.1(c)) or which are claimed to be exempt from Subject Access (see paragraphs 4.5.1 to 4.5.6)? How does the recipient Data User deal with Subject Access to personal data received in this way?

(c) How is the Data User to assess whether allowing Access to personal data could seriously harm the Data Subject or another person? If, amongst the various agencies concerned, there are differing professional viewpoints on 'serious harm', is there a mechanism for allowing these viewpoints to be reconciled?

(d) How will a Data User department indicate, to a different department or to another Data User, that the personal data being disclosed are deemed to fall within the scope of a Subject Access exemption?

(e) At what stage should legal or other professional opinion be sought concerning Subject Access to the personal data in question?

4.3 **Comment: the Social Work Order**

4.3.1 Studying the history of the Social Work Order, which (together with the Health Order) was only approved by Parliament one week before the date from which Subject Access became possible, gives some idea of the difficulties which it presented to Government. A 1985 consultation paper entitled 'Subject Access to Social Work Records, Personal Social Services - England and Wales', started from the viewpoint of **providing** access to records, a position promoted in 1983 by Government circular LAC 83(14). However, the 1985 paper concluded that an Order for Subject Access exemption should:

(a) 'designate health authorities and voluntary organisations under it as the need arises to safeguard the flow of information between authorities;

(b) withhold information about a third party whose identity, although not given, could be deduced;

(c) withhold information given expressly in confidence by a third party;

(d) protect provisional opinions of social work departments where Subject Access would prejudice social work;

(e) withhold information that would harm the Data Subject.'

4.3.2 Had these proposals been incorporated into an Order this could have totally restricted access. For example, personal data received from a third party could routinely be coded as 'given expressly in confidence' and thus become exempt from Subject Access.

4.3.3 And what is a 'provisional' opinion? Although the DHSS paper stated that social work clients could have access to the decisions affecting them and to the reasons for these decisions, it did not define a 'provisional' opinion. By contrast, the LAMSAC Code of Practice for 'Personal Information in Social Services', issued in January 1987 to Social Work practitioners, suggested that such Social Work opinions should be 'examined every twelve months' and 'irrelevant, trivial or outdated material' deleted.

4.3.4 Acknowledgement of these diverging viewpoints could be found in DHSS 'Notes', on

'Construction of the Social Work Order', circulated in November 1986. These outlined the consultation process since 1985, and showed that only 9% of the profession wanted total Subject Access exemption for Social Work personal data. Conclusions regarding the four principal grounds on which Access might be withheld were summarised as follows:

(a) 'Where identity of third party could be deduced: as proposed, uncontroversial (those who opposed did so because they thought the Act already allowed for this; it does not).

(b) If information provided in confidence by third party. Those consulted favoured this safeguard but it would be a major change to the Act. Moreover the other safeguards should cover this position.

(c) If confidential provisional opinion. Many favour the proposal but saw difficulty in distinguishing such opinion from final decision. And protection in (d) below could be sufficient.

(d) If subject would be harmed. Generally accepted and possibly extended to cover another person. Therefore it is proposed that information may be withheld if data subject or another person may suffer **serious** harm if access were granted.'

4.3.5 These findings were reflected in the final version of the Social Work Order (SI 1987 No. 1904) which modified the Subject Access provisions (in Section 4 of the Order) to allow for:

(a) personal data to be withheld from the Data Subject if Access is likely to cause serious harm to the Data Subject or to any other person. Pertinent examples of 'any other person' (who was likely to be seriously harmed by some action of the Data Subject following Subject Access) could be friends or family of the Data Subject (eg if the information provided would cause the Data Subject, a mother, to desert her children). Additionally, this provision of the Order can be used to protect an employee of the Data User, or a 'relevant person' acting in a Social Work capacity (see paragraph (b) below), who may be at risk following Subject Access (eg if Access is likely to cause the case worker to be assaulted);

(b) personal data to be withheld from the Data Subject if the identity of another individual is disclosed or could be deduced from the context of the data. This provision does not apply if the other individual concerned is a 'relevant person' as defined in paragraph 4(6) of the Order (eg an employee of the Data User working in a Social Work capacity, or any other person paid for providing a similar service), or if the other individual has consented to the disclosure of the data.

4.3.6 These aspects of the Order allow an exemption to Subject Access if the Data Subject's special knowledge **can be used** to infer the source of the data (**other** than an employee etc as referred to above). In practical terms, for instance, the identity of a neighbour who reported a social problem affecting a nearby family can be protected, but **not** the identity of the case worker who made comments in relation to the family. However, as explained in Chapter 4(A) paragraph 4.7.12, should the Data User have firm grounds for believing that Access to the data was likely to result in serious harm to any individual (eg the Social Worker was likely to be attacked by the Data Subject) then the data should **NOT BE DISCLOSED**. The reasons for refusing Access should be fully documented by the Data User, in case refusal has to be defended to the Registrar or before a Court.

4.3.7 The Order thus allows for Subject Access to provisional opinions, and to personal data received in confidence, as long as the limitations outlined in paragraphs 4.3.5 (a) and (b) above are not contravened; however, much information of this kind can contain personal data of the type that would be exempt. Section 3 of the Order defines the meaning of Social Work by listing the many organisations empowered to exercise Social Work functions, together with the relevant statutes - some ten Acts of Parliament.

4.3.8 In determining what constitutes 'serious harm', the Social Work Order specifies 'serious harm to the physical or mental health or emotional condition' of the Data Subject or any other person. If Subject Access is to be refused on these grounds, Data Users will have to document carefully and formally their precise worries concerning 'serious harm', so that the reasons are available to the Courts (or Registrar) if the exemption is contested (in certain circumstances a legal opinion as to the correct course of action may be necessary). Also, since the conditions that can cause 'serious harm' one day might not cause serious harm the next, personal data exempted on these grounds (especially 'emotional condition') may have to be released to the Data Subject on a subsequent Access request. In some cases, the application of the definition of 'serious harm' will have to take into account what counselling will be available to explain the proper meaning of the personal data to the Data Subject; for example, counselling can ameliorate the impact of the personal data and, thus, reduce the chances of 'serious harm' being caused to the Data Subject.

4.3.9 In most cases, therefore, **some** personal data will **have** to be released to the Data Subject, following a Subject Access application: only those personal data that would be likely to result in 'serious harm' can be withheld. Any 'condition' **other** than the three specified in relation to 'serious harm' (eg financial condition, rather than physical, mental or emotional condition) would constitute insufficient grounds on which to refuse Access.

4.3.10 Uniquely amongst the Subject Access exemptions, if **all** the personal data covered by a single Subject Access request are exempt, this fact has to be revealed to the Data Subject, ie the Data Subject is still entitled to be informed **whether** data are held. This situation could occur if a separate Register Entry deals with a controversial topic and arises because, in order to restrict the scope of the exemption, paragraph 4(2) of the Social Work Order confines the exemption narrowly to Section 21(1)(b) of the Act and to paragraph (a)(ii) of the Seventh Data Protection Principle (thus Section 21(1)(a) and paragraph (a)(i), which entitle an individual to be told **whether** data are held, remain valid).

4.3.11 However, if Social Work personal data are supplied in evidence to, and held by, a Court, a specific exemption, via paragraph 4(1) of the Order, from 'the subject access provisions' (ie from the whole of Section 21 and the whole of paragraph (a) of the Seventh Data Protection Principle), applies.

4.3.12 Where exempt Social Work personal data are disclosed to any other Data Users **of a category designated under Section 3 of the Order**, and held by them (eg Health Authorities), the Subject Access exemption may still apply. It is therefore important that these latter Data Users, ie the recipients, know what to do should a Data Subject seek Access to personal data that have been provided by such another Data User. If at all possible a Social Work Department should mark the relevant personal data (eg by means of a code which would alert the recipients to seek the advice of the Social Work Department if Subject Access is requested).

4.3.13 Such a reference back to the originating Social Work Department is not made mandatory by the Order (unlike the Health Order - see paragraph 4.4.5 below). However, Social Work professionals are clearly more likely than anyone else to have up-to-date information on, say, the 'emotional condition' of the Data Subject, and thus to be able to exercise the required professional judgement concerning 'serious harm' or what prejudices 'the carrying out of social work'.

4.3.14 Lastly, Social Workers and others involved with Social Work data should always be alert to the fact that, if such personal data are disclosed to and held by Data Users **not** within the categories designated under Section 3 of the Order, these Data Users would not be able to use the provisions of the Order to exempt any such data from Subject Access.

4.4 Comment: the Health Order

4.4.1 Within the Health Service, the division over policy towards Subject Access is public knowledge. In the appendix to a DHSS paper published in 1985 ('Data Protection Act - Subject Access to Personal Health Data'), the influential 'Inter Professional Working Group on Access to Personal Health Information', chaired by Sir Douglas Black, stressed: 'We support the right of patients and clients to have access to all information which is held about them on their behalf. Such access encourages openness and can improve the quality of record by correcting factual errors and reducing misunderstandings'.

4.4.2 The Group also added that there 'are some situations in which the unregulated release of the entire clinical or social records could cause distress or harm'. The Subject Access exemption for health records proposed in the DHSS paper was, in general, along these lines, and suggested that the criteria for restricting Access should be expressed in relation to 'harm to the subject'.

4.4.3 Although the Council of the British Medical Association supported this approach, the BMA meeting in June 1986 voted, by a small majority, to deny patients Access to their medical records. Some commentators noted that an undercurrent of the debate was the use patients could make of their medical records when taking legal action for malpractice - for example, according to one press report (ComputerScope, September 1987) many Subject Access applications in France are from certified lunatics who wish to identify the medical practitioner who committed them to an institution.

4.4.4 Following the BMA meeting, the Data Protection Registrar stated (The Guardian, 16.7.86) that the removal of the right of Subject Access to medical records held on computer:

'would not be consistent with the spirit or intent of the Act, or the Council of Europe Convention the Act seeks to ratify. The modification of the right in particular circumstances, where to give an individual medical information would seriously damage him or her, could be consistent with the Act and the Convention, both of which seek to benefit the individual. The right of access might perhaps be delayed to give a doctor time to counsel his or her patient. The mechanism by which a modification could be implemented would need careful consideration. There should be a right of appeal by the individual to the registrar or the courts; this would be consistent with other 'tests of prejudice' in the Act.' (These conclusions were repeated on page 21 of the Registrar's Third Report, dated June 1987).

4.4.5 As a result of all these differing viewpoints, the DHSS, in effect, handed the problem of Subject Access to health data back to the relevant health professional. The Health Order (SI 1987 No.1903) states (in Section 4 of the Order) that the Subject Access provisions shall not have effect (ie Health personal data may be withheld):

(a) if the release of personal data is likely to cause serious harm to the physical or mental health of the Data Subject. (Note that, unlike in the Social Work Order, the phrases 'emotional condition' and 'or any other person' are not present);

(b) if the identity of another individual is disclosed or could be deduced from the context of the data (even following the omission of names or other identifying particulars). This provision would not apply if the individual is a health professional who has been involved in the care of the Data Subject, or if the other individual has consented to the disclosure of the data.

(c) if the data are Health personal data held by person who is not a health professional, until an 'appropriate health professional' has been consulted as to whether (a) or (b) above applies.

4.4.6 Note also that, in contrast to the Social Work Order (see paragraph 4.3.10), if **all** the Health personal data are exempted then the Data Subject is not entitled to know **whether** such data are held, since the exemption covers 'The subject access provisions' as a whole (paragraph 4(1) of the Order).

4.4.7 The Subject Access procedures for Health personal data thus differ from those for Social Work data on three key issues - the absence of any right to know whether relevant data are held by a Data User, the obligation of certain Data Users to consult a health professional, and the disregard of the effect of Subject Access on anyone other than the Data Subject. The latter two items are discussed in more detail below.

4.4.8 If Health personal data are held by a Data User who is **not** a health professional (the Schedule to the Order defines who **is** a health professional) an 'appropriate health professional' (as defined in paragraph 4(6) of the Order) **must** be consulted prior to the release of the data. The individual to be consulted is the health professional responsible for generating the information in question (note that this approach is open to criticism since there is always the possibility that the interests of the Data Subject do not coincide with those of the health professional; see paragraph 4.4.3 above). If such consultation is likely to prove impossible (eg within the Subject Access time limit), the Order stipulates consultation with a suitably experienced and qualified health professional.

4.4.9 Data Users should, therefore, have contingency arrangements in case the appropriate health professional is not available; in rare instances this could mean paying consultancy fees. It follows from these considerations that personal data received from a health professional should always be recorded and disclosed with sufficient details to determine their origin (ie health data require at least a primitive 'disclosure log'). If all else fails, and given the time constraint of 40 days to complete Subject Access, DHSS Circular LAC(88)16 dated July 1988 advises that 'in the absence of a response to a request to the appropriate health professional on whether information should be withheld, the authority as the data user is obliged to provide access to the applicant'. Note that in critical cases of likely serious harm, and where the health professional's advice cannot, for good reason, be obtained in time, it would be prudent to keep formal records of the attempts to consult the health professional.

4.4.10 As noted in paragraph 4.4.5(a) above, there is no provision in the Health Order for protecting 'any other person' from serious harm; this reflects the text of the Council of Europe 'Regulation for automated medical databanks' (Recommendation No. R(81)1; see also Chapter 5, paragraph 7.3) which does not include any such provision. The **Order**, therefore, cannot be used in **any** circumstances to withhold

Health personal data from Subject Access on the grounds that they reveal (directly or by deduction) the identity of the health professional. However, as explained in Chapter 4(A) paragraph 4.7.12, should the Data User have firm grounds for believing that Access to the data was likely to result in serious harm to any individual (eg the source of the data was likely to be attacked by the Data Subject) then the data should **NOT BE DISCLOSED**. The reasons for refusing Access should be fully documented by the Data User, in case refusal has to be defended to the Registrar or before a Court.

4.4.11 Furthermore, the omission of 'or any other person' may well lead to anomalies. For instance, in contrast to the example for Social Work personal data given in paragraph 4.3.5(a), **Health** personal data that were judged likely to cause the Data Subject (a mother) to desert or injure her children could not be exempted from Subject Access on these grounds (an argument that such action by the mother could only follow if she herself had first been seriously harmed might be difficult to sustain!).

4.5 Health and Social Work personal data: some problems in common

4.5.1 As in the case of the Section 28 exemption (see paragraph 3.2.24 above), refusal of Access raises the problem of what to tell the Data Subject. In the case of personal data covered by the Health Order, particular care would need to be taken to ensure that the form of a reply was not likely, in itself, to cause 'serious harm' to the Data Subject, and the Data User could say something on the lines of 'These are the personal data to which you are entitled under Section 21 of the Data Protection Act'.

4.5.2 As far as the Social Work Order is concerned this statement alone would not suffice if **all** the personal data are exempt, since this fact itself would have to be revealed (see paragraph 4.3.10 above). As a result, some Data Users may have structured their Register Entries in a way that does not permit individual identification of sensitive databases. Such structuring may, however, then be open to the criticism that it contravenes the spirit of the Act, or is designed to frustrate Subject Access expressly permitted by the Order.

4.5.3 Some Social Work Departments may also take the view that an ambiguous reply could undermine their open-file policy towards their clients. For example, if the form of reply led clients to suspect that some Social Work personal data were being withheld, they might also conclude that data were being held on other secret files. To avoid such a situation, the Data User might want to be more explicit, eg 'These are all the personal data which relate to your Social Work record, except for Health personal data which can only be released to you following consultation with the appropriate health professional'.

4.5.4 Such a statement by the Data User could, however, be in breach of the exemption, and the reaction of the health professional should first be ascertained, since if the

Health personal data are **subsequently** exempted by the health professional, the Data Subject might draw a damaging inference from this.

4.5.5 The mandatory consultation with a health professional can sow the seeds of future dispute. For example, suppose a Social Work Department receives personal data from a health professional, and subsequently receives a Subject Access request for these data. What happens if, following discussions between the two organisations concerning the nature of 'serious harm' to the Data Subject, the Social Work Department wants to give Access, but the health professional advises that Access should be refused?

4.5.6 Since the Order specifies 'consultation', and not 'consent', the Social Work Department could still decide to release the personal data. However, this could lead to a conflict which, if unresolved, could impede subsequent collaboration between the two parties.

4.5.7 A further potential source of problems is the fact that Health personal data are defined in paragraph 3(1) of the Health Order as being held or first recorded by a health professional (and thus are covered by the Order irrespective of who eventually holds the data), whereas Social Work personal data are defined as such only if held by a Data User described in Section 3 of the Social Work Order (see paragraphs 4.3.12 and 4.3.14 above). As Health and Social Work personal data often form part of the same file it is advisable to hold discussions, between all those concerned, regarding shared data. Files should be structured so that Health personal data can be distinguished, and disclosure procedures should be standardised, so that **any** personal data likely to be covered by a Section 29 exemption can be recognised **by all parties** who hold such data. In addition, it will be useful to establish procedures to deal with problems that may arise from Subject Access, especially those that result from differences in professional attitudes towards 'serious harm'.

4.5.8 It should not be overlooked that access to Social Work manual files, held by 'a local social services authority', is now provided by an Order made under the Access to Personal Files Act 1987 (SI 1989 No 206, which came into force on 1.4.89). The Regulations differ in a number of aspects from those established for Social Work personal data, notably as regards the exemption from access to Health personal information (ie not data) held by such an Authority and which originated from or was supplied by a health professional. In this case not only must the local authority seek the advice of the health professional but, if the advice is in writing and if it clearly states that the information **must** not be disclosed, then the Authority has no option but to withhold the information.

4.5.9 As far as information in Health manual records is concerned, the 'Access to Health Records Act 1990', which gives individuals the right to see their own records, came into force on 1st November 1991 and covers Health records compiled after that date.

(The provisions of the Act are explained in 'A guide for the NHS' which was issued by the Department of Health in August 1991.)

4.5.10 The Act defines Health manual records as those compiled by a 'health professional' in connection with the care of the patient, and thus excludes, for example, information obtained for litigation or criminal investigations. The equivalent provisions of the Data Protection Act, and of the Subject Access Modification (Health) Order 1987, have been incorporated, eg to protect the privacy of third parties (but not the identity of a health professional); to protect the health of patients who could be seriously harmed by Access (prior consultation with 'the appropriate health professional' is mandatory); to provide Access within 40 days (with a special provision of 21 days if information had been recorded less than 40 days prior to the Access application). Additionally, the Act provides for Access, 'where the patient has died', by 'the patient's personal representative and any person who may have a claim arising out of the patient's death'.

4.5.11 Mention must also be made of the 'Access to Medical Reports Act 1988' which relates to any such report, on an individual, which is to be, or has been, supplied by a medical practitioner for employment purposes or insurance purposes (the Act does not apply to reports prepared before 1.1.89). The Act gives individuals the right to see their reports **before** they are supplied, to withhold consent to the supplying of the report, and to request amendment of any part which the individual considers to be incorrect or misleading (or to attach a statement to this effect). Exemptions under this Act are generally similar to those in the Data Protection Act, and include the crucial provision that if part or all of the medical report is exempted, ie is to be withheld from the individual, then the latter has to be informed of that fact (again, **before** the report is supplied, so that consent to this can be refused).

4.5.12 The problem of Subject Access by minors, or by parents, legal guardians, etc on behalf of their children, is noted here since a Data User will have to exercise particularly sound judgement when Access is requested to a young person's Health or Social Work personal data. In general, Subject Access under these circumstances should be in the child's interests (see Chapter 4(A) paragraphs 4.3.3 and 4.3.4); in some cases a legal opinion may be necessary before Subject Access is granted. The Children Act 1989, referred to in this paragraph, provides the following useful list of points to be considered in relation to children (Section 1(3) of the Act):

(a) 'the ascertainable wishes and feelings of the child concerned (considered in the light of his age and understanding);

(b) his physical, emotional and educational needs;

(c) the likely effect on him of any change in his circumstances;

(d) his age, sex, background and any characteristics of his which the court considers relevant;

(e) any harm which he has suffered or is at risk of suffering;

(f) how capable each of his parents, and any other person in relation to whom the court considers the question to be relevant, is of meeting his needs;

(g) the range of powers available to the court under this Act in the proceedings in question'.

4.5.13 **Checklist for Action**: Health and Social Work personal data

(a) Does the Data User hold personal data that are covered by a Subject Access Modification Order under Section 29 of the Act?

(b) If so, are the personal data received from another Data User, or disclosed to any other Data User(s)?

(c) If so, how are those personal data marked to identify the source of the data and to ensure that staff know (or the recipient Data User knows) that a Subject Access exemption may apply to some or all of the data?

(d) How are Subject Access requests going to be handled, especially as regards the form of the reply to the Data Subject?

(e) Is the source of the personal data described or can it be deduced from the information? If so, should the personal data which describe the source be withheld from Access? Should the consent of that individual be sought before Access is provided? Is the identity of another individual described or can it be deduced from the information? If so, should these personal data be withheld from Access? Should the consent of that individual be sought before Access is provided?

(f) If the personal data held contain exempt data supplied by another organisation, how would Subject Access be dealt with? Are consultations with that organisation necessary?

(g) How is a Subject Access request by a child or young person to be handled?

(h) How is a Subject Access request by a parent or guardian, on behalf of a child, to be handled (especially if the personal data requested include information that a parent may find disturbing, eg comments about the home, sexual lifestyle of the 'child', etc)?

(i) What is the procedure as regards Access to personal data the release of which would be likely to cause 'serious harm'? What formal procedure will document the decision to refuse Access?

(j) If personal data are to be released, would any special counselling be necessary to explain the data to the Data Subject?

(k) Note that any personal data disclosed to a Data Subject under the Subject Access provisions must be 'intelligible' to that Data Subject (Section 21(1) of the Act). Will this create difficulties (especially with medical records), for example where abbreviations, Latin terms or technical information is concerned? (see Chapter 4(A) paragraph 4.7.15).

(l) Are there special problems, with respect to the use or disclosure of personal data, that will result from a multi-agency approach to caring?

(m) Are there new legal provisions, or Departmental Circulars, which affect the disclosure of Health personal data (eg on the grounds of confidentiality; see paragraph 4.6.1 below)?

(n) At what juncture should legal advice be obtained? Refusal to give Subject Access? Challenges to that refusal? When personal data are challenged for accuracy? When the Data Subject seeks erasure of personal data? When it seems possible that Access would expose the Data User to proceedings 'for any offence other than an offence under this Act' (see paragraph 9.2.12 of this Chapter)?

4.6 **Other relevant statutes or guidelines**

4.6.1 **Code of Confidentiality**

(a) Via Section 2(3) of the Act, Orders can be made to modify or supplement the Data Protection Principles for the purpose of providing additional safeguards in relation to the kinds of personal data often held by caring agencies. In particular, there has been an ongoing debate since the Act came into force as to whether the confidentiality of Health personal data requires such additional, statutory, safeguards.

(b) The British Medical Association, generally supported by an Inter Professional Working Group set up to advise the Department of Health, claims that health service officials, acting on behalf of Health Authorities who have registered as Data Users for Health personal data, may now disclose such data without first having to obtain the consent of the patient or the patient's doctor (previously the Secretary of State was able to enforce a Code, made under the National Health Services Act 1977, which prevented such disclosures, irrespective of the form in which the information was held).

(c) As a result, the BMA and others favour legislation to close this disclosure 'loophole', and in 1987 the DHSS carried out a consultation exercise on the draft text of an appropriate Statutory Instrument, linked to a detailed 'Handbook of guidance' on the principles and practice involved. No agreement could be reached by the various professional bodies, patients' representatives etc whose advice was sought on these issues and further consultations followed in the latter half of 1989. In the light of the fact that there have been no reports of substance concerning breaches of confidentiality (and that existing laws dealing with the Duty of Confidentiality, together with professional Codes of Ethics may, therefore, offer adequate protection), the Department of Health then prepared a non-statutory Code which is significantly shorter and less detailed than the previous provisions, and permits a certain degree of local discretion (the Department hopes to be in a position to consult on this Code in the autumn of 1991).

(d) The Code is intended to apply both to Health Authority employees and to General Practitioners. Note that whilst ownership **and** control of certain Health personal data rests with Health Authorities, the definition of Data Users (in Section 1(5)(b) of the Act) involves only **control** of the contents and use of the data, and many health professionals, for instance, could well be Data Users in their own right (and certainly so in the case of Health personal data which relate to their private patients). The Data Protection Registrar has also pointed out (News Release dated 3.4.90) that 'day to day control' of patients' records 'is undoubtedly in the hands of the practitioner'.

4.6.2 Mentally ill Data Subjects

(a) Via Section 21(9) of the Act the Secretary of State can define who exercises Subject Access rights on behalf of a person who is incapable of doing so by reason of mental disorder. Currently, the requisite authority to apply on behalf of such a person is provided by an Order of the Court of Protection or by an enduring power of attorney (see also Chapter 4(A) paragraph 4.1.9).

(b) An Order under this Section could define additional avenues to exercise these rights (eg a specific type of medical certificate combined with a statutory declaration); this will be considered by the Registrar and the DSS if experience with Subject Access identifies such a need.

4.6.3 Research and statistical analysis

(a) Personal data which are held only for the purpose of research and statistical analysis may be exempt from Subject Access if the conditions outlined in Section

33(6) of the Act are obeyed (see paragraph 8.2.10 of this Chapter).

4.6.4 **Human fertilisation and embryology**

(a) Scientific advances in this field can pose difficult ethical problems, for example a child may wish to trace its genetic parents or vice versa, or when the child becomes an adult and wishes to have children there may be the need to obtain genetic information about its parents.

(b) Section 32(8) of the Human Fertilisation and Embryology Act, which received Royal Assent on 1st November 1990 and comes into force in stages, amends the Data Protection Act by adding a new Subject Access Exemption (Section 35A of the Data Protection Act). The Exemption ensures that the Access provisions of the Data Protection Act are not used as a 'backdoor route' to obtain genetic information other than that specified in the Human Fertilisation and Embryology Act. Section 30 of the latter Act obliges the Human Fertilisation and Embryology Authority to keep a register of information (including a great deal of personal data) relating to the donors of eggs or sperm, the patients receiving treatment and any child born as a result. Disclosures are regulated using powers given to the Secretary of State. Sections 30 to 32 of the Act describe the kind of information to be collected, the information that can be provided to individuals, and the several restrictions on the disclosure of information.

4.6.5 **Restriction in the interests of an individual**

(a) Via Section 34(2) of the Act the Secretary of State may exempt from Subject Access certain personal data if he considers that a prohibition or restriction of Access ought to prevail 'in the interests of the data subject or of any other individual'.

(b) An Order under this Section (SI 1987 No.1906, 11.11.87) relates to personal data held for adoption purposes, and for special educational needs, and cites the relevant enactments and instruments which prohibit or restrict Subject Access, in order to protect the subjects of the data or some other individuals.

(c) The basic procedure for withholding personal data, covered by this Order, from Subject Access should be:

(i) check that the personal data to be withheld conform to the precise legal rules and statutes specified in the Schedules to the Order;

(ii) document and be prepared to justify the application of the exemption with respect to these rules and statutes;

(iii) release to the Data Subject those data that do not fall within the Order.

5. Section 30: Regulation of financial services, etc

5.1 Text of Section 30 of the Data Protection Act (1984)

(1) Personal data held for the purpose of discharging statutory functions to which this section applies are exempt from the subject access provisions in any case in which the application of those provisions to the data would be likely to prejudice the proper discharge of those functions.

(2) This section applies to any functions designated for the purposes of this section by an order made by the Secretary of State, being functions conferred by or under any enactment appearing to him to be designed for protecting members of the public against financial loss due to dishonesty, incompetence or malpractice by persons concerned in the provision of banking, insurance, investment or other financial services or in the management of companies or to the conduct of discharged or undischarged bankrupts.

5.2 Text of Section 190 of the Financial Services Act (1986)

An order under section 30 of the Data Protection Act 1984 (exemption from subject access provisions of data held for the purpose of discharging designated functions conferred by or under enactments relating to the regulation of financial services etc.) may designate for the purposes of that section as if they were functions conferred by or under such an enactment as is there mentioned:-

(a) any functions of a recognised self-regulating organisation in connection with the admission or expulsion of members, the suspension of a person's membership or the supervision or regulation of persons carrying on investment business by virtue of membership of the organisation;

(b) any functions of a recognised professional body in connection with the issue of certificates for the purposes of Part I of this Act, the withdrawal or suspension of such certificates or the supervision or regulation of persons carrying on investment business by virtue of certification by that body;

(c) any functions of a recognised self-regulating organisation for friendly societies in connection with the supervision or regulation of its member societies.

5.3 **Comment:**

5.3.1 Section 30 (and Section 190 of the Financial Services Act) empower the Secretary of State to describe, by Order, the circumstances under which personal data held for purposes associated with the supervision of financial services can be exempted from the Subject Access provisions. The exemption is needed in order to prevent anyone who is suspected (eg by a supervisory body) of financial impropriety from using the Subject Access provisions to frustrate investigation or other appropriate action. As with the Subject Access exemption for the prevention of crime etc, there is a test of prejudice: the exemption applies if the Access in question would prejudice the public interest in relation to financial probity.

5.3.2 Such supervisory bodies include the Government (usually the Secretary of State) and the independent bodies (eg the Bank of England) established by the Financial Services Act (1986); the exemption can also apply to personal data held by liquidators. Other bodies covered by these Sections are those established by the Banking Act (1987) to oversee the workings of the banks, and similar supervisory bodies established by the Lloyds Acts (1871-1982), Companies Act (1985), Building Societies Act (1986) etc (over 230 functions relating to 30 Acts; Hansard 3.11.87 and 19.2.90). All bodies of this nature collect personal data on people who transgress or are thought to transgress the relevant rules, or who can or cannot operate a financial service, or who wish to provide a financial service.

5.3.3 Each circumstance to which the exemption applies is narrowly drawn. Firstly the personal data have to be held by a specified Data User; secondly the exemption has to relate to specified functions, and finally the exemption has to relate to a specified part of another statute. For example, in one circumstance the Secretary of State can apply a Subject Access exemption if the personal data relate (a) to functions under Section 160A of the Financial Services Act 1986 and (b) to exemption of advertisements from the provisions of Sections 159 and 160 (of the Financial Services Act).

5.3.4 The Financial Services Act (Section 190) allows personal data used by the self-regulatory bodies established by this Act to be exempt from the Subject Access provisions. As the Financial Services Act allows the Secretary of State to transfer his regulatory powers to the self-regulatory bodies, Section 190 was necessary to ensure that the Subject Access exemption could be transferred.

5.3.5 The first Order establishing these provisions was entitled the 'Data Protection (Regulation of Financial Services etc) (Subject Access Exemption) Order' (SI 1987 No.1905); it came into force on 11.11.87 and listed 230 circumstances in which the exemption could be applied. Three years later, these were amended and seven more were added to the list via the 'Data Protection (Regulation of Financial Services etc) (Subject Access Exemption) (Amendment) Order' (SI 1990 No. 310).

6. Section 31: Judicial appointments and legal professional privilege

6.1 **Text of Section 31:**

(1) Personal data held by a government department are exempt from the subject access provisions if the data consist of information which has been received from a third party and is held as information relevant to the making of judicial appointments.

(2) Personal data are exempt from the subject access provisions if the data consist of information in respect of which a claim to legal professional privilege (or, in Scotland, to confidentiality as between client and professional legal adviser) could be maintained in legal proceedings.

6.2 **Comment**:

6.2.1 Subsection (1) allows Government Departments, and the Lord Chancellor's Department in particular, to exempt from Subject Access certain personal data relevant to the purpose of appointing judges, magistrates and other judicial functionaries. Note that the personal data must satisfy three tests: (a) they are held by a Government Department; (b) they come from a third party; and (c) they are relevant to judicial appointments.

6.2.2 Subsection (2) maintains legal privilege and the confidentiality of the legal case made by a solicitor on behalf of a client. It stops a third party (for example the 'accused' or 'co-respondent') from having access to any personal data about the third party. For example, a man in a divorce case cannot have Subject Access to those personal data about him which were given to the solicitor acting for the man's wife.

7. Section 32: Payrolls and accounts

7.1 **Text of Section 32:**

(1) Subject to subsection (2) below, personal data held by a data user only for one or more of the following purposes -

(a) calculating amounts payable by way of remuneration or pensions in respect of service in any employment or office or making payments of, or of sums deducted from, such remuneration or pensions; or

(b) keeping accounts relating to any business or other activity carried on by the data user or keeping records of purchases, sales or other transactions for the purpose of ensuring that the requisite payments are made by or to him in respect of those transactions or for the purpose of making financial or management forecasts to assist him in the conduct of any such business or activity,

are exempt from the provisions of Part II of this Act and of sections 21 to 24 above.

(2) It shall be a condition of the exemption of any data under this section that the data are not used for any purpose other than the purpose or purposes for which they are held and are not disclosed except as permitted by subsections (3) and (4) below; but the exemption shall not be lost by any use or disclosure in breach of that condition if the data user shows that he had taken such care to prevent it as in all the circumstances was reasonably required.

(3) Data held only for one or more of the purposes mentioned in subsection(1)(a) above may be disclosed -

(a) to any person, other than the data user, by whom the remuneration or pensions in question are payable;

(b) for the purpose of obtaining actuarial advice;

(c) for the purpose of giving information as to the persons in any employment or office for use in medical research into the health of, or injuries suffered by, persons engaged in particular occupations or working in particular places or areas;

(d) if the data subject (or a person acting on his behalf) has requested or consented to the disclosure of the data either generally or in the circumstances in which the disclosure in question is made; or

(e) if the person making the disclosure has reasonable grounds for believing that the disclosure falls within paragraph (d) above.

(4) Data held for any of the purposes mentioned in subsection (1) above may be disclosed -

(a) for the purpose of audit or where the disclosure is for the purpose only of giving information about the data user's financial affairs; or

(b) in any case in which disclosure would be permitted by any other provision of this Part of this Act if subsection (2) above were included among the non-disclosure provisions.

(5) In this section "remuneration" includes remuneration in kind and "pensions"

includes gratuities or similar benefits.

7.2 **Comment:**

7.2.1 In the Registrar's Guideline 6 (Second series, February 1989) the following clarification is provided (pages 10-15):

'A.5.1 So long as two conditions are observed, personal data are exempt from Parts II and III of the Act if they are held by a data user only for one or more of the payroll purposes and accounts purposes mentioned below. If the data are held or used for any other purpose, the exemption is lost. The two conditions are explained in A.5.4, A.5.5 and A.5.6.

A.5.2 **The payroll purposes are**

- calculating amounts payable as remuneration for service in any employment or office
- calculating amounts payable as pensions for service in any employment or office
- paying remuneration or pensions
- paying amounts deducted from remuneration or pensions.

A.5.3 **The accounts purposes are**

- keeping accounts relating to any business or other activity carried on by the data user
- keeping records of purchases, sales or other transactions in order to ensure that any necessary payments are made by or to the data user for those transactions or in order to make financial or management forecasts to assist the data user in the conduct of any business or activity he carries on.

A.5.4 **The first condition** is that the personal data may only be disclosed in very limited circumstances. If any other disclosure is made, then the exemption is lost. To qualify for the exemption, personal data held for the exempt accounts purposes or for both the exempt accounts and payroll purposes may only be disclosed

- for the purpose of audit
- for the purpose of giving information about the data user's financial affairs

- in circumstances covered by one of the exemptions from the non-disclosure provisions of the Act. These are dealt with in detail in Part B of this Guideline but stated briefly they cover disclosures made

  — because they are required by law or the order of a court

  — in order to obtain legal advice or for legal proceedings in which the person making the disclosure is a party or witness

  — to the individual whom the information is about, or to a person acting on that individual's behalf

  — to employees or agents of the data user in the course of carrying out their duties

  — at the request or with the consent of the individual whom the information is about. The request or consent may be from another person acting on that individual's behalf. The request or consent must be to the particular disclosure in question - a general consent is not sufficient

  — to meet an urgent requirement for information to prevent injury or damage to the health of any person

- when the disclosure is required for the purpose of safeguarding national security

- when a failure to disclose would be like to prejudice

  — the prevention or detection of crime

  — the apprehension or prosecution of offenders or

  — the assessment or collection of any tax or duty.

A.5.5 Personal data held only for the exempt payroll purposes may also be disclosed in the circumstances set out above. In addition, provided that they are **not** also held for the exempt accounts purposes, they may be disclosed

- to any person, other than the data user, by whom the remuneration or pensions in question are payable

- in order to obtain actuarial advice

- for research into occupational diseases or injuries
- when the data subject (or a person acting on his behalf) has requested or consented to the disclosure of the personal data. In this case the consent need not be to the particular disclosure but may be given generally or may be related to the circumstances of the disclosure.

A.5.6 **A second condition** must also be observed if the exemption is to be available. This is that the personal data must only be used for those purposes described in A.5.2 and A.5.3.

A.5.7 The Registrar expects that this exemption is likely to apply only to some very small businesses. Such businesses might have their own small computers or may have their work done through a general computer bureau or a professional accountancy firm. More sophisticated users - which will inevitably include most large businesses and many small ones - will find that the exemption does not apply to them because they cannot observe the conditions about use and disclosure of the personal data. Examples of situations about when a data user could not rely on the exemption include the following

- when records of time-keeping and absences used to calculate an employee's pay are also used to judge the employee's performance
- when records of trade union membership used to deduct dues from salary and pay them to the union are also used to monitor which employees belong to a trade union
- when records held by pension fund trustees in order to pay pensions are also used by an employer considering a possible programme of early retirement
- when records of past sales to an individual are also used for marketing purposes
- when an individual's address kept for accounts purposes is also used to distribute articles or information not connected with the accounts
- when a trader keeps a credit limit figure with the accounts information
- if information is given to a debt collection agency not simply to enable the agency to collect debts but so that it can be used to build up credit reference information
- if information about individual bad debtors is, without their consent, shared with other traders

- if, without the individual's consent, personal data are disclosed to a computer maintenance organisation in order to recover data or re-establish the use of equipment or computer programs after a failure.

A.5.8 The Registrar is sometimes asked whether a data user who holds a particular item of information - for example the date of birth or home address of an employee - is entitled to rely on this exemption. It is impossible to answer such a question. The exemption does not depend on the nature of the personal data held but on the uses and disclosures which are made of the personal data. So, for example, a date of birth may be relevant to calculating pay and if it is only used for that purpose then the exemption would not be lost. But if that information is used for a non-exempt purpose - for example in order to decide when the employee is due to retire - then the exemption is lost.

A.5.9 If a data user is entitled to the exemption, it is not lost by a breach of one of the conditions as to use or disclosure if the data user can show that he has taken all reasonable care to prevent that breach. In practice, however, a data user who has deliberately committed or authorised such a breach could not rely on this provision.'

7.2.2 From the above it will be abundantly clear that to rely on this exemption is to embark on a veritable minefield, and perhaps not worth the attempt - even if the 'prize' is not having to register the relevant personal data and, consequently, not having to worry about Data Subjects' rights or the Registrar's powers.

7.2.3 The Registrar provides a very plain hint to this effect in Section A.5.7 of Guideline 6 (see above), by stating that 'this exemption is likely to apply only to some very small businesses', and by following this comment with a list of pitfalls of which the last is probably the worst: abandon hope all ye who have your computers maintained or serviced.

7.2.4 Note also that, as set out in Section A.5.4 of Guideline 6, Data Users who have not registered such data cannot **refuse** to disclose them on the grounds that the exemption would be invalidated thereby, **if** the disclosure would be covered by any one of the non-disclosure exemptions.

7.2.5 This was forcefully illustrated by 'Rowley v Liverpool City Council' (The Times, Law Reports, 26.10.89). The case arose because the litigant, a former employee of the Council (the Data User), was seeking compensation following a personal injury. Solicitors acting on behalf of the litigant asked the Court to enforce a previous ruling that allowed them to obtain personal data, from the Data User's payroll system, relating to three other individuals, so that an earnings comparison could be made. Access to these personal data was an important part of assessing the totality of the claim for compensation. The Data User had refused to act on the previous ruling, claiming that the disclosure would breach the terms of the exemption.

7.2.6 Their Lordships disagreed, and concluded that the Data User should have considered the wording in Section 32(4)(b) of the Data Protection Act, which states that a disclosure would be possible if it was 'among the non-disclosure provisions'. Since this Section contains a relevant non-disclosure exemption (ie 'required by or under any enactment, by any rule of law or by the order of a court') the Court ruled that the Data User could disclose the personal data without being in breach of Section 32.

7.2.7 In summary, many Data Users will find Registration to be the best option. Even though the terms of this exemption remove the enforcement powers of the Registrar, it seems paradoxical for the exemption to be valid only if the computer is not maintained by an outside organisation. After all, the Data Users should still comply with the relevant Data Protection Principles (via Section 2(2) of the Act): the Eighth Principle, which calls for appropriate security measures, must surely include some computer maintenance to guard against accidental loss or destruction of data.

7.2.8 Thus for any organisation that uses sophisticated payment and accounting systems, this exemption is unlikely to apply. Its stringent conditions make it appropriate solely for those Data Users who utilise basic financial, accounting or pension procedures and who have no need to exceed the limitations on the use and disclosure of the personal data that the exemption imposes. If the exemption is used, the work involved in monitoring procedures to ensure that it still applies can prove a significant burden. If the exemption is infringed (eg by one of the disclosures listed by the Registrar in Section A.5.7 quoted above), the use of the personal data is unlawful until they have been registered.

8. Section 33: Domestic or other limited purposes

8.1 Text of Section 33:

(1) Personal data held by an individual and concerned only with the management of his personal, family or household affairs or held by him only for recreational purposes are exempt from the provisions of Part II of this Act and of sections 21 to 24 above.

(2) Subject to subsections (3) and (4) below -

(a) personal data held by an unincorporated members' club and relating only to the members of the club; and

(b) personal data held by a data user only for the purpose of distributing, or recording the distribution of, articles or information to the data subjects and consisting only of their names, addresses or other particulars necessary for effecting the distribution,

are exempt from the provisions of Part II of this Act and of sections 21 to 24 above.

(3) Neither paragraph (a) nor paragraph (b) of subsection (2) above applies to personal data relating to any data subject unless he has been asked by the club or data user whether he objects to the data relating to him being held as mentioned in that paragraph and has not objected.

(4) It shall be a condition of the exemption of any data under paragraph (b) of subsection (2) above that the data are not used for any purpose other than that for which they are held and of the exemption of any data under either paragraph of that subsection that the data are not disclosed except as permitted by subsection (5) below; but the first exemption shall not be lost by any use, and neither exemption shall be lost by any disclosure, in breach of that condition if the data user shows that he had taken such care to prevent it as in all the circumstances was reasonably required.

(5) Data to which subsection (4) above applies may be disclosed -

(a) if the data subject (or a person acting on his behalf) has requested or consented to the disclosure of the data either generally or in the circumstances in which the disclosure in question is made;

(b) if the person making the disclosure has reasonable grounds for believing that the disclosure falls within paragraph (a) above; or

(c) in any case in which disclosure would be permitted by any other provision of this Part of this Act if subsection (4) above were included among the non-disclosure provisions.

(6) Personal data held only for -

(a) preparing statistics; or

(b) carrying out research,

are exempt from the Subject Access provisions; but it shall be a condition of that exemption that the data are not used or disclosed for any other purpose and that the resulting statistics or the results of the research are not available in a form which identifies the data subjects or any of them.

8.2 **Comment:**

8.2.1 Section 33(1) exempts an individual's personal data from Registration, from the Registrar's supervision, and from the Subject Access provisions, if those personal data are held for that individual's domestic or recreational requirements. The exemption does **not** cover personal data processed at home, by that individual, on behalf of any other Data User (ie such data are not exempt simply by virtue of the fact that the processing is carried out on domestic premises), nor does it apply to that individual's business or professional purposes.

8.2.2 The Registrar's 'Review' of the Act (published in the 5th Report, June 1989) records no queries concerning this exemption (see Section B.1.6) and in Section B.2.6 he recommends 'complete exemption from the Act' for relevant data. However, the arguments in support of this omission are open to criticism on the same grounds as those that support the omission of 'small' Data Users from the Act (see Chapter 3, paragraph 1.5).

8.2.3 Given the inexorable proliferation of home computers, electronic notebooks and the like, and the facilities these offer for holding and processing this wide range of exempted information, it is more than likely that Data Subjects have already suffered damage from what might, in other circumstances, be deemed breaches of Data Protection Principles.

8.2.4 The contention that **any** personal data, in the wrong context or in the wrong hands, are capable of causing harm, certainly has force when one considers 'domestic' lists such as baby-sitting rosters (which may well specify where, and at what time, occupants at a particular address may be particularly vulnerable to an intruder); the names and addresses of disabled friends in the neighbourhood of the (disabled) Data User, and the many similar examples of quite innocently held time-bombs. It is not surprising that arguments are being put forward to switch emphasis from the concept of 'sensitive' personal data, defined as such, to recognition that it is the **context** in which the personal data are used that really matters.

8.2.5 In relation to Section 33(2)(a), the Registrar points out in Guideline 6 (Second series, February 1989) that the exemption for the personal data of members of an unincorporated club, where the club is the Data User, hinges on two conditions:

'A.6.2 The first condition is that all members of the club must be asked whether they object to the personal data relating to them being held by the club. If any member does object then either

- the personal data relating to that member should be taken off the computer. So far as the Act is concerned, that information can be held and processed manually or

- the club should register in respect of the personal data. Having registered, it may continue to hold the personal data whether or not members object.

A.6.3 For existing members, objections might be sought by sending each of them a standard letter or by including a request for objections in a prominent position in a newsletter sent to every member. After this initial trawl for objections the club should establish some procedure so that objections are sought before information is recorded about new members. For example, it may wish to include a question in its membership application forms - 'do you object to the club holding your membership record on computer?'

A.6.4 The second condition is that the personal data about members may only be disclosed in very limited circumstances. These are

- when the member, or a person acting on behalf of the member, has requested or consented to the disclosure. This consent may be given either generally or in the circumstances in which the disclosure in question is made

- when the disclosure falls within one of the non-disclosure exemptions described in Part B. (Note: the Part B referred to here is that found in Guideline 6, and not the Part B form used in registration).

A.6.5 To comply with the second condition it would be sensible for the club to identify the circumstances in which it may wish to make disclosures and to obtain the consent of the members. Consent might be incorporated in membership application forms or in a rule of the club. Disclosures might include, for example

- the publication of a list of members of the club

- disclosures to affiliated clubs and societies

- disclosures to computer maintenance organisations when this is necessary in order to repair the equipment or computer programs

- other disclosures for the purpose of the club which its governing body decides are necessary.

A.6.6 The exemption does not apply

- to any personal data held by the club about individuals who are not members of the club

- if the club is a corporate body (for example, if it is a registered company)

- to a club which is not owned by its members - a proprietor's club.'

8.2.6 The 'Mailing lists' exemption is defined in Section 33(2)(b) of the Act, and is qualified by four conditions, of which two have essentially the same effect as those which apply to unincorporated clubs. The full text of the Registrar's comments in Guideline 6 is as follows:

'A.7.2 The first condition is that the personal data must consist only of the names and addresses of the individuals or of other details needed for making the distribution. These other details might include, for example, telephone numbers or telex numbers. If more information is held - for example as to the occupation, status , interests or preferences of the individual - this exemption does not apply.

A.7.3 The second condition is that the personal data must only be used for the purpose mentioned above. If they are used for any other purpose then the exemption is lost.

A.7.4 The third condition is that all the individuals must be asked whether they object to the personal data relating to them being held by the data user. If an individual does object then either

- the personal data relating to that individual should be taken off the computer. So far as the Act is concerned, the information can be held and processed manually; or

- the data user should register in respect of the personal data. When registered, the personal data may continue to be held whether or not the individual objects.

A.7.5 For individuals already on the list, objections might be sought by including a request in a prominent position in the next mail shot which is to be sent to them. After this initial trawl the data user should establish some procedure so that objections are sought before information is recorded about any other individuals.

A.7.6 The fourth condition is that the personal data may only be disclosed in very limited circumstances. These are

- when the individual, or a person acting on his behalf, has requested or consented to the disclosure. Consent may be given either generally or in the circumstances in which the disclosure in question is made

- when the disclosure falls within one of the non-disclosure exemptions described in Part B. (of Guideline 6)

A.7.7 It would be sensible for data users who wish to rely on the exemption

- to identify the circumstances in which they may wish to make disclosures, and
- to consider whether these are expressly permitted by the non-disclosure exemptions. If not, the data users will need to obtain the individuals' consent to those disclosures.'

8.2.7 The stringent conditions of the Section 33 exemptions are particularly relevant to work carried out on a home computer (whether, voluntarily, by a member of a club or, for example, by a teacher or lecturer taking work home).

8.2.8 Whilst the Act does not prevent individuals from carrying out this sort of work, formal arrangements may be required to establish, where appropriate, that the organisation, and not the individual, is the Data User. It may be necessary to appoint such individuals as officers of the club or association so that they are bound by its Registration, and the Data Protection Principles, when processing on its behalf.

8.2.9 In these circumstances, individuals using their own equipment would not be a 'Computer Bureau' within the terms of the Act. For instance, as long as teachers do not breach the conditions of their contracts, their home computer can now be regarded as a normal 'tool of the trade'.

8.2.10 Section 33(6) means that personal data held solely for the purpose of statistics or research are exempt from the Subject Access provisions (note that whilst a disclosure for any other purpose would invalidate the exemption, disclosures to other research bodies may still be within the 'research' purpose). If the statistical or research information is published, the exemption would also be lost unless the information is presented in an anonymised form. Even if a Data User only holds personal data of this type, that Data User must register, is subject to the Data Protection Principles, and is liable for damages under Sections 22 and 23 of the Act. In addition, the exemption does not include disclosure for the purpose of computer maintenance. Thus the exemption will be lost if the computer hardware or software is maintained by an external contractor who, in the course of his duties, requires access to relevant personal data held by the Data User.

9. Section 34: Other exemptions

9.1 **Text of Section 34:**

(1) Personal data held by any person are exempt from the provisions of Part II of this Act and of sections 21 and 24 above if the data consist of information which

that person is required by or under any enactment to make available to the public, whether by publishing it, making it available for inspection or otherwise and whether gratuitously or on payment of a fee.

(2) The Secretary of State may by order exempt from the Subject Access provisions personal data consisting of information the disclosure of which is prohibited or restricted by or under any enactment if he considers that the prohibition or restriction ought to prevail over those provisions in the interests of the Data Subject or of any other individual.

(3) Where all the personal data relating to a Data Subject held by a data user (or all such data in respect of which a data user has a separate entry in the register) consist of information in respect of which the Data Subject is entitled to make a request to the data user under section 158 of the Consumer Credit Act 1974 (files of credit reference agencies)-

(a) the data are exempt from the subject access provisions; and

(b) any request in respect of the data under section 21 above shall be treated for all purposes as if it were a request under the said section 158.

(4) Personal data are exempt from the subject access provisions if the data are kept only for the purpose of replacing other data in the event of the latter being lost, destroyed or impaired.

(5) Personal data are exempt from the non-disclosure provisions in any case in which the disclosure is -

(a) required by or under any enactment, by any rule of law or by the order of a court; or

(b) made for the purpose of obtaining legal advice or for the purposes of, or in the course of, legal proceedings in which the person making the disclosure is a party or a witness.

(6) Personal data are exempt from the non-disclosure provisions in any case in which -

(a) the disclosure is to the Data Subject or a person acting on his behalf; or

(b) the Data Subject or any such person has requested or consented to the particular disclosure in question; or

(c) the disclosure is by a data user or a person carrying on a computer bureau to his servant or agent for the purpose of enabling the servant or agent to perform his functions as such; or

(d) the person making the disclosure has reasonable grounds for believing that the disclosure falls within any of the foregoing paragraphs of this subsection.

(7) Section 4(3)(d) above does not apply to any disclosure falling within paragraph (a), (b) or (c) of subsection (6) above; and that subsection shall apply to the restriction on disclosure in section 33(6) above as it applies to the non-disclosure provisions.

(8) Personal data are exempt from the non-disclosure provisions in any case in which the disclosure is urgently required for preventing injury or other damage to the health of any person or persons; and in proceedings against any person for contravening a provision mentioned in section 26(3)(a) above it shall be a defence to prove that he had reasonable grounds for believing that the disclosure in question was urgently required for that purpose.

(9) A person need not comply with a notice, request or order under the subject access provisions if compliance would expose him to proceedings for any offence other than an offence under this Act; and information disclosed by any person in compliance with such a notice, request or order shall not be admissible against him in proceedings for an offence under this Act.

9.2 **Comment:**

9.2.1 Section 34(1) states that any personal data held for a purpose that requires the data to be made public **by law** are exempt from Part II and Sections 21 to 24. Note that this refers **only** to those personal data which the Data User has a **statutory duty** to make public. The fact alone that a Data User makes the personal data public does **not** entitle the Data User then to claim the exemption.

9.2.2 Examples of personal data covered by this provision are

(a) the Electoral Register (not including any administrative or other personal data which are held, by the Electoral Registration Officer, to support this Register)

(b) the list of a company's shareholders (via Section 356 of the Companies Act 1985)

(c) the Public Extract of the Community Charges Register.

9.2.3 When Section 34(2) was debated in Committee the Minister said that the purpose of this clause was to prevent Subject Access in specific, odd, cases. For example, if twins brought up separately could use the Act to find each other, and if the Secretary of State concluded that the reasons why they were brought up in this way were still valid, Subject Access could be denied. There was concern that the words 'any enactment' could refer to the Official Secrets Act 1911, and thus enlarge the scale of secrecy within government. However, the Minister refuted this argument, noting that any order under this subsection must be made by affirmative resolution of both Houses of Parliament.

9.2.4 An Order in relation to personal data held for adoption purposes and for children's special educational needs (SI 1987 No. 1906) was laid before Parliament on 9.11.87 and came into force on 11.11.87; it exempts from the Subject Access provisions any personal data 'the disclosure of which is prohibited or restricted by certain enactments and subordinate instruments', specified in the Order, 'in the interests of protecting the subject of the data himself or some other individual'. A brief checklist for Subject Access covered by this type of Order is in paragraph 4.6.5(c) of this Chapter.

9.2.5 Section 34(3) establishes that access to information kept on the files of credit reference agencies shall be guided by the provisions of the Consumer Credit Act (1974), ie that access requested via the Data Protection Act will be treated as access under the Consumer Credit Act. This is because the Consumer Credit Act, by virtue of Section 158(5), allows access to 'all the information .. kept (about the consumer) ... regardless of how the information is stored', ie the information comprises relevant manual files as well as personal data (including, for example, sources of the information, if stored). In addition, the maximum £10 fee for Subject Access under the Data Protection Act is substantially higher than the fee for access under the Consumer Credit Act - which currently stands at £1.

9.2.6 Failure to give credit can upset and antagonise customers, especially if information about one individual has been confused with someone else's, or if the information is inaccurate or ambiguous (see Appendix 1 for detailed comment on current legal issues in this respect). The press feed on such cases, and the publicity can be damaging to image and to business. If credit is refused to an individual on the basis of an adverse report from a credit reference agency, and this report is **not** stored by the Data User, then it would still be good practice, conducive to good customer relations, to reveal the source of this information (ie which agency was used).

9.2.7 Promotion of such procedures, used in a positive and helpful way, can take the 'sting' out of adverse credit ratings, and mollify justly enraged customers if mistakes have been made, since the agency can then be contacted so that the information can, if necessary, be corrected. If the information is covered by the Consumer Credit Act, the customer should be referred to procedures that allow access to, and correction of, the information (these procedures should already have been established).

9.2.8 Section 34(4) exempts from Subject Access any personal data used for 'back-up' purposes. **Note that archived data are generally not back-up data** and that, as a consequence, Subject Access must be provided to archived personal data. The commonly held misconception that 'archives are exempt' is usually founded on either:

(a) an interpretation of Section 1(5)(c) of the Act - namely that archived data are **not** 'held', as here defined, 'with a view to being further so processed on a subsequent occasion' and are, therefore, outside the scope of the Act, or

(b) an interpretation of Section 34(4) - namely that archived data provide back-up and hence 'are kept only for the purpose of replacing other data in the event of the latter being lost, destroyed or impaired', and are therefore exempt from the Subject Access provisions.

9.2.9 Caution is necessary in trying to use Section 1(5)(c) in this way, which hinges on whether the Data User intends to process the data again, since it can easily be claimed that by archiving data rather than destroying them, the Data User demonstrated an intention to process the data in the future. (It should also not be forgotten that scanning hardware, combined with appropriate software, can bring printouts and other printed material within the Act's definition of 'data', at a cost which is now easily affordable by a high proportion of Data Users). Regarding Section 34(4), caution is again advised since it would normally not be possible to sustain the argument that archived data are kept **only** for the purpose of replacement. Furthermore, the **sufficiency** of the archived data to 'replace ... lost, destroyed or impaired' data also needs to be considered, since 'archiving' is likely to be equivalent to 'taking out of current circulation' and such data may well not be able to 'replace' the data left 'live'. Obviously, in many cases, archived data provide no certain means of correcting an 'impairment' to the live file; for example, a corrupt payroll file is not usually restored from records two years old! In short, 'archived data' are **definitely not** 'back up' data in most applications.

9.2.10 Sections 34(5) and 34(6) are discussed at length in Chapter 3, Section 3.2.7. They relate to disclosures that need not be identified in the Register Entry, and involve the Data User in the duty to ensure that the disclosee is the person satisfying the requirements stated in these Sections. If such disclosures **are** identified through Registration, the Data User could be conveying to the public a potentially misleading and damaging message about the activities described by the Entry.

9.2.11 Section 34(8) raises some of the problems that also apply to other disclosures for narrowly defined purposes. Employees of the Data User should be able to recognise when disclosures for 'emergency health' purposes can be made, and be trained to adequately document such disclosures (normally after a disclosure has taken place).

9.2.12 Section 34(9) establishes the 'right of silence' (ie not to be forced by statute to incriminate oneself) concerning a disclosure of personal data which would expose the Data User to criminal proceedings - **other** than for an offence under the Data Protection Act. Any information that **is** released to a Data Subject via the Subject Access provisions cannot be used as evidence in proceedings under the Act; however, the evidence may be used in civil cases. It will be thus advisable, in appropriate cases, for the Data User to obtain legal advice on the personal data to be released under the Subject Access provisions. If data are withheld, it will be essential to keep a formal record of this advice, and of the data.

10. Section 35: Examination marks

10.1 **Text of Section 35:**

(1) Section 21 above shall have effect subject to the provisions of this section in the case of personal data consisting of marks or other information held by a data user

(a) for the purpose of determining the results of an academic, professional or other examination or of enabling the results of any such examination to be determined; or

(b) in consequence of the determination of any such results.

(2) Where the period mentioned in subsection (6) of section 21 begins before the results of the examination are announced, that period shall be extended until -

(a) the end of five months from the beginning of that period; or

(b) the end of forty days after the date of the announcement, whichever is the earlier.

(3) Where by virtue of subsection (2) above a request is complied with more than forty days after the beginning of the period mentioned in subsection (6) of section 21, the information to be supplied pursuant to the request shall be supplied both by reference to the data in question at the time when the request is received and (if different) by reference to the data as from time to time held in the period beginning when the request is received and ending when it is complied with.

(4) For the purposes of this section the results of an examination shall be treated as announced when they are first published or (if not published) when they are first made available or communicated to the candidate in question.

(5) In this section, 'examination' includes any process for determining the knowledge, intelligence, skill or ability of a candidate by reference to his performance in any test, work or other activity.

10.2 **Comment:**

10.2.1 This Subject Access 'exemption' (if that is the correct term) applies particularly to examining institutions (especially those who are concerned with large public examinations) who normally amend raw marks, perhaps several times, in the process of arriving at the final results. Such amendments could be aimed at achieving consistency over the years, for instance, or be due to reviews performed by external assessors and the like. In fact, the 'exemption' is a Subject Access 'deferment'; if it applies it gives the Data User two basic choices:

(a) to satisfy the request within 40 days of validating it

(b) to satisfy the request within 40 days of the announcement of the exam results, or within five months of receipt, whichever is the earlier. In these two latter instances the marks, and any other associated personal data, which are held at the time the request is **received** (any time taken to validate the request is **not** relevant in this particular instance), **and** all adjustments and variations during the period up to the response date, must be provided to the Data Subject.

10.2.2 If the Data User is presented with these options, because the Subject Access request is received before publication of the examination results (note that 'publication' is defined by Section 35(4) and 'examination' by 35(5) of the Act), other factors will also need to be considered, eg:

(a) the timing of the request in relation to computerisation of the relevant marks;

(b) the extent of the interval between computerisation and finalisation of the results (an extended period will increase the liability for disclosure of raw marks);

(c) the nature of the 'examination' (ie whether this is a single event or consists of multiple assessments), and the date of any 'final' assessment in relation to the effective date of the request.

10.2.3 The right to see the **marks** (interim and final) of any examination or assessment (established by Section 35(1)) as well as the ultimate **grade** may well increase the number of appeals from students who have narrowly failed to achieve a particular grade; the problems of Subject Access by children (see Chapter 4(A), paragraphs 4.3.3 and 4.3.4) may also be a significant issue in this context.

10.2.4 Some Universities (as reported in New Statesman, 28.5.86, and in The Guardian,

13.10.86) considered options to frustrate Subject Access, by holding examination marks on computer for **no longer than 40 days**. The procedure for such a 'routine computer purge' is outlined in the 'Code of Practice for Universities' (April 1987) and criticised in the foreword supplied by the Registrar. However, whilst noting that the procedure was 'likely to give rise to difficulties', he states that it is 'not wrong in law'.

10.2.5 Depending on the circumstances, Section 10(4) of the Act may indeed not offer the Registrar the option, in this instance, to serve an Enforcement Notice in relation to the Seventh Data Protection Principle. However, whether a **new** procedure to purge personal data of all marks within a 40 day period was a contravention of this Principle could, nevertheless, become a matter to be decided by case law.

10.2.6 This is because an individual student is not bound to complain to the Registrar via Section 36(2). Using Section 21(8), a student could ask a Court to enforce Subject Access on the grounds that 'the Data User in question has failed to comply with the request'. If this happens, the case would hinge on whether the Court decides that the procedure adopted by the University falls within routine amendments or deletions allowed for by Section 21(7), or whether the procedure was aimed at contravening the Subject Access provisions. In addition, since individual cases may differ from each other, a University could face repeated Court appearances. This would do little for the University's public image, and could be counterproductive as regards future student enrolment. Clearly, student unions can be expected to fight any attempt to reduce students' new rights of access to examination marks, and it has already been noted (eg in The Times, 8.7.87) that a challenge could arise via the European Court.

10.2.7 An alternative strategy would be for a group of students to arrange for Access requests to be presented every day over a period of time, so that at least some of the relevant 40 day periods would end on dates when raw marks were being held on computer (ie prior to deletion of the marks). In these circumstances, some students would be bound to obtain at least some of their raw marks (since not providing the information would bring Section 35(3) into play), and this would give weight to complaints of 'unfair processing' (under the First Data Protection Principle) by the other students.

10.2.8 Finally, it is interesting to record that 'a more detailed breakdown of course marks was common in Europe', and that in relation to applications for employment outside the UK, 'British students might be disadvantaged if all they have to show is a certificate indicating an overall classification' (Guardian 2.5.91).

10.3 Student records held by schools in manual files

10.3.1 The Education (School Records) Regulations 1989 (SI No. 1989/1262), which apply to all schools in England and Wales, came into force on 1st September 1989. They state that it is the role of the governing body of the school to ensure that a 'formal record of a pupil's academic achievements, his other skills and abilities and his progress in school' is kept and updated every year. Since 1st September 1990, these Regulations have allowed access by the pupil (and in many cases the parent of the pupil) to this 'curricular record'.

10.3.2 The origin of these Regulations can be found in the commitment made by the Government to Archy Kirkwood MP during the Committee stage of his Private Member's Bill (now the Access to Personal Files Act 1987), when the Secretary of State (then David Waddington) stated that existing powers in the Education Acts could be used to allow individuals, who are the subject of a manual file, access to their own school record (Hansard, Standing Committee C, Access to Personal Files Bill, 25th March 1987, col 6). Accordingly, the Committee removed Education Departments (and, for other reasons, many other organisations that hold personal files in manual form) from the Bill, leaving a measure which only covers access by individuals to the files about them held by Housing and Social Work Departments.

10.3.3 There are significant differences between these Regulations and the access provisions made under the Data Protection Act and Access to Personal Files Act; this may cause problems and confusion. These problems are:

(a) Education records are not usually organised in a way that allows for the simple identification of 'curricular records'. Usually such records are integrated into one file with respect to a school pupil, and segregation of curricular records may prove difficult in practice. This problem is especially acute if extracts of Social Work, Medical, Educational Special Needs or Probation files form part of the curricular or other educational record. The implication is that careful weeding of the information prior to Access may be necessary.

(b) Under the Regulations, access hinges on the age of the young person, whereas under the Data Protection Act access depends on the 'legal capacity' (see Guideline 5, paragraph 2.33 produced by the Data Protection Registrar) of the young person, as assessed by the Data User, to understand the nature of an access request. Thus a parent could have access to information, in manual files, that relates to a young person, whilst access to the same information, held as personal data, could be refused. The Regulations thus make **who** has access conditional on **how** the school stores information.

(c) Despite the exemptions provided under the Regulations, these age-related rules could generate a further source of conflict. For example, suppose a 17 year old school pupil's relationship with another person was a factor bearing on educational performance. It could be that the parental right of access would disclose to the parent the nature of the relationship, thus undermining the common law status re-iterated in the well known Gillick case: parental rights yield to those of young persons when the latter are capable of organising their own affairs.

(d) As a consequence of these differing rules of access, Local Authorities must adopt procedures for Education that are different to Housing and Social Work (and different again if personal data are involved). This will undoubtedly cause confusion, and will further complicate procedures in those difficult cases where information in a young person's files is shared by the caring services of an Authority.

10.3.4 These School Records Regulations define the record-keeping duties of the 'Governing Body' in considerable detail. They support the view that the Government's policy of placing more responsibility on School Governors will eventually mean that the Governors become the Data User with respect to more and more personal data in the school. In addition, Head Teachers may find they are Data Users with respect to some information (eg truancy and disciplinary records). Add the fact that the Parent Teacher Association may use a school's computer, and each school in the state sector could eventually involve four Data Users!

Chapter Eight: Computer Security

1. Introduction

1.1 Inappropriate security of personal data has serious legal implications. The Data Protection Act provides the Registrar with the power to serve Supervisory Notices to improve security; unauthorised disclosure of personal data can be a criminal offence (Sections 5 and 15 of the Act) as can neglect of duty (Section 20), and individuals can obtain compensation if damage results from a breach of security surrounding personal data (Section 23). In addition, many organisations are becoming increasingly aware that serious malfunctions within their computer operations can not only incur financial loss and undermine credibility, but can also lead to business failure or even bankruptcy. Similar threats to an organisation arise through fraud or sabotage, and through improper or mismanaged procedures associated with routine operations. In brief, computer security is a problem of many dimensions and aspects.

1.2 This Chapter is designed to highlight the security obligations that arise as a consequence of the Data Protection Act, and describes the relationship between that Act and other legislation which impinges on computer security matters. In practice, these obligations should be part of a process that considers security of **all data and processing activities under one coherent policy and one security management structure**. Such an integrated approach will not only help compliance with any relevant legislation, but will also ensure the safety of the organisation's operations as a whole. This unified approach cannot be detailed in one Chapter; it is a subject which could easily fill a further 400 pages.

1.3 What could well be a comprehensive legal examination of the internal security procedures of a Data User or Computer Bureau can follow from an action under Section 23 of the Data Protection Act, when an individual applies to a Court for compensation for damage that has resulted from the loss, unauthorised destruction or unauthorised disclosure of personal data, or from unauthorised access to such data. A key defence against such a claim for compensation is for the Data User or Bureau to prove that they 'had taken such care as in all the circumstances was reasonably required to prevent the loss, destruction, disclosure or access in question'. Note that if a User or Bureau relies on this condition in Section 23(3), they will need to convince the Court that adequate procedures applied at the time. By contrast, the claimant will attempt to prove negligence, for instance by producing evidence that similar organisations employ a far more stringent approach to security, or that some specific security procedure was inadequate.

1.4 A similar spotlight could also be trained on security procedures if there is a prosecution, under Section 5(5) or Section 20 of the Act, following an unauthorised disclosure made 'knowingly or recklessly' in contravention of particulars described in the Register Entry (or where such a disclosure arises as the result of 'the consent or connivance' or 'any neglect' of any senior member of staff). In this case, the final 'guilty or innocent' verdict could well depend on whether the relevant security procedure, that should have been associated with disclosures of personal data, was 'knowingly' broken, 'recklessly' ignored, or 'neglected'. Thus in attempting to prove a Section 5(5) or Section 20 offence the prosecution could, as a deliberate tactic, hold current security procedures (in relation to the unauthorised disclosure in question) up to public ridicule.

1.5 Thus an action before a Court could well see a Data User's or a Computer Bureau's approach to the management of computer security, or to security procedures, being 'torn apart', in public, by hostile barristers. This prospect, if combined with unfavorable publicity in the media, could cause serious long term damage to a business or to an organisation's credibility.

1.6 Under Section 36(2) of the Act, the Data Protection Registrar can probe an organisation's security procedures even if no damage to an individual has occurred. The Registrar's annual reports indicate that complaints are running at around 2,500 per year and, as can be seen from the examples in Section 10 of Chapter 4(B), several of the reported incidents are of the type which could lead to complaints about the security of personal data. In investigating such complaints, the Registrar recognises that 'no security policy can be foolproof' and the 'mere fact that there has been a breach of security will not cause him to take formal action'. However, the Registrar 'will want to be satisfied that the computer user has done everything which could reasonably be expected in order to avoid the breach' (Guideline 4, paragraph 8.5).

1.7 When attempting to assess whether 'everything which could reasonably be expected' to be done has actually been done, the Registrar will request the Data User or Computer Bureau to provide its own version of the events. This will oblige the organisation to explain, for example, the relevant procedures associated with the access to or disclosure of personal data, or the appropriateness of those procedures to the personal data, or the effectiveness of the procedures for the destruction of the data. Thus the burden of proof could well lie with the Data User or Computer Bureau to demonstrate that proper procedures were in place at the material time, and that management actively monitored the effectiveness of these procedures. Note that in relation to **all** actions that arise from the Data Protection Act following a breach of security, **without reliable documentary evidence** it will be difficult to prove that security procedures were instigated, checked, changed, or even reliably managed.

1.8 Because the Eighth Data Protection Principle obliges Data Users or Computer Bureaux to be responsible for the security of the personal data that are processed, there should be periodic security reviews to guard against 'unauthorised access to, or alteration, disclosure or destruction of, personal data and against accidental loss or destruction of personal data'. The mere fact that a formal review takes place will strengthen the defence in any civil action for compensation that may follow a breach of this Principle.

1.9 In Guideline 4, paragraph 8.2 the Registrar indicates that Data Users and Computer Bureaux should adopt a rigorous and formal approach towards the security of personal data processed by computer. This advice states that:

> 'The prime responsibility for creating and putting into practice a security policy must rest with the computer user. The policy should seek to achieve:
>
> - that personal data can only be accessed, altered, disclosed or destroyed by authorised people
> - that those people only act within the scope of their authority and
> - that, should the data be accidentally lost or destroyed, they can be recovered so as to prevent any damage or distress being caused to data subjects'.

1.10 However, the most important change encouraged by the security implications of the Act could be one of attitude. The Act requires management to consider not only the price, the software, the training support and the hardware when buying a computer, but also whether the personal data to be processed will be adequately protected by appropriate security measures. Data Users and Computer Bureaux should anticipate that the legislation may call them to account for the security of personal data, and that somebody will then have to defend their security management and procedures in open Court. Who that somebody is can be an interesting question to pose; certainly the answer needs to be found **before** the event.

2. Security implications in detail

2.1 Through the Eighth Principle and its Interpretation, the Act is quite clear on the security implications. The Principle states that Data Users and Computer Bureaux shall take 'appropriate security measures against unauthorised access to, or alteration, disclosure or destruction of, personal data and against accidental loss or destruction of personal data'. Determining the limits of 'appropriate' is, in the first instance, the responsibility of the Data User or Computer Bureau (whether they have done this 'responsibly' may, of course, be the issue that is challenged). The word 'unauthorised' used in conjunction with 'access to, or alteration, disclosure or destruction of' implies that procedures to 'authorise' such activities should be established. Note, too, that the Principle does **not** describe particular instances of 'accidental loss or destruction', implying that appropriate security procedures should protect personal data from **all** types of accidents, ranging from the foreseeable (eg disk head crash) to the complete mischance (eg struck by lightning).

2.2 The Interpretation of the Eighth Principle states that:

'Regard shall be had

(a) to the nature of the personal data and the harm that would result from such access, alteration, disclosure, loss or destruction as are mentioned in this principle; and

(b) to the place where the personal data are stored, to security measures programmed into the relevant equipment and to measures taken to ensuring the reliability of staff having access to the data'.

2.3 Reference to 'the nature of the personal data and the harm that would result from such access, alteration, disclosure, loss or destruction as are mentioned in this principle' implies that an assessment of the security risks faced by the personal data needs to be undertaken (eg by means of a risk analysis). This would include an assessment of:

(a) procedures that relate to the security of personal data stored in the computer centre, on microcomputers, at remote sites and in the office;

(b) security procedures with respect to management structure and staff responsibilities, and to authorised access, authorised alteration, authorised disclosure or authorised destruction of personal data;

(c) whether the personal data are of a kind that warrants special safeguards;

(d) the operation and management of any access control security software, and the effectiveness of audit, logging and monitoring procedures;

(e) the security risks to personal data that arise via any network connection;

(f) the risks associated with destruction or disposal of personal data;

(g) any plans or procedures to assist recovery from the loss of personal data (eg following a major disaster or minor catastrophes such as accidental deletion of some personal data held in a micro), and the cover provided by any relevant insurance policy;

(h) appropriate countermeasures to any perceived risk.

2.4 The phrase 'to the place where the personal data are stored' defines in broad terms the physical location where the data can be found. Thus a detailed assessment of physical security would be required to determine who can enter locations where:

(a) personal data are awaiting input, processing, collection or disposal;

(b) personal data can be accessed, altered, destroyed or stored via a terminal or computer;

(c) personal data can be available via a network or an external dial-up line.

2.5 Any one of these assessments could require weeks of work. For example, with respect to microcomputers, the Act requires Data Users and Bureaux to be able to demonstrate that they are fully in control of the security situation, and to do this could involve the evaluation of items from the following list:

(a) **physical access** to the micro, personal data and programs, and determining who has access to the computer within an office;

(b) **other problems** associated with the location of the micro (eg static electricity, power supply, magnetic fields from other electronic equipment, health and safety aspects such as Repetitive Strain Injury and VDU hazards). Evaluation of such problems is a consequence of the Eighth Principle: staff reliability could be impaired if the location of the micro is unsuitable;

(c) **secure disposal** of data, output, manuals, disks, tapes, source documents, programs, old equipment etc;

(d) **staff training** (eg in relation to the use of equipment, programs, data, procedures, Copyright, Computer Misuse, avoiding the introduction of computer viruses, and Data Protection);

(e) **safe use of disks** (eg disk management, storage and transportation, lifespan and use, disposal of disks, access control systems, access and repairs by external agents such as maintenance engineers);

(f) **contingency planning** which involves consideration of: back-up of data, recovery from hardware failures (eg communications interrupt or head crash), recovery from software malfunction or data corruption, accidental deletion of files, threat from computer viruses, taking back-ups before moving a micro, theft, and personnel aspects (eg who manages the recovery process);

(g) **networks**: if a micro is connected to a mainframe or Local Area Network then some security problems (eg integration with mainframe security policies and security controls, physical security of the network, access controls to the network, audit trails on a network, contingency plans to include the network, telecommunications security and the network) become more acute.

2.6 The reference to 'security measures programmed into the relevant equipment' focuses on software that controls access to personal data; this also includes security devices that are used in conjunction with such software (eg smart cards, security cards etc), or hardware devices controlled by software (eg electronically controlled locks on security doors that require a special card and PIN number to be presented before the door opens).

2.7 With respect to access control software, this should control:

(a) access to personal data on the system and to data storage devices. This means that the software security system should be able to allocate a user's right of access to specified disks, terminals, tapes, specific lines of a network and all other elements of hardware;

(b) initiation of transactions, programs or commands. Software operations, execution of the commands of the operating system, (especially the ability to read, write, delete, copy, rename, allocate disk space or execute programs) should be capable of restriction to identifiable and authorised users;

(c) access to data files. The security software should protect a collection of records in a data file, and allow the definition of user rights or permissions (ie whether a user has read access, write access, amend, update, delete or copy permissions). The file handling utilities should always refer to these rights or permissions before executing the utility, and the access control system should report important violations of these rights.

2.8 An alternative way of considering the phrase 'security measures programmed into the relevant equipment' is to consider that every Data User or Computer Bureau should, where 'appropriate' (of course) determine 'Who can do what, to which personal data, when and from where'. Taking each 'W' word in turn, any Data User or Computer Bureau should be able to define:

(a) **Who** All individuals who use data or programs must be known and positively identified by the access control system, at the least through a user number plus password combination. Other identifying particulars may combine something one owns with something one knows or some personal attribute (such as a signature or fingerprint). For example, automatic teller machines use software and hardware to check a cash-card (something one owns) against a Personal

Identification Number (something one knows); a more sophisticated approach uses a smart-card (something one owns) to generate the Number which is used only once. Everyday equipment cannot, at present, identify the image, fingerprint, or voice of the user (ie the personal attribute), but there are many developments towards this goal.

(b) **What** Following positive identification, the type of operation that users are allowed to perform on data files, and the range of computer facilities and/or commands that they are authorised to use, should be defined and translated into access rights.

(c) **Which** All users should be restricted to those particular data files and facilities that have been defined as being needed for their work. This procedure can be used to enforce the proper segregation of duties within an organisation, by controlling the type of information and process that any particular user is authorised to handle. It is a management function to define this apportionment carefully.

(d) **When** A number of time controls can be employed, for example the times of day that certain computer operations can be performed, or when information becomes available. Other controls of this type ensure that user identifiers or access rights allocated to contract or temporary personnel are removed after a period of time, or specify the length of time before users are required to change their password. Similar controls limit the length of time that a terminal is allowed to be logged onto the system without a key depression, and automatically determine when the terminal is logged off the system. (Note that this is different to the blanking out of the screen which is sometimes set within the terminal by the manufacturer, to preserve the screen from excess wear).

(e) **Where** In this case controls can be used to ensure that certain computer operations can only be carried out at specified places (for example the operator console function should be restricted to specified secure terminals).

2.9 Any access control software would be useless without its accompanying **principles of password usage** (for convenience, the word 'password' includes any Personal Identification Number etc), and unless staff are trained to respect password security. These principles should include the following rules:

(a) passwords should be unique to each user and should not be displayed or echoed on the VDU display or printed on computer output or hard copy devices;

(b) every password violation should be recorded, and the software should respond appropriately by shutting out or warning the user if there are repeated attempts to access the system with the use of a wrong password. This is essential to stop unauthorised access by a 'trial and error' method of guessing passwords;

(c) the software should pause for an interval of several seconds after a wrong password has been entered, before processing another password entered from the same ID. This is to deter any automated, high speed, 'trial and error' method of guessing passwords;

(d) the software should record all log-on attempts. This log should be regularly examined by management, and particular note should be taken of long log-ons and log-ons made at unusual hours;

(e) staff should be trained to appreciate the importance of keeping their password secure, and also their own responsibilities generally in maintaining the security of the installation. For example, passwords should never appear on computer output, be written into diaries, be disclosed to colleagues etc;

(f) managers who allow staff to share passwords should be aware of the problems that sharing may create. Sharing of passwords **should be strongly discouraged if not outlawed** (the practice is only defensible as a last resort where management has consciously decided that many staff can safely perform the same **READ ONLY** operations from the same location);

(g) only security management should be able to allocate new passwords, including replacement in cases of loss.

2.10 The passwords themselves should:

(a) have the option of being alphanumeric and at least six characters long. There should only be one password for each user;

(b) not be easy to guess. Because people are concerned that they may forget their passwords they tend to choose a password that they feel is impossible to forget - for example first names, flowers, initials etc. Many people choose a very short password for convenience: one to three letters, or often a short word; this means that a knowledgeable person can often guess common passwords and can, by automated trial and error methods, gain unauthorised access;

(c) be protected. Staff should be trained to act responsibly in selecting and changing passwords and to report any infringement;

(d) be changed (or removed) by management if access is no longer required. Checks should be made to remove any default passwords supplied with the system. Access rights (or passwords) belonging to ex-employees, or to contract staff who have completed their work, should always be deleted immediately (even when automatic deletion of the passwords would follow on a specified date), or after a time period during which they are unused;

(e) be changed by staff on or before expiry of a specific period. Software to force the periodical changing of passwords should be used, and old passwords should become part of the password vetting procedure. Staff should not be able to alternate between two or even three passwords. Passwords should be changed frequently by their respective users and, under normal circumstances, should be known only to such users;

(f) be changed frequently, if necessary, especially if they facilitate access to special privileges. All 'standard' passwords that come with the operating system should be changed immediately.

2.11 The final phrase of the Interpretation: 'and to measures taken for ensuring the reliability of staff having access to the data', raises three issues. Firstly, are staff 'reliable' in the sense that they have security clearance to access the data in question (eg have been positively vetted or granted specific authority to access certain personal data, or chosen for some work because of their proven integrity). Secondly, have staff been made reliable through training programmes (eg to heighten awareness of security issues, or to inform staff how best to use the equipment, data or computer programs). Finally, what are the penalties if staff do not follow the security procedures (are they disciplined?), and what is management's attitude towards a breach of security policies by staff.

3. Computer Bureaux security and the Data Protection Act

3.1 Although this Chapter generally deals with security from the point of view of both Data Users and Computer Bureaux, the Data Protection Act does outline specific requirements for Computer Bureaux. As most Data Users will also register as Computer Bureaux, these legal constraints on the operation of a Bureau need special emphasis. These constraints require a Computer Bureau:

(a) **to register** the fact that it operates as a Bureau; failure to do so is a criminal offence;

(b) **not to disclose** personal data without the authority of the Data User (ie the client); an unauthorised disclosure can be a criminal offence and can lead to a claim of compensation via Section 23 of the Act;

(c) **to conform** to all aspects of the Eighth Data Protection Principle dealing with security;

(d) if, in addition to the provision of Bureau services, it acts as a the servant or agent of the Data User, **to apply** the restrictions imposed by the Register Entry for the Data User (eg it could be a criminal offence for the Bureau or any of its employees to knowingly or recklessly process, obtain or disclose personal data not covered by the Register Entry);

(e) **to be liable** to pay compensation for any unauthorised loss, destruction or access to personal data, as specified in Section 23 of the Act.

3.2 A Bureau must have some knowledge of the 'nature of the personal data' processed, so that appropriate security can be determined. It may also need to know what disclosures are authorised through the Data User's Register Entries, and generally to ensure that it only makes those disclosures which the Data User has specifically authorised it to make. Nevertheless, for example, a Computer Bureau is free to disclose personal data (held by its clients) under the terms of any non-disclosure exemption (for example to the Police, if the non-disclosure provisions described in Section 28 of the Act apply), despite the fact that a Data User's policy towards such disclosures could be different to that adopted by the Bureau. So, for example, whilst a Bureau's disclosure of a client's personal data to the Police may please the Police, and satisfy the requirements of the non-disclosure exemption, such action might completely upset the relationship between the Bureau and its client, the Data User.

3.3 The Registrar has provided advice on a Bureau's relationship with its clients: in Section 2.7 of Guideline 8 he includes the following statement:

> 'If a bureau causes personal data to be processed on behalf of its customers the bureau must consider whether the customer is a registered data user and the contents of their register entry. If that person is a registered data user and if the bureau uses, obtains, discloses or transfers personal data on behalf of that person, it must not knowingly or recklessly depart from the terms of the data user's register entry. At the very least, to avoid an accusation of recklessness, the bureau should obtain an assurance from its customers who are registered data users that any such act which it performs on their behalf is covered by their register entries.
>
> In cases where a person is a bureau solely because he allows others to use equipment in his possession for the processing of personal data, the bureau need only be concerned with whether its customers are registered data users.'

3.4 Except for the fee, registration of a Bureau is comparatively 'painless'; it just requires the name and address of the Bureau and the completion of some of the questions in a Part A. Registration is, of course, unnecessary if the data processed are not personal data, or if they are personal data but are exempt from Part II of the Act (eg via Section 32: 'Payrolls and accounts'). However, if such an exemption is relied on by a Bureau, the Bureau should seek assurance that the Data User (ie the Bureau's client) will adhere rigorously to the terms of the exemption. (Note, for example, that the Section 32 exemption would be invalidated if, without the consent of each Data Subject, personal data were to be disclosed to a hardware maintenance engineer; see Chapter 7, Section 7).

3.5 Criminal offences involving a Bureau can occur when:

(a) an unregistered person knowingly or recklessly supplies Bureau services with respect to personal data;

(b) a Bureau, or its servants or agents, knowingly or recklessly discloses personal data without the authority of the Data User (unless a non-disclosure exemption applies);

(c) a Bureau fails to comply with an Enforcement Notice.

3.6 In summary, a suitable mechanism has to be established whereby a Computer Bureau:

(a) obtains details of its clients' Register Entries, and is kept informed of any relevant changes to these Entries;

(b) obtains sufficient knowledge (if not contained in the Register Entries) about the personal data to be processed so that it can assess what security is appropriate;

(c) if additionally acting as agent of a Data User, can ensure that **all** staff are aware of the limitations imposed by that Data User's Register Entries;

(d) only acts with the authority of the Data User when processing, accessing, and disclosing personal data;

(e) if additionally acting as agent of a Data User, can ensure that **all** procedures satisfy the Data User's requirements with respect to any Data Protection Principle.

3.7 All procedures reviewed above(in particular the security provisions) have to be kept under review to ensure that the Bureau cannot be held responsible for any unauthorised disclosure of, or access to, clients' personal data or for unauthorised destruction of such data. Back-up procedures have to be monitored to ensure that a Bureau does not lose clients' personal data following a major breakdown. All these issues should be formally expressed through contractual agreements between Data Users and Bureaux.

3.8 Finally, Computer Bureaux should exercise care to clarify the legal position with respect to Section 39 of the Act. If bureau services are provided in the UK to an overseas client, then the bureau is a Bureau as defined by the Act; however, depending on the nature of the contract, the Bureau could be providing additional services which could also make it a Data User under the Act. If such services are provided abroad to a client based in the UK (ie even if the processing takes place abroad), the Bureau may still be subject to the Act. Such situations can be very complex (see Chapter 1, paragraphs 3.7.11 and 3.8.5; Chapter 3, paragraphs 3.2.8 and 3.2.9; and Appendix 6), and may even result in the personal data being subject to two Data Protection jurisdictions. Note that the Computing Services Association have produced a Code of Practice for Computer Bureaux (see Chapter 5, Section 6).

4. The Computer Misuse Act 1990: a security enforcement aid

4.1 On 29th August 1990, the following activities became a criminal offence: unauthorised access to computer material (eg by employees who intentionally exceed their level of authorised use of a computer, or by a hacker who breaks the security of a computer); unauthorised access to a computer in order to facilitate a further offence (eg hacking in order to facilitate a fraud, or accessing sensitive data in order to blackmail an individual); and unauthorised modification of a computer program or data (eg planting a 'logic bomb' so that a computer program executes in an unauthorised way, or deliberately infecting a computer with a 'virus', even if the 'virus' is 'harmless'). The Computer Misuse Act 1990 thus established three new offences, of which one, unauthorised access to computer material (Section 1 of the Act) was new in scope and can apply to many misdemeanours that involve a computer. The other two offences, in essence, remove previous doubts as to whether existing criminal law applied.

4.2 The Section 1 offence in the Computer Misuse Act could prove a useful weapon in the armoury of those Data Users who wish to involve the criminal law to deter staff from misusing personal data, especially in those circumstances when there is unauthorised access to a computer in order to make an unauthorised disclosure of personal data. Under the Data Protection Act, there is no equivalent offence of 'unauthorised access to personal data', and individuals can only be prosecuted if they 'knowingly or recklessly' contravene the particulars described in the Register Entry (Section 5), or if the offence is committed 'with the consent or connivance or ... any neglect' of a senior employee (Section 20).

4.3 An offence under the Data Protection Act can be a fiendishly difficult matter to prove, particularly if a Data User's Register Entries are littered with intended disclosures (one of the problems of ticking boxes in the Entry is that each extra tick enlarges the authorised activities of the Data User, under the Act, and thereby diminishes what can be defined as unauthorised). In addition, since Registration does not link specific personal data to specific disclosees, many Disclosure categories (eg D206 'Suppliers, providers of goods or services') can be interpreted as **authorising** disclosures that the Data User might class as **unauthorised**: in this case, D206 may have been ticked to authorise disclosures to **one** particular supplier, whilst in fact it can be interpreted as authorising disclosures to **any** supplier 'associated with the Data User'. Similar problems arise when the non-disclosure provisions apply: for instance a D203 tick in a Data User's Entry (legitimising disclosures to employees or agents directly associated with the Data User) can be interpreted as legitimising the disclosure of personal data to staff who have **no need to know**, since Section 34(6)(c) allows personal data to be disclosed (without the need to register the disclosure) to staff who **need to know**. If the prosecution were attempting to prove, under the Computer Misuse Act, that an individual had gained unauthorised access to a computer, it would be embarrassing if the Register Entry under the Data Protection Act permitted the disclosure of personal data to that individual.

4.4 In general, a Section 1 offence under the Computer Misuse Act gives Data Users the chance of creating a clearer policy to control unauthorised access. The offence is committed if staff intentionally use a computer to secure unauthorised access 'to any program or data held in any computer', and staff who deliberately disclose their password in order to allow somebody else to gain unauthorised access could be aiding and abetting the unauthorised access. However, it is important to realise that there must be a **deliberate** attempt to use a computer in order to access material held on a computer. Thus staff who make unauthorised use of a printout, or who gain unauthorised access by accident (eg following a software failure), or who abuse their **authorised** access to a computer are not committing this offence.

4.5 It is, therefore, essential to train staff about keeping within the limits of their authorised level of access, about the importance of security procedures for safeguarding passwords, and about the constraints determined by the Register Entries that relate to their work. By keeping the signed attendance records of such seminars (including induction courses), the Data User can demonstrate who has been trained, and has an indication of the type of training and advice that has been provided. As the authority of staff to access a computer can usually be tightly defined by access control software, the range of reports generated by this software should provide an efficient way of logging the use of the system, and an effective method of revealing possible abuse. Finally, if staff are not trained or instructed about the authorised disclosures, it might be difficult to prove that an unauthorised disclosure was 'knowingly' made.

4.6 As with the Data Protection Act, it might be useful to discuss with the Data User's (or Bureau's) legal advisor the formal procedures that are to be adopted by the organisation should evidence from access control software be required for use in Court. As the defence will attempt to rubbish the procedures and the reports, it might be prudent to identify the relevant responsible person (or expert) who may have to appear in Court to rebut such attacks. Finally, the Register Entry should be scrutinised to remove unnecessary disclosure ticks (**especially** D203; see paragraph 4.3 above and Chapter 3, paragraph 3.2.7(e)); conditions of employment should be modified if necessary, in order to bring unauthorised use of a computer or personal data formally to the attention of all staff, and reminders should periodically be issued to staff concerning all these matters (eg via 'messages of the day' etc).

4.7 The Computer Misuse Act creates some anomalies because it is limited to computers; for example, it makes the unauthorised use of a computer to access a Sonnet by Shakespeare a crime, leaving unauthorised access to the most sensitive of manual files unpunished (similarly the Data Protection Act is restricted to personal data and does not cover any personal information). Despite its title, there is no definition of computer in the Act, and there are worries that it could apply in unusual circumstances; for example, if a microchip controls the use of a photocopier by means of access codes, is the member of staff who uses the access code allocated to another employee, committing a criminal offence? There are several important references; these are **References (Debates)**: Commons Hansard, 9th February 1990 (Second Reading), 4th May 1990 (Report and Third Reading); Lords Hansard, 15th May 1990 (Second Reading); Official Report, Standing Committee C, 14th, 21st and 28th March 1990 (Commons Committee Stages: there were no amendments tabled for the Lords Committee Stage and therefore no debate in the Lords), and **References (Law Commission Papers)**: 'Criminal Law. Computer Misuse' (Cm 819); 'Working Paper No. 110, Computer Misuse' (highly recommended).

5. The Police and Criminal Evidence Act 1984: Sections 68 and 69

5.1 During the 1980s there was much activity to plug gaps in the laws which apply to computer fraud, and to provide extra resources to enable the Police to improve its effectiveness in this area. A Serious Fraud Office, which concentrates on major cases, was set up, and every Police Force in the UK now has a specialist Fraud Squad, building up expertise in collecting the detailed and often technical evidence necessary for a successful prosecution.

5.2 The Police has been assisted in this process by the Police and Criminal Evidence Act (1984), which establishes rules of admissibility of evidence specifically in relation to evidence held on computers. In effect, this changes the traditional assumption that where an individual's liberty is at stake, any evidence must be capable of being tested in Court, and be supported by the relevant witness; the problem is that in today's society the only witness may be a record in the computer.

5.3 It was a ruling by the Court of Appeal in 1980 that precipitated the change in the law, when the Law Lords had to rule on the admissibility of evidence from a document produced by a computer belonging to the Bank of England. The Bank had a computer system that sorted bank notes by rejecting defective bank notes, bundling good notes in batches of one hundred, and recording the serial numbers of all the good notes in each batch. The Appeal Court had to answer the question: was the record of the serial numbers in the computer, evidence that the bank notes were 'good'?

5.4 The Law Lords ruling started from first principles. They argued that all evidence must be tested in open court, and therefore asked the supplementary question: which individual could verify this evidence? They concluded that since there was no one person with first-hand personal knowledge of the evidence (and obviously the computer could not be cross-examined in the witness box), the evidence could not be tested and was therefore inadmissible.

5.5 This immediately created a legal problem. Many computer systems which record transactions and events automatically, in much the same way as a thermocouple can automatically record temperature, were in danger of producing evidence that would be ruled inadmissible, should an issue come to Court. However, unlike the thermocouple whose temperature reading can be checked independently against another thermometer of a different kind, the operation of one computer system is generally not verifiable against another.

5.6 This legal dilemma was solved by Sections 68 and 69 of the Police and Criminal Evidence Act. Section 68 restates the general rule: any documentary evidence must be presented in Court, supported, wherever possible first-hand, by a witness. However, if there are documentary records held on computer that **cannot** be presented in this fashion, there are strict tests that apply before the computer record is held to be admissible as evidence.

5.7 These tests are outlined in Section 69. It states that it must be shown that 'there are no reasonable grounds for believing that the statement is inaccurate because of improper use of the computer', and that 'at all material times the computer was operating properly'. If the computer had some failure it must be shown 'that any respect in which it (the computer) was not operating properly or was out of operation was not such as to affect the production of the document or the accuracy of its contents'.

5.8 The Act also requires a witness to be a 'responsible person' who can be cross-examined, and who can sign a certificate which states that, to the best of the witness's knowledge, the operating conditions of the computer were those outlined in Section 69 during the production of the documentary evidence. To ensure that the 'responsible person' takes the issue seriously the law provides a simple test. If that person 'makes a statement which he knows to be false or does not believe to be true', that person shall be guilty of an offence that could carry a 'term of imprisonment not exceeding two years'. To put it another way, 'responsible' people would be advised not reach too eagerly for their pens.

5.9 Who then are these 'responsible' people who are willing to endure the delights of cross-examination? Clearly they will have to have a good working knowledge of the computer system, its controls and the associated procedures, and how these are relevant to the matter before the Court. Thus a 'responsible' person is likely to be an Auditor, or a Data Processing Manager or other senior manager within the computer department. However, as computer systems become more accessible, via distributed systems, local area networks etc, the only 'responsible' person who is appropriately qualified could well be the local manager in charge of the office computer.

5.10 In practice, the clause presents further problems. Before 'computer evidence' can be admitted, the organisation must have in place all the necessary operational procedures, standards and audit trails. These are, after all, the preconditions that allow a 'responsible' person to sign a statement which says 'I believe these documents produced by the computer to be a true statement of the facts'. It will be embarrassing, to say the least, if evidence that a person has committed a fraud is found through cross-examination to be 'inadmissible'.

5.11 In other pieces of legislation, the law is steadily beginning to make computer owners responsible for security measures. For example, if unauthorised access was gained to a computer that controlled machine tools or robots, and this access threatened the safety of staff (eg by causing a robot to function dangerously), then the employer could be liable under the Health and Safety at Work Act 1974. If a defective product (eg consumer electronics controlled by a software running on a microchip) was sold to the public, the manufacturer of the product could be liable under the Consumer Protection Act 1987. If there were insecure procedures that allowed unauthorised copies of proprietary software to be made, then this could lead to an action under the Copyright, Designs and Patents Act 1988.

5.12 In summary therefore the trend is clear: legislation that relates to computers or data makes it inevitable that attention will be focused (by the defence or the prosecution, depending on the case before the Court) on security, to demonstrate that an organisation had totally inadequate procedures in this respect. Equally inevitable is that any security weakness will be brutally exposed in order to undermine evidence to the contrary. Thus those responsible for information technology must anticipate these problems and be able to prove to a Court that they:

(a) established a consistently managed security policy and developed the appropriate procedures to deal with every aspect of security of data, programs and equipment;

(b) trained staff and management in the use of those procedures, and in the safe use of data, programs and equipment;

(c) reviewed, managed, audited and changed procedures periodically;

(d) retained detailed and relevant documentary evidence that describes all security activities (without these vital pieces of paper, any case in Court could be fatally compromised).

6. Security training for staff

6.1 It is important to ensure that training programmes, induction courses, staff notice boards, messages of the day etc all work together to ensure that staff know what procedures to follow, why these procedures have been established, and to whom to turn if there is a problem. Staff must know of any specific obligations in law (eg to the Data Protection Act, Computer Misuse Act, Copyright Act etc) and their duty towards confidentiality of data in general.

6.2 One method of ensuring that staff take the issue seriously is to get all computer users to formally acknowledge receipt of a brief Security Statement; this can be issued to each user when the user identifier is allocated (a draft Statement is provided in Section 7 below), or sent to all staff as a circular. An equivalent Statement of management responsibilities is in Section 8.

6.3 It is important that staff receive proper instruction as to the procedures to be followed and the equipment or programs to be used. This enables staff to understand the 'why' behind a procedure and, if in doubt, to challenge its efficacy. Staff should be encouraged to report to line managers any failings or suspected failings that impact on security. It is far easier for staff to integrate security from the outset than to impose security constraints at a later date.

7. A draft 'Computer security statement for staff'

1. INTRODUCTION

1.1 In view of this organisation's heavy reliance on data processing systems, the confidentiality, security and accurate processing of data are of considerable importance. To help maintain equipment, systems and data in a sensibly controlled and secure environment, a number of requirements must be observed which are briefly described in this Statement.

1.2 The Statement is being sent to you as an authorised user (or potential user) of computing equipment, to alert you to your responsibilities for computer security. The Statement is also part of the organisation's response to the requirements of the Data Protection Act.

1.3 Staff are reminded that the Staff Code states:

> 'Employees shall not disclose or make use of for their private advantage any information which they may acquire in the course of their duties and which is not available generally to the public'.

2. BASIC RESPONSIBILITIES

2.1 Staff are to follow all procedures that ensure the proper use of computer equipment and data.

2.2 Equipment, programs and data are only to be used for purposes directly concerned with the organisation's business.

2.3 Only authorised persons may operate equipment or access data.

2.4 Any computing equipment, program or data obtained by the organisation must be in accordance with existing advice and guidelines.

2.5 Staff must play their part in following and monitoring the security procedures to ensure that computers, data and facilities are adequately protected.

3. COMPUTER SYSTEMS AND DATA

3.1 All computer programs and data developed, purchased, or rented for the organisation are for the sole use of the organisation or its clients.

3.2 Deliberate unauthorised access, copying, alteration, destruction or interference relating to computer programs or data are expressly forbidden; each can be a criminal offence.

3.3 Unwanted output must be disposed of with due regard to its sensitivity. Confidential output must be shredded, or destroyed by other appropriate, authorised means. Individual departments are responsible for ensuring that the required facilities are provided.

3.4 Staff should ensure that there is an up-to-date copy of all (important) data.

3.5 Any access, disclosure, destruction or operation involving data or programs belonging to a client of the organisation must only take place in accordance with the client's written instructions.

4. TERMINALS AND PASSWORDS

4.1 Terminals must not be left unattended when 'signed-on'.

4.2 Passwords must not be disclosed to unauthorised persons.

4.3 Unauthorised use of user identifiers is expressly forbidden.

4.4 Passwords should comprise a minimum of 6 characters, be changed periodically, and also conform to all other adopted standards for passwords.

4.5 Forgotten passwords will be reset only by the designated Computer Security Manager, following a written request by the authorised user.

4.6 Terminals and microcomputers should only be connected to the mainframe by authorised installation staff.

5. SECURE AREAS

5.1 Unauthorised persons are not allowed in secure areas unless accompanied by an authorised person.

5.2 The transfer of keys, identity cards, access cards, or codes to unauthorised personnel is expressly forbidden.

5.3 Any loss of access devices, and breaches or attempted breaches of security must be reported to the Computer Security Manager.

6. GENERAL

6.1 All identity cards, keys, manuals and equipment must be returned to the appropriate location when staff leave the employment of the organisation.

6.2 Periodic checks will be made by the Computer Security Manager to ensure compliance with these rules.

6.3 The requirements contained in this policy statement are of a general nature and cover all computers; there may be additional requirements designed for specific locations, data or applications.

6.4 This Computer Security Statement may be modified from time to time in response to changing circumstances. If this happens you will receive a copy of the new Statement.

8. A draft 'Computer security statement for managers'

1. INTRODUCTION

1.1 The increasing reliance placed on data processing systems means that the confidentiality, security and accurate processing of all data and software are of considerable importance.

1.2 To help maintain equipment, systems and data in a sensibly controlled and secure environment, and in order to respond to the Data Protection Act and other relevant legislation, managers must observe a number of requirements which are briefly described in this Statement.

2. MANAGEMENT RESPONSIBILITIES TOWARDS STAFF

2.1 Managers should ensure that staff receive adequate training in the proper use of equipment and programs, in proper data processing procedures, and in 'Health and Safety' issues with regard to electrical equipment.

2.2 Managers should ensure that their staff know what their responsibilities and liabilities are under the Data Protection Act and the Computer Misuse Act, and assess whether additional training is required.

2.3 Managers should ensure that their staff are aware of the contents of any Register Entries which relate to personal data handled by the staff.

2.4 Managers should ensure that their staff are aware of the organisation's policies on computer security, and on the safe use of equipment.

2.5 Managers should notify the Data Protection Officer of any modification to the use or disclosure of Personal Data that may require a change in the relevant Register Entry.

3. MANAGEMENT RESPONSIBILITIES TOWARDS THE USE OF COMPUTING EQUIPMENT

3.1 Any data processing equipment should be obtained, installed, tested, and used in accordance with the organisation's standard procedures.

3.2 Managers should keep a description of all equipment, including: the manufacturer, the equipment type or function, the serial numbers (if any), and links to other equipment. This will help to identify the equipment if it is stolen, and to describe its capabilities when a replacement is required.

3.3 Managers should know who the authorised users of the equipment are. This will assist the identification of staff training requirements, the distribution of information relevant to particular staff, and also effective auditing.

3.4 Managers should know who has access to equipment and data, note any potential environmental problems and keep a record of any movement of equipment. This information will help to evaluate the physical security of particular equipment.

3.5 Managers should position terminals and microcomputers so that they cannot be subject to unauthorised use or disclosures.

3.6 Managers should ensure that there is proper maintenance of equipment.

3.7 Managers should ensure that any data storage media, disks and tapes are stored, used and maintained in accordance with the manufacturer's instructions.

3.8 Managers should ensure that provision is made to adequately back-up and restore any data, especially from microcomputers, to implement recovery should there be a failure.

3.9 Managers should ensure that equipment is not left without adequate supervision.

4. MANAGEMENT RESPONSIBILITIES TOWARDS COMPUTER SOFTWARE

4.1 Managers should determine what computing facilities are being made available to their staff.

4.2 Managers should know how to use the software security system, to help them administer the computing facilities made available to their staff.

4.3 Managers should ensure that passwords conform to adopted standards.

4.4 Managers should encourage staff to act responsibly in selecting and changing their passwords, and to ensure that passwords are not displayed on equipment.

4.5 Managers should ensure that password violations are recorded, reported, and acted upon.

5. GENERAL

5.1 Managers should formulate contingency plans in case computing facilities are unavailable for a long period of time.

5.2 Managers should arrange for the secure disposal of data that are no longer required.

5.3 Managers should ensure the retrieval of all keys, identity and/or access cards when staff leave.

5.4 Managers should make provision to cope with visitors, cleaners, engineers, auditors, and other persons who may occasionally have access to data-processing and to data-handling areas.

5.5 Managers should integrate computer security procedures with their routine office procedures, make periodic checks, as necessary, to ensure compliance with standards, and report any operational or procedural problems.

Chapter Nine: Need for a Change?

1. Data protection: why should I worry?

1.1 Data protection is concerned with why and how information held on computer is collected, how it is processed and used, how its accuracy is checked and validated, who will see it and under what conditions, and how the security arrangements protect that information. Over the last two decades a number of data protection proposals were put forward, notably by the Younger Committee on Privacy (1970-72), the Lindop Committee on Data Protection (1976-78), the Council of Europe Convention (1981) and, late in 1990, by the European Commission's Proposal for a Data Protection Directive (COM (90) 314). As will be seen, the UK approach, as expressed in the Data Protection Act 1984, differs significantly (in some respects) from all the above.

1.2 Developments since the publication of the Lindop report (1978) show that the Government was in no hurry to legislate. Following the lukewarm response to the Lindop recommendations, the Home Office proposed that a panel of Home Office officials could perform the functions of the data protection body required by industry, pressure groups and international law. The implication was that the responsibilities of the Home Office, which include the sensitive data collections held by the Prison, Probation, Immigration, Police and Security Services, would not conflict with supervision of computerised information as a whole. Eventually the Government, after considerable lobbying, relinquished this idea and published a White Paper in 1982. The Home Office, perhaps not surprisingly, drafted a Bill that did not fully apply to the many sensitive data collections under its control; it was decided to legislate for an independent Registrar, whose powers would be restricted to supervising personal information that was processed automatically, and which would also be qualified by strict conditions or exemptions regarding access to sensitive personal data.

1.3 The driving force for legislation in 1983 was not a desire to provide individuals with control over the use of their computerised information, but rather to allay fears that, without a Data Protection Act, protectionist measures would be applied against the UK. In 1981, eleven European states (including the UK) had signed a Data Protection Convention, 'The Convention for the Protection of Individuals with regard to Automatic Processing of Personal Data', which concerns the automated handling of personal information. (The Convention, which was originally published by the Government as Cmnd 8341 and republished as Cm 1329 in December 1990, came into force on 1.10.85 when it had been ratified by five states. Ratification by the UK became effective on 1.12.87, and by January 1991 ten states had ratified with a further eight committed to ratification).

1.4 The Convention sets out broad guidelines to protect the privacy of individuals with regard to information processed on computers, and obliges signatories to introduce data protection legislation. Furthermore, the Convention allows member states to prevent personal data reaching, or being processed in, those states whose laws do not satisfy the Convention. As transborder data flow is extensive and a significant source of income to the UK computer services industry, its prohibition would result in the loss of valuable contracts, and lead to the UK falling behind in the considerable information trade that takes place (in 1981 it was rumoured that some European Countries were considering arguments about 'protection of the individual' to justify not processing personal data in the UK).

1.5 However, the Data Subjects involved generally do not concern themselves with international trade in personal data; they usually give information to organisations or to the State for a specific purpose, and assume that it will not be used for a different purpose, or by another organisation, without their knowledge and approval. Thus from the standpoint of the individual, the UK approach to data protection was inherently weak; the driving force for legislation was commercial interest. It can be argued that this problem still remains; it was the then Secretary of State for Trade and Industry (Lord Young) who in 1988 pressed for an inter-departmental review of the Data Protection Act. The terms of reference placed particular emphasis on 'the impact on data users of the registration requirements' and on dealing 'first with the registration aspects' (ie the impact of the Act on holders of personal data took priority over the impact of the Act on Data Subjects).

1.6 Yet two decades earlier, individual privacy was deemed to be very important. In the late 1960s the Younger Committee commissioned a survey which asked if people approved of a freely available list of properties coupled with the names of the residents; over 30% of the replies expressed disapproval - yet this list was none other than the Electoral Register which, in its political context, raises few objections. By the late 1980s about 90% of the population were concerned about 'controlling the information that can be kept about you', or about 'stopping organisations passing your information to others' (Third Report of the Data Protection Registrar).

1.7 In most cases individuals do not object to bona fide uses of information; for example the names and addresses held in the Electoral Register or telephone directory are not seen as any threat to privacy, because the reason for the existence of these lists (and their public availability) is understood and approved by everybody who chooses to appear on them. However, the processing of the Electoral Register by a computer adds a new dimension; it allows personal data that were collected for electoral purposes to be used (or matched against other data) for completely different purposes (eg employers might wish to check the political affiliations of prospective employees by consulting a database which combines the Electoral Register with canvass returns held by a constituency party). As a result, if data protection legislation is to be effective, information collected for purpose X should not be used for purpose Y without public approval and controls.

1.8 A clear example of this kind of problem was the delayed West German census of 1983. People were to be asked their employment status, religion, race and how much living space they occupied. This information, it was argued, could enable the authorities to determine priorities for social welfare or building programmes. However, the same information could be used to determine the identity of those Turkish guest-workers who were unemployed and living in overcrowded conditions, and who could therefore be targeted for enforced repatriation to Turkey. Whatever the purpose of these questions, its aim was not assisted by Munich City Council paying a bounty to census workers of £2 for every illegal immigrant found, or £1 for every West German found who was not registered with the Police. In this case there was an active 'Volkszählungsboykott', legal appeals to the Constitutional Court, and a realisation that the Census would become meaningless if individuals did not answer questions voluntarily or, even worse, gave false answers. There were echoes of this in the London Borough of Haringey, when the Office of Population Censuses and Surveys (OPCS) gave a trial run to the ethnic origin question before the 1981 Census; it was discovered that one third of the ethnic population refused to answer and that only 14% of West Indians gave usable replies (The Economist, 1.8.87). There was, clearly, major concern that such ethnic data could be used as a basis for repatriation. In both cases, approval, consent and cooperation of the Data Subject was crucial to the integrity and accuracy of the personal data.

1.9 Such issues are repeatedly raised in relation to an Identity Card. For example, a plastic card embossed with an individual's National Insurance (NI) number could be an efficient device to ensure accuracy and speed of benefit payments; on the other hand, the unique number, once accurately recorded, could be the basis of linking files of many government departments. In general, worries about identity cards do not concern the card itself, but rather the purposes for which the card could be used through technological developments in the future, and the lack of control by the individual over the use of the card. On these grounds, when the concept of an identity number was discussed in the Lindop Committee's Report on Data Protection published in 1978, the Committee drew attention to the 'risk of drifting towards a Universal Personal Identifier, which could evolve without legislation if a particular identity number came to be widely used', and to the consequent 'reduction of the British Citizen's traditional anonymity'; the Committee concluded that 'special legislation should be enacted' (ie the political process, with its concomitant public debate and ultimate democratic decision, should determine events).

1.10 Often, however, arbitrary decisions by administrators may increase information exchange between government departments with the aim of improving efficiency or for administrative convenience. For example, the Driver Vehicle Licensing Agency (DVLA; formerly the DVLC) computer holds up to date addresses of all vehicle keepers, which are transferred on a regular basis to the Police National Computer

(PNC). This has allowed the Police to perform nearly 25 million vehicle checks per year. Additionally, the DVLA operates a service to local government and the Police, and in 1990 they divulged names and addresses over 13 million times to these and other organisations (including some as diverse as the RSPCA, universities and Malvern Hill Conservators). These procedures are justified primarily by requirements such as the need of the Inland Revenue to find tax evaders or the DHSS to trace those who have defaulted on maintenance payments. This type of transaction is well established, and the DVLA and Inland Revenue have been exchanging names and addresses since 1931, long before computers and data protection. Computerisation, it is argued, is nothing to worry about: it simply makes the exchange a little quicker. After all, the argument continues, it is clearly in the public interest to catch tax evaders, maintenance defaulters and car thieves.

1.11 However, such cross-linking makes possible many additional checks and controls that were impossible using manual systems. For example, the cross-referencing of records of the DHSS and Department of Employment could lead to simple computer programs to compare those people who work (ie pay NI contributions), against those who claim social security (ie draw benefit), as happened in the USA. A simple political decision could be taken to investigate all such matches with a view to prosecution; this leads to automatic checks, not because there is tangible suspicion of fraud or even evidence of an actual fraud, but because the checks are easy to make. Consequently such procedures lead to targeting (or profiling) and the selective treatment of those whose details are recorded. For example, the Social Security fraud squad often target their enquiries on unemployed people with specific skills (eg motor mechanic, carpenter) or on, say, single women. The assumption is that unemployed people with skills may be earning on the 'black economy', or that single women may be living with, and being supported by, a man. Computer programs can be written to identify such individuals, and the squad can then begin to investigate, on the basis that people who meet the criteria of a **potential** fraudster, are **likely** fraudsters requiring investigation. It is not surprising, therefore, that some individuals feel uneasy at the increased threat to individual privacy that this use of computerised personal files can pose; a future Government could easily select target groups, on the basis of different criteria, for different purposes.

1.12 In addition, such techniques strike at a fundamental tenet of Human Rights: the presumption of 'innocence' until found 'guilty'. Targeting philosophies raise the prospect of having to prove one's innocence as they will always identify people who satisfy the criteria, but who have not committed any crime. The result is that individuals who satisfy the selection criteria will feel obliged to provide explanations as to how this came about: there is always the seductive argument that 'those who have nothing to hide have nothing to fear'. Thus if data protection is to be effective in protecting privacy, it must be able to establish whether it is fair to use personal data in such a way, and to arbitrate on the use of, or the relevance of, the personal data in such new circumstances.

1.13 Data protection must also arbitrate in areas which are affected by traditional attitudes to secrecy. Many members of certain professions (eg doctors, social workers, lawyers, police officers, teachers) argue that professional requirements necessitate immunity for their files from inspection by those concerned. Doctors say that such access would be detrimental to health care, social workers say it would harm the provision of advice, and the Police say that it could enable criminals to avoid detection. To support these claims, hypothetical cases are generally constructed, often involving a cancer patient, a stressed single parent, a rapist etc (in doing so, the fact that such examples are rare, rather than the norm, tends to be overlooked).

1.14 But this emphasis on restricted Subject Access to files ignores the gradual change of use of personal information held by the professions. Initially, notes were written as aides memoire, or concerned facts known only to one individual, for example the sole doctor in a practice or the constable on the beat. Now such notes, often containing subjective assessments of individuals, tend to be available to a much wider audience, for example through multi-agency policing or multi-agency caring. Information, fully understood by the observer, may be disclosed to others who are unaware of the context in which the original record was made, thereby leading to problems of interpretation.

1.15 There will always be cases where a person wonders how an interviewer obtained some personal detail, or whether all the information known to the interviewer is, in fact, correct. This might occur in a job interview and result in the applicant becoming suspicious about not being appointed; similarly, where a person is deprived of the custody of children, or of priority housing or other benefit, there can always be a feeling that somebody, at some time, has passed on information that has been detrimental to the case of the individual concerned. Consequently it is important that any data protection legislation insists that, wherever possible, records are kept of the interchanges of information between organisations, so that any inaccuracies or misinterpretations can be corrected, and that there is a right of access to the data by the individual concerned (or, at the very least, access by an independent person).

1.16 To summarise, the components of satisfactory data protection legislation are:

(a) the setting of limits, known to the public, on the content, use and disclosure of any collected information;

(b) the application of accepted principles of data protection to all information, irrespective of how or where the information is held;

(c) the establishment of access to information, powers of correction and, in the case of exemptions to such access, the right to have problems investigated independently;

(d) wherever possible, the ability to trace information through the maze of exchanges that exist between information systems (eg by using the computer to log data transfer automatically, so that corrections can be passed on);

(e) the right for individuals to exercise a measure of control over the use of their information, and to obtain an independent assessment as to whether it is fair, relevant or appropriate to use information, collected for one purpose, in different circumstances;

(f) the ability of a supervisory authority to monitor and enforce legal controls and technical standards (eg security systems, encryption etc) that maintain the confidentiality of the information.

1.17 As will be seen, it can be argued that the Data Protection Act fails to meet many of these tests, and that changes are necessary: the data protection debate is far from over.

2. The Data Protection Act: a Data Subject's critique

2.1 The first part of the Act deals with basic definitions: 'Data Users' (persons or organisations who control the contents and use of the information); 'Data Subjects' (living individuals whose details are recorded); and what constitutes 'data' and 'personal data'. The complex definition of data hinges on the form in which the information is recorded, and limits the legislation to information that can be processed automatically (eg on computer). Manual files, which currently contain the bulk of personal information and, additionally, most of the sensitive information, are generally outside the scope of the Act. As the Data Protection Principles do not apply to such records, there is little redress should manually held information be inaccurate, irrelevant, used or disclosed at whim, retained indefinitely, out of date, or kept in conditions of total secrecy or insecurity.

2.2 This leads to obvious anomalies when dealing with dual information systems, where part of the information is held on computer and part on paper file. Systems of this kind are a natural progression in moving to fully automated procedures, and during the transition the active manual records are generally condensed to an abstract, which is placed on computer together with information as to where the complete manual file can be found. This abstract is comprehensively indexed (via the data fields of a database), so that references to the manual record are fully catalogued. Computer programs are then able to manipulate the index to cross reference many manual files and, via the index, to link together data held within the manual files.

2.3 Mixed systems allow the manual files to be used in many different ways (for example, the HOLMES system used by the Police deals with the vast amounts of data collected during major incidents). In a completely manual system, structured files can only answer specific questions such as 'Where is the criminal record on X?', or 'Where is the file on 24 Smith Street?'. With the files indexed and with abstracts on computer, it is possible to refer to these files by using more speculative questions which are useful to detect crime. For example 'Which crime reports refer to males aged between 20 and 24 living with their mothers?' or 'What incidents refer to red-haired men driving blue Cortinas?'. The difference between the two is that a completely manual system can only be organised around a few specific enquiries, whereas mixed systems, because they contain an abstract or index on computer, can allow the manual files to be used to answer many questions.

2.4 This flexibility could encourage those organisations using manual systems to keep the sensitive information on paper and to index the material with the aid of a computer - since in a mixed system using manual and computer records, only the computer records come under the jurisdiction of the Act. A Data Subject, for example, may be able to find from the computer record that an extensive paper file exists in a filing cabinet on the 10th floor of, say, the Department of Social Security, but the Act's provisions mean that there is no right of Subject Access to that file. Many people have alleged that the Economic League, an organisation that holds records of 'left wing trade unionists' etc, favours a manual system in order to keep the personal information outwith the provisions of the Data Protection Act.

2.5 Within the Act itself, the definition of personal data separates 'intentions' and 'opinions'. The Act defines opinions (eg 'I think Fred Smith is uncreditworthy') as personal data. Intentions (eg 'I shall not offer Fred Smith credit') are not personal data even though the fact that credit will not be given would normally be based on an opinion of uncreditworthiness. Because an 'intention' is not personal data, the data are not subject to the Act. Thus these definitions not only allow a Data User to restrict access to personal data, under the Subject Access provisions, if the data express an intention towards the Data Subject, but also allow such data to escape the provisions of the Data Protection Principles (eg intentions can be based on, or consist of, wholly inaccurate or irrelevant information). Since the Registrar's powers relate specifically to 'personal data', he cannot pursue a complaint about any personal information (eg personal details in manual files, or in intentions) that is not personal data.

2.6 The protection which the Act offers to Data Subjects rests on the eight Data Protection Principles and on the Registrar. The Registrar's function, established by the Act, is to ensure that the Data Protection Principles are upheld by all Data Users, and to maintain a public Register of these Data Users and of their activities that deal with personal information. However, the Act prevented the Registrar from refusing an application (unless there was an error in filling in the Registration forms), or from using any of his powers for a start-up period of two years - which expired 11.11.1987 (this meant that the Registrar had to wait until then before taking effective action against Data Users, other than on the grounds of non-registration). Furthermore, it is difficult to see how the Registrar could pay detailed attention to the facts submitted in the initial Registration process, when over 130,000 applications were submitted within nine months.

2.7 Registration of personal data is itself full of ambiguities for the Data Subject. For example, the Act says that every Data User must provide a description of all sources from which the Data User 'intends or may wish to obtain the data', a description of all persons to whom the Data User 'intends or may wish to disclose the data' and a description of overseas transfers that the Data User 'intends or may wish' to make. The phrase **'intends or may wish'** draws attention to an inherent ambiguity; the fact that an event **may** take place does not mean that it **does** take place. In fact the Act exacerbates this problem. The interpretation of the Third Data Protection Principle states that the Principle cannot be contravened if the disclosure is to a registered person. In addition, a Data Subject cannot claim compensation for damage, on the basis that it was caused by an unauthorised disclosure, if that disclosure was to a registered person. Thus to avoid the legal threats in the Act consequent on unauthorised disclosures, many Data Users use their crystal ball to register every conceivable disclosure that they are likely to make, just to ensure that all are authorised as defined by the Act. This is completely different from describing clearly to the Data Subject what disclosures **actually** take place as part of the Data User's normal, legitimate, activities.

2.8 This confusion is deepened by the 'non-disclosure' exemptions, which establish a number of circumstances under which disclosures of personal data need not be described in a Register Entry. Combined with the above, this means not only that a Data Subject cannot tell from the registered disclosures whether those disclosures actually occur, but also that conversely (or perhaps perversely), the absence of a description from the list of disclosures does not preclude such a disclosure.

2.9 Although the Registrar can act if he is satisfied that a Data User has contravened one or more of the Principles, he has no power to obtain information from a Data User, and the only way the Registrar can act against an 'uncooperative Data User' is to obtain a search warrant. To obtain a warrant, the Registrar must have enough evidence (presumably from aggrieved Data Subjects) to persuade a Circuit Judge to issue one. Thus it can be argued that if the Registrar can convince a Court, he already has enough information to serve an Enforcement Notice anyway. Note that the Registrar has no simple power to inspect personal data or to obtain other information, as recommended by the Lindop Committee; a serious omission from the Act. Even when the Registrar serves a Notice, the Act allows a Data User, who thinks the Registrar is being unfair, to appeal to a Tribunal whose decision is final except on a point of law; by contrast a Data Subject cannot appeal to the Tribunal over the Registrar's decision not to act against a Data User.

2.10 A Data Subject who is seeking compensation must find redress through a Civil Court (the Registrar has no formal part to play in these proceedings, except that any investigation by the Registrar may be used as evidence). There are many defences provided for the Data User; for example, the use or disclosure of third party information, even if unsubstantiated gossip, cannot incur damages as long as the information has been accurately recorded and is always identified as having been obtained from a third party. Similarly, should the Data Subject challenge the accuracy of the data, damages cannot be awarded if the Data User always draws attention to that challenge when using or disclosing the information. Under Section 23 of the Act, compensation cannot arise from a disclosure that has been registered; thus the larger the number of registered disclosures, the more the Data Subject's ability to obtain recompense is reduced (ie the more 'imaginative' the Entry, the less risk the Data User runs of being liable for compensation).

2.11 In other cases surrounding compensation outlined in Sections 22 and 23 of the Act, it is a defence for the Data User to show that 'reasonable' steps were taken (eg as far as security procedures are concerned) to prevent the damage that was caused. In determining what is 'reasonable', evidence from expert witnesses for Data Users will be difficult to contradict, except via expensive expert witnesses for the Data Subject. In these costly circumstances, many Data Subjects will find it difficult to obtain redress. Some Data Subjects, perhaps a majority, may find it more convenient to forego any claim, but rather to complain to the Registrar in the hope that he will act in pursuance of a violation of the Data Protection Principles. That, in any event, will not financially compensate for damage caused to the Data Subjects.

2.12 It is, however, the exemptions from the Act that make it even more controversial. It establishes three kinds of exemption: from Part II (Registration and Supervision of Data Users) and Sections 21 to 24 (Rights of Data Subjects); from the Subject Access provisions as a whole (Section 21) or in specific circumstances (eg Section 29); and from the various non-disclosure provisions. Where appropriate, the first kind of exemption effectively means that the provisions of the Act do not apply; a Subject Access exemption means that the Data User can refuse Data Subjects access to all or some of their own personal data; and a non-disclosure exemption relates to disclosures which do not have to be registered.

2.13 Consider the payroll and accounts exemption in Section 32 of the Act: its aim is to relieve small businesses of the obligation to register, on the basis that, within the tight limitations set by the exemption, the use and disclosure of personal data would be essentially innocuous. Thus the exemption could be used by a newsagent to manage the accounts, and to indicate the income anticipated against a customer's name and address. However, a forecast reduction of income against a particular address for a summer month could well imply that this address will then be unoccupied (people normally stop papers when they take their holiday), and this would be valuable intelligence for a burglar. If the newsagent disclosed such information inadvertently (eg by poor disposal of output), because of the extent of the exemption (Part II and Sections 21-24) the Act offers no opportunity to claim compensation from the newsagent.

2.14 A similar wide exemption applies to data required for the purpose of safeguarding national security, such as data held by the Security Services (MI5, MI6, GCHQ, Special Branch, etc) for this purpose. Not only is Subject Access to such data denied, but the non-disclosure provisions also apply so that a Data User can disclose any personal data for this purpose without the disclosure having to be registered. Since the Registrar cannot monitor compliance with the Data Protection Principles in this case, the legal incentive for checks within the Security Services on the accuracy or relevance of the information is, clearly, substantially diminished.

2.15 In the case of national security, the exemption (Part II and Sections 21-24) is determined by means of a certificate signed by a Minister of the Crown. These certificates are 'timeless', and need not be signed by the relevant Minister (ie a Minister other than the Home Secretary could sign a certificate for MI5); even a broad description of the contents of a certificate has been refused to Parliament on the grounds of national security. This contrasts with the Lindop Committee recommendation that a special person be appointed, with relevant Security Services clearance, to deal with data protection aspects of the sensitive data held by the Security Services. The exemption for safeguarding national security must be viewed with concern, given the reported plans for many Government Departments to be linked via a Government Data Network. As this Network involves the Home Office, and possibly the Police National Computer Network, the allegation by an ex-MI5 operative (Peter Wright, in the book 'Spycatcher') that MI5 had computer links to the DHSS computer in Newcastle becomes a pertinent issue.

2.16 Data Subjects' rights to obtain all their own personal data held by a Data User can also be limited by the cost involved. Since a fee can be demanded for Access to each Register Entry (and since large Data Users, in particular, may have many Entries) quite a substantial sum of money may be required.

2.17 The exemptions defined by Section 28 of the Act ('Crime and taxation') will result in well-publicised and contentious cases surrounding 'the prevention or detection of crime; the apprehension or prosecution of offenders; or the assessment or collection of any tax or duty'. In these cases, the only redress available to the Data Subject if the Police or Inland Revenue were to refuse Subject Access (which can only be done on the grounds that these purposes would be prejudiced thereby), would be to complain to the Courts, under Section 25(2) of the Act, and to run the risk of paying the considerable costs involved, or to complain to the Registrar that the Seventh Data Protection Principle has been contravened, in the knowledge that the Registrar may have to work in the dark (see paragraph 2.9 above).

2.18 Personal data required for 'the prevention or detection of crime; the apprehension or prosecution of offenders; or the assessment or collection of any tax or duty' are also subject to the non-disclosure provisions of the Act. This means that a Data User can disclose personal data to the Police or to tax officials for these specific purposes and does not need to register such disclosures if satisfied that failure to provide the particular data 'would have been likely to prejudice' any of these purposes. Consequently, the Police and tax officials, like the Security Services, can delve into any database if they can persuade Data Users that the test of 'prejudice' can be met (the use of a standard form by the Police to certify this can make such disclosures a bureaucratic formality). Thus, in summary, the Registrar could be ignorant of many sensitive disclosures that will affect personal privacy.

2.19 Subject Access exemptions for health and social work records could, in practice, offer wide scope to withhold information (see Chapter 7, Section 4). Certainly, application of the exemptions can be uneven across the country as Access depends on the viewpoint of the professionals concerned: 'serious harm' in Bradford may not be considered 'serious harm' in Barnsley, or vice versa.

2.20 The Subject Access provisions can be used as a mechanism through which employers check on the criminal record of potential employees. During the Commons Committee stage, the Government rejected an amendment which would make it a criminal offence for an employer to require an individual to make a request for Subject Access (in this case to the Police) before offering employment. The Minister (David Waddington), in reply, said that 'there seems in principle to be nothing criminal in asking the applicant to confirm the details he has supplied by means of a printout' (Committee Hansard 27.3.84, column 469). It is obvious that this process can extend to other vetting situations, which need not all be as valid as, say, the vetting of employees whose work involves substantial access to children. There is nothing in the Act to prevent 'forced' Subject Access and this has become an increasing problem.

2.21 Overall, scrutiny of the small print of the Act shows that in many cases, notably in the public sector, some kind of exception or exemption negates the important safeguards established by the legislation. This has considerable legal implications for the personal data used in connection with Community Charges Registers, the Electoral Registers, and the Government Data Network.

2.22 Consider the First Data Protection Principle which states that personal data shall be obtained and processed fairly and lawfully. In relation to this Principle, the Data Protection Registrar (Guideline 4, paragraph 1.4) advises Data Users to ensure that individuals 'are not misled as to why the information is required or why it will be used or disclosed'. The Registrar even states that 'it would be unfair for a Data User to process an automated mailing list with the result that advertising material is sent to an individual who has informed the Data User that he does not wish to receive such material' (Guideline 4, paragraph 1.6). The reason for this advice is quite simple: the public are very sensitive about who uses their names and addresses. Since 1987, successive Annual Reports of the Data Protection Registrar have shewn that between one fifth and one third of all complaints from Data Subjects concerned unsolicited mail.

2.23 However, in Schedule 1, Part II of the Act, the 'Interpretation' of the First Principle stipulates that information is 'in any event' obtained fairly 'if it is obtained from a person who is authorised by or under any enactment to supply it; or is required to supply it by or under any enactment ...'. Thus if a Data User has statutory authority to use the data for another purpose, then any reason originally given for collecting the personal data has no relevance to the subsequent use since the First Data Protection Principle cannot be contravened.

2.24 This situation has implications for a Community Charges Register, as any relevant information (names, addresses, dates of residence) in the possession of the Charging Authority (eg derived from applications for free bus passes or library tickets, from housing registers, planning records, education records etc) can lawfully be copied to compile this Register. Because of the 'by or under any enactment' condition in the First Principle, all these personal data will have been obtained 'fairly' even though their use in compiling the Register is kept secret (and such use for Community Charge purposes may thus be without the knowledge or consent of the Data Subject, and may also be at odds with the original reason for the collection of the data).

2.25 The legal position with respect to disclosing personal data is similar. For example, Section 34(5) of the Act relates to a disclosure which is required 'by or under any enactment'. Such a disclosure does not have to be described in an Entry in the Data Protection Register, and is not subject to the enforcement powers of the Registrar with respect to 'any Data Protection Principle inconsistent with the disclosure in question' (Section 26(3)(b) of the Act). In this situation the Registrar cannot use his enforcement powers under **any** Data Protection Principle, and there is no obligation to tell the Data Subject about the disclosure.

2.26 To understand how these regulations can work in practice, consider a disclosure which consists of the sale of names and addresses from the Electoral Register. Because both collection and disclosure of the personal data fall within the definition of 'under any enactment', the sale can proceed without reference to the Guidelines issued by the Data Protection Registrar, despite the evidence of some dubious procedures. For example, according to the Daily News (17.4.87), some Councils have sold special lists derived from the Electoral Register (eg single women living in a certain area). In addition, Parliament has been told that the Electoral Register is legally used by the Police to vet juries, by DHSS special squads to investigate fraud, by the BBC to hunt TV licence evaders, and by immigration authorities to trace illegal immigrants, as well as for normal electoral purposes! It is hardly surprising, therefore, that there is evidence that some people do not want their data to be recorded on publicly available Registers. In a similar instance, and according to a survey carried out by the University of Bradford in certain inner city areas (The Guardian, 8.6.87), as many as 11% of eligible voters did not register because they did not want to be traced for one reason or another, whilst in Aberdeen South, according to the local MP, the number of registered electors dropped by 5,000 in 1987 (Hansard, col 326, 8.12.87) following the introduction of the Community Charge.

2.27 Two Parliamentary questions relating to personal data obtained and disclosed by the Driver Vehicle Licensing Agency (DVLA) in Swansea provide a typical example of how the Data Protection Act can, in certain circumstances, apply differently to the public and the private sectors. The answer to the first question (Hansard, col 585, 18.7.90) is factual; it describes that under Regulation 15 of the Road Vehicles (Registration and Licensing) Regulations 1971 (SI 1971 No. 450), over 13 million names and addresses were disclosed by the DVLA to the Police, Local Authorities and other organisations during the financial year 1989/90. As these disclosures are determined by statutory regulations the non-disclosure provisions apply, and Section 26(3) of the Act means that the disclosures effectively escape the Registrar's supervisory powers. Similarly, the collection of information to be contained in the personal data is 'in any event' fair as the information is obtained under statute (for example in the case of the name and address on a Driving Licence, 'there is a maximum penalty of £400' for failure to inform the DVLA of any change of address). The second question (Hansard, col 101, 19.2.91) asked whether application forms produced by the DVLA would, in future, carry a statement, to inform applicants that their information would be disclosed to the Police: the provision of such explanatory detail is, under ordinary circumstances, recommended practice with respect to the First Principle (eg Guidance Note 19: 'Clearly, simply, honestly and fully'). The response to this question was rather startling (although of course accurate with respect to personal data subject to statutory regulation): 'The DVLA registrations ... indicate that details ... are given to the police. Copies of the registrations are freely available from the Data Protection Registrar. There is no requirement under the Data Protection Act to include additional references on application forms to inform individuals and, at present, the DVLA has no plans to do so'. The Registrar's Guideline 4, paragraph 1.3 states that 'The law does not assume that individuals know the contents of the Data Protection Register'. As the DVLA transfers personal details about vehicle keepers to the Police National Computer (details of licence holders are similarly to be transferred), it can be argued that, in such cases, individuals are obliged to register their address with the Police. Since this happens now, it can also be argued 'what is the objection to extending this principle to other databases?'.

2.28 More generally, the problems mentioned above are endemic to many Government databases. This is because, unlike in the private sector, every task, operation or function within the public sector must be authorised by an Act of Parliament, since it would otherwise be illegal. Consequently, if there is a new initiative from Government, it must either be supported by previous legislation, or new powers have to be sought from Parliament. Thus, as in the case described above, the new use would be subject to the 'under any enactment' clauses of the Data Protection Act, and would therefore be outside the scope of many of the Registrar's enforcement powers. Should a new enactment be required, then its passage through Parliament would, again, reduce the Registrar's supervisory role over the collection and disclosure of the relevant data throughout the Network.

2.29 It is not surprising that many individuals look to aspects of legislation implemented in other countries as potential improvements to the UK Data Protection Act. These aspects, some of which may be incorporated into the eventual Directive on Data Protection from the European Commission (see Section 4 of this Chapter for details of these proposals) include:

(a) Denmark: permission has to be obtained from the Data Surveillance Authority before an automated file containing sensitive data can be processed in the private sector (as against mass registration, without prior evaluation of data protection requirements, permitted in the UK, Sweden and France).

(b) West Germany: the general right to privacy ensures that individuals can themselves determine the limits within which their personal data can be used, and this right can only be restricted when the legitimate interests of the general public (not necessarily represented by the interests of the private sector) override those of the individual.

(c) Canada: since the Privacy Act forbids the use of personal information except for the purpose for which it was obtained, or for use consistent with that purpose, computer matching (the comparison of information for different purposes) contravenes this provision, since it can turn the traditional presumption of innocence into a presumption of guilt (see paragraph 1.11 above).

(d) Austria: the right to know, in many cases, the actual source of the personal data.

2.30 Because of the obstacles, enshrined in the UK legislation, which Data Subjects have to surmount in order to achieve their legitimate objectives, Data Subjects may pursue other avenues of 'attack'. These include:

(a) complaints to their local MP, or to an MP who takes an interest in Freedom of Information or Data Protection issues. Cases before MPs can be raised directly with responsible Ministers and often action can be quick. If the case is strong enough, the MP could pass the complaint to the Parliamentary Commissioner or Health Commissioner. These 'ombudsmen' have the advantage that their investigative track record has been well established, and although they cannot award compensation, their 'suggestions' for such recompense are usually obeyed;

(b) complaints to journalists working for the local, trade or national press. Although it does not produce compensation for the Data Subject, such adverse publicity can damage a Data User's image;

(c) complaints to consumer organisations, Citizens Advice Bureaux, trades unions or professional bodies, who will support cases of direct relevance to them;

(d) complaints to special government bodies such as the Police Complaints Board, or to Councillors in the case of local government;

(e) complaints to specialist pressure groups such as MIND (mental health), Consumers Association (especially on consumer issues such as credit allocation) or Liberty (civil liberties), who may be prepared to cover legal costs to establish a point of principle.

2.31 In summary, the Data Protection Act fails to satisfy many of the needs of Data Subjects. The Act is limited to data processed by computer, there are numerous limitations on Subject Access, and the Act does not offer proper control of sensitive data collections, or even the security of knowing in time where disclosures have occurred and who has received the personal data. It could prove very expensive for Data Subjects to obtain a copy of all their own personal data since Data Users may require a fee to be paid for access to each Register Entry. Legislation that pre-dates the Data Protection Act and which defined rules for the uses and disclosures of personal information, also legitimises the same uses and disclosures when that information has been converted to data. Given the flexibility with which computers can manipulate personal data, such legislation, which did not take account of privacy aspects, could then work to the detriment of Data Subjects.

2.32 Thus it can be argued that the words found in the 1975 White Paper 'Computers and Privacy' (Cmnd 6353): 'the time has come when those who use computers ... can no longer remain the sole judges of whether their own systems adequately safeguard privacy' still do not apply in the many cases in which Data Users are, in effect, judge and jury with respect to the personal data they obtain and disclose. In such cases the words 'protected personal data' really mean protected from the supervision of the Data Protection Registrar, and from the legitimate concerns of Data Subjects.

3. Annual reports from the Data Protection Registrar

3.1 Those involved with Data Protection are well advised to obtain a copy of the Data Protection Registrar's annual reports: it is one important way of keeping abreast of developments in the field, and of anticipating areas of special interest. For example, several of the concerns raised in the Fifth Report (June 1989) resulted in the serving of well publicised Enforcement Notices (eg against Community Charges Registration Officers, Consumer Credit Industry), and the reports set out the reasoning behind the Registrar's actions. Subsequent to 1987, when the Act came fully into force, each report has contained a section on 'Complaints from Individuals'; for example in the Sixth Report there is an outline of 30 cases taken up by the Registrar's officers. These provide valuable information on how Data Users contravened the Act, and on the remedial action that has been taken.

3.2 The Registrar uses these reports to comment on current issues, to ensure that current data protection aspects are fully considered. In his Third Report (June 1987), he mentioned the need to develop policy on 'Issues of Public Debate' such as the use of lists of names and addresses (found in Share Registers, Electoral Registers and Community Charges Registers) or the Government Data Network. In the Sixth Report, the Registrar indicated areas of special concern for the coming year, involving work by his office to establish a 'position'. In addition to the 'hardy annuals' (credit referencing, direct mail, community charge) he noted that he would focus on public sector areas that include: the implications of NHS Reform, Police National Computer upgrade, the Government Data Network, computing developments in the Inland Revenue and the Department of Social Security, the 1991 Census, and DNA fingerprinting. In the private sector, he considered central insurance registers, itemised billing for telephone calls, remote monitoring surveillance devices, EFTPOS, the use of expert systems, and profiling to be of particular importance. How much cognisance is taken of the many questions raised by this report has yet to be seen; however, the degree of involvement of the Registrar in computer projects of this kind is potentially very extensive.

3.3 The annual reports are a good source of information concerning the number (and type) of complaints (for example, in the year of the Sixth Report (1989/90) the number of complaints rose from 1122 to 2698). Most complaints relate to Consumer Credit (17%) and Direct Mail (45%), with Community Charge a new entry (7%); in the report the Registrar writes of an 'unacceptable backlog' of 310 complaints that have to be looked at. The Registrar uses the reports to make announcements: for example, in the Sixth Report, in anticipation of further increases in complaints, the Registrar stated that he had started a telephone service to advise complainants directly (this will weed out those that do not need a formal process and will offer immediate advice to complainants); he has also placed an index to the Register Entry in 262 libraries (this may stimulate more interest than those unused microfiches, which have been withdrawn).

3.4 The reports also indicate areas of frustration. For example, in his Third Report the Registrar noted 'I was not asked for comments on the (Community Charge) legislation for Scotland'. In the same report, the Home Office told the Registrar, in relation to allowing voters the choice whether their name and address could be sold by local authorities without their knowledge or consent:

> 'The Home Office considered my request but concluded that, for reasons connected with the way in which the forms are completed (eg by a head of household) and because of the design of the form, they were unable to accede to it. The Minister assured me that careful thought had been given to my suggestion and he was disappointed that practical difficulties prevented it from being adopted. He also felt that, since the Electoral Register was in the public domain, there was no unfairness or breach of privacy in supplying it in the form of data.' (Third Report, June 1987). However, a month before the report was issued, the Home Office told one MP (Hansard, 5.5.87) that the reason was 'A warning notice might discourage people from registering' (see Chapter 4(B), paragraphs 1.2.13 to 1.2.17).

3.5 Three years later, in the Sixth Report, the Registrar stated that he was 'disappointed that the position of individuals was weakened' by new regulations that allowed increased sales of the Electoral Register, without the knowledge or consent of voters, for purposes other than those associated with elections. The Registrar complained that the Regulations had effectively 'forced (individuals) by statute to supply their names and addresses to those who care to buy these registers'. The Registrar is thus politely making the point that such legal abrogations of the standards for 'fair obtaining', (as outlined in Guidance Note 19 on the First Data Protection Principle) leaves much to be desired, if the best that Ministers can offer with respect to the sale of the Electoral Register is that 'they will consider the possibility of EROs publishing, from time to time, a list of those who have bought their registers'.

3.6 In the Sixth Report, the Registrar still showed signs of being concerned that Data Protection issues are not being raised with his Office before they happen. Although couched in positive language, addressed both to the public and private sector, 'It is **clearly helpful** to my Office ... to have early discussion on new developments' (our emphasis), it is the Government that is the intended target of this plea (for example, the sentence 'I was pleased that a number of government departments were seeking views' raises the issue of those that did not!). Although the Registrar has made progress and is exploring with the Home Office 'the possibility of obtaining regular notification of the introduction of relevant legislation', realistically he is 'less sanguine about the situation as a whole' (if any Government is determined to legislate, then Data Protection issues are unlikely to provide overriding objections).

3.7 Reports also contain valuable surveys and analyses; for example half of the Fifth

Report was devoted to the Registrar's public consultation about the performance of the Act itself. In relation to Subject Access fees the Registrar noted, in the Third Report, that he had carried out research which discovered that 66% of people thought a fee for Subject Access was reasonable (28% said any fee was unreasonable), and that of the 66%, 7 out of 10 said that £10 was an unreasonable fee. If this proportion is recombined with the 28%, it can be said that 74% of the population thought a £10 fee to be unreasonable.

3.8 As multiple Register Entries would allow multiple fees to be charged, the Registrar noted in the Third Report:

> 'During debates in Parliament, the Minister suggested a maximum subject access fee of between £3 and £8. In the light of the research results, this seems an appropriate sort of range. A fee towards the bottom end of this range would meet the public's requirements, be comparable with fees in other European countries and be not too dissimilar from the charge of £1 made for access to credit reference files under the Consumer Credit Act. The Home Secretary will set the maximum fee which may be charged for subject access and I have passed the results of the research, referred to above, to the Home Office'.

3.9 Two weeks after the publication of this report the £10 fee was announced.

3.10 The Registrar indicated in the Sixth Report that he was very concerned about the potential uses of Personal Identification Numbers (PINs) and the possibility they offered to merge unrelated personal data (the risk may be reduced if the proposed European Directive is enacted). Underlying the PIN controversy are huge social and political issues: the Identity Card debate (most European Countries have compulsory ID Cards and many MPs support 'voluntary' ID cards: see the Home Affairs Committee, Seventh Report, Practical Police Co-operation in the European Community, HC 363); the regulation of the free movement of people, between Member States, from 1992; the exchange of benefit or health personal data between Member States; immigration control, and the prospect of a European-wide 'wanted persons index' for Police Forces.

3.11 With respect to the UK, the Registrar's research (see the very useful Appendix AA1 in the Sixth Report) shows that surname, first forename and address identify 99.1% of the population; this, the Registrar argues, should point more towards research into the use of second names, and into which surnames cause the most problems, than towards acceptance of a widely used PIN. Although the Registrar concedes that an identification number provides a useful shorthand reference, he argues that this number should be 'context specific' and not used for unrelated purposes (as this would facilitate data matching). It is these arguments that helped him dissuade the Student Loans Company (who contacted him 'late in the day') from using the National

Insurance Number as an identifier, and form the basis of his objections to the Consumer Credit Industry holding Dates of Birth.

3.12 The Registrar also stated in the Sixth Report that 'in future years (he) will publish a list' of those Data Users who are involved in prosecution or supervisory action under the Data Protection Act; in the Seventh Report (June 1991) he gave effect to that warning. He is of the opinion that it is unfair for some Data Users to receive headline treatment (Police and Community Charge Data Users know what he means) whilst others get off far more lightly (for example, the 'Theatre trust' referred to in the 'Table of Cases Brought' of the Sixth Report was found guilty of an offence under each of Sections 5(2)(a)-5(2)(d), was fined £2,000 with £900 costs and escaped a mention even in the local paper).

3.13 The First Report of the Home Affairs Committee ('Annual Report of the Data Protection Registrar', HC 115, Session 1990-91) was also the first formal study, by backbench MPs, of the Data Protection Registrar's Office and of the Act. Like most parliamentary examinations of public bodies, the First Report includes: a Memorandum from the Registrar (this was culled from his Sixth Report); a verbatim record of the cross examination of the Registrar and his senior officials by the Select Committee; and a series of conclusions from the Committee. The conclusions were that:

(a) early contact by Government with the Registrar's Office 'in respect of proposed legislation' is important. Ministers should 'ensure that their Departments initiate this contact automatically when Bills and other relevant policy initiatives are being drawn up'

(b) the Government should 'issue guidance to all local authorities and other public bodies recommending that, where they have not done so, they should make early contact with the Registrar and, more importantly, give full consideration to his guidance'

(c) 'the harmonisation of data protection practice throughout Europe should be given priority in any proposed legislation'

(d) although the Registration framework may change (see the discussion of the 'Report on Structure' in Section 5 below) the Government should 'take account of the Registrar's concerns on the need to maintain contact with persons holding sensitive information'

(e) legislation should prohibit the use of Third Party information by credit referencing agencies (the Committee explicitly supported the Registrar's enforcement action against four agencies). As regards trading in personal information, legislation may also be necessary to reinforce the Registrar's view that 'an organisation must give broad details to anyone submitting personal information as to the future uses of that information'

(f) 'clear procedures (should be) established governing the merging of files of data' (the Registrar, in his evidence ('Examination of Witnesses', Q31) stated that the Third Data Protection Principle, which would be relevant to data matching (ie what the Committee calls 'file merging'), is "in practice ... very severely weakened, if not in fact almost wished away, by the Act")

(g) 'the Home Office should initiate a comprehensive study - which would necessarily involve a number of Government Departments - of the case for and against a common national identification number' (the Registrar outlined his objections to PINs in the Sixth Report: the Committee, by contrast, 'believe that the case for one identification number may have some merit' (paragraph 20))

(h) the 'decisions about disclosure of criminal records must be the same throughout the country. They should not be subject to the idiosyncrasies of the 52 police forces of the United Kingdom', and the 'efficiency scrutiny currently under way should establish guidelines both on the length of time different types of criminal records should be held and on the organisations that should have access to them'

(i) 'Although the creation of a DNA database on the whole male population would undoubtedly be expensive, we consider it a development that would provide considerable benefits for the police'

(j) the committee 'look forward to the development of technology which could enable different files of data on individuals to be kept on the same card and accessed independently, and reiterate our previous recommendation' (this was a reference to the Committee's Seventh Report: 'Practical Police Co-operation in the European Community', Session 1989-90, HC 363, that 'Government employ the services of those with sufficient technical imagination to produce a machine-readable identity card' that could control access to different kinds of data stored on the card)

(k) 'the improvement of public awareness of the Act should remain a high priority for the Registrar, not least because it would make his task of enforcing good practice that much easier', and that the 'growing importance of data protection and the increasing problems which Data Protection Commissioners throughout the world will face' means that it is vital that the Registrar's Office 'continues to receive an adequate level of funding from the Home Office'.

3.14 In its published response to the Home Affairs Committee (Cm 1485, ISBN 0-10-114852-6), and apart from the comments about the Directive (see paragraph 5.10 below), the Government reinforced the Committee's view that 'the Registrar's office is successfully fulfilling its purpose'. In further detail the Government:

(a) has instigated procedures for closer liaison between Departments and the Registrar's Office

(b) considers that the Community Charge problems arose 'because Government guidance was not followed' and is not 'convinced that it would be appropriate for it to issue separate general guidance on data protection to other public bodies'

(c) will not consider amending the law in order 'to prohibit the use of third party information (to assess the credit-worthiness of an unconnected individual who happens to be a previous owner of the applicants house)', until the final outcome of the cases involving the Credit Reference Agencies has been determined (see Appendix 1 for details to date)

(d) 'has no present intention of commissioning detailed work' on the case for and against a common national identification number', has rejected the idea of introducing 'voluntary' identity cards, but is 'considering a number of important legal and ethical questions relating to the establishment of a DNA database'

(e) will fund the Registrar's Office 'in the light both of expenditure bids and of overall public spending constraints'

(f) sidestepped the Committee's suggestions (eg on data matching, consultations about the Act, removing unnecessary criminal offences) by saying that these issues can only be resolved when the final form of the European Directive becomes apparent. In summary, the Government 'believes that amending legislation (to the Data Protection Act) is best considered once the Directive has been adopted' (see below).

4. Proposals for change (European Commission)

4.1 According to the European Commission, a common approach to Data Protection is vital to the success of the free market in 1992. The Commission argues that without safeguards to maintain the equivalent level of individual privacy across Europe, Member States could restrict transborder data flow, create obstacles to economic activity, distort competition, or even impede the Commission's supervisory functions. Thus to protect the free market, the Commission distributed a Draft Directive in 1990 (COM (90) 314 SYN 287): 'Draft proposal for a Council Directive approximating certain laws, regulations and administrative provisions of the Member States concerning the protection of individuals in relation to the processing of personal data') which outlines some very tough proposals for Data Protection legislation.

4.2 The Commission's Draft Directive adds to the pot-pourri of Data Protection reviews and international initiatives. In the UK, the Registrar submitted his proposals for legislative changes to Government (following his 'What are your views' exercise) in early 1989 (these proposals were fully discussed in the Fifth Report of the Data Protection Registrar: June 1989). The Home Office, encouraged by the then Secretary of State for Trade and Industry (Lord Young), established its own interdepartmental review in July 1988. Its terms of reference were to concentrate 'particularly with regard to the impact on data users of the registration requirements' and to deal 'first with the registration aspects'; the Data Protection Registrar was present only 'in an advisory capacity' (Releasing Enterprise, Cm 512, page 29: the recommendations are discussed in the Section 5 below). In the international arena there are several Data Protection standards to choose from: the OECD Guidelines (which are usually adopted by the economically advanced countries outside Europe); the Council of Europe Recommendations (which are establishing on a sectoral basis, eg Police sector, Direct Marketing sector, what the international standard should be); a Data Protection initiative started in the United Nations, and the Commission's Draft Directive.

4.3 An eventual Directive, if adopted by the Member States, will cut across all these initiatives and will dictate the nature of Data Protection for years to come. As the Commission regulates one of the major economic power blocks in the world, its standards will oblige other nations to legislate equivalent safeguards; otherwise those nations risk the prohibition of transborder personal data flow from Europe. A common European standard could aim high, by adopting the strongest aspect of the Data Protection legislation of each Member State, or low, by choosing a 'Data Protection baseline' derived from the weakest aspects. As four Member States (Italy, Portugal, Greece, Belgium) do not have any established Data Protection laws (although in some cases there are Government Bills before respective Parliaments), such a baseline could not achieve the Commission's stated policy objectives (eg on transborder data flow). In addition, adopting a low standard could involve some Member States in legislation to lessen individuals' rights (something not necessarily attractive to elected politicians). In practice, the Commission seems to have been guided largely by the International Conference of Data Protection Commissioners of 30th August 1989 (see Appendix AA3 of the Sixth Report of the Data Protection Registrar for fuller details).

4.4 Manual files containing personal information are included within the scope of the Draft: in France, Germany, Austria and in a number of other countries, data protection law already covers manual files. In the UK, three different access to manual files statutes have been enacted (via Private Members Bills) in successive years, and the Data Protection Act itself could apply to manual files containing personal information, if such files are used in conjunction with OCR readers, automatic microfiche readers or other scanning devices. In the Draft, this extension to manual files follows from: the definition of personal data to include 'any information relating to an identified or identifiable individual', the absence of words such as 'processed by equipment operating automatically' (as found in Section 1(2) of the UK's Data Protection Act), and the definition of 'processing' to include operations 'whether or not performed by automated means'. However, personal data have to be 'structured and accessible in an organised collection' (ie have to be capable of use in a way that relates to individuals), and this excludes those manual files from which personal details cannot be so retrieved. Personal data, as defined by the Directive, makes no reference to 'living individual' (ie includes the dead). Finally, the use of the words 'identifiable individuals' in the definition of personal data implies that data relating to individuals that **could** be identified are covered (eg data about red-haired Spaniards may not directly identify a specific individual but could easily do so indirectly, eg by inference or from the context in which the data are used). **Note** that the phrase 'personal data', used in this Section, has the extended meaning which includes manual personal files and also personal information relating to the dead (ie the Directive is not limited to data relating to identifiable living individuals etc).

4.5 The Draft Directive extends to the whole range of activities that fall within the Commission's remit (eg Goods, Services, Transport, Agriculture, Economy and Social Policy) but does not extend to: the activities that do not fall within the scope of Community law (eg Defence); the personal data that are held by 'an individual solely for private and personal purposes'; the personal data held by certain non-profit making bodies on condition that members of those bodies 'have consented to being included (in the personal data file) and that they (the personal data) are not communicated to third parties'. (Note that, in the last case, the fact that the individual may consent to the disclosure does not seem to matter).

4.6 **The Draft Directive limits the public sector to those functions supported by statutory powers**, as the use of files of personal data held by a public sector entity shall only be lawful if it is 'necessary for the performance of the tasks of the public-sector entity' (Community Charge officials are learning this message the hard way). Public sector personal data can be requested by a private sector organisation which 'invokes a legitimate interest, on condition that the interest of the data subject does not prevail'; however, the controller of the file 'shall inform data subjects of the communication of personal data'. Note that this would reverse Government policy towards the sale of the the Electoral Register, and could require a 'warning' notice on the Registration form (see paragraph 3.4 above). However, since the Directive uses the plural 'data subjects', it is unclear whether the Electoral Registration Officer will have to inform voters individually (eg by a warning notice), or whether more global means of communication (eg press notices, public notice boards etc) can be used.

4.7 **The Draft Directive requires the private sector to obtain prior consent of the Data Subject for the holding, use and disclosure of personal data**. Consent is valid only if the Data Subject has been provided with: the reasons why personal data are stored; the types of data stored; the identity of the recipients of the data (it is unclear whether this includes internal as well as external recipients); and the name and address of the controller of the file. Consent can be withdrawn at any time, but 'without retroactive effect'. An organisation can process personal data (without the consent of the Data Subject) only in accordance with the Directive and if the processing (a) occurs within the framework of a contract with the Data Subject; or (b) if the data originate from 'sources generally accessible to the public'; or (c) 'the controller of the file is pursing a legitimate interest, on condition that the interest of the data subject does not prevail'. However, Member States are free to specify the conditions under which the processing of personal data by the private sector is lawful, and this may offer a degree of flexibility in certain sectors. Such specification could also overcome the prospect that a privatised cum public sector service (eg schools, nursing and old people's homes etc) could be covered simultaneously by different data protection obligations.

4.8 Article 9 of the Draft requires private sector users to inform Data Subjects of the first communication (ie disclosure) of their personal data, or if these data become available for on-line consultation. The objective is to assist Data Subjects in exercising their rights (these are considerable; see paragraph 4.11 below), by making them aware of who accesses their personal data. There is no obligation to inform Data Subjects in this way if the data are generally available to the public **and** their processing is intended solely for correspondence purposes, or if the communication of personal data is required by law.

4.9 In most cases, **both the public and private sector will have to register** (at least): the name and address of the controller of the file; the creation of a personal data file; the reason why the file was created; a description of the types of data stored in the file; to whom the data might be disclosed, and a description of the security measures taken to protect the personal data. One potential problem is that the Draft Directive states that Registration has to be made with the Data Protection Authority where the file is physically located (if in a Member State). So if the London office of a multi-national company has on-line access to a data file stored in France, any personal data would be subject to French registration procedures (unlike the application of Section 39 of the Data Protection Act which makes the location of the Data User the prime consideration). Thus Registration could become quite involved (English translations of French registration forms hopefully available?) and, if personal data were to be transferred across national boundaries, they could become subject to different Data Protection Authorities (and Registration regimes). The definitions of public and private sector are not simple: activities are judged from the standpoint of the type of function performed, and not on the basis of the ownership of the enterprise. Thus it is possible to have a privately owned concern (eg a private nursing home) operating under the 'public sector rules', or a public sector initiative (eg a marketing campaign for a Council service) operating under 'private sector rules'.

4.10 At the point of collection of information, Member States shall guarantee that the individuals from whom personal data are collected have the right to be informed about: why the data are being collected; the obligatory or voluntary nature of the reply; the consequences if the Data Subject fails to reply; the recipients of the information (it is unclear whether this includes internal as well as external recipients); the right of access and rectification of data; and the name and address of the controller of the file. The Data Protection Authority has the power to authorise a derogation from the above, should contact with Data Subjects prove too difficult to put into practice. There is an exception to this guarantee: if providing information to the Data Subject would 'prevent the exercise of supervision and verification functions' of public authorities, or the maintenance of public order.

4.11 As well as the familiar Data Subject rights (access, correction, erasure, compensation for damages), the Draft:

(a) proposes a right 'to oppose, for legitimate reasons, the processing of personal data'. Thus if a Data Subject can demonstrate adequate objection to the use or disclosure of personal data, then the relevant processing must cease (unless the controller of the file is authorised, by law, to continue). This provision is akin to that put forward by the Registrar in Section 1.9 of Guideline 4, which includes 'consequences for the individual' as one of the criteria for judging 'fair processing'

(b) extends the right of correction of data, by providing the right to insist that third parties, to whom erroneous personal data have been disclosed, are notified of 'rectification, erasure or blocking' (this implies a disclosure log)

(c) provides for individuals 'not to be subject to an administrative or private decision involving an assessment' (of a Data Subject's conduct) 'which has as its sole basis the automatic processing of personal data defining his profile or personality' (eg refusal to provide credit, based only on a credit scoring system, or to appoint to a post via psychological test scoring). Note that this paragraph is not particularly clear in meaning and, if applied literally, could be very restrictive: for example, could the fact that a Data User holds names and addresses of customers mean that these form a 'profile' (if used for a special kind of mailshot, it can be argued that such a decision is a consequence of knowing that the customer has specialist interests)

(d) provides for the erasure, free of charge, of personal data held 'for market research or advertising purposes'

(e) states that Member States shall prohibit, unless there is an overriding public interest, the automatic processing of particularly sensitive data (religious or philosophical beliefs, racial origin, political opinions, health, sexual life, trade union membership) without 'the express and written consent, freely given, of the

Data Subject' (note that the prohibition does not apply to manual files which contain such data, although these files would be subject to the rest of the Directive, eg to the right to oppose the processing of personal data)

(f) states that criminal conviction data can only be held in public-sector files.

4.12 Computer Bureau will have to be more involved in the processing performed on behalf of their clients, as the Draft states that 'any person who collects or processes personal data on behalf of the controller of the file shall fulfil the obligations provided for in Articles 16 and 18 of this Directive'. Article 16 relates to the obligation of a controller of the file to adhere to various (familiar) data protection principles (Subject Access excepted), whilst Article 18 relates to obligations for the controller to take 'appropriate and organisational measures to protect personal data'. The clear implication is that the person who provides services for the controller should check compliance with the principles and with security requirements. In addition, the controller of the file must 'where processing is carried out on his behalf, ensure that the necessary security and organisational measures are taken and choose a person or enterprise who provides sufficient guarantees in that respect'. Note that this gives added importance to the security requirements, details of which have to be registered (see above).

4.13 The Draft Directive confirms that the Data Protection Authority in each Member State would have significant powers of supervision (applied to the UK, it would strengthen the Registrar's powers considerably). In general, each Authority 'shall have investigative powers and effective powers of intervention', 'the right of access to files covered by this Directive', and the 'power to gather all the information necessary'. With respect to policing, national security, defence, public safety and other state-sensitive areas, the Data Protection Authority 'shall be empowered to carry out, at the request of the Data Subject, the necessary checks on the file' (at the least, resistance to the inclusion of national security can be expected in the UK).

4.14 The Commission seeks to supervise application of the Directive by Member States by establishing a Working Party on the Protection of Personal Data to monitor events, to report on 'significant divergences' between Member States and to report annually to the Commission. The Commission (not each Data Protection Authority) would, in the first instance, examine the policy implications that arise from the transfer of data to countries not subject to the Directive, and would have rule-making powers to adopt technical measures in certain sectors. The Commission asks Member States to encourage business sectors to draw up codes of conduct on the basis of the principles set out in Article 16 (see paragraph 4.12 above: these principles are almost the same as the UK Act's Data Protection Principles); it is not clear whether these codes are to be statutory or voluntary. Member States can grant derogations from the Directive to allow a balance to be struck between press freedom and invasion of privacy.

4.15 Software designers have to consider how they could satisfy European standards as the free market in 1992 approaches. Study of the Draft Directive confirms that they will need:

(a) to go beyond mere technical and computing considerations and include manual files in their concept of an integrated information system

(b) to check that the design of any public-sector information system (including its data fields, processing, disclosures, and user-options) limits the system to the lawful tasks of the relevant public-sector body. Without such checks, any feature that is 'extra' or 'special' could, if used, lead the public-sector body into performing an unlawful action

(c) to consider carefully the security measures taken to protect the personal data, as the controller of the file may be held accountable for any security infringement (a safe procedure is formally to agree the desired level of security controls during the design stage, in order to identify where responsibility lies)

(d) to integrate a Subject Access module within any software, so that all personal data (including those data stored in archive) can be easily retrieved; codes used in conjunction with personal data will require explanation. The Subject Access module needs to be protected by the appropriate level of security (if this module is insecure then all personal data could be at risk of unauthorised access)

(e) to design software that could hold, as part of the data, the express consent of the individual who is the subject of the data (certain sensitive personal data fields cannot be held unless such consent has been provided)

(f) to consider whether an automated method to log or monitor disclosures of personal data is required, as the Data Subject has the right to insist on the notification of those who have received personal data that require 'rectification, erasure or blocking'

(g) to ensure that expert systems are not designed to lead to an administrative or private decision which has as its sole basis the automatic processing of personal data defining an individual's profile or personality

(h) to keep documentary evidence of meetings with clients, and of agreements, program enhancements etc, as these might be needed to demonstrate that the system had been designed with all reasonable care.

4.16 There is a long political path ahead of the Draft before it becomes a Community Directive (though from the timetable provided, it can be inferred that the necessary new legislation in the UK should be enacted by January 1st 1993), and there are likely to be strong objections from the private sector (eg the Direct Mail industry considers that restricting the use of profiles will result in more unsolicited mail because mailshots will be less well targeted). Some Governments may also not enthusiastically embrace certain elements of the Directive (eg those that impose checks on certain functions of the State), and arguments will no doubt rage over the subtle distinctions between various translations. Additionally, Member States, especially those with no tradition in Data Protection, may argue that to adopt the high standards set by the Commission is too great a first step. Consequently, we expect that inter governmental horse-trading could produce a much weaker animal; whether it is of the kind usually designed by a committee, only time will tell!

4.17 Published by the Commission at the same time as the Data Protection Directive (COM (90) 314 SYN 287) was a Data Protection Proposal relating specifically to telecommunications: 'Proposal for a Council Directive concerning the protection of personal data and privacy in the context of public digital telecommunications networks, in particular the integrated services digital network (ISDN) and public digital mobile networks' (COM (90) 314 SYN 288). The main reason for this is that the Data Protection problems associated with the telecommunications industry are beginning to mount. For example, even at the simplest level an itemised telephone bill contains personal data that are ripe for misuse; add in the location details of a mobile telephone, then who has called whom, when, for how long and from where becomes recorded. If the contents of new telecommunications services (eg videotex) are combined with, say, listings of telephone contacts made, then the potential for direct marketing by phone ('junk phone calls?'), the establishment of profiles, deductions as to personal behaviour, and many other invasions of privacy can become a reality.

4.18 The rationale for the Directive is the same as that for Data Protection: a level playing field for Europe that will allow the free movement of telecommunications equipment and services. However, in the Telecommunications Directive personal data can include manually held information in unstructured form. The main proposals state that:

(a) the 'collection, storage and processing of personal data by a telecommunications organisation is justified for telecommunications purposes only' (eg to establish connections, produce bills, rectify faults)

(b) 'the telecommunications organisation shall not use such data to set up electronic profiles of the subscribers or classifications of individual subscribers by category'

(c) 'after termination of the contract the data are to be erased' (unless required to deal with complaints, unpaid bills etc)

(d) 'the contents of the information transmitted must not be stored by the telecommunications organisation after the end of the transmission' unless required by law to do so (eg lawful interception of communications)

(e) the subscriber has the usual rights of Subject Access, correction and erasure

(f) personal data shall not be disclosed outside the network of the telecommunications organisation 'without specific authorisation by law or the subscriber's prior consent', nor inside the network to those 'who are not dealing with the relevant services provided'. The provision of services must not depend on such consent being granted

(g) organisations should advise subscribers of the potential security breaches, and provide adequate, state-of-the-art protection of personal data against unauthorised access and use

(h) only limited categories of personal data for billing purposes and for managing the traffic on the network can be processed (examples of such personal data are provided in Articles 9 and 10)

(i) the ability to obtain itemized call statements which record the telephone numbers (without the last four digits) called by subscribers, to have numbers ex-directory, to limit incoming calls to specific callers, and to remove the identification on incoming calls should be part of the service offered to the caller and called. This last feature can assist callers to some helplines (eg Aids Helplines) who might not want to be identified from the connection

(j) providers of teletext and videotex services are prevented from establishing a consumer profile; senders of unsolicited messages have to establish procedures to respect privacy should recipients indicate that they no longer want to receive such messages.

4.19 Also published in the same series of documents as SYN 287 and 288 is a 'Proposal for a Council Decision in the field of Information Security'. This document is tacit recognition by the Commission that information security is an important component of any computer operation; it sets out to initiate research into the establishment of security standards on a sectoral basis. There are six components: the development of a framework for an information security strategy; the analysis of security requirements; the identification of solutions to meet immediate and interim security needs; the production of specifications, standards and verification procedures; the development of security devices within a general strategy; and the integration of certain security functions in information systems.

5. Proposals for change (Home Office)

5.1 In announcements made to Parliament (Hansard, col 418, 28.11.90 and col 351, 11.12.90), the Government stated that it was consulting 170 UK organisations with respect to the European Commission's proposal for a Data Protection Directive (COM (90) 314 SYN 287) and noted that the 'need for legislation will be considered when negotiations on the directive have been completed' (the relaxed wording imply that the European Commission's optimistic time scale could slip). Together with a copy of the Directive, the Home Office then distributed the Report (dated October 1990) of the interdepartmental committee appointed to review the operation of the Data Protection Act. A study of this 'Review of the Data Protection Act: Report on Structure' provides an indication of how far the Government's data protection views diverge from the Commission's (for convenience, the paragraphs below follow the sequence of the discussion of the Directive in the previous section).

5.2 **The Review rejects the argument that manual files should be subject to the Act**. 'Extension to all manual records would substantially increase burdens across government and business alike (ie to monitor compliance with the various Principles); subject access would require special correspondence, weeding and/or physical facilities for inspection', and 'the fact that personal data can be held by other means does not amount to a conclusive argument that it should always be subject to statutory protection' (paragraph 16). Extension of Data Protection to legal persons (as in some other countries) is rejected, as 'the thrust of data protection policy is to apply safeguards in the interest of individuals' privacy and sense of security; not to protect data relating to their public personae in the business world or to provide a form of commercial confidentiality' (paragraph 17).

5.3 The terms of reference were 'To review the implementation of the Data Protection Act, particularly with regard to the impact on data users of registration requirements; and to make recommendations'. Issues thus **excluded** from the Report (complete list in Annex F) include: statutory interpretation of all the Data Protection Principles; existing Subject Access exemptions; possible new Subject Access exemptions (eg private electronic correspondence about a third party, routine personnel information, contact lists, bibliographies, product or service descriptions); Registrar's powers (ie lack of them!) when a Subject Access exemption applies; problems with Subject Access (specifically enforced Subject Access, logging of Subject Access refusals, identification of third parties); existing non-disclosure exemptions; possible new non-disclosure exemptions (eg computer maintenance personnel); personal data held overseas; Registrar's resources; the Definitions; sanctions against servants and agents; and a few other procedural issues dealing with supervision of the Registrar. However, with reduced registration requirements (see below) or indeed, 'with the disappearance of registration' (paragraph 58), the Principles would be made 'directly applicable to data users', ie to all Data Users, including those Data Users that are currently 'outside the formal mechanisms of the

Act' (those Users exempt from Part II and Sections 21-24), except for 'strictly limited' exemptions (paragraph 26).

5.4 The Review states that 'so far as the UK is concerned we do not consider that the public sector now poses a greater risk to the individual than the private sector does; and indeed transfers between private sector data bases are much more common than in the public sector'. Consequently 'the same level of protection should continue to apply to public and private sector data alike' (paragraph 18). By contrast, the Directive has specific rules which 'are based on the nature of the service provided by the body concerned, regardless of its private or public status' (ie a single body might 'have to apply the rules specific to the private sector or to the public sector according as to whether it carries on commercial activities or performs public-service duties' (from 'Discussion of the Provisions', Article 2, paragraphs g) and h) of the Directive).

5.5 The Review considers that there is a case for seeking 'lighter touch' alternatives to Registration. Instead, the Data User would have to send to a Data Subject, on demand and free of charge, a copy of a 'standard declaration' (or specification) which described who holds the data, the purposes for which he holds them, whether he transfers data overseas, and the address(es) for Subject Access requests (paragraph 35). To ensure that Data Users produce a declaration, options for the specification of purposes would have to be on a statutory basis, 'but the choice of method could be left to the data user' (paragraph 44). The Review envisages an Order empowering the 'supervisory authority (or Secretary of State)' to prescribe how specification could take place, and thereby provide a choice of methods as to the format of the specification; the Registrar could also 'recommend how it might be done' (paragraphs 35 and 44). Whilst a small organisation might prefer verification (of the specification) by 'a professional person such as a banker, solicitor or accountant', a retailer could specify (and satisfy the 'fair obtaining' requirements) by displaying 'permanent and clearly visible notices at all tills'. However, 'the burden of proof would have to fall on the data user ... to show that he had specified by a method listed in statute' (paragraph 44). With the disappearance of Registration 'the statute might deem' certain purposes to have been specified (eg to assume that the Data User holds personal data for certain 'innocuous business and administrative purposes', for example payroll and accounts, own customer credit control, unincorporated members' clubs and limited distribution lists) (paragraph 60). Certain disclosures could be made compatible with the specified purpose through deeming legislation 'if the uses and disclosures concerned would have passed the 'fair obtaining' test' (paragraph 47, and see immediately below). The Review authors have taken legal advice to ensure that the above procedures are consistent with the specification requirements of the Council of Europe Convention; by contrast the Directive proposes an obligation to notify the Registrar of far more details than those of a 'declaration'. The only reference to 'Computer Bureau' notes the removal of the criminal offences for unregistered operation of a Computer Bureau and for unauthorised disclosure of personal data by a Bureau (Annex E).

5.6 Paragraph 41 expands on the requirement (in the Council of Europe Convention) that personal data be 'fairly obtained': 'essentially this means that when he obtained them (the personal data) the data user should have had a particular purpose in mind; and the data subject should know that purpose either from information he received before he imparted the data or from the nature of the transaction'. This seems to support the Registrar's views in the controversy, surrounding the First Principle, as described in the Advertising Association's Code of Practice.

5.7 As before, there would be a fee for Subject Access, to be enclosed (Annex D) with the Application (enclosing a fee at that stage is not an obligation at present); however, with a copy of the personal data, the Data Subject would receive 'details of sources and disclosures'. The Review admits that research will be necessary as to the form these details would take (if 'unreasonable administrative burdens' are not involved then sources and disclosures could be specific to the Data Subject), but at the minimum there would be a 'standard list of sources and disclosures'. Presumably this list would be at least as comprehensive as the information one can obtain by looking at the relevant Part B of a current Register Entry; however, if the list were only available via the Subject Access provisions (ie after possible payment of a fee), or if the list were to be withheld if there were no personal data, **this would be a significant step backward from having such information in the public domain**, as at present. In addition there would be a statement that 'any matters of concern ... should be pursued with the data user' paragraphs 37 and 38), the idea being that the Data Subject should first try and resolve problems with the Data User, and then 'if he is not happy with the reply he would have the right to approach the Registrar' (paragraph 39). It is not clear from the Review whether the latter procedure would also reduce an individual's present rights. For example, the Review does not refer to those circumstances when it might be difficult to complain directly to the Data User (eg complaining to one's employer), nor does it deal with the case where a valid complaint may arise from an individual who is not a Data Subject (Section 36(2) of the Data Protection Act which states that the Registrar may consider any complaint that raises 'a matter of substance' does not say that the complaint has to come from a Data Subject: this can allow the Registrar to take up a 'substantial' case from other sources). The Review recommends that an 'enforcement notice issued in respect of inaccurate data should require the data user to take all reasonable steps to pass the correction on to the source of the information and those to whom it has been disclosed' (paragraph 56). This is not as strong as the Data Subject's right to insist that corrections are notified to third parties who have received the erroneous data (as outlined in the Directive) but, in compensation, the Review's recommendation does include sources of the data as relevant third parties (which the Directive does not).

5.8 The Review proposes (paragraph 55) that the Registrar (to be renamed the Data

Protection Commissioner) should be able to serve an 'Information Notice' to oblige a Data User to provide information (instead of having to obtain a search warrant for this purpose). This is because the Registrar's power to seize evidence by warrant can, at the moment, only be invoked **after** the Data User has refused entry to the Registrar (so that all helpful Data Users who allow access cannot have evidence seized!). The Registrar should also be able to seize any material (including personal data exempt from Registration) if there is reason to believe that the Act is being contravened. In the absence of Registration, a De-registration Notice would be replaced by a 'Processing Prohibition Notice', and many of the registration offences would become redundant; however, there would be an offence of 'failure to specify purposes' (if not a 'deemed' purpose: see paragraph 5.5 above). Refusal to comply with the two new Notices, as with all enforcement notices, would be an offence. Note that the implied reduction in scope to prosecute a Data User (or employee or agent of a Data User) could contrast with individual prosecutions under the Computer Misuse Act 1990: it would look strange if individuals who obtain personal data via unauthorised access to a computer are prosecuted, whilst individuals can no longer be prosecuted for 'knowingly or recklessly' making an unauthorised disclosure of personal data from a computer.

5.9 The Review concludes that 'changes would require consultation and comprehensive legislation' and that 'officials would need to do further work on consequential and non-structural issues' (ie see paragraph 5.3 above); 'parliamentary time for a medium size Bill' would be required. To conclude the discussion of the Report with a 'lighter touch': what appears to be a proposal for an interesting new non-disclosure exemption: 'Disclosure to person not described in register entry', should **not have appeared** under 'Possible new exemptions' in Annex F!

5.10 **It thus seems increasingly likely that the Government will oppose much of the Commission's Proposal for a personal data Directive** (SYN 287) as described in Section 4 above. In its response to the Home Affairs Select Committee (see Section 3), the Government 'regards it as desirable that states should implement the 1981 Council of Europe Convention, the OECD Guidelines and the United Nations Guidelines, as appropriate'. It states that 'in discussion with other Member States and the Commission, it will wish to draw attention to the rather different emphasis of the text of the Convention - which requires transparency and compliance with good handling principles and to the need for a sensible working balance between free flow of information and individuals' interests'; the implication being that the Directive is the wrong vehicle to achieve these aims. In answer to a Written Question (col 278, 22.2.91) the Government emphasized that 'it supports any move by the Commission to ensure that all Community states ratify the European Convention on data protection and introduce national implementing legislation'. Finally, in evidence to the Select Committee on European Legislation which examined the Directive (Fourth Report, HC 29-iv, ISBN 0-10-279291-7), the Government said that it was 'considering whether all the provisions of the draft Directives are within

Community competence' and that the Directive would 'increase costs to data users, and affect the business practices of those who currently process personal data without the informed consent of the data subject'. In summary, the Government's strategy seems to be based on the following views:

(a) not all Member States have Data Protection laws, therefore the Council of Europe Convention (not the European Commission's Directive) is the appropriate standard in the first instance;

(b) UK law already satisfies the Convention;

(c) any change could follow suggestions made in the Structure Report as these also satisfy the Convention

(d) agreement to the Directive needs to be delayed, and this will postpone the date for implementation of legislation in the UK (we expect legislation by late 1994 at the earliest, followed by time for Data Users to readjust to new rules).

5.11 Given the increased importance placed by Government on the Council of Europe Convention (ie the Government's view on where the Data Protection 'line in the sand' will be drawn), readers might want to obtain copies of the 'Recommendations' issued by the Council of Europe. These are discussed in Chapter 4 and are available from HMSO. The references are:

(a) 'Regulations for automated medical data banks', Recommendation R (81) 1 (1981), ISBN 92-871-0595-2

(b) 'Protection of personal data used for scientific research and statistics', Recommendation R (83) 10 (1984), ISBN 92-871-0317-8

(c) 'Protection of personal data used for the purposes of direct marketing', Recommendation R (85) 20 (1986), ISBN 92-871-0876-5

(d) 'Protection of personal data used for social security purposes', Recommendation R (86) 1 (1986), ISBN 92-871-0924-9

(e) 'Regulating the use of personal data in the police sector', Recommendation R (87) 15 (1988), ISBN 92-871-1587-7

(f) 'Protection of personal data used for employment purposes', Recommendation R (89) 2 (1989), ISBN 92-871-1714-4

(g) Two other useful Council of Europe documents are: 'Computers and Law. Study on new technologies: a challenge to privacy protection?', ISBN 92-871-1616-2;

and 'Computer-related crime', ISBN 92-871-1792-6.

6. Proposals for change (Data Protection Registrar)

6.1 In a separate section of his Fifth Report ('Part B: A Review of the Data Protection Act', June 1989), the Data Protection Registrar outlines at length his own views on how to improve the Act. These views remain important because, unlike the Proposal for a European Directive (which does not consider UK law in isolation) or the Home Office Structure Report (which mainly considers the Registration aspects of UK law), the Registrar's Review relates to the whole of the Data Protection Act.

6.2 With respect to Registration, the Registrar proposed (in paragraphs 176 - 184 of Part B in the Fifth Report):

(a) a limited Registration regime which would apply to specific types of persons, or persons who hold specific types of personal data that are deemed (by Parliament) especially sensitive. Types of personal data that would require Registration include: those already listed in Section 2(3) of the Act (eg health, sexual life, criminal conviction data); personal data used in credit referencing, direct marketing, the provision of financial services, or employment vetting. Types of persons who would register include: all public bodies (eg local authorities, police forces, government departments), those who conduct public examinations, those who transfer personal data abroad, and all professional regulatory bodies. The Secretary of State would be empowered to change, by Order (ie without primary legislation), the categories of persons and types of personal data

(b) a reduced Registration scheme for those who need to register

(c) that unregistered Data Users would be under a duty to maintain an up to date list of purposes for which they hold personal data

(d) that the criminal offences under the Act that related to Registration (eg Sections 5(1) and 5(5)) would not apply to unregistered Data Users

(e) that **complementary powers** (eg a Data Holding and Processing Prohibition Notice) would be necessary to regulate those Data Users who breached the Principles but did not need to Register. The Registrar noted (paragraph 174) that his proposed Registration scheme would 'thus be confined to relatively few data users', and that 'the smaller number can more readily be advised and visited by the Registrar'.

6.3 With regard to the Data Protection Principles the Registrar took the view that they formed a good code of practice, but that some changes in their interpretation were required in some instances. The major changes proposed were (paragraphs 103 - 149):

(a) to relate the issue of 'fair obtaining' in the First Principle to the question whether 'an individual was given any choice as to the uses or disclosures to be made of the information' (this consolidates the Registrar's views expressed in Guidance Note 19). With respect to personal data obtained 'by or under any enactment' (ie personal information obtained or disclosed in accordance with statute; paragraph 1(2) of the Interpretation of the First Principle), the Registrar suggested a test of 'whether the application of the First Principle was likely to prejudice the statutory purpose'. The Registrar thus argues that 'this complete exemption for those acting under statutory authority is too sweeping and may licence practices which on their merits **would be unacceptable in other circumstances'** (our emphasis)

(b) to add to the interpretation provisions of 'fair processing' that 'regard shall be had to the purpose of the processing and the foreseeable consequences of the processing for the individual data subjects whose data are being processed' (note that the Registrar has incorporated this test into his Guideline 4 since March 1987)

(c) to change the interpretation of the Second Principle (which, even under a restricted Registration regime, would still require purposes to be specified) so that regard should be had to '(i) whether the purpose is in a form approved by the Registrar; and (ii) the circumstances in which and purposes for which the information constituting the data were (sic) obtained' (thereby creating a link to the 'fair obtaining' implications of the First Principle)

(d) to remove the interpretation of the Third Principle whose effect is that registered uses and disclosures **cannot** be incompatible with the purpose. Any question of incompatibility could then be determined by the Courts (or Tribunal) on a case by case basis. However, the Registrar states that 'it would also be valuable ... in determining whether a disclosure is incompatible or not' to have regard 'to the purposes for which the data are to be used by the person to whom they are disclosed' (thereby obliging Data Users to assess the uses of personal data prior to disclosure)

(e) to change the impact of the Fourth Principle (there is no interpretation in the Act) so that 'adequate, relevant and not excessive' related not to purposes but to the circumstances of the individual who brought the complaint (note that it is possible for personal data to be relevant to a particular purpose, but irrelevant to a particular individual)

(f) to leave the interpretation of the Fifth Principle unchanged, but to give the

Registrar the same powers as those given to a Court by Section 24 (ie to require the rectification of inaccurate personal data, even if markers are used as described in Section 23 of the Act). Additionally (in paragraph 208), the Registrar seeks powers to allow an Enforcement Notice 'to require a data user to take all reasonable steps to inform any source of information and those to whom it has been disclosed of the inaccuracies found'

(g) to change the effect of the Sixth Principle (there is no interpretation in the Act) so that the length of time personal data were kept could be related not the purposes for which the personal data are held but to the circumstances of an individual who brought the complaint (cf the Fourth Principle).

6.4 No changes were proposed to the interpretation of the Seventh and Eighth Principles, and the Registrar suggested that **all** Data Users had a clear duty to apply the eight Principles to all personal data held by them.

6.5 Other major changes suggested were:

(a) to give the Registrar the power to seize evidence when lawfully on premises (ie without a warrant) (paragraph 199)

(b) to allow a Data Subject to appeal to the Tribunal on the Registrar's failure to take enforcement action (paragraph 213), and to allow the Registrar to support Court applications by individuals (paragraph 235)

(c) to reduce the fee for Subject Access (especially in relation to multiple Entries); to oblige Data Users to keep a log of those cases in which a Subject Access exemption is used; to consider the use of disclosure logs in appropriate cases; to provide details to the Data Subject, as part of Subject Access, about the uses, disclosures, and sources of personal data (in a universal Registration scheme these appear in the Register) (paragraphs 215-224)

(d) to limit 'complete exemptions' from the Act to personal data held for 'personal, domestic and recreational purposes'; the Registrar assumes that 'an exemption on current lines' will continue for National Security (paragraph 226). Criticism of the exemption 'for things done under statutory authority' could be reduced by the test of prejudice introduced into the First Principle (paragraphs 119 and 234)

(e) to give those Codes of Practice that have a formal endorsement by the Registrar a raised status akin to that of the Highway Code, so that such Codes could be cited, and taken into account, by the Tribunal (paragraph 238)

(f) to remove the distinction between 'opinion' and 'intention' in the definition of personal data, and to introduce a new Subject Access exemption (if this was still thought appropriate by Parliament) relating to 'the confidentiality of personnel succession planning data'; to clarify any doubt as to the meaning of agent (so that it related to any person acting as 'an intermediary through whom someone effects an action'); and add to the definition of data so that it could relate to data held in transient form (eg in memory; this would remove doubts as to whether data transmissions by cable, satellite, radio etc are subject to the Act) (paragraphs 242-251)

(g) to make the practice whereby individuals are required to access personal data in order to disclose those data to a third party (eg Subject Access to personal data held by the Police, in order to disclose these data to an employer), a criminal offence (paragraph 240).

7. Proposals for change (Labour Party)

7.1 The Labour Party policy document 'The Charter of Rights' outlines major changes to the Data Protection Act should there be a change of Government. Endorsing the European Commission's Draft Directive, the document proposes: the Data Protection Act should extend to manual files in key sectors (the Directive applies to nearly all sectors); registration with the Data Protection Authority for defined categories of Data User (the Directive requires registration of nearly all Data Users); Data Users should provide a clear undertaking about uses and disclosures before the collection of personal data; the Data Protection Principles should apply to all Data Users; powers of inspection for the Data Protection Registrar (to include those personal data held for national security purposes); a single fee for Subject Access, with some Data Users possibly prevented from charging for Access (under the Data Protection Act a fee may be charged per Register Entry); a criminal offence associated with 'forced' Subject Access; finally, strict adherence to the Council of Europe Recommendation with respect to Direct Marketing.

7.2 Some indication of the Party's concerns can be deduced from the two Data Protection (Amendment) Bills laid before Parliament by Harry Cohen, Labour MP for Leyton. The Bills (which are almost identical) give the Registrar more flexibility to regulate Data Users, strengthen the role of Codes of Practice and also remove the need of many Data Users to register, thus lessening the bureaucratic burden, in particular on small businesses. In addition, the Bills eliminate the provision for non-disclosure exemptions.

7.3 In greater detail, the proposed legislation:

(a) gives Data Subjects an uncomplicated right of Access to their own personal data, and allows exemptions only if the purposes for which personal data are held might be prejudiced by Access;

(b) allows the Registrar, in the circumstances surrounding a Subject Access exemption, to inspect the exempt personal data before deciding whether to exercise his powers;

(c) brings personal data held for a national security purpose fully under the power of the Act;

(d) allows the Registrar, subject to the issuing of a warrant signed by a circuit judge, powers of inspection of any Data User's computer installations if a breach of the Data Protection Principles is suspected;

(e) ensures Registration of specific personal data that are of public concern (eg public sector personal data, Police, national security, ethnic records, credit agencies, education, etc: the Bill has a short list);

(f) reduces the need of many Data Users to register under the terms of the Act (if they do not process personal data that fall under the categories mentioned in (e) above) whilst not absolving these Data Users of their responsibilities - they will have to provide Subject Access to their personal data, can be sued for damages, and are subject to the enforcement powers of the Registrar should they breach the Data Protection Principles;

(g) gives a statutory role to Codes of Practice, which are developed and subject to certification by the Registrar;

(h) allows the Registrar to assist in a limited way (but **not** by using his powers to gain evidence) a civil action brought by a Data Subject;

(i) removes the restrictions on the Registrar found in Part IV of the Data Protection Act, on his use of Enforcement Notices in relation to the First, Third and Seventh Data Protection Principles.

Appendix 1: 'DATA PROTECTION NEWS'

Data Protection News is a quarterly newsletter produced by the authors of this book. This Appendix comprises important articles from each issue of the newsletter in order, beginning with Spring 1990; the fourth item on Consumer Credit is a combination of the articles that appeared in the Spring and Summer 1991 issues. Subscription is currently £95 per year; for a sample copy and subscription details please write to Dr. C. N. M. Pounder, IPMC, Security Division, Hoskyns Group plc, 95 Wandsworth Road, London SW8 2LX.

LEGAL RULING: Not an unlawful disclosure

Summary

In the first case of its kind, the Courts have ruled that the Data Protection Act does not prevent a Data User (in this case Liverpool City Council) from disclosing personal data (The Times, Law Reports, 26th October 1989).

The litigant's case

The case arose because the litigant, a former employee of the Data User, was seeking compensation following a personal injury. Solicitors acting on behalf of the litigant asked the Court to enforce a previous ruling that allowed them to obtain personal data, from the Data User's payroll system, relating to three other individuals, so that an earnings comparison could be made. Access to these personal data was an important part of assessing the totality of the claim for compensation.

The Data User's argument

The Data User had refused to act on the previous ruling, claiming that as they had used the payroll and accounts exemption (ie exempt from Part II and Sections 21-24 of the Data Protection Act via Section 32), they were subject to the strict conditions surrounding the exemption. Thus, they could not use or disclose personal data for purposes other than those specified in Section 32. Accordingly, the Data User argued that they could not disclose personal data to the litigant's legal advisors, as the disclosure would breach the terms of the exemption.

The judgement

Their Lordships disagreed, and concluded that the Data User should have considered the wording in Section 32(4)(b), which states that a disclosure would be possible if it was 'among the non-disclosure provisions' (ie a disclosure from personal data covered by the payroll exemption **may** take place, if the disclosure in question satisfies the conditions that relate to **any** non-disclosure exemption). Since Section 34(5)(b) defines a relevant non-disclosure exemption (ie 'required by or under any enactment, by any rule of law or by the order of a court'), the Court ruled that the Data User could disclose the personal data without being in breach of Section 32. The judgement also supports the Data Protection Registrar's advice (Guideline 6, paragraph A.5.4) which indicates that personal data, subject to Section 32, can be disclosed 'in circumstances covered by **one** of the exemptions from the non-disclosure provisions of the Act' (our emphasis). Note that a provision in Section 33(5)(c) corresponds to that found in Section 32(4)(b) to cover the domestic purposes and 'simple' mailing lists exemption from Part II and Sections 21-24.

Other actions for 'discovery'

The case also raises interesting problems with respect to actions for 'discovery' which are not limited to industrial compensation. For example, personal data (relating to several individuals) may be required by a complainant who seeks redress under legislation covering equal opportunities, equal pay, sexual discrimination etc, or in other circumstances that can be resolved by a direct comparison of personal data, relating to the complainant, with personal data relating to other individuals whose circumstances are similar to those of the complainant.

Policy considerations

Data Users that actively take the lead on these kinds of issues **cannot** rely on a non-disclosure exemption when disclosing personal data to an independent body to perform any comparison (or to assess the effectiveness of a policy), unless the disclosure is required under an order from a Court or other statutory authority, or until the consent of all the Data Subjects involved has been obtained. Otherwise, the disclosure **must** be registered and procedures that are consistent with the First Data Protection Principle (see Guidance Note 19 from the Data Protection Registrar's Office) **must** be in place.

Unsuitability of Section 32

It is also surprising that a large Data User should use the Section 32 exemption. When this exemption was discussed by Parliament, it was made clear that it was intended for use by small businesses with a basic payroll system. Most large organisations use payroll (or accounts) data for purposes other than those specified in Section 32 (eg maintaining a staff or customer telephone directory, linking payroll data to personnel functions etc) and the Data Protection Registrar's advice (Guideline 6, paragraph A.5.7) shows that the exemption would be invalid in several common circumstances (eg a disclosure of personal data to Trades Unions, or to software or hardware engineers).

Nothing to do with the Register Entry

It is well known that any disclosure by a registered Data User is made lawful under the Data Protection Act so long as it appears in the relevant Register Entry (and is made 'fair' by procedures to comply with the First Data Protection Principle), or is covered by the non-disclosure provisions. Their Lordships' judgement means that when the non-disclosure provisions apply, it is irrelevant whether the Data User has registered the particular purpose or not.

Concluding comments

The judgement overturns the argument that 'this cannot be disclosed because of the Data Protection Act', as the Act only defines the conditions that must apply to make a disclosure lawful. The Act does not stop disclosures from occurring, and even the fact that a disclosure is registered with respect to the Data Protection Act does not mean that the disclosure actually takes place; these are matters for the Data User's own internal policy. Finally, note that the Data Protection Act can **never** legalise a disclosure if it is prohibited by other legislation (eg as in the case of the Community Charge).

EMPLOYMENT VETTING: increasingly controversial

What a lot

The need to vet seems insatiable. According to the Home Affairs Select Committee (Third Report, 'Criminal Records', HMSO, £7.85), Government and Local Authorities make over half a million official vetting enquiries, each year, to Police records (this represents 1% of the adult population per year). In addition, the Departments of Education and Health also have to be notified in cases involving serious professional misconduct, and offer advice on the suitability of candidates for employment (eg via 'List 99'), and instances are on the increase whereby Local Authorities, the Security Industry and Employers oblige prospective applicants for licences, jobs etc to exercise their Subject Access rights to any personal data held by the Police before issuing a licence etc. Finally, there are private organisations such as the Economic League who, for an annual subscription, assist the vetting process by providing information about prospective employees to employers.

Conflicting demands

The vetting procedure has several major Data Protection implications. Is it proper or fair for Subject Access rights to be used in vetting? Can it safely be assumed that the information is accurate and that it relates to the person who is being vetted? How should the individual being vetted be involved in the vetting process? How can the concerns of the public (eg to prevent the employment of paedophiles in a Children's Home; sex offenders as taxi drivers etc) be accommodated? Many of our readers represent organisations who face this dilemma: this Section attempts to clarify the issues.

Known problem areas

Despite safeguards, people have been refused jobs because of minor or irrelevant offences. In one case, a part-time worker lost her job following the disclosure of a conviction for growing a cannabis plant thirteen years ago; another case referred to an Oxford undergraduate who had lost a temporary maths teaching post due to a caution for criminal damage following a schoolboy prank; and a man lost a job as a bus driver when a conviction in 1969 for importuning (homosexuality was legalised in 1967) became known (The Guardian, 26.9.88). It took a Court case (Local Government Chronicle, 3.3.89) to remove information from Local Authority files that branded a plumber as a child molester, when in fact he had been cleared by the Police.

Uncomfortable discretion to disclose

Except for a few statutory reasons (eg in relation to adoption, some licence applications etc) that oblige the Police to disclose personal data, the disclosure of information is at the discretion of the individual Chief Officer of Police. The general principle governing disclosures is that information should **not** be disclosed 'unless there are important considerations of public interest to justify departure from the general rule' (Home Affairs Committee Report, paragraph 17). It is this arrangement that has been used to allow the vetting of all new employees (including employees who change jobs) who, as part of their employment, have significant access to children. Note that this places a Chief Constable in the constitutional position of deciding what is in the public interest; such matters are usually determined by Parliament.

Safeguards

Following recognition that procedural errors had occurred, the relevant Home Office Circular (HOC(86)44) was revised to include safeguards and procedures designed to mitigate some of the effects of the misinterpretation of Police records (HOC 102/88 'Protection of Children: Disclosure of Criminal Background of those with Access to Children'). The Circular is important as it offers an official role model on how to balance conflicting interests, and protect (a) the individual (against unfair practice), and (b) society (against the employment of unsuitable persons). The Circular outlines principles of good practice to be used in all vetting circumstances, and with respect to the vetting of those who will have access to children suggests that:

- the nature of the job should be evaluated: is there one-to-one contact with young children? is the position supervised? is the position an isolated one? is there regular contact with children? are the children particularly vulnerable?

- the relevance of the conviction should be evaluated: what is the nature of the conviction? what is the nature of the appointment? when did the offence occur? what is the frequency of the offence?

Open procedures

The Circular makes it clear that the vetting procedure should be open. If there is a disagreement between the vetting and the information provided by the prospective employee 'the local authority **must** discuss the discrepancy with the person before reaching a decision to appoint' (paragraph 19 of HOC 102/88). To minimise the number of people checked against Police records, the Circular states that 'requests for checking must not therefore be made when interview short lists are being drawn up, but only when the final candidate has been selected and in respect of that candidate alone' (paragraph 10); thus the prospective employee knows the vetting results and can use appeal procedures if necessary. Finally, on appointment the 'information should be destroyed' (paragraph 20), and that only 'a senior nominated officer' (paragraph 22) should be responsible for making requests to Police Forces: this implies that any information disclosed by the Police should only be used in conjunction with the appointment.

'Forced' Subject Access

In contrast to the safeguards that apply in the case of those who wish to work with children, there is no protection for Data Subjects who are forced to use Subject Access to provide information, and it has been known for Data Subjects to be asked to hand over the information received from the Police without first opening the (presumably distinctive) envelope. This use of Subject Access, first employed by Local Authorities with respect to applications for taxi licences, is now being extended to people who work with the elderly, or with the mentally handicapped (or 'to see that applicants had not been convicted for stealing books'; Guardian 25.6.90), and is also used by employers in the Security Industry (Home Affairs Committee Report, paragraph 20). Such abuse of an individual's rights has been criticised by the Data Protection Registrar in his Fifth Report (in paragraph 290 he states that the practice should be made a criminal offence) and also in his evidence to the Committee ('an undesirable manipulation of the Data Protection Act'). Both the Registrar and Select Committee recommend that **only** Parliament should determine when vetting can take place.

Registrar's guidance

The increasing use of such procedures (eg the 'Report of the Commissioner of Police of the Metropolis 1989' states that, as a result, during 1989 Subject Access requests rose from 2,600 to 8,759) has caused the Registrar to issue Guidance Note 21 (The Use of the Subject Access Provisions of the Data Protection Act to check the Criminal Records of Applicants for Jobs or Licences), in which the Registrar also raises several other problems. For example, the spirit of the Rehabilitation of Offenders Act may be broken, as a Subject Access request to a Police computer will reveal details of offences that are spent under the terms of that Act (the Police may keep personal data on convictions for 20 years). In addition, the vetting procedure itself could be unfair to the individual, as there is no right to be involved (or to appeal) if the personal data are interpreted in a way that is detrimental to the Data Subject (unlike those procedures that apply with respect to those individuals who will be employed with young children).

False sense of security

Organisations who use this vetting process should realise that the procedure could be flawed, as the details of some convictions may not be personal data (information held on microfiche or manual files is not accessible via the Subject Access rights), or the Police may withhold personal data whose disclosure is likely to prejudice the prevention or detection of crime etc (Section 28(1) of the Act). In addition, forced Subject Access has led to legal battles (Cook v Southend Borough

Council, The Weekly Law Reports, 19.1.90), when a taxi driver, who had a blackmail conviction, successfully used the Courts after the Council had revoked his hackney carriage licence.

Compensation and the recipients of information

Despite safeguards, errors can and do occur with the result that a person can wrongly be refused an appointment. In this case compensation for damage (via Section 22), or enforcement of the Data Protection Principles by the Registrar, will not apply to the organisation that receives the information from the Police, as that organisation is unlikely to become a Data User (ie to 'hold' the information as personal data or to cause the data to be 'processed'). As the Circular suggests that any information received from the Police should be destroyed after appointment, to retain such information as personal data could lead to breaches of the First, Fourth and Sixth Principles.

Compensation and the disclosers of information

The Police are also unlikely to be liable for damages. Either the Police are meeting a Subject Access request, or they provide the information (a) with an undertaking from the employer that the job-applicant being vetted **has consented** to this, and (b) with an important disclaimer covering any information disclosed (the Police provide details about a particular individual X with the wording 'The subject may be identical with' the X who is applying for work); this wording should alert recipients of information that they need to check that it refers to the applicant). The Police can thus argue that they have acted reasonably, and cannot be held accountable if recipients of information do not follow procedures that are designed to safeguard the Data Subject.

THE HALIFAX BUILDING SOCIETY: unresolved issues

Introduction

On 17th December last, the Halifax Building Society case was thrown unceremoniously out of Leeds Crown Court: the Judge decided to halt the proceedings mid-trial after hearing the prosecution's evidence. The Halifax Press Release of that date stated that the Judge had described the prosecution case as a 'complete nonsense' and had directed the jury to find the Society 'not guilty'. A triumphant and naturally relieved Society was delighted that it had been 'completely vindicated' and that there was 'no case to go to the jury'. This Section deals with the legacy of the case and the several important Data Protection strands that still need to be tied together.

Problem for the prosecution

To understand the prosecution, one first must consider how the Registrar can police the Act. Besides achieving compliance with the Principles, eg by means of Enforcement Notices, the Registrar can prosecute Data Users for a breach of Section 5(1) (the absolute offence of not having an Entry in the Register) or Section 5(2) (in this case there is at least one Entry, but in accordance with Section 5(5) the Data User has to have contravened, 'knowingly or recklessly', the description contained within a particular Entry). Most of the Registrar's prosecutions (see the Annual Reports) have been against 'small' Data Users and under Section 5(1): a relatively easy case to establish as a Register Entry either exists, or it doesn't. As could be expected of a 'large' Data User, the Halifax had registered, and the prosecution was brought under Section 5(2)(b) (ie the Registrar claimed that the Halifax should have registered a further purpose); this meant that 'knowingly or recklessly' had to be proved. As these words are not defined in the Data Protection Act, their meaning has to be determined by their use in common parlance (ie by the understanding of that mythical 'man on the Clapham Common omnibus'). Consequently, a successful prosecution would require the Registrar to prove beyond reasonable doubt that the Halifax Building Society had deliberately ignored the Act, in this case the provisions which oblige all Data Users to place in the public domain a description of all the purposes for which they hold and process personal data.

Queries for all

The case raises a fundamental (and complex!) question for all Data Users: when does a specific activity fall outside the range of activities that can reasonably be declared as being consistent with, or similar to, those quoted in 'NOTES to help you apply for Registration' (the brown book that comes with the Registration pack) as typical of each Standard Purpose title? In the 'Background information' issued with its Press Release, the Halifax claimed that it, like any sensible financial institution, would 'use computer held information to counter fraud and other crime'. This was 'a normal part of the prudent administration of customer accounts', and consequently came under the relevant Standard Purposes already registered by the Society. It can be argued that the Registrar has accepted the essence of this point, as the description of all Standard Purposes includes 'analysis for management purposes and statutory returns', and one 'management purpose' could include the prevention or detection of crime (ie fraud). To support the view that 'to counter fraud' is a secondary activity (ie not a primary purpose), it could be claimed that whilst millions of transactions are carried out weekly to administer the accounts, perhaps only a proportion may specifically relate to the prevention of fraud. (Note that this argument can extend to almost any Data User and Standard Purpose: eg 'prudent administration of Community Charge Benefits' could include personal data collected on those who defraud or who are suspected of fraud; similarly the 'prudent administration of employee records' could require sensitive personal data, collected by the Auditor, to be held about certain employees. However, Note 3 of Standard Purpose P016 'Research and Statistical Analysis' makes it clear that 'analysis for management purposes' has been included in **every** Standard Purpose specifically to avoid having to register the **P016 Purpose in every case** when 'analysis for management purposes' is carried out). In addition, the Halifax has established a recognised Data Protection function, and indeed argued in its Press Release that it does 'far more than many other organisations in complying with (the Act's) complex provisions'; a point which, the Society implied, supported the case that it had accidentally overlooked (rather than say deliberately avoided) the provisions of the Act. The Society also stressed in the Press Release that it had acted responsibly, for as soon as the Registrar raised the problem (in August 1988), the Society had amended the Entry to comply with his views and also notes that the Registrar had, in February 1989, 'changed his Guidelines to make them clearer' (this is a reference to Guidelines 1-8; the 'NOTES' booklet has not been changed).

An outline of the facts

In February 1987, the Society decided to keep information 'about transactions from all its branches and cash machines indefinitely on computer tapes ... for the future use in the prevention of fraud and crime and (to) assist in the prosecution of offenders' (Yorkshire Post, 12.12.90). A customer, who was dissatisfied with the personal data provided by the Society via Subject Access (The Guardian, 10.2.90), complained to the Registrar (under Section 36(2) of the Act): a subsequent investigation by the Registrar revealed that the Society had withheld details of cash withdrawals (Daily Telegraph, 13.12.90). Two actions by the Registrar followed: (a) a prosecution on the grounds that a considerable amount of personal data had 'knowingly or recklessly' been used for an unregistered purpose (Standard Purpose P058 'Crime Prevention & Prosecution of Offenders') for over a year (until 10.10.88 when Registration of P058 was effected on behalf of the Society), and (b) an Enforcement Notice in relation to the Seventh Data Protection Principle (the Enforcement Notice is under appeal to the Data Protection Tribunal; the Tribunal hearing was postponed until after the prosecution).

Extrapolating on the major issues

If the word 'purpose' in Section 28 of the Act means 'separate purpose', then to claim any of the Section 28 exemptions **would require registration** of P057 'Policing' or P058 'Crime Prevention & Prosecution of Offenders'. On the other hand, if it became established in law that many Standard Purposes could legitimately contain the purposes 'prevention or detection of crime, or apprehension or prosecution of offenders', this could in each case permit the application of any relevant exemption **without having to register those purposes**. Thus, under the Subject Access exemption, the majority of Data Subjects could never know for certain that the Access request had been fully complied with. Since any Subject Access exemption (see Section 21(1)(a) of the Act) allows the Data User to conceal that personal data are held, the rights of Data Subjects could become severely curtailed. This problem is exacerbated by the Act which does not provide the Data Protection Registrar with the power to see the exempted personal data in order to test whether a Subject Access exemption has been applied properly (he can however, examine the grounds on which the exemption is claimed, and access to personal data in order to test the exemption is available to the Courts under Section 25(2)). Further curtailment would occur if the non-disclosure provisions found in Section 28 (and generally defined in Section 26(3)) were applied by a Data User, as any enforcement power of the Registrar 'to the extent to which it is exercisable by reference to **any data protection principle** inconsistent with the disclosure in question' is removed (our emphasis). Finally, there is the impact of Section 28(4) of the Act. This can, subject to a test of prejudice (which can only be scrutinised by a Court, or by the Tribunal under Schedule 3, Section 4(2)(c)) remove all enforcement powers of the Registrar in relation to the First Data Protection Principle (ie fair obtaining and processing of personal data used for Section 28 purposes).

The importance of Registration

As far back as 1985, the Registrar advised his preferred solution to this problem **(ie before any Data User had to register)**. In the 'NOTES to help you apply for Registration' the Registrar differentiated between Standard Purpose P057 (to be used only 'by recognised police forces') and P058 (to be used by other agencies that can prosecute). Additionally, Note 3 associated with Standard Purpose P058 states that: 'This purpose may be used, in appropriate circumstances, by the investigating departments of private organisations such as banks and major retailers'. If a Data User has to register the P058 Purpose, the Registrar can exert some supervisory influence through the Registration mechanism, or through the exercise of the enforcement powers that could apply to personal data held for that Purpose (depending on whether the Subject Access exemption applies to all, or only to some, of the personal data). However, if the Purpose is not registered then the Registrar may never be able to ascertain the extent of one of the most sensitive uses of personal data. Finally, the Registrar has a potential credibility problem: if he indicates (as he has) in successive Annual Reports that he intends to flex his muscles to enforce the the Act, he can not be deemed to be acting equitably if he largely restricts his use of enforcement powers to the minnows.

Not Guilty

Whilst the 'Not Guilty' verdict was returned in rather embarrassing circumstances for the Registrar, the issues outlined above have not been resolved. As the Registrar points out (Press Release, 17.12.90), the acquittal was 'on the grounds that, as a matter of law, the evidence was insufficient to prove the knowingly or recklessly requirement'; furthermore, in such circumstances, 'the jury are not asked to consider the facts of the case'. Thus if any lessons are to be learnt, they are being learnt within the Registrar's Office and not by Data Users in general. This means that to consider that 'Crime Prevention & Prosecution of Offenders' is 'a normal part of the prudent administration of customer accounts' (or of any other purpose) could still be ill advised, and the fact that a prosecution against one Data User has collapsed will only ensure that the Registrar will try to be better prepared against the next Data User.

Any xtra comments?

Because many Data Users have expressed interest in the issues explored above, we have asked both the Halifax and the Data Protection Registrar to comment, if they so wish, in the next issue. For instance, will the Enforcement Notice be withdrawn? Watch this space.

CONSUMER CREDIT: An insight into 'fair' processing

A conflict in the making

Since 11th November 1987, when the Data Protection Registrar's supervisory and enforcement powers came into effect, a dispute has been simmering between the Registrar and the big four Credit Referencing Agencies (CCN, Infolink Ltd, CDMS Ltd and Wescot Data Ltd) over the use of 'third party' personal data. Third party information in the context of its use by the Credit Reference Industry is those personal data that relate not to the Data Subject seeking credit, but to another individual who is linked to the Data Subject either directly (eg as a present or former member of the household), or indirectly (eg through having occupied the same address, not necessarily at the same time as the Data Subject). During these four years, attempts to find common ground over the use of third party data have failed with the result that in the autumn of 1990 Enforcement Notices in relation to the First Principle were served on all four Agencies. Each Agency appealed to the Tribunal against its Notice and the first of four Tribunal hearings (CCN's) took place in January 1991. The result was a claim of 'victory' by the Registrar; however, as both sides now claim that the Tribunal erred in law in reaching some of its conclusions, the next round is set for the High Court in about six months time. This Section examines the background to the case as it has profound implications for **all** Data Users. (**References**: the Registrar's various Annual Reports; Registrar's Press Releases 27th February 1991, 22nd March 1991; the Appeal Decision of the Tribunal; Grounds of Appeal to the High Court by the Registrar).

Differing degrees of fairness

The case is particularly important since the Registrar's Enforcement Notice was based on his interpretation of the First Data Protection Principle, and the appeal will therefore oblige the Courts to establish case law in relation to the meaning of 'fair' and 'unfair' processing as implied by the second part of the First Principle (' ... and personal data shall be processed, fairly and lawfully'). Although the Registrar claims that 'unfairness' is an inherent consequence of the use of **any** third party information in the assessment of credit risk, the Registrar's action raises several questions that have answers which are far from obvious. For example, is it **inevitably** 'unfair' to process information about one person in relation to another's credit application **(ie in every instance)**? Suppose there is a close family relationship (eg son, niece) between the credit applicant and the third party? Is the processing 'unfair' when the family relationship has been strained to breaking point but 'fair' if the relationship is amicable? If it is 'fair' to use personal data irrespective of the 'family' circumstances, how is 'family' defined? Husband - wife - children may be obvious examples of family; but does a definition of family include a common law wife, a distant let alone estranged cousin, a stable homosexual relationship? How are such cases to be distinguished from a tenant or an au-pair? Finally, could there be 'unfair' consequences for other individuals by not using such third party information, and should such consequences then be relevant to any assessment of 'fair' or 'unfair'?

A matter of interpretation

In the absence of case law, the only 'official' guidance is the Registrar's interpretation found in his Guideline 4, paragraph 1.9 which states that 'fairness will need to be judged by reference to the purpose of the processing, the nature of the processing itself and to its consequences for the individual affected by it' (see also Guidance Note 19). This interpretation is founded on the concept of 'fairness' to the Data Subject and takes a potentially broad view of relevant criteria; it could call into question the very business itself, by allowing a challenge to the use of the personal data that support the business. Such a prospect should not be seen as exceptional; it is similar in effect to Article 14 of the European Commission's draft Directive (see DPN 3), which suggests that a Data Subject should have the right 'to oppose, for legitimate reasons, the processing of personal data relating to him'. One such legitimate reason could be that the processing discriminates unfairly against the Data Subject's interests.

A little bit of history

An early mention of credit referencing as a data protection problem is in relation to a National Credit Register, in the Third Report of the Data Protection Registrar (June 1987, page 5). By May 1988 (five months after his powers to investigate substantial complaints came into effect), the Registrar was so concerned that he called a meeting of representatives of the Credit Industry to attempt to sort out the problems (Fourth Report, pages 5-9, give a comprehensive exposition of the Registrar's concerns). The following year (Fifth Report, covering 1988/89) confirmed the trend; approximately 400 of the complaints during that period (35% of the total number of complaints) were about credit referencing. Although the Registrar indicated in the Fifth Report that the Industry had made some 'positive proposals', an impasse had been reached; he wrote that 'the industry takes the view that the way in which they process third party information is fair: I take the view it is not' (pages 6-8). Armed with advice from 'leading counsel' and the tacit support of the Office of Fair Trading (Fourth Report, page 6), he served Preliminary Notices on the four Credit Referencing Agencies in June 1990 (Sixth Report, page 6), by which time the number of complaints had risen to 450 per year (17% of the total number of complaints received). Formal Enforcement Notices were served in August that year, to take effect by 31st July 1991.

The facts of the case

The complaint that resulted in the enforcement action revolved around a Mr J who sold his House to a Mr W. Three years later, Mr J applied to a building society for a cheque guarantee card; this was refused after a credit reference had been sought from CCN. Mr J applied to CCN under Section 158 of the Consumer Credit Act 1974 for a copy of his file which showed a judgement against Mr W; this was followed by action under Section 159 of the Consumer Credit Act to remove that part of the record that related to Mr W. CCN refused this request on the grounds that the information about Mr W was factually correct; however they agreed to add a statement of correction stressing that the information on file relating to Mr W had nothing to do with Mr J. This preference for correction over deletion is a matter of policy; as far as CCN is concerned such information is required by their customers (ie the creditors) (Registrar's Press Release 27th February; paragraph 10 of the the Appeal Decision).

Addressing the problem

The third party information arises from the address-based structure of CCN files; CCN annually purchases copies of the Electoral Register and, every quarter, information about the post-code from the Post Office. To this are added Court judgements, bankruptcy information and other information about credit risks from CAIS (the Credit Account Information Sharing scheme) and CIFAS (Credit Industry Fraud Avoidance Scheme); information from CAIS and CIFAS is only available to CCN customers who are also members of these services. CCN customers search the database by name and address (eg as provided by an individual shopper before purchase), and once these details have been confirmed the system searches for other data (eg Court judgements) that relate to that address. Larger firms have remote terminal connections to the database and some organisations integrate their own credit-selection techniques with the personal data held by CCN so that a decision (eg 'accept', 'reject' or 'second opinion') can be reached automatically. The Tribunal noted that 'no enquiries are made to supplement the information received' (paragraphs 20-31 of the Appeal Decision). **Note**: the European Commission proposes in Article 14 that an individual should not be subject to an assessment 'which has as its sole basis the automatic processing of personal data defining his profile ... '.

Don't blame me; blame the customers

CCN argued that it provides the means by which its customers could assess credit risk, and that it does not make any judgement about the individual seeking credit. Thus the processing carried out by CCN was neither fair nor unfair, as any unfairness 'would be the result of the acts of CCN's customers, not of CCN, which was merely a conduit pipe for the supply of information' (paragraphs 25 and 41 of the Appeal Decision). In addition, CCN's customers gave evidence that third party data played a useful part in assessing credit risk, especially when there was no other information (ie other than the name and address) available. If such information was unavailable 'the judgements of credit grantors would be less reliable', with the inevitable consequence that either the number of defaulters would rise (and such losses would be passed on via higher premiums from those who did not default), or credit grantors, in the absence of third party information, would not provide credit (thereby restricting the freedom of some individuals to make a purchase). Thus any concept of 'fairness' towards an individual had to be balanced against the utilitarian concept of 'fairness' towards other individuals (ie the public) who could be adversely affected (eg by the increased cost of credit: paragraphs 48, 49). Finally, 'witnesses for CCN, who included representatives of banks, mail order companies and other credit grantors, were adamant that third party information could be used and was statistically valid even though there appeared to be no causal connection with the applicant' (paragraph 33).

A 'clear conclusion': the Tribunal's decision

The Tribunal firmly rejected all aspects of CCN's case (including the statistical arguments). It stated that 'in our judgement the presence of third party information can lead to an applicant being refused credit' (paragraph 37); rejected 'the notion ... that CCN, with its wide specialist knowledge of and experience in credit reference and credit scoring, is a mere "conduit pipe" ' (paragraph 53); and took the view that 'in deciding whether the processing we have described is fair we must give the first and paramount consideration to the interests of the applicant for credit - the "data subject" ' (paragraph 52). The Tribunal came to the 'clear conclusion' that 'it is unfair for a credit reference agency, requested by its customers to supply information by reference to a named individual, so to program the extraction of information as to search for information about all persons associated with a given address or addresses notwithstanding that those persons may have no links with the individual the subject of the enquiry or may have no financial relationship with that individual' (paragraph 53).

Not quite so clearly concluded!

Despite having given the Registrar his 'victory on behalf of thousands of credit applicants' (Press Release, 27th February), the Tribunal also considered that 'unfair' processing could be 'fair' in some circumstances; consequently the Registrar's Enforcement Notice was varied (via powers in Section 14 of the Act) in two important ways. Firstly the Tribunal changed the implementation date of the Notice from 31st July 1991 to January 1st 1993: evidence from CCN (given in January 1991) indicated that 'it could take CCN as long as 12 months to change their computer programs so as to comply' (paragraph 47 of the the Appeal Decision). Secondly, the Tribunal allowed the use of third party information under certain circumstances: instead of the complete ban sought by the Registrar, address-based searches would be 'fair' if the third party shared the same address as the Data Subject at the same time (ie concurrent addresses; paragraph 60) and if the personal data extracted comprised information relating to:

- 'the subject of the search'
- 'a person with similar names reasonably believed to be the subject'
- 'a person with the same surname, clearly not the subject, who is reasonably believed to be living as a member of the subject's family ... in a single household' (paragraph 67)
- persons who have a different surname 'but, on the basis of information obtained before such processing, are reasonably believed to live as members of the family of the subject in a single household' (paragraph 66).

An appeal against 'victory'

Within a month of the Tribunal's adjudication, the Registrar appealed to the High Court on points of law (this obliged CCN to issue a counter-appeal, in order to have its side of the story heard by the Court). The Registrar's full grounds of appeal can be summarised as follows:

- that having arrived at a 'clear conclusion' (see above), the Tribunal then varied the Enforcement Notice in ways that were 'inconsistent with the Tribunal's findings' (ie by varying the Notice the Tribunal did not follow the logic of its conclusion that 'we must give the first and paramount consideration to the interests ... of the "Data Subject" ' (paragraph 52)

- the arguments adduced by the Tribunal for varying the Enforcement Notice were not raised by CCN in **any** of its evidence, nor by the Registrar. Consequently, the lack of opportunity for the Registrar to comment on the effect of the variation was 'in breach of natural justice'

- that the Tribunal erred in law by varying the Enforcement Notice in a way which would determine what 'was not unfair' (ie determine what was 'fair'), since it had no status 'in the case of fair extraction' (ie it is the Tribunal's function to adjudicate whether the serving of an Enforcement Notice was correct in relation to the specific circumstances surrounding an alleged breach of a Data Protection Principle; it is not its role to determine those situations when a Notice need not be served)

- that the Tribunal's variation of the Notice was 'neither definite, clear nor precise in its terms, and is too obscure to be included in an enforcement notice' (ie raises all the awkward questions posed in the paragraph **Differing degrees of fairness** above).

What about the Fourth Principle?

One interesting feature was that the Registrar's Notice was served under the terms of the First rather than the Fourth Principle, for at first sight it seems obvious that personal data about one Data Subject, when applied to another, are irrelevant. However, the Tribunal was clearly worried about the meaning of the word 'relevant' and noted that it was being used in two different senses: firstly from the Registrar's viewpoint that personal data to be relevant must relate 'to the individual applicant for credit' (ie to the Data Subject); and secondly, from CCN's viewpoint, that relevant meant 'relevant to the question whether the credit applicant was a member of a group or class of persons of whom a certain percentage would be likely to default' (paragraph 37). It could be that the Registrar anticipated that CCN might put forward a case based on statistical evidence (at the Tribunal the Registrar employed a statistician as expert witness on his behalf), and was concerned that, in practice, defining the word 'purpose' in the Fourth Principle ('Personal data held for any purpose or purposes shall be adequate, relevant and not excessive in relation to that purpose or those purposes') could weaken the case for enforcement action (ie personal data about third parties could be relevant to the purpose, even though they were irrelevant with respect to the Data Subject). We are not aware whether the Registrar avoided enforcing the Fourth Principle for the reasons mentioned here, but if the arguments are valid, the protection afforded by the Fourth Principle seems distinctly weak.

Consumer Credit: two more Tribunal Decisions

Two more Tribunal Decisions (Infolink and Equifax) have followed the CCN Decision; the Registrar has gained approval for most of his enforcement action. With only one Appeal to hear (as we go to press the CDMS Appeal is being heard), it seems that Credit Reference Agencies will have to adhere to the Registrar's Enforcement Notice by January 1st 1993, and reduce their reliance on third party information (except in a few cases where there is concurrency of location and time, and the third party data are reasonably believed to relate to a family member: see DPN 5). A settlement that avoids a High Court conflict is a distinct possibility.

The Infolink Decision: public domain data

The arguments before the Tribunal were close to the CCN case (see DPN 5); however there was one important implication for the use of data in the public domain. Counsel for Infolink argued that since judgments in County Courts were a matter of public record, the provision of data about such judgments was fair (the issue being determined by the fact that, as a matter of public policy, Courts and their records are open to the public). This being so, Infolink 'advances this public policy by making the information accessible' (paragraph 66 of Tribunal Decision). The Tribunal **did not** object to this argument, but stated that it did not apply to Infolink as they did not make data accessible in general terms, but made data **accessible for a specific purpose** (ie the provision of credit). Those who hold personal data derived from public sources (eg Electoral Register, company shareholder registers etc) will find it difficult to argue that that they can never process the data unfairly.

The Equifax Europe (formerly Wescot Data) Decision

The Tribunal's Decision relating to Equifax Europe **is very important**. It clarified the law in relation to the application of the exemption found in Section 28(4) of the Act (this removes the powers of the Registrar in relation to the First Principle **'in any case** (our emphasis) in which the application of those provisions to the data would be likely to prejudice' the prevention or detection of crime, or the apprehension or prosecution of offenders), and in relation to the definition of 'Processing' in Section 1(7) of the Act (especially the meaning of the words 'by reference to the data subject'). In summary, the Tribunal established that Section 28(4) only applies on an individual case-by-case basis, and that in relation to Section 1(7), the important factor was whether the processing took place in order to find out something about an individual. In further detail:

- in relation to Section 28(4), Equifax argued that an important part of any credit reference system was the prevention and detection of fraud, and Equifax had recently registered **P058 Crime Prevention & Prosecution of Offenders** in their Entry. Thus, if personal data had to be removed, this could reduce the effectiveness of the fight against fraud. Since the potential for fraud exists every time credit is offered, Equifax claimed that, in general, **all of the personal data** could be potentially useful for crime prevention. If this is so, Section 28(4) could be applied to the data, with the result that the Registrar had no powers to pursue his Enforcement Notice under the terms of the First Principle. The Tribunal accepted the argument that **some** personal data could be useful for crime prevention, **but only on an individual basis** (ie in any **(single)** case) and not for **'the vast majority'** of cases (paragraph 41). The Tribunal thus 'rejected Equifax's argument based on the crime exemption' (paragraph 42) except for those cases where it could be shown that compliance with the Notice would prejudice prevention of crime etc;

- in relation to the definition of processing 'by reference to the data subject', the argument depended on whether these words were limited to the actual manipulation of the data performed by the computer during processing, or had a wider meaning. Equifax retrieved the data by address: thus, if an address input into the system was that of a single parent then only one name might be attached to the address. However if the address related to, say, a student's Hall of Residence, then details on scores of Data Subjects could be retrieved. Equifax then argued that because the processing started by inputting an address, they were instructing the computer to manipulate the data to select details linked to a specific address. Accordingly, they were not 'processing by reference to the data subject' but processing by address. As the personal data were not 'processed' it followed that they could not be held; consequently Equifax was not Data User with respect to these data and the application of Registrar's powers in relation to these personal data did not arise. The Tribunal rejected this idea and argued that the reason for the processing was important; since the processing was undertaken in order to focus on a particular data subject, the object of the exercise was 'to learn something about individuals' (ie process by reference to the data subject).

Appendix 2: The Disclosure of Personal Data

1. Introduction

1.1 To complement the numerous references to disclosures made in the body of the text of this book, the following advice is intended to help management to establish general procedures, within an organisation, that will enable staff to deal more easily and consistently with requests for disclosures of personal data. These requests can be generated by Data Subjects (who are the individuals to whom the personal data relate), by the requirements of the organisation (the Data User), or by Third Parties who are outside either of these categories.

1.2 Sections 2 to 4 of this Note apply to **all** disclosures, and must be adhered to before personal data can be disclosed, whilst Sections 5 to 10 outline some specific responsibilities.

1.3 In general, a disclosure may only take place if:

(a) it is made to the Data Subject (when identification of the Data Subject is not in doubt), or if the permission of the Data Subject has been given for a disclosure to someone else; or

(b) it is made within an organisation for the authorised functions (ie registered purposes) of that organisation; or

(c) it is made outside an organisation to persons registered under the Data Protection Act as recipients of personal data held by that organisation (note that there can be certain exceptions to this condition; for important examples see paragraphs 5.3, 7.1 and 9.2(a)); or

(d) where the disclosure is by order of a Court, or a statutory duty.

1.4 Unless explicitly required by law, there is no duty to respond to a request for disclosure of personal data.

2. Disclosing personal data

2.1 Disclosures commonly occur at public enquiry desks, via the telephone, in letters, by electronic transmission of information, through the distribution of print-out etc.

2.2 In all cases of oral requests for personal data (eg when somebody phones or appears at an enquiry desk), staff will need to confirm the identity of the caller. If the data relate to the caller, then the information can usually be provided once identification has been confirmed. If the data relate to a person other than the caller, staff will need to confirm the caller or the caller's organisation against a list of those authorised to receive the personal data. If authorisation is confirmed, only those data of direct relevance to a legitimate enquiry should be released. If the caller is not on the list, staff should not disclose any personal data, but discuss the matter with their line manager.

2.3 Staff should take care not to disclose information over the telephone before the caller's identity has been properly verified (eg by phoning back on a known number, or by confirming a known reference number, or by discussing some reference details known only to the organisation and the caller). This may be difficult if the caller is agitated or angry, but usually callers will divulge information that will help to assess their identity. Difficult problems can also arise when callers claim to be 'friends' or 'partners' of Data Subjects; in every case the best advice is: 'If in doubt, do not disclose personal data'.

2.4 If the caller is unable or unwilling to provide adequate identification, staff should ask whether it is possible for the caller to obtain additional evidence of identity and to phone again (or to be phoned back), or whether the caller can wait until staff have obtained the necessary authority to disclose the personal data (see also Section 3). Staff should try to be patient and calm, and not to become embroiled in arguments!

2.5 If common sense suggests that a particular disclosure should be an exception to the rules outlined in paragraph 1.3 above (eg where someone's health might be at risk), staff should be trained to accurately record, immediately after the event, both the disclosure and to whom it was made, to record the circumstances that made the disclosure necessary, and to provide full details to their manager as soon as is practicable (see also Section 7).

2.6 All disclosures of sensitive personal data may have to be recorded on the appropriate files or case papers. In some cases (eg medical records, social work records, police records etc) there may be restrictions on the access to information; if so, special procedures to deal with enquiries will be necessary.

2.7 The confirmation of personal data that callers say are in their possession (for example the Home Office may request a College to confirm that a student is registered as a full-time student) is in itself a disclosure of personal data. Even if the answer is just "yes", the disclosure must follow the rules outlined in this Section.

2.8 Careful reading of written requests for personal data is essential; close inspection may show that an official-looking letter is not what it purports to be.

2.9 Any letter which says there is a statutory duty to disclose information should:

(a) refer to the relevant parts of the statute which define that duty to disclose, and

(b) satisfy the reader that the writer is entitled, by statute, to request the information.

2.10 Procedures for the disclosure of personal data by electronic mail, by the distribution of print-out etc, must similarly incorporate appropriate and adequate safeguards, to ensure that the information only reaches those who are entitled to receive it.

2.11 If a disclosure is authorised, staff should take care only to disclose information that has been requested, and no more.

2.12 Staff should be trained to draw the attention of their line manager to any unusual request for the disclosure of personal data.

2.13 The confidential nature of any personal information supplied must be stressed at all times; staff should not take short cuts and should always follow the correct procedure. In summary, again: 'If in doubt, do not disclose'.

2.14 Any new disclosure of personal data may require **prior** amendment of the relevant Register Entry, so as to ensure that every disclosure of personal data remains compatible with its relevant Register Entry (see paragraph 1.3(c) and also Section 10).

2.15 Some organisations who represent Data Subjects (eg student bodies in the case of students' personal data) may seek assurance that all disclosures are in the interests of the Data Subjects, and this may lead Data Users (eg education establishments) to consider whether they need to establish agreed guidelines on the disclosure procedures.

3. Refusing to disclose personal data

3.1 Whether orally or in writing, staff should always be polite and explain that they are not allowed to disclose personal data unless the enquirer's credentials to receive the data have first been verified. Staff should make it clear that the reason why they are refusing to give information is one of confidentiality, and protection of the Data Subject. The following is suggested as the basis for a standard explanation, when inadequate identification is the issue:

> 'The 1984 Data Protection Act regulates the use of personal data. It is the organisation's policy to respect the confidentiality of the personal data in its possession, and because you have not been able to identify yourself properly, I cannot help you. However, if you can provide satisfactory identification in future, I may be able to comply with your request'.

4. Forwarding letters

4.1 In some circumstances, staff may wish to offer to forward letters on behalf of an enquirer, but they should make it clear that they can give no guarantee of locating the person in question. Only if this offer is taken up (ie a letter actually arrives for forwarding) should staff take time to try to trace the addressee and to send on the letter.

4.2 Staff should ask the enquirer to enclose the letter in a sealed envelope, and to provide a further and larger stamped envelope endorsed with the name of the recipient, together with a formal written request for the letter to be forwarded. In this way, the confidentiality both of any forwarded letter and of the address of the recipient can be maintained. The request should contain the last known whereabouts of the recipient, and should be marked for the attention of the section or department who will deal with the request.

4.3 Staff should ensure that the letter to be forwarded is accompanied by a note which explains this action, and stresses that the recipient's address has not been disclosed to the writer of the letter; staff should also keep a formal record of their actions.

5. Disclosure of personal data to prosecuting agencies and other public agencies

5.1 If staff receive a request for personal data from a police officer, customs official, Community Charges Registration Officer, social security or immigration official etc, they should refer the request to their line manager who will be responsible for ensuring compliance with the Data User's established procedure. As disclosures in response to such enquiries can be controversial, the options available are explained below.

5.2 Disclosures of personal data to agencies that have power to obtain information usually fall within one of the following:

(a) the Data User has a statutory duty to provide the personal data (eg a warrant or a Court Order has been issued, or the agency exercises a statutory power);

(b) disclosures to these agencies have been registered;

(c) the Data Subject has consented to the disclosure.

5.3 If none of these criteria apply, Section 28 of the Data Protection Act allows for personal data to be disclosed to certain prosecuting agencies (eg Police, Inland Revenue, Customs and Excise, Public Health Authority etc) for the purposes of:

'(a) the prevention or detection of crime;

(b) the apprehension or prosecution of offenders; or

(c) the assessment or collection of any tax or duty'

so long as Data Users can prove that they 'had reasonable grounds for believing that failure to make the disclosure in question would have been likely to prejudice any of those matters.' (see (a), (b), (c) immediately above).

5.4 It is likely that only agencies with a statutory duty to investigate the matters mentioned in paragraph 5.3 will use this Section of the Data Protection Act, and it is for senior management, usually at a level such as Director or Assistant Director, to decide whether or not to release personal data to these agencies (note that in these circumstances there is no compulsion to comply with a request for personal data).

5.5 In practice the Police, for example, are fully prepared to put such a request in writing. Thus it is suggested that, to be consistent, all agencies who may want a Data User to disclose personal data under Section 28 of the Data Protection Act should be asked to put this in writing. Disclosures of personal data to prosecuting agencies should not be made orally.

5.6 The procedure for disclosure would be:

(a) the request for disclosure must be received in writing from the agency, and must explain satisfactorily why the personal data are required by the agency;

(b) the disclosure is discussed by senior management (usually Director or Assistant Director of the Department concerned);

(c) the disclosure is either approved or denied.

5.7 If the disclosure is approved, management should formally record the decision and file this with the written request. The record should include the time and date of the approval, who made the decision, who was involved in the discussions about the disclosure, and a copy of the personal data disclosed.

5.8 If the disclosure is denied, a formal note explaining why the personal data were not released should be sent to the agency, and copied to the Data User's Legal Services in case there is subsequent legal action by the agency.

5.9 If in doubt, a senior manager should:

(a) discuss the matter with Legal Services or the Data Protection Officer in the Data User organisation;

(b) attempt to find out more information from the agency as to why the personal data are required.

6. Calling in a prosecuting agency

6.1 The procedures mentioned in Section 5 above still apply if a member of staff uncovers a crime and informs the Police. For example, an auditor may come across an irregularity that warrants Police involvement or a member of staff may hear of some impropriety. At this point evidence may have to be disclosed to the Police to enable them to apprehend the culprit, and this could involve the disclosure of personal data.

6.2 As before, when such a disclosure does take place, it will be necessary to take note of details of any meeting, who was present, the nature of the irregularity and what personal data were disclosed to the Police.

7. Emergencies

7.1 There may be circumstances where staff have to disclose personal data in emergencies. If an emergency involves a threat to a Data Subject's health, or to prevent injury to a Data Subject, then the disclosure can take place (by virtue of Section 34(8) of the Act).

7.2 A proper record of the disclosure must be made, either at the time or as soon as possible after the disclosure has occurred. In other urgent situations, staff will have to use their judgement but in all cases they should keep a formal record of their decision to disclose, and send a note of the disclosure to their line manager.

8. 'Subject Access' to personal data

8.1 Staff may be consulted by an individual who wishes to apply formally for Subject Access. In these cases, the Data Subject should be referred to the Data Protection Officer or, if this is impossible, to the line manager.

8.2 All staff should be aware that Subject Access is a separate and formal procedure which involves legal responsibilities, and through which personal data are disclosed to the Data Subject.

9. Access to personal data by Councillors (or Elected Members)

9.1 Staff should refer any request for personal data from Councillors (or Elected Members) to their line manager. As disclosures of this kind can be difficult to handle, further explanation is provided below.

9.2 The common law principles concerning Councillors (or Elected Members) can be summarised as follows:

(a) A Councillor, by virtue of this office, is entitled to have access to all documents in possession of the Local Authority, but only as far as such access is reasonably necessary to enable relevant duties to be performed properly (ie the Councillor is acting in an authorised capacity as a manager of the Authority).

(b) A Councillor has no 'roving commission' in respect of Local Authority documents and mere curiosity is not a sufficient basis for access to information.

(c) In the case of a Committee of which the Councillor is a member, there is a presumption that the Councillor has good reason for access to all the information and documents which pertain to the functions of that particular Committee.

(d) In the case of a Committee of which the Councillor is not a member, the Councillor has no automatic right of access to material and has to demonstrate a 'need to know' (eg Councillors may have to show that they are acting on behalf of a constituent in sorting out a problem).

(e) The decision about whether a Councillor has good reason for access to the material of a Committee of which the Councillor is not a member is ultimately one to be taken by the Elected Members themselves. The Local Authority can delegate to officials the right to decide whether an application for access to material ought to be granted, subject, however, to Councillors having a right of appeal to their peers.

9.3 Particular care must be taken to discriminate between the reasons for disclosures. Disclosures that relate to duties on behalf of a Local Authority must be differentiated from those that relate to a Councillor's political party, business etc.

10. Responsibilities of line managers

10.1 Line managers should supervise their staff in relation to disclosures of personal data, and ensure that staff are trained in the correct procedures. Line managers should liaise with the Data Protection Officer to ensure that staff have available to them a list of permitted disclosure categories and of the related procedures that need to be adopted.

10.2 All other disclosures of personal data may be unlawful. Consequently, if a line manager concludes that the legality of a disclosure is in doubt, reference should be made to the Data Protection Officer before the disclosure proceeds. If there is concern about any disclosure, reference should always be made to the Data Protection Officer.

Appendix 3: Data Protection and the Auditor

1. Aims

1.1 The Data Protection Act establishes certain rights in relation to personal information, about living individuals, which is held in the files and databases of any computer. These new rights include the right of individuals to obtain a copy of these data, the right to have inaccurate personal data corrected or erased and, where appropriate, to seek redress for any damage caused.

1.2 The Act obliges all organisations and individuals who process personal data ('Data Users') to provide a brief description of these data (in standardised form, covering uses, sources and disclosures) to a public body – the Office of the Data Protection Registrar. Data Users also must follow eight internationally accepted 'Data Protection Principles' on which the Act is based, and which together define a code of conduct for the processing of personal data. To ensure compliance, the Act establishes criminal offences if these responsibilities are neglected.

1.3 The Act recognises that information is power, particularly when information involves personal data which relate to living individuals and are capable of being processed by computer in many different ways for many different purposes. Misuse of this power (whether intentionally or accidentally) can cause considerable damage or distress to those individuals whose data are recorded, since personal data are often of a very sensitive nature.

1.4 This Guide is intended to outline those Data Protection issues on which management may look to Auditors for comment, including advice on whether existing procedures comply adequately with the provisions of the Act. In particular, Auditors may need to:

(a) assist management to understand its obligations under the Act (eg to take reasonable precautions to ensure the accuracy of personal data)

(b) indicate the practical steps to be taken by management to improve appropriate procedures

(c) assist management to understand the obligations which relate to the rights of Data Subjects, and what steps can be taken by management to reassure Data Subjects that their own personal data are professionally handled

(d) help to promote common standards within a Data User with respect to all aspects of the use of personal data.

1.5 Section 2 of this document outlines the role of Auditors in dealing with some general issues; Section 3 quotes each Data Protection Principle in turn, explains what that Principle means in practice, and provides a checklist for each Principle which Auditors can use to examine current procedures. **If Auditors are unsure on any aspect, they should discuss the matter with a Data Protection Officer.**

1.6 Section 4 raises an issue not limited to the Data Protection Act. It discusses how Auditors' wide powers to inspect data and programs could be controlled; indeed, whether they should be controlled!

1.7 In summary, Auditors should be able to alert Data User management to the obligations described below, to evaluate management structure from the viewpoint of these obligations, and to monitor compliance with the Data Protection Principles. To improve working practices, a review of the relevant activities should be carried out where necessary. Security aspects may require consideration of whether staff are properly trained in such practices and are fully aware of their responsibilities towards personal data. Auditors should aim to ensure that any procedure adopted to comply with any Principle, includes the means by which the effectiveness of the procedure can be assessed.

2. The role of Auditors in Data Protection work

2.1 Auditors have a general duty to ensure the probity of financial systems, and to measure the efficiency and effectiveness of all activities and of management. In relation to Data Protection, the Auditor will want to ensure that the Data User's procedures comply with the law, and that managers are able to maintain compliance in future.

2.2 In particular, the Auditor will be concerned with the Data User's Registration, to ensure that it accurately reflects the use of personal data, and that all appropriate staff are aware of the Register Entries relevant to their work (Sections 5, 15 and 20 of the Act). In addition, the Auditor will want to be satisfied that the Data User can organise a defence with respect to compensation (Sections 22 and 23), and can deal with enquiries from the Data Protection Registrar in relation to the Principles. Where Computer Bureau services are provided, the Auditor may wish to check the requirements of the contract with the Bureau's clients. Finally, the Auditor will want to ensure that procedures relating to all Data Protection Principles, particularly with respect to data accuracy and security, are supported by the management process, and that staff have been instructed to alert management to any changes that are required.

2.3 In practice, therefore, the Auditor will monitor independently how the Data User copes with the obligations imposed by each Data Protection Principle. In many cases, the Auditor will want to investigate problem areas and examine relevant documentation.

2.4 It should be noted that an Auditor's status in exercising these functions can vary – for instance, the Auditor can be an employee of the Data User, or an independent consultant, or an official having a statutory duty to perform with respect to the Data User. Such status can itself have a bearing on how disclosures to the Auditor are treated in the Data User's Registration; notably since, in many cases, the disclosures could be covered by a non-disclosure exemption and therefore not require to be registered.

2.5 **Checklist of general issues**

(a) Is there a Data Protection Policy?

(b) What is the reporting structure that supports and reviews the Policy and its effectiveness?

(c) Is that Policy sufficiently resourced?

(d) Are data protection procedures formally documented and reviewed by management (eg records of changes, or minutes of meetings, that could assist in a defence to an action under the Act)?

(e) What is management's awareness of the Act in general?

(f) How are Data Protection problems resolved and timetabled for action?

(g) How effective is the Data User's procedure for maintaining a comprehensive and up to date census of personal data (see also paragraph 3.2.2)?

(h) Do contractual relationships between Data User, Computer Bureau, contract staff etc specify Data Protection requirements?

(i) How does management recognise particularly 'sensitive' personal data that may require a special procedure?

(j) Are the Principles taken into account during system design, during the development of methodologies, and before the purchase of hardware or software?

(k) Are staff adequately trained in the necessary procedures?

(l) Has the Data User any special statutory powers (eg Environmental Health, Electoral Register, Community Charge) in relation to the obtaining and disclosing of personal data and, if so, is there satisfactory proof as to whether these powers are exercised properly?

3. Specific obligations to the Eight Data Protection Principles

3.1 The First Principle

'The information to be contained in personal data shall be obtained, and personal data shall be processed, fairly and lawfully'.

3.1.1 The Auditor needs to be satisfied that management:

(a) ensures that any person from whom personal data are obtained is not deceived or misled as to the purposes for which such data are held, used or disclosed. An indication of the purpose(s) should appear on any form used to collect data, and staff should be trained to explain, where necessary, why personal data are being collected and to whom data may be disclosed

(b) ensures that no unfair pressure is used in order to obtain the information (eg an unjustified threat to withhold a service unless the form is completed).

3.1.2 **Checklist for Auditors**

(a) Are people advised at the time the information is obtained of the various purposes, uses or disclosures involved?

(b) Do any forms need to be redesigned?

(c) Do any staff require training in the proper techniques of collecting personal data (eg to ensure that no unfair pressure is used)?

(d) Are special powers to obtain personal data used properly (see paragraph 2.5(l))?

3.2 The Second Principle

'Personal data shall be held only for one or more specified and lawful purposes'.

3.2.1 The Auditor needs to be satisfied that management:

(a) plays its part in ensuring that the information which the organisation has contributed to the Data Protection Register is properly maintained. This means that the Auditor may need to review the personal data used by the organisation, to ensure that its Register Entries contain

(i) particulars that adequately describe all its processing of personal data (see also paragraph 3.2.2(g))

(ii) sufficient detail to explain as fully as possible the reason(s) for which the personal data are held by the organisation, and that the purpose(s) involved are, in themselves, lawful

(iii) sufficient detail to fully define the sources, disclosures and types of personal data

(iv) information that, to the extent permitted by the Registration format, is neither ambiguous nor confusing to the Data Subject

(b) has designated a person to be responsible for Registration (or part of a Registration), and for answering questions that pertain to any of the organisation's Register Entries, and that this person is fully resourced and of sufficient seniority. As it is the Register Entry that sets the legal limits of the use, collection and disclosure of personal data by the organisation, the Auditor may need to check the mechanism for raising any query or doubt with a Data Protection Officer.

3.2.2 Checklist for Auditors

(a) Does each registered purpose comply with any legal constraints to which the Data User may be subject?

(b) Does each registered purpose adequately explain the reason for which the personal data are held, or are further details required?

(c) Can the person(s) responsible for Registration be identified within the Data User organisation?

(d) How is a new purpose, disclosure or source notified to the person responsible for Registration?

(e) How are the particulars contained in the Register Entries kept up to date?

(f) How are staff made aware of which Register Entries relate to their work?

(g) Is the census paperwork convincing (see also paragraphs 2.5(d) and 2.5(g))?

(h) Does the census include all equipment which can automatically process information (eg automatic retrieval devices, or electronic scanners that can process manual records)?

3.3 The Third Principle

'Personal data held for any purpose or purposes shall not be used or disclosed in any manner incompatible with that purpose or those purposes'.

3.3.1 The Auditor needs to be satisfied that:

(a) all disclosures are lawful and compatible with established procedures and Register Entries

(b) personal data are only disclosed after proper identification of the disclosee(s)

(c) disclosures are regularly monitored and reviewed to see if they are appropriate

(d) staff are aware at all times of the particular responsibilities pertaining to the disclosure of personal data, are properly trained, and will not disclose personal data without following established procedures

(e) procedures are established to formally record disclosures where appropriate (eg disclosures of sensitive personal data, disclosures which are required by law, or those disclosures of personal data which may appear to be controversial; see also paragraph 2.5(l)).

3.3.2 Checklist for Auditors

(a) What checks are there to monitor whether all disclosures are compatible with internal procedures and with Register Entries and Codes of Practice?

(b) What steps are taken by managers to ensure that personal data can safely be disclosed?

(c) Are staff aware of all the disclosures which they are authorised to make?

(d) Are staff trained to cope with difficult (eg aggressive) enquiries involving personal data?

3.4 The Fourth Principle

'Personal data held for any purpose or purposes shall be adequate, relevant and not excessive in relation to that purpose or those purposes'.

3.4.1 The Auditor needs to be satisfied that management:

(a) ensures that the terms 'adequate, relevant, and not excessive' have been defined in relation to every purpose for which personal data are processed. The Auditor may need to ask management to justify why personal data are held, and to check that any item of personal data is within the scope of the relevant registered purpose (this could be especially important in the case of free text fields)

(b) has established procedures to check the relevance of personal data, and to train staff to be able to explain to Data Subjects why particular data are required.

3.4.2 Checklist for Auditors

(a) How are personal data tested as to whether they are 'adequate, relevant, and not excessive' in the context of each particular registered purpose?

(b) Are any personal data held merely because 'they could be useful'?

(c) What procedures are there to sample personal data, at intervals, to check their adequacy and relevance, and to remove irrelevant personal data?

3.5 The Fifth Principle

'Personal data shall be accurate and, where necessary, kept up to date'.

3.5.1 The Auditor needs to be satisfied that management:

(a) ensures that adequate procedures exist to validate all personal data for accuracy, and to keep personal data up to date

(b) has established procedures to identify personal data that require correction, to rectify or erase such data, as may be necessary, and to advise disclosees of such changes if appropriate. Where personal data have been received from a third party, any change should only be implemented following a check with that third party

(c) has established procedures to use 'markers' (if feasible) in the way specified in Section 22 of the Data Protection Act, to create a defence for the Data User against any action for compensation brought under the Act

(d) formally reviews actions which were based on personal data later found to be inaccurate

(e) has considered whether there should be provision for a Data Subject to indicate any disagreement with the personal data held; whether a marker should be added to such data to indicate their 'challenged' status, and whether such disagreements, or agreed corrections, can be notified to all recipients of the original data

(f) reminds all staff, at appropriate intervals, of the importance of maintaining the accuracy of personal data, and of following procedures to ensure this.

3.5.2 Checklist for Auditors

(a) Are the sources of personal data (ie Data Subject, Data User, or third party) 'marked' where necessary?

(b) How, and how often, are personal data checked for accuracy (including validation of data input)?

(c) What procedures are there to rectify or erase personal data, in compliance with requests from Data Subjects and/or Court Orders?

(d) What procedures are there to determine whether personal data require updating?

(e) Are personal data evaluated to establish the degree of damage that could be caused by inaccuracy or being out of date?

(f) Are there procedures to monitor the factual relevance, accuracy and timeliness of free text opinions or comments about individuals?

3.6 The Sixth Principle

'Personal data held for any purpose or purposes shall not be kept for longer than is necessary for that purpose or those purposes'.

3.6.1 The Auditor needs to be satisfied that management:

(a) has established procedures to review the length of time that personal data are kept and to monitor whether personal data are still required. These procedures should adhere to any legal requirements that may be in force for retaining certain personal data

(b) ensures that personal data which are no longer required should be deleted. Where personal data are kept for historical or statistical purposes, management should be able to justify the grounds for this decision.

3.6.2 Checklist for Auditors

(a) Are personal data reviewed at appropriate intervals, to establish whether they are still required for the stated purpose(s) or as a consequence of legal requirements?

(b) Are there procedures to record the dates on which relevant personal data were generated and/or obtained?

(c) Are personal data reviewed periodically to determine if retention in archive is necessary or if they can be anonymised (eg if kept only for historical or statistical purposes)?

3.7 **The Seventh Principle**

'An individual shall be entitled -

(a) at reasonable intervals and without undue delay or expense -

(i) to be informed by any data user whether he holds personal data of which that individual is the subject; and

(ii) to access to any such data held by a data user; and

(b) where appropriate, to have such data corrected or erased'.

3.7.1 The Auditor needs to be satisfied that:

(a) Subject Access procedures have been formally established, additionally to any procedures that already allow Data Subjects access to some of their own personal data, and that a clear distinction is drawn between routine requests for information and applications for formal Subject Access

(b) procedures to identify a Data Subject are thorough, and appropriate to the sensitivity of the data; that whilst details to help locate the personal data in question may be requested from Data Subjects, neither the verification nor the location provisions are too stringent; and that, once these provisions are satisfied, the procedures enable a copy of a Data Subject's personal data to be provided to that Data Subject within 40 days

(c) the procedures take into account that some personal data may contain information which is exempt, by law, from Subject Access, or which is exempt because it relates to other living individuals

(d) any codes or other data not likely to be intelligible to the Data Subject can be explained

(e) provision has been made, following Subject Access, to allow such rectification or erasure of personal data as may be appropriate, in compliance with requests from Data Subjects (see the Fifth Data Protection Principle for details), and that some kind of appeals procedure has been established for use in cases of dispute

(f) advice and assistance is available with the interpretation of a Data Subject's personal data, as may be necessary in special circumstances (eg where a Data Subject has English as a second language or suffers from a disability that impairs reading)

(g) if a fee is charged by the Data User for Subject Access, a procedure for handling such fees has been established

(h) as Subject Access is a legal right, management always follows the procedure for dealing with an Access request.

3.7.2 Checklist for Auditors

(a) What are the existing procedures which allow Data Subjects to access their personal data?

(b) How effective are the procedures for locating the personal data to which Subject Access is required?

(c) What procedures are there to ensure that personal data which

  (i) identify another individual

  (ii) describe the intentions of the Data User towards the Data Subject

  (iii) contain other information which might also be exempt from Subject Access

  are not disclosed to Data Subjects until any necessary deletions have been effected?

(d) Who is responsible for providing written explanations, to the Data Subject, of any codes or other unintelligible information?

(e) Is there a procedure for monitoring compliance with Subject Access to ensure that the data are released within the prescribed 40 days?

(f) What are the procedures for handling any Subject Access fees that may be levied under this legislation?

3.8 The Eighth Principle

'Appropriate security measures shall be taken against unauthorised access to, or alteration, disclosure or destruction of, personal data and against accidental loss or destruction of personal data'.

3.8.1 The Auditor needs to be satisfied that:

(a) security of personal data has a high priority and profile, as part of a comprehensive security policy

(b) management evaluates the security of personal data held by the organisation, taking account of the potential harm to a Data Subject that would result from a security breach, and implements appropriate security measures

(c) staff training in security procedures, and the suitability of staff for particular posts, is considered an integral requirement for ensuring the security of personal data

(d) equipment, network, programs, data and documentation are made sufficiently secure, and that access to data and equipment is at all times restricted to appropriate staff

(e) security procedures are monitored and reviewed and include provisions for preventing accidental disclosures, for disaster recovery and for emergency standby

(f) management and staff responsibilities towards security are taken seriously.

3.8.2 Checklist for Auditors

(a) **Physical security**

(i) Are the locations of all equipment, on which personal data are held or can be accessed, known to management?

(ii) How is access to the buildings and equipment safeguarded?

(iii) How are the magnetic media used, stored and disposed of?

(b) **Software security**

(i) How is access to equipment, programs and personal data restricted to appropriate staff?

(ii) How sensitive are the data?

(iii) Are there any security implications arising from a network?

(iv) How is the security software supervised?

(v) How is password security maintained?

(vi) How are the access controls supervised?

(vii) How regularly are access and use monitored?

(viii) Are security copies of programs and data taken?

(ix) Is there a recovery plan to cover situations when processing is impossible?

(c) **Printed matter** (input, output, documentation etc)

(i) Where is input/output stored?

(ii) How is input/output distributed?

(iii) How is input/output disposed of?

(iv) Where is relevant documentation kept?

(v) How is access to documentation controlled?

(vi) How is documentation disposed of?

(d) **Contingency planning**

(i) Are personal data adequately backed-up in a secure location?

(ii) What procedures (including manual office procedures) are there to ensure recovery from fire, flood and other disasters?

(iii) What procedures (including manual office procedures) are there to cover lesser accidents such as loss of personal data, unavailability of equipment or network, corruption of personal data etc?

(e) **Staff awareness**

(i) What precautions are taken to prevent accidental disclosures?

(ii) Are staff and management aware of security issues?

(iii) Are staff and management given training, periodically, in security issues?

(iv) Have security guidelines been distributed to all staff?

(v) How and when is security reviewed by management?

(f) **Staff reliability**

(i) How is staff integrity evaluated prior to any activity that involves access to personal data?

(ii) Are staff properly trained to process personal data?

(g) **Contracts**

(i) Do the conditions of service embody a statement that informs staff of their responsibilities towards personal data held by the Data User?

(ii) Do contractors, external agents or consultants have in their contract with the Data User a written obligation towards the requirements of the Data Protection Act?

4. Finally: who audits the Auditor?

4.1 Auditors have a unique role. They act independently to ensure the quality of administrative and managerial procedures, and have a duty to ensure financial probity and the proper performance of information systems. In addition, a Computer Auditor has a specific duty to 'protect' an organisation by checking that computer systems, applications and personnel operate efficiently in the interests of that organisation.

4.2 To achieve this, the Computer Auditor in particular has unique powers of access to data and equipment. This access generates some questions that should be addressed by the organisation as a whole:

(a) how independent should the Auditor be?

(b) what limits (if any) of access should there be on the Auditor?

(c) what access controls should be placed on the Auditor to ensure that these powers are not abused?

(d) how can management best use the Auditor to improve the organisation's computing performance?

(e) what is or what should be the relationship between Computer Centre Management, Computer Security Management and Auditor?

4.3 Questions (b) and (c) above give rise to further issues that the organisation should consider:

(a) does the organisation approve of the Auditor having general access to data:

(i) without the data owner's knowledge?

(ii) without the Security Manager's knowledge?

(b) If not:

(i) under what circumstances should access be obtained without the knowledge of the data owner or Security Manager?

(ii) is the organisation satisfied with the procedures that allow the Auditor use of such facilities?

(iii) should there be further security procedures (eg software monitoring) or logs within the Auditor's section?

(c) In summary, is the organisation happy with the current procedures?

4.4 In many organisations, getting a forum in which to raise these issues will be a challenge in itself. However, such problems must ultimately be resolved, and Auditors can play their part in ensuring that security provisions apply to all users of an organisation's computers.

Appendix 4: Data Protection and Software Design

1. Introduction

1.1 This paper describes how the Data Protection Act influences the design of applications programs, and provides a check-list to aid software design. In summary, any computer application or scheme, or any procedure which supports an application, must satisfy the requirements of the eight Data Protection Principles. Many of these requirements will be familiar to you in current operational procedures.

1.2 The various implications of these Principles have been grouped into eight Sections. For ease of reference, the text of the Principles is provided below, together with references to the relevant Sections in which the requirements of each Principle are discussed.

1. The information to be contained in personal data shall be obtained, and personal data shall be processed, fairly and lawfully. (See Section 4).

2. Personal data shall be held only for one or more specified and lawful purposes. (See Sections 5 and 9).

3. Personal data held for any purpose or purposes shall not be used or disclosed in any manner incompatible with that purpose or those purposes. (See Sections 5 and 9).

4. Personal data held for any purpose or purposes shall be adequate, relevant and not excessive in relation to that purpose or those purposes. (See Sections 4, 5 and 9).

5. Personal data shall be accurate and, where necessary, kept up to date. (See Sections 2, 4 and 5).

6. Personal data held for any purpose or purposes shall not be kept for longer than is necessary for that purpose or those purposes. (See Sections 4 and 5).

7. An individual shall be entitled –

   (a) at reasonable intervals and without undue delay or expense –

      (i) to be informed by any data user whether he holds personal data of which that individual is the subject; and

      (ii) to access to any such data held by a data user; and

(b) where appropriate, to have such data corrected or erased. (See Sections 2, 4, 5 and 6).

8. Appropriate security measures shall be taken against unauthorised access to, or alteration, disclosure or destruction of, personal data and against accidental loss or destruction of personal data. (See Sections 3, 7, 8 and 9).

1.3 Contravention of these Principles, whether the Data User is an organisation or an individual, can lead to legal action, criminal prosecution and award of compensation. In particular, the Act provides for compensation to be paid if a Data Subject can prove to a Court's satisfaction that damage resulted from

- unauthorised loss, disclosure, access or destruction of personal data, or
- the use of personal data which were incorrect or misleading as to any matter of fact.

1.4 The best defence will be to prove to the Court that all the steps that could reasonably be taken to prevent the damage were in fact taken. The burden of proof will be on the defendant (ie that the organisation had the proper procedures in place at the material time, and actively monitored the effectiveness of these procedures).

1.5 Thus to prepare a defence against legal actions that might be founded on the Data Protection Act, an organisation should ensure the development of adequate quality controls, and of security and privacy procedures in relation to the use of all personal data. As a consequence, this document will overlap with others, as many of the topics or questions raised here will also be relevant to existing procedures. For example, security practices already established in relation to access, destruction, disclosure and alteration also fall within the ambit of the Eighth Data Protection Principle. The development of audit trails and verification processes is encouraged by the Third and Fifth Data Protection Principles, which deal with disclosure and accuracy of personal data.

2. What are 'accurate' personal data?

2.1 Section 22 of the Data Protection Act establishes a Data Subject's entitlement to compensation if personal data are 'incorrect or misleading as to any matter of fact', **and** if it can be proved to a Court's satisfaction that use of the inaccurate data caused damage to the Data Subject. As mentioned in paragraph 1.4, it will be up to the Data User to prove to a Court's satisfaction that the User's operational procedures were of sufficient quality to establish the defence of 'reasonable care', and included procedures to ensure data accuracy.

2.2 Further means are available to the Data User to guard against having to pay compensation. As long as input procedures reach adequate standards, no damages could be awarded if the personal data have been marked as received from a Data Subject or third party, as appropriate, and if the personal data are always used with these markers. As long as its meaning is explained, a marker need not be complex; it may be a simple character, or the name of the actual source of the data, or perhaps a set of initials.

2.3 In many cases, a system of markers may be very difficult to design, especially if personal data are received from many different sources outside the organisation. In addition, for existing systems, a change in data structure may create more problems than it solves. However, it is clear that the use of markers, to record from whom personal data are obtained, should be considered for new systems.

2.4 The Data Protection Registrar has offered some advice on this topic; it is quoted in full below (Section 3.6 from Guideline 5; our emphasis).

'There is another case when no compensation would be payable even though the personal data are inaccurate. This is where

- the data accurately record information received from the Data Subject or a third party **and**

- the fact that the information was so received is apparent whenever the information is extracted from the data **and**

- any challenge to the accuracy of the information made to the Data User by the Data Subject is also apparent whenever the information is extracted from the data.

This provision is not easy to understand. It is clear that, whenever the received information is displayed on a screen or is printed out, then some indicator of the matters mentioned above must also appear. But the type of 'indicator' which a court might consider to be sufficient is not clear. For example:

- it has been suggested that the letter 'R' displayed next to an item of information is a sufficient indicator that the information was obtained from the Data Subject or a third party. However, this argument might be difficult to sustain when the meaning of 'R' has not been explained to the person seeing the information

- an indicator which expressly states 'this item of information has been received by X Limited from the Data Subject or a third party' would be sufficient. Its meaning would be clear to any person who sees it. But to produce an indicator like this may well present difficulties in practice.

This provision does not give protection if the information is made inaccurate by the

Data User or his staff when the data are being entered. A cautious Data User who intends to rely on this provision may, therefore, wish to keep a separate record of the information received and its source in case of any later dispute as to the validity of the indicator'.

2.5 To ensure the accuracy of personal data, care should also be taken over the setting of default values. For example, one commercial package sets the default status to 'married' and default date of birth to '1.1.1945'.

3. An overview of the necessary design considerations

3.1 **Design considerations in relation to the processing of data or use of programs are a standard part of internal procedures.**

3.1.1 Although in some cases the operating systems or other procedures external to the application will take control of error handling, the designer should always be aware of what action should follow discovery of an error. In particular, the designer of the application should know what happens if any of the following occur:

- errors detected during processing by the program
- hardware failure
- system software failure
- operator mistakes
- invalid or corrupt data
- mathematical overflow or underflow
- program error or failure
- access control violation.

3.1.2 In addition, consideration should be given to:

- clear diagnostic messages to aid efficient use of the program
- use of the access control system to increase security
- support of the application with adequate documentation
- how the application is to be backed-up easily

- satisfactory archive and audit procedures for the application
- proper protection of any audit trail information
- ensuring that access to shared files is controlled, and that file enquiries can be logged if necessary
- the formulation of a disaster recovery plan (including manual office procedures) should there be a failure in the application.

3.2 Design considerations in relation to end-users

3.2.1 The design should take into account how an end-user will use the application. In particular, consideration should be given to:

- the personnel who will use the program
- the environment in which the program will run
- the administrative procedures that will support the application
- the appropriate involvement of the Data Protection Officer, Auditor and Security Manager in the design process.

3.2.2 Other design factors should include:

- the appropriate involvement of all interested parties to meet end-users' specifications and needs. Such specifications should be agreed formally
- the legal status of end-users. If an end-user is a separate legal entity (ie another Data User), there must be formal arrangements for the processing and use of the application. Should this be the case, the Data Protection Officer must be consulted
- proper control over the use of the live data, programs, and test data (ie to the same level of security)
- consideration of encryption for sensitive data
- whether the application is covered by a Register Entry, if personal data are to be processed
- whether facilities are to be provided for dealing with requests from Data Subjects for access to their own records on a routine basis

- how formal Data Subject Access, to archived as well as to current personal data, is to be achieved

- care over the default values assigned to personal data.

4. Design checks for data input

4.1 The questions detailed below will, in many cases, be very familiar. They outline some of the basic requirements of quality control. For example, how are data to be verified, kept accurate and of the highest quality? The checklist details some obvious attempts to reduce operator or end-user error. For example, it should be impossible to obtain another valid identifier, or to instigate a valid process, through an accidental interchange of two digits, or characters, of an identifier used by the application.

4.2 Where possible, checks should be designed for data entry, to verify the fields that are entered.

4.3 Finally, any internal check that can examine whether the data are self-consistent should be considered. For example, if a person's date of birth and age are recorded, these data should, when taken together be consistent with the current date (ie present year minus age in years should give the year of birth plus or minus one year).

4.4 **Design checks:**

- are personal data 'captured' as close to the source as possible?

- how is the quality of personal data checked?

- is the quality of personal data variable?

- should any special procedures be designed for confidential personal data?

- are personal data verified before processing?

- are there internal checks that can ensure consistency of personal data?

- are the 'default' values chosen with care?

4.5 **Other checks:**

- do all input documents have a unique identity?

- are there input standards that staff can follow?

- are forms designed to suit the needs of the end-users?
- are instructions and documentation for the program written in simple and clear language?
- should there be a checksum (eg a modulus check)?
- how are input records verified for completeness, content and field sequence?
- what prevents duplicate, missing or unauthorised input?
- should there be a full reconciliation system linking input data to all output (eg reconciliation of the request for a cheque and the production of this cheque)?
- what controls ensure key fields are entered correctly?
- how are all fields validated for range format and size?
- how are rejections in the data validation process checked, controlled and recycled?
- should it be possible for transactions to be cancelled or reversed?
- how is the system restarted correctly, following a failure?
- is there appropriate provision for an audit trail?
- what are the end-user's stand-by arrangements and manual office procedures when data input is impossible?

5. Design checks in relation to the use of personal data

5.1 The issues listed below are particularly important and involve the general queries: 'Who can access the personal data; how are these data backed up; how are these data kept timely?' Consequently, the checks examine access to data, updating procedures, dating the data and purging obsolete data.

5.2 Dating and purging are vital aspects if free-text comments are entered about Data Subjects. For example, the free-text field which may contain comments like 'Joe Bloggs was smelling of drink when last visited' should always be accompanied by the relevant date, and the identifier of the person entering the comment. Since without these details the data are unattributable and lack context, they are potentially misleading and therefore useless. If the end-user needs free-text fields, it will be good practice to enable these fields to be sampled, and to ensure that the end-user has standards and procedures that vet free-text comments.

5.3 **Design checks:**

- do the uses of personal data reflect the differing responsibilities of end-users?
- who can update personal data?
- who can disclose personal data?
- how are personal data archived and backed up?
- should the despatch and receipt of personal data be recorded?
- should any disclosure of personal data or output from the application be accounted for by a log? (This could be very important if data are disclosed to other organisations)
- how are personal data to be purged at a later stage?
- should personal data be dated to assist purging?
- what are the retention criteria for the fields within the personal data?
- can the reason for holding every personal data field be justified?
- are any personal data held merely because 'they could be useful'?
- are the purposes for which all personal data fields are held, and all data sources or disclosures, covered by the Register Entries?
- can the personal data be sampled at intervals to check their relevance? (This is important if there are free-text areas in a record)
- does the end-user require training, to ensure that staff do not enter personal data that do not relate to 'matters of fact'?
- should there be an indication of the source of the personal data? (See Section 2 about the use of markers).

6. Design checks in relation to Subject Access provisions

6.1 Program design should take account of the fact that access to personal data is the rule. Even if a Subject Access exemption can be applied to the data, the data may have to be produced for inspection by a Court of Law. In general, Data Subjects are able, as a legal right, to obtain copies of personal data that relate to them, and to ask for these data to be corrected or erased; a Court of Law could direct either of these actions to be taken. In addition, personal data may often be disclosed as a matter of routine (eg to a customer or client who queries a payment).

6.2 Discussion should therefore take place with end-users to determine how access is currently achieved, or is to be achieved. Thus the design should anticipate how personal data can be made available to Data Subjects – and not just under the provisions of the Data Protection Act.

6.3 The questions listed below outline the basic requirements of providing access. If there are difficulties or doubts, the problems should be discussed with the Data Protection Officer. This is especially true for certain cases (eg in the personnel, health or social work areas where some personal data may be exempt from Subject Access). Particular care may need to be taken if one Department shares such personal data with other Departments.

6.4 **Design checks:**

- are there requirements which allow Data Subjects routine access to their personal data (eg to provide details of accounts to customers)?
- how easy is it to locate the personal data to which access may be requested?
- is there a need to note who has accessed the personal data and when?
- do special access routines need to be designed?
- is there information, in the personal data, which identifies another living individual?
- do the personal data contain any other information which might be exempt from Subject Access?
- could personal data, covered by a Subject Access exemption, be disclosed to another Department within the organisation?
- are there any codes that require explanation?
- can compliance with Subject Access be monitored to ensure that the data are released within the prescribed 40 days?
- are there any difficulties in giving Subject Access to archived data?
- is there provision for a Data Subject to indicate any disagreement with the

personal data held by the Data User?

- are such disagreements, or agreed corrections, notified to all disclosees who have received the original data?

- can personal data be rectified or erased in compliance with formal requests from Data Subjects and/or Court Orders?

- does the Data Protection Officer need to be consulted about any of the queries in this section? (In case of doubt concerning any of the above questions, **consultation is recommended)**.

7. Checks in relation to software obtained from manufacturers

7.1 **Software checks:**

- is data protection, Subject Access or security considered when the software is bought?

- are there adequate procedures to ensure the integrity of the software?

- are controls adequate to ensure only authorised changes or modifications can be made to the software?

- are there checks on all such changes to see they are made accurately?

- are there any 'hidden features' which can be abused (eg 'trapdoors' which enable maintenance to be carried out)?

- how is the software backed up?

- does the manufacturer offer a software maintenance or updating service that should be used?

- is the manufacturer's documentation complete?

- is there a back-up copy of the manufacturer's documentation?

- does the software offer any facility that may require a change to a Register Entry?

- are the 'default' values going to cause problems?

8. Design checks in relation to documentation

8.1 **Design checks:**

- is there documentation and, if so, who is responsible for it?
- is the documentation written for a specific reader?
- is the documentation comprehensive and clearly written?
- is the documentation kept up to date in line with any amendment?
- does the documentation cover all major functions?
- is the documentation tested as part of the software testing procedure?
- are manuals designed to be 'user friendly'?
- are there sufficient copies of the documentation?
- should there be additional staff training, specifically to assist with the understanding of the documentation?

9. Maintenance and review of applications programs

9.1 Most program changes arise in four ways:

- as part of the normal running of the system, when errors are found
- when users ask for improvements
- when external requirements change
- as a result of specific investigations or reviews of systems performance.

9.2 A major security objective is to ensure that applications staff do not have unauthorised access to production programs or data. This is necessary to ensure proper management controls over access to data and programs, and has nothing to do with staff integrity. For example, without such separation of staff functions it would be difficult for evidence from computer records to be admissible in a Law Court under the terms of the Police and Criminal Evidence Act 1984.

9.3 Procedural requirements in relation to the program changes in paragraph 9.1 above must be designed to ensure that:

- any member of staff is encouraged to report all malfunctions which may require an amendment
- any amendment or change in procedure receives a proper written level of authorisation (this is especially important where external clients are concerned)
- any amendment is either consistent with the Register Entry pertaining to the application, or results in appropriate change(s) to the Entry
- each amendment is scrutinised independently
- any persons holding documentation or files are always kept up to date with other work involving changes to the same system
- any procedure is capable of handling several concurrent amendments with different timescales
- any procedure does not violate existing channels of communication
- all amendments are properly tested and that the testing covers all aspects of the system
- documentation is updated where necessary
- end-users know that an amendment has been made
- all amendments are recorded, documented and dated
- any bureaucratic procedures are minimal, so that implementation of amendments is not delayed
- where necessary, the Data Protection Officer or Security Manager is informed.

9.4 Personal data or live data should, as far as possible, never be used for testing purposes. Data should be extracted from personal data so that the test data are either anonymous or relate to fictitious Data Subjects. Be careful of randomising personal data in the hope that they are no longer personal data; in some cases, all that has happened is that the personal data have been rendered inaccurate by the randomising process.

Appendix 5: Data Protection Census Form

DATA PROTECTION ACT 1984

CENSUS OF THE USE OF PERSONAL DATA BY (DATA USER NAME)

THIS FORM IS FOR INTERNAL USE ONLY

When complete please return to:

Name: ....

Location:.......................................

Telephone: ....

Note: The information that you provide in this form is required to ensure that (Data User name) can use personal data lawfully within the terms of the Data Protection Act.

1. IDENTIFICATION OF CONTACT

Name of contact:-
(for any queries regarding the details found on this form)

Section: ....

Division: ....

Business address: ....

Business telephone number: ....

Signature and date of completion:..

2. TITLE OF SCHEME OR ACTIVITY

Please supply a general description or title of the computer scheme or activity. A name that is widely known, recognised or commonly used will suffice.

....

....

....

3. PURPOSE(S) FOR WHICH PERSONAL DATA ARE PROCESSED

Please describe each purpose for which personal data are processed by you**(*)**. Please use the prefixes (A),(B),(C) etc in subsequent sections to identify the purposes concerned.

eg	(A)	Mailing list of customers
	(B)	Accounts administration
	(C)	Personnel administration
	(D)	Cost Centre management

....

....

....

....

....

....

....

....

* IF NONE, state 'NONE', and return the signed form.

4. TYPES OF DATA SUBJECT

Please describe the type(s) of **individual** about whom personal data are to be held for each of the purposes (A), (B), (C) etc. Please list **ALL** such Data Subjects and indicate whether current, past or potential (eg current, past and potential customers, current and past suppliers, past debtors, potential employees etc).

Using the example of (A) Mailing list of customers

(B) Accounts administration

(C) Personnel administration

(D) Cost Centre management

the **types of Data Subject** could include:

(A) Current, past and potential customers

(B) Current and past customers, current contractors

(C) Current and past employees

(D) Current employees

....

....

....

....

....

....

....

....

....

....

5. CLASSES OF PERSONAL DATA

Please describe the **classes of data** held for each of the purposes (A), (B), (C) etc. An item by item description of **ALL** such data fields is required. A sample form or computer printout may be attached to clarify the description.

Using the example of (A) Mailing list of customers

(B) Accounts administration

(C) Personnel administration

(D) Cost Centre management

the **classes of data** could include:

(A) Name, address, status of customer

(B) Name, address, bank account number, debtor status

(C) Name, work location, telephone number, next of kin

(D) Name, salary, expenses

....

....

....

....

....

....

....

....

....

....

6. SPECIAL CLASSES OF PERSONAL DATA

For each of the purposes (A), (B), (C) etc please indicate **whether and why** personal data are held which relate to a Data Subject's criminal convictions, mental health, sexual life etc (see below for full list).

Using the example of (A) Mailing list of customers

(B) Accounts administration

(C) Personnel administration

(D) Cost Centre management

the reasons for holding **special classes of data** could include:

(A), (B), (D):	No special classes of personal data held
(C) Physical health:	absenteeism due to illness
(C) Ethnic origin:	monitoring equal opportunities

Criminal convictions ....

Mental health ....

Sexual life/orientation/activity ....

Physical health ....

Religious or other beliefs ....

Political opinions ....

Ethnic or racial origin ....

If you are not sure or hold other sensitive data (eg concerning social work, court orders, personal or family problems etc), please describe the circumstances

....

....

7. SOURCES OF PERSONAL DATA

Please describe each type of person or organisation from which the personal data may be obtained for **each** of the purposes (A), (B), (C) etc. Please list **ALL** such Sources (eg customers, employers, Data Subjects, Department of Social Security), including those from within (Data User name).

Each Source quoted must contribute to the personal data held. So, for example, if employees provide information about **other** individuals, then employees would be a Source of personal data. If employees only provide information about **themselves** then they would be a Source. However, if employees only transcribe personal data into a file (eg as in data prep) they are **not** a Source.

Using the example of (A) Mailing list of customers

(B) Accounts administration

(C) Personnel administration

(D) Cost Centre management

the types of **Sources** could include:

(A) customers, electoral registers, surveys

(B) customers, credit reference agencies

(C) Data Subjects, employers, referees, employment agencies

(D) employees associated with the Cost Centre

....

....

....

....

....

....

8. DISCLOSURES OF PERSONAL DATA

Please describe each type of person or organisation to whom these personal data may be disclosed for each of the purposes (A), (B), (C) etc. Please list **ALL** such Disclosures **including** those within (Data User name).

Note that a Disclosure of personal data can be made by means of printed output, telephone calls, direct conversation, networks, access to VDU screens, files, disks, tapes etc.

Using the example of (A) Mailing list of customers

(B) Accounts administration

(C) Personnel administration

(D) Cost Centre management

the types of **Disclosures** could include:

(A) customers, employees, Central Marketing (internal)

(B) customers, debt collecting agencies, Inland Revenue

(C) Data Subjects, employees, banks, building societies

(D) Head Office (internal)

....

....

....

....

....

....

....

....

9. TRANSFER OF PERSONAL DATA OUTSIDE THE UNITED KINGDOM

Only complete this part of the Census if personal data are transferred outside the UK in machine readable form (eg on disk or tape, via electronic mail etc). A laptop computer containing personal data which is taken abroad would also be an overseas transfer of personal data. An Overseas Transfer usually means that a Disclosure of personal data must also be shown in Section 8 of this Census Form.

Please list **ALL** the relevant countries or territories. The Isle of Man, Jersey, Guernsey (and other Channel Islands) are all **outside** the UK whilst Wales, Scotland, England, Northern Ireland, Isle of Wight are within the UK. If transfers of personal data to many countries are described in a generic way (eg 'worldwide', 'European Community', 'Channel Islands') please give reasons for these transfers as the Data Protection Registrar usually asks for them.

Using the example of (A) Mailing list of customers

(B) Accounts administration

(C) Personnel administration

(D) Cost Centre management

the examples of Overseas Transfers could include:

(B) to Head Office in Germany

(C) Worldwide: As associated companies exist in several countries, personnel personal data will need to be transferred between companies.

....

....

10. Use this space if you wish to make any further comments

....

....

11. Please return this form to the address shown on the first page

Appendix 6: Transborder Data Flow

1. Cause for confusion

1.1 Four key problems can arise when countries take different views of what should be covered by data protection legislation, and adopt different rules with respect to who is responsible for the personal data and under what circumstances (note that some countries have no data protection legislation at present). This appendix outlines some of the basic steps that need to be taken before information relating to a person is transferred abroad (this is not limited to information in a form that can be processed automatically and could also include information about 'legal persons' (eg companies) or individuals who are dead).

1.2 The first problem is to recognise under what circumstances different jurisdictions can come into play. For example:

(a) in the UK, if the contents and use of personal data are **controlled** from the UK, any data **used** in the UK are fully subject to the UK Data Protection Act (in Austria, Eire, Guernsey, Isle of Man and Jersey data protection legislation takes a similar stance);

(b) in France, the application of the French data protection law is restricted to **processing activities** which take place, in whole or in part, on French territory (Danish and German legislation takes a similar stance);

(c) in the Netherlands, the law comes into effect when a **file** of personal data is **located** in that country.

1.3 The second problem is that the definition of what is covered by data protection legislation can vary considerably. For example:

(a) in Austria, Denmark, France, Finland, Germany, Netherlands and Norway **manual** files containing personal information are also subject to legislation;

(b) in Eire, Guernsey, Isle of Man, Israel, Jersey, Luxembourg, Sweden and the UK legislation only relates to personal information that can be processed **automatically**;

(c) in Austria, Denmark, France, Iceland, Luxembourg and Norway data relating to **legal persons** are also subject to legislation.

1.4 The third problem is that some countries have special rules: some covering the export of information (usually personal data), and others which relate to other legislation. For example:

(a) in all Scandinavian countries, Portugal and Austria, permission is required to export certain kinds of personal data. This invariably includes specific 'sensitive' data (eg criminal convictions, health data), but can cover other kinds of data (eg credit referencing, trades union membership), or personal data from which sensitive data can be inferred (eg personal data, recorded for billing purposes, that identify purchases from a sex shop);

(b) in the Netherlands there are special provisions that relate to nationals (eg in cases where personal data, relating to persons resident in the Netherlands, are transferred abroad for processing but remain under the control of a person in the Netherlands);

(c) the right of access remains under Danish law if the personal data are controlled and processed abroad but are used by a person in Denmark;

(d) in the UK, many data protection type issues are dealt with by other legislation (eg Access to Personal Files, Access to Medical Reports, Consumer Credit Act);

1.5 The fourth problem is that several countries within Western Europe have no legislation; as we go to print this includes Belgium, Greece, Spain, Switzerland (who have each introduced Data Protection Bills) and Italy. Most countries outside this area (eg in Eastern Europe, and countries such as USA) do not have specific data protection legislation, although other laws (eg on Privacy) may be relevant in certain circumstances. Most West European countries have signed the 1981 Council of Europe 'Convention for the Protection of Individuals with regard to Automatic Processing of Personal Data', an act that committed them to legislate. However, even here the picture is complex; for example, Switzerland has a Bill but has **not** signed the Convention, Spain has **ratified** the Convention but has no Act, while Finland has a Data Protection Act but has **not** signed the Convention.

1.6 Given such diversity, it becomes feasible to imagine complex situations under which personal data may be subject to three data protection laws (eg a UK subsidiary of a company causes the processing of personal data in France of which a back-up copy is also located in the Netherlands), or under which information which is not subject to data protection legislation in one country is covered by another country's legislation following a transborder transfer (eg the transfer from the UK to Norway of a manual file containing personal information, or the processing in Denmark of data relating to Irish companies). The special rules that relate to nationals (see paragraph 1.4) add further weight to the need to take care.

1.7 The Council of Europe Convention is important as it is the driving force behind all European data protection legislation; adherence to the terms of the Convention is a major objective outlined in the European Commission's proposals for a Directive (to take effect, in theory, in 1993) to harmonise data protection within the European Community. Article 12 of the Convention states that a Party to the Convention 'shall not, for the sole purpose of the protection of privacy, prohibit or subject to special authorisation, transborder flows of personal data going to the territory of another Party'. This implies that a country which is **not** a Party to the Convention risks such a prohibition on the transfer of personal data, across its national borders, from Parties to the Convention. Similarly, such a country **could freely impose** a prohibition on the transfer of personal data, to these Parties, across its borders.

1.8 Article 12(3b) of the Council of Europe Convention could further complicate matters; this specifically places an obligation on Parties to the Convention to ensure that transfers of personal data across national boundaries do not result 'in circumvention of the legislation' of a Party to the Convention. The result is that the status of related organisations (eg companies within the same group) can come under particular scrutiny, especially as regards to the provision of processing services with respect to personal data transferred across national borders. This can lead to a situation whereby a legal entity which **only processes** personal data in a particular country is made to assume the obligations of a **controller** of personal data in that country. Such an outcome is almost certain if that legal entity is able to intervene on behalf of the business interests of the related (controller) company which is located in another country, as the personal data are then also being independently controlled by the provider of the processing services.

1.9 The potential for circumvention of the Convention is high, especially as it is possible to create situations where the minimum (or no) legislation applies. For example, if the decision were to be taken to process personal data from France and the Netherlands in a Computer Bureau in the UK, then French and Netherlands laws might not apply as neither processing nor file location are within their respective jurisdictions. Assuming that the data are not used in the UK, and since control is not exercised in the UK, the responsibilities under UK law could be restricted to those of a Computer Bureau.

1.10 Some countries' laws have anticipated such problems. For example, using the scenario outlined in the paragraph above, if the French or Netherlands Data Protection Authorities formed the view that the personal data were being processed in the UK as a tactic to avoid legal obligations, then one could expect them to use their powers of intervention at every available opportunity. There would be ample scope for this, since Netherlands law has provisions that can be applied to transfers of personal data (relating to Dutch nationals) out of the Netherlands, whilst French law can force a foreign Data User to appoint an agent, in France, who then becomes accountable, under French law, for the processing carried out in another country.

1.11 The Commission's proposals for a Data Protection Directive (for detail see Chapter 9, Section 4), will also affect the transfer of data across borders. The Commission (not each Data Protection Authority) would, in the first instance, examine the policy implications that arise from the transfer of data to countries not subject to the Directive, and would have rule-making powers to adopt technical measures in certain sectors. Member states 'shall provide in their law that the transfer to a third country .... may only take place if that country ensures an adequate level of protection' (Article 24). Although the Commission may decide that a particular country that is not a Member of the Community has implemented equivalent protection, quite clearly it may, on occasion, decide otherwise.

2. Cause for action

2.1 Despite a confused picture, it can be concluded that several practical steps need to be taken before data are transferred across a national boundary. The first step is to examine whether the data become subject to none, one or two data protection laws. Four of the most likely scenarios are evaluated below:

(a) data, even though they are not subject to legislation in the country of origin become, on transfer, subject to the legislation of the recipient country;

(b) data, subject to legislation in the country of origin, are not, on transfer, subject to the legislation of the recipient country;

(c) data are transferred from a country which has data protection legislation, to another country which has no such legislation or has not signed the Council of Europe Convention;

(d) data are transferred from a country which does not have data protection legislation or has not signed the Council of Europe Convention, to another country which has such legislation or has signed the Convention.

2.2 If (a) or (d) applies, the transfer of data is likely to result in **more** data protection controls. As the recipient will be a separate legal entity, that entity will have some data protection expertise which satisfies the requirements of national legislation. It will be necessary to discuss the nature of the transfer with the staff member responsible, and possibly also with the Data Protection Authority itself as there may be a need to set up specific procedures to meet the requirements of the recipient country's legislation.

2.3 If (b) or (c) applies, the transfer of data is likely to result in a **reduction** in data protection controls. Thus **before** data are transferred abroad, it could be important to make a detailed appraisal of the status of relevant data protection legislation, to ascertain whether this might prohibit the transfer of the data. Strategic business decisions may also play a part in this process; for example, customers might resent a reduction in controls, and might fear that the confidentiality of their data could not be maintained. These issues become especially important in the circumstances of a transfer to a country that has neither data protection legislation nor has signed the Council of Europe Convention (and thus risks a prohibition to the transfer of data).

2.4 If there is a transfer of data **into** the UK, procedures are similar to those that should already be in place to deal with a new use of personal data. If the data are not 'personal data' (as defined in Section 1(1) of the Data Protection Act 1984) then no action is required under UK law (however, it might be useful to discover whether action is necessary in the other country if it has a higher standard than the UK's Data Protection Act). If the data are personal data, but the control of the contents and use of the data is being exercised from outside the UK **and** the data are not used in the UK, then the legal entity carrying out the processing in the UK is a Computer Bureau (the Registrar's Guideline 8 details the responsibilities of a Bureau). However, if some (or all) of the personal data are used in the UK, then the person carrying out the processing may be a Data User with respect to these personal data; in this case all uses of the personal data, items of personal data imported and sources of the personal data will need to be checked against the Data User's current Register Entry, as changes may be required.

2.5 If there is a transfer of data **from** the UK, **and** if the data are not personal data (as defined by Section 1(1)), **and** the destination is a European country with established data protection legislation, then it would still be necessary to alert the recipient of the data that action might be required in accordance with the recipient's national data protection legislation. If the transferred data are personal data, then the Data User's Register Entry will need to be checked with respect to Overseas Transfer and Disclosure; if the transfer is a new initiative then future sources of personal data may need to be alerted to the circumstances (as a consequence of the First Principle: see Guidance Note 19). Note that even if the transfer is registered, the Registrar can still serve a Transfer Prohibition Notice with respect to any particular instance (in contrast to a registered disclosure, when the Registrar's scope for action is very limited). Finally, if control of the contents and use of the personal data remains in the UK, and the data are for use in the UK, then the person transferring the personal data remains a Data User.

2.6 As the European Commission's proposals are intended to harmonise data protection laws, progress and debate surrounding its Data Protection Directive should be closely followed. Any state that joins the Community (eg Austria, Finland, Norway, Sweden, Switzerland and Turkey) has to harmonise domestic legislation with that of the Community.

3. List of Data Protection Authorities

3.1 The following are useful sources of further advice within Europe:

AUSTRIA: Republik Österreich Datenschutzkommission; Ballhausplatz 1 (Hofburg); 1014 Vienna; Telephone: 010(43) 153 115 2525.

DENMARK: Registertilsynet; Christians Brygge 28[4]; 1559 Copenhagen V; Telephone: 010(45) 331 43844

EIRE: Data Protection Commissioner; Block 4; Irish Life Centre; Talbot Street; Dublin 1; Telephone: 0001 748 544;

FINLAND: Data Protection Ombudsman; Kauppakartanonkatu 7, P.O.B. 31; SF-00931 Helsinki; Telephone: 010(358) 034 32455.

FRANCE: CNIL; 21 Rue Saint-Guillaume; 75007 Paris; Telephone: 010(33) 145 444 065.

GERMANY: Der Bundesbeauftragte für den Datenschutz; Stephan Lochner Strasse 2; 5300 Bonn Bad Godesberg; Telephone: 010(49) 228 819 950.

GUERNSEY: The Data Protection Officer; States Advisory and Finance Committee; States Office; Guernsey; Telephone: 0481 24411.

ICELAND: Chairman; Datatilsynet; Arnarhvoll; 150 Reykjavik; Telephone: 010(354) 160 9010.

ISLE OF MAN: Data Protection Registrar; PO Box 69; Douglas; Telephone: 0624 661030.

JERSEY: Data Protection Registry; c/o Judicial Greffe; Cyril Le Marquand House; The Parade; St Helier; Telephone: 0534 32273.

LUXEMBOURG: Data Protection Commission; Ministère de la Justice; 16, Boulevard Royal; Luxembourg 2910; Telephone: 010(352) 479 4423.

NETHERLANDS: Registratiekamer; Data Protection Authority; P.O. Box 3011; 2280

GA Rijswijk; Telephone: 010(31) 703 190 190.

NORWAY: Datatilsynet; Postboks 8177 Dep; Oslo 1; Telephone: 010(47) 242 1910.

SWEDEN: Datainspektionen; Box 8114; S 104 20; Stockholm; Telephone: 010(46) 857 6100.

UNITED KINGDOM: Data Protection Registrar; Springfield House; Water Lane; Wilmslow, Cheshire SK9 5AX; Telephone: 0625 535777.

3.2 Non-European Data Protection Authorities include:

AUSTRALIA: Privacy Commissioner; Level 24; American Express Building; 388 George Street; Sydney; New South Wales 2000; Telephone: 010(61) 2229 7600.

CANADA: Privacy Commissioner of Canada; 112 Kent Street, 14th Floor; Ottawa; Ontario KLA 1H3; Telephone: 010(1) 613 995 2410.

ISRAEL: Registrar of Data Bases; Ministry of Justice; P.O. Box 2180; Jerusalem 91021; Telephone: 010(972) 225 5650.

JAPAN: Government Information Systems; Management and Coordination Agency; Prime Minister's Office; 3-1-1 Kasumigaseki; Chiyoda-Ku; Tokyo 100; Telephone: 010(81) 3581 2078.

NEW ZEALAND: Privacy Commissioner; Wanganui Computer Centre; P.O. Box 10094; Wellington; Telephone: 010(64) 472 2059.

INDEX

The index is organised by Chapter (in bold type) and Section or paragraph number (in brackets). Thus **7** [4.5.9] means Chapter 7, paragraph 4.5.9; **8** [2.7-2.9] means Chapter 8, paragraphs 2.7 to 2.9; and **4** [3] means Chapter 4, Section 3 (in this case the reference is to all paragraphs beginning with the number 3, for example 3.1, 3.1.1, 3.2 etc).